PUBLIC BUDGETING SYSTEMS

Fourth Edition

Robert D. Lee, Jr.
The Pennsylvania State University
University Park, Pennsylvania

Ronald W. Johnson
Research Triangle Institute
Research Triangle Park, North Carolina

AN ASPEN PUBLICATION®
Aspen Publishers, Inc.
Rockville, Maryland
1989

Library of Congress Cataloging-in-Publication Data

Lee, Robert D.
Public budgeting systems/Robert D. Lee, Jr., Ronald W. Johnson.
p. cm.
Bibliography: p.
Includes index.
ISBN: 0-8342-0070-8
1. Budget--United States. 2. Program budgeting--United States.
I. Johnson, Ronald Wayne, 1942- . II. Title.
HJ2051.L4   1989   350.72'2'0973--dc20   89-14933
CIP

Editorial Services: Marsha Davies

Library of Congress Catalog Card Number: 89-14933
ISBN: 0-8342-0070-8

Printed in the United States of America

1 2 3 4 5

*This book is dedicated to those
who suffered the loss of family time:*

*Barbara, Robert, Craig, and Cameron;
Sally, Ron, and Jennifer.*

Table of Contents

Preface

This is a general book on public budgeting. Its purpose is to survey the current state of the art among all levels of government in the United States. We emphasize methods by which financial decisions are reached within a system and ways in which different types of information are used in budgetary decision making. The book emphasizes the use of program information, since budget reforms for decades have sought to introduce greater program considerations into financial decisions.

Budgeting is considered within the context of a system containing numerous components and relationships. One problem of such an approach is that, since all things within a system are related, it is difficult to find an appropriate place to begin. We have divided the text into chapters, but the reader should recognize that no single chapter can stand alone. Virtually every chapter mentions some issues relevant to the chapter that are treated elsewhere in the book.

A discussion of budgeting may be organized in various ways. Historical or chronological sequence is one method of organization, although this approach would require discussing every relevant topic for each period of time. Another method is by levels of government, with separate sections for local, state, and federal budgeting. Such an approach again would involve extensive rehashing of arguments at each level. Still another approach is by phases of the budget cycle, from preparation of the budget through auditing past activities and expenditures. Rigid adherence to this approach would be inappropriate, because the budget cycle is not precisely defined and many issues cut across several phases of the cycle. Another approach would be to organize the discussion around the contrast between the technical and political problems of budgetary decision making.

The organization of this book is based upon a combination of these approaches. The Introduction is a general discussion of the nature of budgetary decision making, including distinctions between private and public budgeting, the concept of responsibility in budgeting, the possibility of rationality in decision making, and the nature of budgeting and budget systems. Chapter 2, The Public Sector in Perspective, reviews the scope of the public sector, the magnitude of government, the sources of revenues, and the purposes of government expenditures. Budget cycles are the topic of Chapter 3, which summarizes the basic steps in budgeting—preparation and submission, approval, execution, and audit. Together these chapters provide a basic framework for the remainder of the book.

The next three chapters focus upon the budget preparation process. The purpose of these chapters is to provide the reader with an understanding of the types of deliberations involved in developing a proposed budget. Chapter 4, Budget Preparation: The Revenue Side, which is new to this edition, considers the different sources from which governments obtain their funds and the special concerns associated with limitations on taxing and spending and with estimating revenue for the next budget year. Chapter 5, Budget Preparation: The Expenditure Side, discusses early budget reform efforts and contemporary approaches to developing proposals for funding governmental programs. Chapter 6, Budget Preparation: The Decision Process, examines the process of putting together a budget proposal that includes recommended revenue and expenditure levels and then reviews the types of budget documents that are used in government.

Chapter 7, Policy and Program Analysis, is a transitional chapter that discusses the role of analysis in both budget preparation and approval. Techniques of analysis are discussed as well as their usage in the executive and legislative branches.

Chapters 8 and 9 deal with the budget approval process. Chapter 8, Budget Approval: The Role of the Legislature, covers in general the processes used by legislative bodies. Chapter 9, Budget Approval: The U.S. Congress, which is new to this edition, treats separately the special factors and problems associated with congressional budgeting.

The next three chapters concentrate on the execution phase of budgeting. Chapter 10, Budget Execution, considers the roles played by the chief executive, budget office, and agencies and treats separately the topics of tax administration, cash management, procurement, and risk management. Chapter 11, Financial Management: Accounting, Auditing, and Information Systems, presents the basic features of accounting systems and processes, explains the types of audits that are conducted, and discusses the nature of information systems used in budgeting and finance. Chapter 12, Financial Management: Capital Budgeting and Debt, examines capital budgeting as a decision process and the financing of long-term capital investments through debt instruments.

The final three chapters deal with special topics in governmental budgeting. Chapter 13, Government Personnel and Pensions, reviews the effect of personnel expenditures on budgets, with particular attention to public pension systems. Chapter 14, Intergovernmental Relations, examines the financial interactions among governments, the types of fiscal assistance in use, and possible means of restructuring intergovernmental relationships. Chapter 15, Government, the Economy, and Economic Development, surveys the federal government's role in managing the economy and the ways economic conditions affect state and local governments.

The fourth edition of *Public Budgeting Systems* closes with some brief Concluding Remarks on themes that can be expected to receive considerable attention from budgeting students and practitioners in the next several years. The Bibliographic Note provides guidance on keeping informed about changes in the field of budgeting.

Overall, this edition retains the topics of the third edition but gives increased attention to some: revenue sources, congressional budgeting, tax administration, cash management, accounting, capital budgets, intergovernmental finance, and selected aspects of economic policy. Text, tables, and figures have been completely updated.

The authors began the first edition as faculty members in the Institute of Public Administration at The Pennsylvania State University. Three editions later, Professor Lee is head of the Department of Public Administration at Penn State, and Dr. Johnson is vice president for Social Sciences and International Development at the Research Triangle Institute. In preparing this edition, the authors worked jointly on a revised outline of chapters and then divided between themselves the drafting of the 15 chapters on a two-to-one basis. Rewrites and editing followed. The result, we think, has been a truly successful collaboration.

Our hope is that this new edition will be useful to readers from many backgrounds and with widely diverse purposes.

Acknowledgments

Having gone through four editions, this book is necessarily the product of numerous individuals and not just two authors. We are indebted to colleagues at our respective institutions—The Pennsylvania State University and the Research Triangle Institute. Colleagues at other institutions, including various colleges and universities, have provided valuable advice as have students at a variety of schools. In preparing the four editions, we received considerable advice from expert practitioners in both the executive and legislative branches of the federal, state, and local governments and from those in nonprofit organizations. In this current edition, two individuals deserve special thanks: Robert Berne, Associate Dean, Graduate School of Public Administration, New York University and David F. Drake, Group Vice President and Secretary Treasurer, American Hospital Association, Chicago. Thank you and our best wishes.

The final product is, of course, our own responsibility.

1

Introduction

Public budgeting involves the selection of ends and the selection of means to reach those ends. It involves the allocation of society's economic and financial resources between government and the private sector, and among competing possible uses in the public sector. Public budgeting systems are systems for making those choices about ends and means, about resource allocation. Those choices are guided by theory, by hunch, by partisan politics, by narrow self-interest, by altruism, and by many more sources of value. Public budgeting systems work by channeling various types of information about societal conditions that budget choices affect and about the values that guide those choices. Complex channels for information exchange exist. These channels process information on what is desired, assessments of what is or is not being achieved, and analyses of what might or might not be achieved. Integral to budgeting systems are intricate processes that link both political and economic values. Use of the sometimes bewildering and often conflicting information about values, about conditions as they are, and about conditions as they might be, in making decisions is a political process that ultimately decides how resources are allocated. This book is an analysis of procedures and methods—past, present, and prospective—used in this resource allocation process.

This chapter examines some basic features of decision-making and budgeting systems. First, some major characteristics of public budgeting are explained through comparison and contrast with private forms of budgeting. Second, the development of budgeting as a means for holding government accountable for its use of society's resources is reviewed. Next, budgets and budgeting systems are defined. Finally, the role of information in budgetary decision making is reviewed.

1

SOME DISTINCTIONS ABOUT PUBLIC BUDGETING

Budgeting is a common phenomenon. To some extent, everybody does it. People budget time, dollars, food—almost everything. The corner grocer budgets, General Electric budgets, and so do governments. Moreover, important similarities in budgeting exist between large public and private bureaucracies.[1]

Budgeting is intended as a mechanism for setting goals and objectives, for identifying weaknesses or inadequacies in organizations, and for controlling and integrating the diverse activities carried out by numerous subunits within large bureaucracies—both public and private. Budgeting means examining how the organization's resources have been used in the past, evaluating what has been accomplished and at what cost per accomplishment, and charting a course for the future by allocating new resources for the coming budget period. Whether this process is done haphazardly with little study or carefully with exhaustive analyses prepared by staff, whether it is carried out by order of the chief executive officer or developed by consensus, it is still budgeting in the corporation or in the government.

Public and Private Sector Differences in Objectives

Resources Availability. Important differences also exist between the private and public spheres. In the first place, the amount of resources available for allocation varies greatly. Both family and corporate budgeting are constrained by a relatively fixed set of available resources. Income is comparatively fixed, at least in the short run; therefore outgo must be equal to or less than income. Of course, income can be expanded by increasing the level of production and work or by borrowing, but the opportunities for increasing income are limited.

Government, on the other hand, is bound by much higher limits, and in the United States at least, government does not use all of the possible resources available to it. Only in times of major crises, such as World War II, has government in the United States begun to approach the limits of its resources. Then, the federal government borrowed an amount that eventually came close to equaling the total production of the economy in a year. During other times, much is left to the private sector. In the late 1980s, government in the United States consumed about 40 percent of society's goods and services.

Profit Motive. Another major distinction between private and public budgeting is the motivation behind budget decisions. The former is characterized by the profit motive, whereas government undertakes many things that are unprofitable in a financial sense. In the private sector, profit serves as a ready standard for evaluating previous decisions—successful decisions are those that produce profits as measured in dollars. The concept of profit, however, can lead to gross oversimplifications about corporate decision making. Sometimes corporations forgo profits in the short run. In the case of price wars they attempt to increase their share of a given market even if it means selling temporarily at a loss. At other times, they incur large debt and take other apparently unprofitable actions to combat a hostile takeover, an attempt by an outsider to purchase enough stock to exercise control over the corporation's assets. Sometimes their major objectives are to produce a good product and to build public confidence in the firm, sure in their pursuit of customer service that the result will be sustained long-run profits for the firm.[2] Even in a private firm with a profit motive, not every budget decision can be guided by this ultimate criterion. Large firms budget significant resources for research and development (R & D) activities, few of which eventually lead to a product that generates large sales. An R & D division can be evaluated over the long term by how many of its developments contribute to profits, but it is not that easy. Often, the products of R & D are subtle improvements in existing products, and measuring the amount of investment relative to the incremental profit gain is impossible. In this regard, private budgeting for R & D is no less difficult than the federal government's support of R & D.

Regardless of the various influences of the profit motive in the private sector of society, governmental decision making, in general, lacks even this standard for measuring its activities. Exceptions to this generalization are governmental activities that generate revenues. State control and sale of alcoholic beverages, whether undertaken for profit or for regulation of public morals, can be evaluated as any other business in terms of profit and loss. Similarly, the operations of a water system, a public transit authority, and a public swimming pool all can be evaluated in business profit-and-loss terms. That does not mean that all of these activities should turn a profit. After all, operating a public swimming pool may be the result of a decision to provide subsidized recreation to a low-income neighborhood whose residents cannot afford other, private recreational alternatives. The budgeting process, however, can be used to assess the operation as a business in order to clarify how much the subsidy costs and aid decision makers in comparing costs with those for other public services provided free of direct charge.

Still, the majority of private sector budget decisions pertain to at least a long-run profit motive, and most public sector budget decisions do not. Governments undertake some functions deliberately instead of leaving them to the private sector. Public budgetary decisions, for example, frequently involve allocation of resources among competing programs that are not readily susceptible to measurement in dollar costs and dollar returns. There is no easy means of measuring the costs and benefits of a life saved through cancer research, although the value of future earnings sometimes is used as a surrogate measure of the value of life. Nor is there a ready means of clearly separating private incentives from public incentives. Although the National Cancer Institute spends millions of public dollars annually on cancer research, the amounts are minuscule compared with the amount spent by private companies on drug research for cancer and prevention treatment. Sometimes public and private sector roles are distinguished on clear-cut, for-profit and not-for-profit motives, but often they are not.

Public and Private Sector Differences in Services Provided

Public Goods. Some governmental services yield public or collective benefits, which are consumed by society as a whole, as distinct from corporate products, which are consumed by individuals and specific organizations. When Ford Motor Company produces automobiles, persons buying the products use them. When the Department of Defense produces a network for detecting a possible launching of intercontinental missiles against the United States, that network is "consumed" by the public in general. Economists call the latter "public goods" that have the property of nonexclusion. Once the detection network is in place, no one can be excluded from its benefits.[3]

Externalities. Another class of governmental services consists of those from which individuals can be excluded, but for which the benefits extend beyond those involved in the immediate service provision. When Ford Motor Company sells a car, its stockholders enjoy the benefits of the profits, and those profits do not spill over to society at large. However, when a child is educated through a school system, not only does the child benefit, but society's productive capacity is enhanced. It certainly is common to have private schools that educate children for a profit, and the owners of the school enjoy the benefits of the profits along with the child and society. However, it seems unlikely that these same for-profit schools would willingly provide equivalent education to all children who cannot make tuition payments. Economists label the benefits that spill over to the rest of society externalities.[4] Governments provide at least a measure of services that produce significant externalities because the private sector would produce those goods or services only to the extent that profit could be made. Education, presumably, would be available only to those who could pay if left entirely to the private sector.

Pricing Public Services. Defining just what is clearly public in nature and determining what the private sector presumably cannot provide is controversial. As the federal government during the 1980s cut back on transfers to state and local governments, and state and local governments faced tax and spending limitations during the 1980s (see Chapter 4), many services once thought to be exclusively public were in fact converted to private services or to public services provided by private firms on a contract basis.[5] Although this conversion was not a new idea, one of the lessons learned from the 1980s in the United States seems to have been that government may grow larger than most feel is beneficial and may be difficult to cut back when unconstrained by any kind of pricing mechanism, such as the private sector ultimately always faces. One consequence of that lesson is that much more extensive user charges and various other fees now force those who benefit directly from a government service to pay for its cost (see Chapter 4). For example, the U.S. Coast Guard no longer provides towing services to disabled boats unless a genuine emergency exists, but notifies private operators who charge the cost to the disabled boat captain. That practice has cut back significantly on calls for towing in general, with prices providing a rationing mechanism.

Other Public/Private Differences. Whatever objectives other than profits private corporations may have, to stay in business they must seek economic efficiency and obtain the greatest possible dollar return on investments. In contrast, governments may be intentionally inefficient in resource allocations, undertaking services the private sector would be reluctant to provide at all. For example, Social Security may be inefficient in the sense that, while other governmental programs might provide greater economic returns to society, it has been agreed that at least some support should be provided to the elderly. Government also is charged with other unique responsibilities, such as intervention in the economy (see Chapter 15). Corporations, on the other hand, depend on economic conditions.

Another difference between private and public organizations lies in the clientele and the owners of the means of production. In theory, at least, both corporations and governments are answerable to their stockholders and clients, but in the private sector these individuals can disassociate themselves from firms. Their counterparts in the public sector are denied this choice, except through the extreme act of emigration. Private stockholders expect dollar returns on their investments, but because government costs and returns are not easily evaluated, the electorate has no simple measure for assessing the returns on taxes they pay.

Finally, corporate budgetary decision making is usually more centralized than governmental decision making. Corporations can stop production of economically unprofitable goods such as Edsels and DeSotos. Given the nature of the public decision-making process, however, government encounters more difficulty in making decisions both to inaugurate programs and to eliminate them. For example, it seems evident that welfare programs intended to aid the poor have not provided the kinds of results desired by either the electorate in general or welfare recipients in particular. Nevertheless, to change existing programs requires years of debate, negotiations, and political bargaining. Passage of the Welfare Reform Act of 1988, which imposed a work requirement on all able recipients of various forms of assistance, took the entire second term of President Ronald Reagan.

RESPONSIBLE GOVERNMENT AND BUDGETING

The emergence and reform of formal government budgeting can be traced to a concern for holding public officials responsible or accountable for their actions.[6] In a democracy budgeting is a device for limiting the powers of government. Two issues recur in the evolution of modern public budgeting as an instrument of accountability—responsibility to whom and for what purposes.

Responsible to Whom?

Responsibility to Constituency. Basically, responsibility in a democratic society entails holding elected officials answerable to their constituents. Elected executives and legislative representatives at all levels of government are, at least in theory, held accountable for their decisions on programs and budgets. In actuality, however, budget documents are not the main source of information for decisions by the electorate. Obviously, most voters do not diligently study the U.S. budget before casting their votes in presidential and congressional elections. However, as the government's share of the total economy approaches 50 percent, it is increasingly clear that voters do hold elected representatives responsible for the overall budget, the budget deficit, and the general performance of the economy. In addition, state and local governments have very specific creditors, the purchasers of bonds issued to finance long-term capital improvements. The interest rates state and local governments have to pay on their bonds are affected by their ability to provide creditors with convincing evidence of their creditworthiness (see Chapter 12).[7] Hence, financial institutions that purchase bonds and ratings institutions that rate state and local bonds are important constituents to whom these governments are accountable.

Because the public in a large society cannot be fully informed about the operations of government, the United States has used the concepts of separation of powers and checks and balances as means of providing for responsible government. Thus, the president is held responsible to Congress for preparation and submission of an executive budget. In most states and many localities, the chief executive has a similar responsibility to recommend a plan for taxes and expenditures. The legislative body passes judgment on these recommendations and subsequently holds the executive branch responsible for carrying out the decisions.

Development of the Executive Budget System. The development of an executive budget system for holding government accountable was a long process that can be traced as far back as the Magna Charta (1215). The main issue that resulted in this landmark document was the concern of the nobility over the Crown's taxing powers. Obviously, the Magna Charta did not produce a complete budget, but concentrated only upon holding the Crown accountable to the nobility for its revenue actions.[8] At the time, the magnitude of public expenditures and the use of these funds for public services were of less concern than the power to levy and collect taxes. It was not until the English Consolidated Fund Act of 1787 that the rudiments of a complete system were established, and it was 1822 before a complete account of revenues and expenditures was presented to Parliament.[9]

The same concern in 18th century England for executive accountability was exhibited in other countries.[10] It was carried over to the American experience even prior to the Constitution. Fear of a strong executive was evidenced by the failure to mention an executive in the Articles of Confederation (1781). Fear of "taxation without representation" probably explains why the Constitution (1789) is more explicit about taxing powers than the procedures to be followed in government spending.

The first decade under the Constitution saw important developments that could have resulted in an executive budget system, but subsequent years were to reverse the trend. The Treasury Act of 1789, establishing the Treasury Department, granted to the secretary the power "to digest and prepare plans for the improvement of the revenue . . . (and) to prepare and report estimates of the public revenue and expenditures." Alexander Hamilton, the secretary of the treasury, interpreted his mandate broadly and asserted strong leadership in financial affairs. Although that legislation did not grant the secretary power to prepare a budget by recommending which programs should and should not be funded, such a development might have subsequently emerged.

Instead, Hamilton's apparent lack of deference to Congress strengthened that body's support for greater legislative control over financial matters. To curtail the discretion of the executive, Congress resorted to the use of increasing numbers of line items, specifying in narrow detail for what purposes money could be spent.[11] The pattern emerged that each executive department would deal directly with Congress, thereby curtailing the responsibilities of the secretary of the treasury. The budgetary function of the Treasury Department became primarily ministerial; the Book of Estimates, prepared by the secretary and delivered to Congress, which could have become the instrument for a coordinated set of budgetary recommendations, instead was simply a compilation of departmental requests for funds. A.E. Buck wrote, "Thus budget making became an exclusively legislative function in the national government, and as such it continued for more than a century."[12]

Modern Executive Budgeting. By the beginning of the 20th century, changing economic conditions stimulated the demand for more centralized and controlled forms of budgeting. E.E. Naylor has written that before this time there was little "enthusiasm for action . . . since federal taxes were usually indirect and not severely felt by any particular individual or group."[13] By 1900, however, existing revenue sources no longer consistently produced sufficient sums to cover the costs of government. At the federal level, the tariff could not be expected to produce a surplus of funds, as had been the case. Causes of this growing deficit were an expanded scope of governmental programs and, to a lesser extent, waste and corruption in government finance. The latter is often credited as a major political factor that stimulated reform.

Local government led the way in acting to establish formal budget procedures. Municipal budget reform was closely associated with general reform of local government, especially for the establishment of the city manager form of government. Two dates are critical. In 1899 a model municipal corporation act, released by the National Municipal League, featured a model charter that provided for a budget system whose preparation phase was under the control of the mayor. In 1906 the New York Bureau of Municipal Research was founded.[14] The following year the bureau issued a study, "Making a Municipal Budget," which became the basis for establishing a budgetary system for New York City. By the mid-1920s most major U.S. cities had some form of budget system.

Reform of state budgeting was particularly notable between 1910 and 1920. This reform was closely associated with the overall drive to hold executives accountable by first giving them authority over the executive branch. The movement for the short ballot, aimed at eliminating many independently elected administrative officers, resulted in granting governors greater control over their respective bureaucracies. Ohio, in 1910, was the first state to enact a law empowering the governor to prepare and submit a budget. A.E. Buck, in assessing the effort at the state level, suggested that 1913 marked "the beginning of practical action in the states."[15] By 1920 some budget reform had occurred in 44 states, and by 1929 all states had a central budget office.[16,17]

Simultaneous action occurred at the federal level, and much of what took place there contributed to the reforms at the local and state levels. Frederick A. Cleveland, who was director of the New York Bureau of Municipal Research and who played a key role in national reform, wrote, "It was the uncontrolled and uncontrollable increase in the cost of government that finally jostled the public into an attitude of hostility."[18] In response to this public concern, President William Howard Taft requested and received from Congress in 1909 an appropriation of $100,000 for a special Commission on Economy and Efficiency. Known as the Taft Commission, the group was headed by Cleveland and submitted its final report in 1912, recommending the establishment of a budgetary process under the direction of the president. This report was to spur great action at the state and local levels.

However, the Budget and Accounting Act, which established the new federal system, was not passed until 1921. In the interim, deficits were recorded every year between 1912 and 1919 except 1916. The largest deficit occurred in 1919, when expenditures were three times greater than revenues ($18.5 billion in expenditures as compared with $5.1 billion in revenues). During this period, vigorous debate centered around the issue of whether budget reform would in effect establish a superordinate executive over the legislative branch. President Woodrow Wilson in 1920 vetoed legislation that would have created a Bureau of the Budget and General Accounting Office on the grounds that the latter, as an arm of Congress, would violate the president's responsibilities over the executive branch. The following year virtually identical legislation was signed into law by President Warren G. Harding.

Thus, an executive budget system was established, despite a historical fear of a powerful chief executive. In 1939 the Bureau of the Budget was removed from the Treasury Department and placed in the newly formed Executive Office of the President. This shift reflected the growing importance of the bureau in assisting the president in managing the government. Ten years later the budgetary task force of the First Hoover Commission on the Organization of the Executive Branch recommended that the Bureau of the Budget be reinstated in the Treasury Department, but the Commission as a whole opposed the recommendation.[19] The Budget and Accounting Procedures Act of 1950 reinforced the trend of presidential control by explicitly granting the president control over the "form and detail" of the budget document. The Second Hoover Commission in 1955 endorsed strengthening the president's power in budgeting as a means for "the restoration of the full control of the national purse to the Congress."[20] A president who had full control of the bureaucracy, then, could be held accountable by Congress for action taken by the bureaucracy.

Responsible for What?

Revenue Responsibility. The earliest concern for financial responsibility centered on taxes. As indicated above, the Magna Charta imposed limitations not on the nature of the Crown's expenditures but on the procedures for raising revenue. This same concern for the revenue side of budgeting was characteristic of the early history of budgeting in this country. The Constitution is more explicit about the tax power of the government than about the nature or purposes of governmental expenditures.

Expenditure Control, Management, and Planning. The larger the public has become, the more the concern has shifted to expenditures. Increasing emphasis has been placed upon the accountability of government for what it spends and for how well it manages its overall finances. Expenditure accountability may be of several different forms. As of the 1960s, expenditure accountability had gone through three stages.[21] The first stage is identified as one characterized by legislative concern for tight control over executive expenditures. The most prevalent means of exerting this type of expenditure control has been to appropriate by line item and object of expenditure. Financial audits, then, are used to ensure that money in fact was spent for the items authorized for purchase. This information focuses budgetary decision making upon the things government buys, such as personnel, travel, and supplies, rather than upon the accomplishments of governmental activities. In other words, responsibility is achieved by controlling the resources or input side.

The second stage is the management orientation, emphasizing the efficiency with which ongoing activities are conducted. Historically, this orientation is associated with the New Deal through the First Hoover Commission (1949). Emphasis was placed upon holding administrators accountable for the efficiency of their activities through methods such as work performance measurement.

The third stage of budget reform is identified with post–Hoover Commission concerns for the planning function served by budgets. Traditional concerns for control of resource inputs may be accommodated in the short time frame of the coming budget year. Managerial concern for efficiency, although aided by a longer time perspective, also may be accommodated in a traditional budget year presentation. When the emphasis is shifted to accomplishing objectives, however, a longer time frame is necessary. Many objectives of governmental programs cannot be accomplished in one budget year. A multiyear presentation of the budget is thus necessary to indicate the long-range implications of current budget decisions.

Financial Management and Financial Condition. While it may be premature to label a fourth stage, the late 1970s and the 1980s showed a significant increase in the concern for sound financial management. Financial management can mean many things. It encompasses the concern for appropriate control over public funds. It certainly includes the concern for efficient public sector management. And financial management entails the cost-effective accomplishment of the objectives of government programs, which has already been labeled a planning emphasis. But a new emphasis has been placed on mechanisms for ensuring that the government remains in a sound financial position. Such mechanisms entail not only budgetary concerns for resource allocation but also the development of soundly based financing plans for meeting both short- and long-term resource requirements.

One of the motivations behind the concern to hold government accountable for its long-run financial position was the New York City budget crisis of the mid-1970s. Following on the heels of that near bankruptcy, both financial institutions that purchased municipal bonds and citizens who wondered about their own cities sought to improve the reporting of the long-term financial position of governments.[22] The issue is that the general operating budget and related accounting reports often do not reveal the overall financial position of the governmental entity. All state governments, most local governments, and of course the federal government have some level of indebtedness. All three levels also have various assets against which to compare that level of indebtedness. However, the long-run planning for debt retirement and the general strategies for managing existing assets do not receive much attention in budgeting systems. Concern at the federal level has led the General Accounting Office to recommend a major overhaul in federal accounting and financial management practices, including the development of capital budgeting.[23] These issues are discussed in Chapters 11 and 12.

The notion of stages can be overemphasized. Budget reform efforts for many decades have attempted to improve the capacity for decision-making systems to concentrate upon accomplishing desired ends. Identifying three, and perhaps four, stages helps focus attention on what government is expected to be accountable for and where the locus of that accountability lies. The first stage would place the responsibility on the legislative branch as the principal authority for determining how values should be allocated. The administrators' job, then, is perfunctory. The second stage may be seen as the beginning of a shift toward broader executive duties but limited to a concern for efficient management rather than program accomplishment. The stage typified by program budgeting and management by objectives reflects the development of executive responsibility for formulating programs that achieve desired ends. The most recent emphasis, on overall financial planning, is on the executive's responsibility for tying budgeting for current operations, capital facilities planning, asset management, and long-range debt financing into an integrated financial and management plan.

Most of the emphasis in this book is on the budget as an instrument for financial and program decision making at all levels of government—federal, state, and local. The one responsibility that most sharply differentiates federal budget decisions from state and local decisions is the federal responsibility for the overall state of the economy. The federal budget not only allocates resources among competitive programs, but it is also an instrument for achieving economic stability. This responsibility has been a part of the federal budgetary process since the Full Employment Act of 1946. The budget as an instrument of economic policy is discussed in Chapter 15.

Budgeting, then, is an important process by which accountability or responsibility can be provided in a political system. As has been discussed, responsibility varies in both to whom the system is accountable and for what purposes. Given these various forms of accountability and the types of choices that decision makers have available to them, different meanings can be attached to the terms budget and budgeting system. Depending on the purposes of a budget, decision makers will need different kinds and amounts of information to aid their choices. The following sections and subsequent chapters therefore focus upon the kinds of information required for different budgetary choices and the kinds of procedures for generating that information.

BUDGETS AND BUDGETING SYSTEMS

What Is a Budget?

Budget Documents. In its simplest form a budget is a document or a collection of documents that refers to the financial condition of an organization (family, corporation, government), including information on revenues, expenditures, activities, and purposes or goals. In contrast to an accounting operating statement, which is retrospective in nature, referring to past conditions, a budget is prospective, referring to expected future revenues, expenditures, and accomplishments. Historically, the word budget referred to a leather pouch, wallet, bag, or purse. Jesse Burkhead observed, "In Britain the term was used to describe the leather bag in which the Chancellor of the Exchequer carried to Parliament the statement of the Government's needs and resources."[24]

The status of the budget document is not consistent from one political jurisdiction to another. In the federal government, the budget is greatly limited in legal status. It is the official recommendation of the president to Congress, but it is not the official document under which the government operates. As will be seen later, the official operating budget of the United States consists of several documents, namely appropriations acts (see Chapters 8, 9, and 11). In contrast, local budgets proposed by mayors may become the official working budgets as adopted in their entirety by the respective city councils.

In still other instances there may be a series of budget documents instead of one budget for any given government. These may include (1) an operating budget, which handles the bulk of ongoing operations, (2) a capital budget, which covers major new construction projects, and (3) a series of special fund budgets, which cover programs that are funded by specific revenue sources. Special fund budgets commonly include highway programs, which are financed through gasoline and tire sales taxes. In such cases, revenue from these sources is earmarked for highway construction, improvement, and maintenance. Other special funds may be user fees for fishing and hunting licenses, with the proceeds used to stock streams and provide ample hunting opportunities.

The format of budget documents also varies. On the whole, budget documents tend to provide greater information on expenditures than on revenues. Usually, revenues are treated in a brief section, with the remainder of the document devoted to expenditures. On the expenditure side, budgets are multipurpose in that no single document and no single definition can exhaust the functions budgets serve or the ways they are used. At the most general level three basic concepts are found in all budgets. They may be understood as descriptions, explanations or causal assertions, and statements of preferences or values.

Budgets as Descriptions. Budgets are first descriptions of the status of an organization—agency, ministry, entire government, or any organizational unit. The budget document may describe what the organization purchases, what it does, and what it accomplishes. Descriptions of organizational activity are also common in budget documents; expenditures may be classified according to the activities they support. For example, a university budget may be divided into such major activities as instruction, research, and public service. Another type of description, organizational accomplishments, states the consequences of resource consumption and work activities for those outside the organization. These statements require external verification of the impact of the organization on its environment.

As descriptions, budgets provide a discrete picture of an organization at a point or points in time in terms of resources consumed, work performed, and external impact. The dollar expenditures, according to these types of descriptions, may be the only quantitative information supplied. Or information may be supplied about the number and types of personnel; the quantity and kinds of equipment purchased; measures of performance such as numbers of buildings inspected and number of acres treated; and measures of impact such as numbers of accidents prevented, amount of increased crop yields, and so forth. Generally, the more descriptive material supplied, the more the organization can be held accountable for the funds spent, the activities supported by those expenditures, and the external accomplishments produced by those activities. Much of the history of budget reform reflects attempts to increase the quantity and quality of descriptive material available both to decision makers and to the public.

Budgets as Explanations. When they describe organizations in all three categories discussed in the preceding paragraphs, budgets also at least implicitly serve a second major function—explanation of causal relationships. The expenditure of a specific amount for the purchase of labor and materials that will be combined in particular work activities alleges a causal sequence that will produce some given results. Regardless of how explicit or how vague the budget document or the statements of organizational officials may be, budgetary decisions always imply a causal process from resources through work activities to external results. Some organizations may have little accurate information about accomplishments, especially public organizations whose accomplishments are not measured as profit and loss. Governments may choose not to be explicit about particular results because they are either difficult to measure, politically sensitive, or both. Regardless of the availability of information or the willingness of the organization to collect and use it, the budget is an expression of a set of causal relationships. These issues are discussed in detail in Chapter 7.

Budgets as Preferences. Finally, budgets are statements of preferences. Whether intended or not, the allocation of resources among different agencies, or among different activities, or among different accomplishments reveals the preferences of those making the allocations. These may be the actual preferences of some decision makers, but more often they may be taken as the collective preferences of many decision makers, produced by complex bargaining. This preference schedule reflects, if not any one individual's values, an aggregate of choices that become the collective value judgment for the local government, state, or nation.

What Is a Budgeting System?

Systems. Budgeting as a decision-making process can best be understood in terms of a system, which can be defined simply as a "set of units with relationships among them."[25] Budgetary decision making consists of the actions of executive officials (both in a central organization such as the governor's office or the mayor's staff and in executive line-agencies), legislative officials, organized interest groups, and perhaps unorganized interests that may be manifested in a generally felt public concern about public needs and taxes. All these actions and interactions are related, and understanding budgeting means understanding these relationships. Such understanding is best achieved by thinking in terms of complex systems.

A complex social system is composed of organizations, individuals, the values held by these individuals, and the relationships among these units and values. A system may be thought of as a network typically consisting of many different parts with messages flowing among the parts.

Budget System Outputs. In a budgetary system, the outputs flowing from this network of interactions are budget decisions that will vary greatly in their overall significance. Not every unit of the system will have equal decisional authority or power. A manager of a field office for a state health department is likely to have less power to make major budgetary decisions than the administrative head of the department, the governor, or the members of the legislative appropriations committee. Yet each participant does contribute some input to the system. The field manager may alert others in the system to the rise of a new health problem and in doing so may contribute greatly to the eventual establishment of a new health program to combat the problem.

Like the outputs of any other system or network, budget decisions are seldom final and more commonly are sequential. Decisions are tentative in that each decision made is forwarded for action by another participant in the process. This does not mean that all decisions are reversible. Major breakthroughs, such as passage of the Elementary and Secondary Education Act of 1965, which provided sizable federal aid to education, are abandoned only with great effort and substantial political pressure. Subsequent budget decisions, therefore, are in large part bounded by previous decisions. These decisions tend to center on the question of changing the level of commitment—allocating more resources, fewer resources, or different kinds of resources to achieve desired levels of impacts or different types of impacts.

System Interconnectedness. Another feature of a system is that a change in any part of it will alter other parts. Because all units are related, any change in the role or functioning of one unit necessarily affects other units. In some instances, changes may be of such a modest nature that their ramifications for other parts of the system are difficult to discern. However, when major budgetary "reforms" are instituted, they assuredly affect most participants. For example, if one unit in the system is granted greater authority, individuals and organizations having access to that unit have their decisional involvement enhanced, whereas those groups associated with other units have diminished roles.[26] Thus, each individual and institution evaluates budget reforms in terms of how political strengths will be realigned under the reforms.

INFORMATION AND DECISION MAKING

Types of Information

To serve the multiple functions described in the preceding section, budgeting systems must produce and process a variety of information. Most of the major reforms, attempted or proposed, in public budget systems have been intended to reorganize existing information and to provide participants with different types and greater quantities of information. Basically, there are two types—program information and resource information. The latter form is traditional. People are accustomed to thinking of budgets in terms of monetary units and personnel. A budget would not be a budget if it did not contain dollar, ruble, or other monetary figures. Similarly, budgets commonly contain data on employees or personnel complement.

Conventional accounting systems have provided for most of the information that most public organizations use for budgetary decisions. This type of information, however, is limited to the internal aspects of organizations—the location of organizational responsibility for expenditures and the resources purchased by those expenditures. When the decision-making system incorporates information about the results or impacts of programs, however, one must leave the boundaries of the organization to examine consequences for those outside. This step requires more extensive and more explicit clarification of governmental goals and objectives (discussed in Chapter 6) and increases the importance of analysis (see Chapter 7). This feature of budget reforms, such as program budgeting, management by objectives, and zero-base budgeting, with their emphasis on program information and priority setting, has generated the most heat among critics of budget reform.[27]

Decision Making

Much of this criticism has involved the argument that decision-making systems must take into account the limitations on human capabilities to use all the information that might be collected. Although there are sometimes subtle differences among theories of decision making, depending on their assumptions about the objectives of a decision system and the capacity of the system to use information, the various theories may be generally classified into three basic approaches—pure rationality, muddling through or incrementalism, and limited rationality.[28] These are both descriptive theories as well as prescriptions for how decisions ought to be made.

Rational Decision Making. Decision making according to the pure rationality approach consists of a series of ordered, logical steps. First, a complete specification of an organization's or society's goals must be ranked by priority. Second, all possible alternatives are identified. The costs of each alternative are compared with anticipated benefits. Judgments are made as to which alternative comes closest to satisfying one's values. The alternative with the highest payoff and/or least cost is chosen. Pure rationality theories assume that complete and perfect information about all alternatives is both available and manageable. Decision making, therefore, is choosing among alternatives to maximize some objective function.

The applicability of the rationality model is limited. It is most consistent with notions of technical or economic rationality, where objectives can be stated with some precision and the range of feasible alternatives is not infinite.[29] Also, the model can be of use where it provides accurate predictions of behavior, such as assuming rational behavior in the private market and predicting future economic trends.[30] As a description of how government budgeting works, pure rationality obviously is inaccurate. The capability to meet the complete requirements of even one of the above steps is nonexistent. It has been argued that the costs of information are so high as to make it rational to be ignorant, that is, to make decisions on the basis of a limited search and limited information. As will be observed in following chapters, some attempts at budget reform have been criticized as attempts to impose an unworkable model, pure rationality, on government financial decision making. The use of program information has been a particular target for criticism.[31]

Incrementalism

The second approach to decision making, muddling through (incrementalism), has been advocated particularly by critics of pure rationality, such as Charles E. Lindblom, Aaron Wildavsky, and others.[32, 33] According to this view, decision making involves a conflict of interests and a corresponding clash of information, resulting in the accommodation of diverse partisan interests through bargaining. "Real" decision making is presumed to begin as issues are raised by significant interest groups who request or demand changes from the existing state.[34] Decision making is not some conscious form of pure rationality, but is the process of incrementally adjusting existing practices to establish or reestablish consensus among participants. This process is known as "disjointed incrementalism."[35] Alternatives to the status quo are normally not considered unless partisan interests bring them to the attention of the decision-making process. There is only a marginal amount of planned search for alternatives to achieve desired ends. The decisional process is structured so that partisan interests have the opportunity to press their desires at some point in the deliberations. Decisions represent a consensus on policy reached through a political power–oriented bargaining process.

The most important characteristic of the muddling through or incrementalist approach as applied to budgeting is its emphasis upon the proposition that budgetary decisions are necessarily political.[36] Whereas a purely rational approach might suggest that budgetary decisions are attempts to allocate resources according to economic criteria, the incrementalist view stresses the extent to which political considerations outweigh calculations of optimality. The strongest critics of many budget reforms have tended to equate those reforms with seeking to establish the pure rationality model. As will be seen throughout the book, any "real" budget reform is forced to accommodate the political nature of decision making.

Limited Rationality. The third approach to decision making, a compromise between the other two theories, is called limited rationality. This model recognizes the inapplicability of pure rationality to complex problems.[37,38] While acknowledging the inherent constraints of human cognitive processes, limited rationality does not suggest that a deliberate search for alternative approaches to goal achievement is of no avail. Search is used to find solutions that are satisfactory as distinguished from optimal or maximal.

Lindblom suggests that incrementalism is a deliberately chosen strategy for decision making and that other strategies short of pure rationality are possible.[39,40] These strategies would involve some form of comparisons among broad alternatives at the planning level and a more focused analysis of the narrower set of alternatives selected. At this lower level, analysts may consider the immediate effects of incremental adjustments in present policies, but explicit attention is also directed at what these immediate effects portend for broader and more long-range concerns. It is possible to be simultaneously incremental and comprehensive with a short- and long-range perspective.

Limited rationality seems to occupy a nebulous middle ground between incrementalism and pure rationality.[41] The reasons for this are that the middle ground is difficult to define with precision and, further, that some of the theorists who support incrementalism and pure rationality may claim some share of this middle territory. The main point, however, is that decision theories are identifiably different in their emphasis upon both the values that decision making serves and the capacities of decision makers to serve those values. One model assumes virtually no limits on human capacities for processing information, another suggests that the only information that decision making should be sensitive to is partisan political interests, and the third attempts to strike a balance between the others. The history of budgeting and budget reform, we argue, reflects the tensions among these approaches to decision making.

SUMMARY

Public budgeting involves choices among ends and means. Private sector and public sector budgeting share many characteristics, but public budgeting often requires the application of criteria for choice that are different from private choices. Chief among the differences is that few public sector decisions can be assessed in terms of profit and loss. Private sector decisions, on the other hand, ultimately must consider the long-run profit or loss condition of the firm.

Budgeting systems involve the organization of information for making choices and the structure of decision-making processes. Public budgeting systems have evolved as one of the means of holding government accountable for its actions. Budgetary procedures are developed to hold the government in general accountable to the public, the executive accountable to the legislature, and subordinates accountable to their managers. Budgetary procedures also are developed to specify for what the executive is accountable. Most recently, concern for the financial solvency of some city governments and the size of the federal budget deficit and total debt has led to reform proposals to use budgeting as a device for holding government accountable for its long-term financial position.

Budgetary systems work through information flows. However, each participant in the budgetary process pays attention selectively to information. The various theories of decision making advanced differ on how much information decision makers are willing and able to consider. The decision-making approach that seems best to characterize budgetary systems is labeled limited rationality. This limited rationality approach underlies the discussions throughout the book.

NOTES

1. Anthony Downs, *Inside Bureaucracy* (Boston: Little, Brown, 1967).

2. Tom J. Peters and Robert H. Waterman, Jr., *In Search of Excellence: Lessons from America's Best-Run Companies* (New York: Harper & Row, 1982).

3. David N. Hyman, *Public Finance: A Contemporary Application of Theory to Policy*, 2nd ed. (Chicago: Dryden, 1987), p. 115.

4. Edgar K. Browning and Jacqueline M. Browning, *Public Finance and the Price System*, 3rd ed. (New York: Macmillan, 1987), pp. 23-51.

5. Gabriel Roth, *The Private Provision of Public Services* (New York: Oxford University Press, 1987).

6. Michael J. White credits W.F. Willoughby's *The Problem of a National Budget* with an early (1919) statement of budgeting as a process for holding government accountable. Michael J. White, "Budget Policy: Where Does It Begin and End?" *Governmental Finance* 7 (August 1978): 2-9.

7. Leo Herbert, Larry N. Killough, and Alan Walter Steiss, *Accounting and Control for Governmental and Nonbusiness Organizations* (New York: McGraw-Hill, 1987).

8. Carolyn Webber and Aaron Wildavsky, *A History of Taxation and Expenditure in the Western World* (New York: Simon & Schuster, 1986).

9. Jesse Burkhead, *Government Budgeting* (New York: Wiley, 1956), pp. 2-4.

10. A. Premchand, "Government Budgeting Forms: An Overview," *Public Budgeting and Finance* 1 (Summer 1981): 74-85.

11. Arthur Smithies, *The Budgetary Process in the United States* (New York: McGraw-Hill, 1955), p. 50.

12. A.E. Buck, *Public Budgeting* (New York: Harper and Brothers, 1929), p. 17.

13. E.E. Naylor, *The Federal Budget System in Operation* (Washington, D.C.: printed privately, 1941), pp. 22-23.

14. Burkhead, *Government Budgeting*, pp. 12-13.

15. Buck, *Public Budgeting*, p. 14.

16. Burkhead, *Government Budgeting*, p. 23.

17. York Willbern, "Personnel and Money," in James W. Fesler, ed., *The 50 States and Their Local Governments* (New York: Knopf, 1967), p. 391.

18. Frederick A. Cleveland, "Evolution of the Budget Idea in the United States," *Annals* 62 (November 1915): 22.

19. Commission on Organization of the Executive Branch of the Government, *General Management of the Executive Branch* (Washington, D.C.: Government Printing Office, 1949).

20. Commission on Organization of the Executive Branch of the Government, *Budget and Accounting* (Washington, D.C.: Government Printing Office, 1955), p. ix.

21. Allen Schick, "The Road to PPB: The Stages of Budget Reform," *Public Administration Review* 26 (1966): 243–58.

22. Ronald W. Johnson and Arie Y. Lewin, "Management and Accountability Models of Public Sector Performance," in Trudi C. Miller, ed., *Public Sector Performance: A Conceptual Turning Point* (Baltimore: Johns Hopkins University Press, 1984), pp. 224–50.

23. General Accounting Office, *Managing the Cost of Government: Building An Effective Financial Management Structure, Volumes I and II* (Washington, D.C.: Government Printing Office, 1985).

24. Burkhead, *Government Budgeting*, p. 2.

25. James G. Miller, "Living Systems: Basic Concepts," *Behavioral Science* 10 (1965): 200.

26. Aaron Wildavsky, *The New Politics of the Budgetary Process* (Glenview, Ill.: Scott, Foresman, 1988).

27. Verne B. Lewis, "Reflections on Budget Systems," *Public Budgeting and Finance* 8 (Spring 1988): 4–19.

28. Garry D. Brewer and Peter de Leon, *The Foundations of Policy Analysis* (Chicago: Dorsey, 1983).

29. The terms "technical" and "economic rationality" are two of five basic types of rationality identified by Paul Diesing, *Reason and Society* (Urbana: University of Illinois Press, 1962).

30. See Milton Friedman, *Essays in Positive Economics* (Chicago: University of Chicago Press, 1953).

31. Aaron Wildavsky, *Speaking Truth to Power: The Art and Craft of Policy Analysis* (Boston: Little, Brown, 1979).

32. Charles E. Lindblom, "The Science of 'Muddling Through,' " *Public Administration Review* 19 (1959): 79–88.

33. Charles E. Lindblom, "Still Muddling, Not Yet Through," *Public Administration Review* 39 (1979): 517–26.

34. The incrementalist approach is most thoroughly applied to the budgetary process in Wildavsky, *New Politics of the Budgetary Process*.

35. David Braybrooke and Charles E. Lindblom, *A Strategy of Decision* (New York: Free Press, 1963).

36. See Lance T. LeLoup, *Budgetary Politics: Dollars, Deficits, Decisions* (Brunswick, Ohio: King's Court, 1977).

37. Herbert Simon, *Administrative Behavior*, 2nd ed. (New York: Macmillan, 1961).

38. Richard M. Cyert and James G. March, *Behavioral Theory of the Firm* (Englewood Cliffs, N.J.: Prentice-Hall, 1963).

39. Lindblom, "Still Muddling, Not Yet Through."

40. Brewer and de Leon, *Foundations of Policy Analysis*.

41. Duncan MacRae, Jr., and James A. Wilde, *Policy Analysis for Public Decisions* (North Scituate, Mass.: Duxbury Press, 1979).

2

The Public Sector in Perspective

A danger of generalizing about the size of the public sector of society is that any single generalization necessarily ignores important information. While the generalization "government is vast" may be valid, it fails to recognize the difficulties in determining what is and is not government or the fact that government is also small in some respects. This chapter provides a long-term view of the size of the public sector, relative and absolute growth rates, and the general level of taxing and spending activity and the societal functions they support.

The chapter explores three main topics. The first is the relative sizes of the private and public sectors of society and the reasons for the growth of government. Second, the magnitude of government and the historical growth of local, state, and federal finances are considered. Third, the purposes of government expenditures are contrasted with the sources of revenue used by the three main levels of government in the United States.

RELATIVE SIZES OF THE PRIVATE AND PUBLIC SECTORS

Basic to all matters of public budgeting is the issue of the appropriate size of the public sector. This issue is inherently political, not only in the partisan sense but also in the sense that it raises fundamental policy questions about what government should and should not do. At stake are congeries of competing public and private wants and needs.

Reasons for Growth

Value Questions. The issue of size relates to values of freedom and societal needs. Keeping government small has been advocated as protecting individuals

21

from tyranny and stimulating individual independence and initiative.[1-3] Faith in the value of the private sector, on the other hand, has been criticized as resulting in the underfinancing of public programs and the failure to confront major social problems.[4] Debates over the rise of the welfare and warfare states have been especially acrimonious during this century.

The political system, of course, is not structured in such a way that an overriding decision is made as to the size of the public sector. The multiplicity of governments makes it virtually impossible to reach any single decision about the appropriate size of the public sector. Decisions relevant to size are made in a political context within and between the executive and legislative branches and among the three major levels of government—local, state, and federal. Each set of decisions contributes to an ultimate resolution of the question, but one must await the tally of all decisions before being able to perceive what has been deemed the appropriate size.

Governmental Responses. Why government expands has been the subject of extended debate.[5,6] The two main reasons advanced have been that government is "responsive" in meeting the needs of society and that it is "excessive."[7,8] In the latter case, government is seen as growing because of empire building by government bureaucrats supported by political leaders.[9,10] Among the numerous factors suggested as stimulating responses from government are:[11,12]

1. **The need for collective goods.** Since defense, flood control, and some other programs benefit all citizens and cannot be readily handled by the private sector, government becomes involved. When wars occur, governments grow in size and after the conflict tend to remain larger than during the prewar period.
2. **Demographic changes.** Increases in total population, newborns, and the elderly stimulate the creation and expansion of government programs.
3. **Externalities.** Air and water pollution produced by industrial firms, which are concerned mainly with making a profit, is a social cost and a condition that government is expected to control. Education also has important externalities; uneducated people impose costs on others through the need for welfare and other social services, while educated people tend to be more productive and increase the total value of the society.
4. **Economic hardships.** Depressions and other economic situations stimulate the growth of government.
5. **High-risk situations.** When risks are high, the private sector is unlikely to invest large quantities of resources, so government is called upon to support programs. One example is the development of atomic energy as a source of electrical power.
6. **Technological change.** With the advent of new technology, government has been called upon to provide support, as in the case of roads and

airports to accommodate improved transportation modes, or to regulate new industries, as in the case of railroads, radio, and television.

While these reasons are helpful in explaining why government enters into the private sector, they do not sufficiently reflect the political considerations at stake when proposals are made for expanding or contracting the scope of the public sector. Any proposal for the expansion of services that results in an increase in taxes is likely to have some unfavorable political repercussions. Therefore, the size issue always relates both to government expenditures and revenues (taxes). Decision makers, no matter how crude or approximate their methods of calculating, attempt to weigh the merits of coping with the current situation with available resources against the merits of recommending new programs that may alleviate problems but at the same time raise the ire of taxpayers.

Private and Public Sector Boundaries

Major problems are encountered when attempts are made to gauge the size of the public and private sectors and to distinguish between one government and another. Government has become so deeply involved in the society that one may frequently have difficulty discerning what is not at least quasi-public. Moreover, governments have extensive relationships with each other, to the point where a discussion of any single government becomes meaningless without a discussion of its relationships with other governments.

Statistical data on government revenues and expenditures fail to reflect adequately the size of government. For instance, the entire political campaign process is clearly governmental in that funds are expended to elect people to political offices, yet most of these monies are not recorded as government expenditures.[13] In other cases, the size of government is understated when some activities require relatively little money and personnel, yet the impact of these activities upon the private sector or other governments can be substantial. This is especially true with respect to regulatory activities, such as the control of interstate commerce, occupational safety, and environmental health by the federal government.

Nonexhaustive Expenditures. Complete reliance on revenue and expenditure data for measuring size is unwarranted for another reason. Sometimes the assumption is made that all government expenditures are a drain upon the private economy. However, government expenditures can be nonexhaustive as well as exhaustive.[14] The latter means that government consumes resources such as facilities and manpower that might otherwise have been used by the private sector. Nonexhaustive expenditures entail the redistribution of resources among components of the society rather than the consumption of resources. Interest payments on the national debt, unemployment compensation, aid to the indigent, and old-age and retirement benefits are some of the major examples of nonexhaustive government expenditures.

Another form of nonexhaustive expenditures is investments for the future, whether for capital facilities or for services, as in educating children. Governmental aid to small businesses, support of research and development, and like activities are forms of investments in future economic development. In light of these kinds of expenditures, then, the cost of government is actually less than the total dollar figures reported in budgets.

Effects on Private Sector. Government expenditures have specific effects upon industries, occupations, and geographic regions. These impacts are especially evident in the field of defense.[15] Clusters of firms and their employees have become highly dependent upon defense outlays, resulting in what President Eisenhower in 1961 decried as the military-industrial complex. A dangerous symbiotic relationship can develop between the military, with its penchant for new weaponry, and corporations that are eager to supply such weaponry. Periodic scandals in defense are seeming confirmation of fears expressed by President Eisenhower.

The impact of defense upon the private sector can be seen in terms of employment. In 1985, defense accounted for 3.2 million jobs in the private sector, or 3.4 percent of the work force. In addition, the federal government hired 2.2 million people for armed forces duty and another 1.3 million as civilian defense workers.[16]

The impact of defense expenditures upon specific occupations also has been significant. Defense expenditures account for over half of the employment in such occupations as precision aircraft assemblers, shipfitters, and electrical installers and repairers.[17] Technical personnel in the aeronautical engineering field, physicists, and a variety of other scientific occupations are heavily engaged in defense-related work. The creation of defense-related jobs has the effect of attracting people into educational programs that develop the requisite skills. The result is that people are attracted into technical career fields that are dependent upon continued defense spending. These people suffer or flourish, depending upon what policies are in operation.

Geographic and Industry Effects. Military research, development, and procurement are of such great magnitude that many specific industries and corporations become quasi-public institutions.[18] Defense purchases 93 percent of the output of the shipbuilding industry, 66 percent of the aircraft industry, and 50 percent of the radio and television communications industry.[19] Besides providers of military equipment, such as Lockheed Aircraft and General Dynamics, numerous consulting and research and development firms are dependent on military expenditures. Employees of these firms are in effect career civil servants, judging from their length of service on government projects. The only difference is that their pay is higher working for "free enterprise" than it would be if they were directly employed by government.

The geographic impact of defense expenditures is equally important, because they are not uniformly distributed throughout the nation.[20] In 1986, defense contract awards totaled $136 billion, and 42 percent of those awards went to corporations in just four states: California was first, followed by Texas, New York, and Massachusetts.[21] The dependence upon defense is hardly a handicap for states when defense expenditures are rising, but declining expenditures can create severe problems.

Defense, while the most striking example of private dependence upon public outlays, is not the sole example. Highway construction is another case involving large sums of public money. The employees of contracting firms specializing in bridge and highway construction are in effect governmental employees. The same is true for suppliers of road-building equipment. It also should be noted that companies of this type are major suppliers of equipment to the Defense Department.

In some cases, the impact of government on an industry is greater in what government does not do than in what it does. This condition exists in housing. The dollar value of public housing and redevelopment construction accounted for less than 1 percent of all housing construction in 1986.[22] Federal Housing Administration and Veterans Administration mortgages covered only 4 percent of the value of housing loans for that year.[23] Although these types of involvement are important, a more significant subsidy to housing is that the federal government allows home buyers to deduct on their income tax returns all interest paid on their loans. Since such deductions are used more by the middle class than the poor and constitute a tax expenditure far greater than government expenditures for low-income housing, the argument can be made that there is a redistributional effect in favor of the middle class.

The lack of clear-cut distinctions between the public and private sectors and between one government and another is evident in education. Elementary and secondary education is a function of local school districts, but about half the funds used by these districts come from state governments, with additional funds coming from the federal government. Public higher education is funded by states with important support from the federal government, especially in the areas of student aid and financing of research. Governments also selectively subsidize private colleges and universities. Private corporations make important contributions to both public and private schools.

THE MAGNITUDE AND GROWTH OF GOVERNMENT

There are many ways to measure the magnitude of government, but dollars and people are generally the easiest measures to apply. By focusing upon revenues, expenditures, and numbers of employees, we can use comparable standards in contrasting governments with each other and with nongovernmental or private organizations. These measures, then, are the main ones used in this section.

A word of caution is warranted. Statistical data used in this and the following section are drawn from several sources, some of which are not even in approximate agreement with each other. Particular problems are encountered in drawing comparisons among nations. Therefore, some of the data reported here must be considered quite approximate.

Revenues

One approach to measuring organizations is to consider their revenues or receipts, thereby allowing comparisons among both private and public organizations.[24] Using this measure, Figure 2-1 ranks the 25 largest organizations in the world. Significantly, 15 of the 25 are governments. Three U.S. bureaucracies are included in the list—the federal government, California, and New York State. New York City came close to making the list, ranking 29th with revenues at $29.4 billion. In a listing of the top 50 organizations in the United States, 10 state governments are included (see Table 2-1). These states, in order of appearance, are California, New York, Texas, Ohio, Pennsylvania, Michigan, Illinois, New Jersey, Florida, and Massachusetts.

An important aspect of these illustrations is that they dramatically underscore the need for caution in generalizing about governments or private corporations. Admittedly, one must recognize the important differences in the functions of government and industry and the methods by which these organizations make decisions. Differences also abound within each of these two types of organizations. Of course, services provided and methods of decision making are not identical in the Soviet Union, West Germany, the United Kingdom, or any other nation.

On the other hand, the standard of size may provide insights into the operations of organizations that are more useful than the designations public or private, national or local, and so forth. Not all industrial firms are like General Motors, nor are all state governments like California's. It may be that all organizations of any given size, regardless of their private or public character, exhibit some common traits.

Although total revenues or expenditures are useful as approximate guides in measuring the size of government, these data need to be assessed in light of the varied capabilities of societies to support government. Unfortunately, reliable international data are often unavailable, and as a consequence drawing useful comparisons among international organizations is impossible or of questionable value.

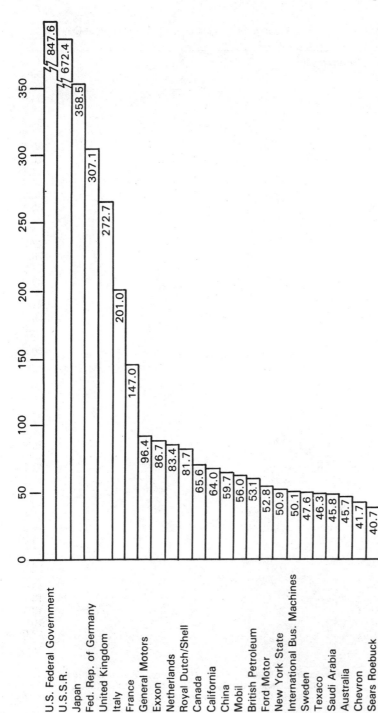

Figure 2-1 Twenty-Five Largest Organizations in the World, by Receipts or Revenues, 1985–86 (Billions of Dollars). *Sources: Government Finances in 1985–86,* Bureau of the Census, Government Printing Office, 1987; "The Forbes 500s Annual Directory," *Forbes,* Vol. 137, pp. 118-119, Forbes, Inc., © April 28, 1986; "The International 500," *Fortune Magazine,* Vol. 114, p. 181, Time, Inc., © August 4, 1986; *The Europa Yearbook, 1988,* Europa Publications, Ltd., © 1988; and *Yearbook Australia, 1986,* Australia Bureau of Statistics, 1986.

1. U.S. Federal Government
2. U.S.S.R.
3. Japan
4. Fed. Rep. of Germany
5. United Kingdom
6. Italy
7. France
8. General Motors
9. Exxon
10. Netherlands
11. Royal Dutch/Shell
12. Canada
13. California
14. China
15. Mobil
16. British Petroleum
17. Ford Motor
18. New York State
19. International Bus. Machines
20. Sweden
21. Texaco
22. Saudi Arabia
23. Australia
24. Chevron
25. Sears Roebuck

Table 2-1 Fifty Largest U.S. Organizations by Revenue, 1985–86 (Billions of Dollars)

1.	U.S. Federal Government	847.6
2.	General Motors	96.4
3.	Exxon	86.7
4.	California	64.0
5.	Mobil	56.0
6.	Ford Motor	52.8
7.	New York State	50.9
8.	International Business Machines	50.1
9.	Texaco	46.3
10.	Chevron	41.7
11.	Sears Roebuck	40.7
12.	American Telephone and Telegraph	34.9
13.	New York City	29.4
14.	E.I. du Pont	29.2
15.	General Electric	28.3
16.	Philbro-Saloman	27.9
17.	Amoco	26.9
18.	Texas	23.1
19.	Ohio	23.0
20.	Citicorp	22.5
21.	K-Mart	22.4
22.	Pennsylvania	22.1
23.	Atlantic Richfield	21.7
24.	Chrysler	21.3
25.	Michigan	20.5
26.	International Telephone & Telegraph	19.9
27.	Safeway Stores	19.7
28.	Illinois	19.4
29.	Aetna Life and Casualty	18.6
30.	U.S. Steel	18.4
31.	New Jersey	17.6
32.	Kroeger	17.1
33.	Cigna	16.2
34.	Florida	15.8
35.	General Telephone and Electric	15.7
36.	Phillips Petroleum	15.6
37.	Tenneco	15.3
38.	United Technologies	15.0
39.	Travelers	14.6
40.	Occidental Petroleum	14.5
41.	Procter & Gamble	14.2
42.	American Stores	13.9
43.	Sun Company	13.8
44.	J.C. Penney	13.8
45.	Boeing	13.6
46.	R.J. Reynolds Industries	13.5
47.	Bank America	13.4
48.	Massachusetts	13.1
49.	Standard Oil	13.0
50.	Southland	12.4

Sources: City Government Finances in 1985-86, Bureau of the Census, Government Printing Office, 1987; *Government Finances in 1985-86*, Bureau of the Census, Government Printing Office, 1987; *State Government Finances in 1986*, Bureau of the Census, Government Printing Office, 1987; "The Forbes 500s Annual Directory," *Forbes*, Vol. 137, pp. 118-119, Forbes, Inc., © April 28, 1986.

Given these limitations, it seems adequate to recognize that the U.S. economy is one of the most prosperous in the world. In 1986, the per capita gross national product (GNP) in the United States was $17,417.[25] This wealth has allowed for both big government and a large private sector. The nation has been able to have large government expenditures ($7,039 per capita expenditures of all governments in the United States) equal to about 40 percent of GNP.[26] The contrasts that can be drawn regarding this great wealth and large expenditures are striking. The government of New York City, for example, normally spends in one year a sum larger than the entire GNPs of many nations having far greater populations.

Historical Trends

Expenditures. Because early records on state and local finance were not kept in any uniform and complete manner, reliance must be placed upon federal expenditure data to obtain some overall perspective of the growth of government since the 18th century. Table 2-2 shows federal spending from 1789 through 1994 (estimated). During this period of two centuries, expenditures rose from only $4.3 million in the first few years to more than $1 trillion annually.

The 20th century has seen important differences between expenditure patterns of the federal government and those of state and local governments. Federal expenditures have fluctuated most, primarily because of war-related

Table 2-2 Federal Government Expenditures, Selected Years, 1789–1994 (Millions of Dollars)

1789–1791	4	1865	1,298	1935	6,412
1800	11	1870	310	1940	9,468
1805	11	1875	275	1945	92,712
1810	8	1880	268	1950	42,562
1815	33	1885	260	1955	68,444
1820	18	1890	318	1960	92,191
1825	16	1895	356	1965	118,228
1830	15	1900	529	1970	195,649
1835	18	1905	567	1975	332,332
1840	24	1910	694	1980	590,920
1845	23	1915	761	1985	946,316
1850	40	1920	6,403	1990	1,151,848*
1855	60	1925	3,063	1994	1,311,601*
1860	63	1930	3,440		

*Estimates.

Sources: Historical Statistics of the United States, Colonial Times-1957, Bureau of the Census, Government Printing Office, 1960; and *Budget of the United States Government:* Historical Tables, Office of Management and Budget, Government Printing Office, 1989.

activities. The first year in which federal expenditures exceeded $1 billion was 1865, the peak year of the Civil War. For World War I, federal expenditures jumped from $0.7 billion in 1916 to $18.5 billion in 1919, then dropped to $6.4 billion the following year. For World War II, expenditures increased from $13.3 billion in 1941 to $92.7 billion in 1945, then declined to $33.1 billion in 1948. For the Korean War, expenditures rose from $42.6 billion in 1950 to $74.3 billion in 1953, then dropped to $68.4 billion in 1955. In general, federal expenditures have risen during wartime and then declined, but not to the prewar level, thereby resulting in a cumulative increase over time. The Vietnam War era departed from this pattern; federal expenditures rose during and after the war.

State and local expenditures, on the other hand, have fluctuated less. They have increased annually, except for a period of slight decline during World War II.

Important shifts have occurred in the extent to which the nation relies upon different levels of government. At the turn of the century, local governments were by far the biggest spenders, followed by the federal government and then the states. During the Depression, federal spending spurted above local expenditures, and the gap has since been widening. As of 1987, federal expenditures stood at $1,148.6 billion compared with $455.7 billion for states and $466.8 billion for local governments.[27] Caution should be exercised in interpreting these numbers in that each includes intergovernmental transfers, namely grants from one government to another.

Just as total expenditures have increased, so have per capita expenditures. In 1902 the total of all government expenditures in the United States was only $20 per capita; in 1987, the comparable figure was $7,436 per capita, an increase of more than 35,000 percent. These data, however, overstate the rising cost of government by not deflating for general price increases or inflation that has occurred.

One means of controlling for price changes over time is to consider government expenditures as a percentage of GNP (Figure 2-2). From 1902 to 1986 the cost of government rose from 7.0 percent to 40.1 percent of GNP. Slight increases were recorded throughout the early 1900s, until a noteworthy increase to 21.4 percent occurred in 1932. The 20 percent level continued throughout the 1930s. World War II brought expenditures to an all-time high, in excess of half of GNP, but a sharp cutback followed in the postwar years. A much smaller increase occurred during the Korean War. During the 1960s and 1970s, government expenditures were almost constant at 30–35 percent of GNP. In the 1980s, the percentage climbed to 40 largely owing to federal expenditures.

Public Employment. The rise of big bureaucracy in the federal government can be measured in terms of public employees. In 1816 there were less than 5,000 full- and part-time civilian employees in the federal service. Following

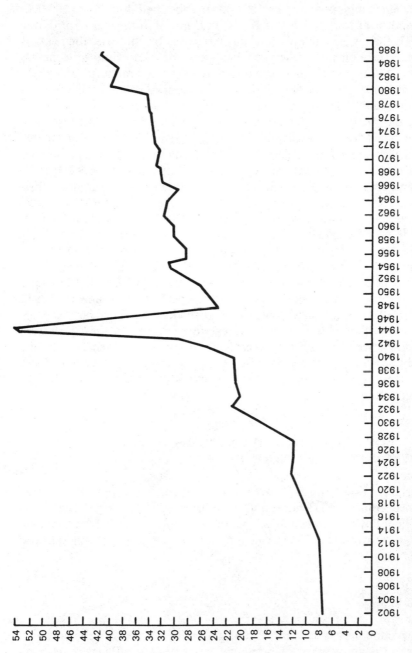

Figure 2-2 All Government Expenditures as a Percentage of Gross National Product, 1902–87. *Sources: Historical Statistics on Governmental Finances and Employment*, Bureau of the Census, pp. 1, 36–47, Government Printing Office, 1969; *Special Analyses: Budget of the United States Government, Fiscal Year 1982*, Office of Management and Budget, p. 253, Government Printing Office, 1981; *Government Finances in 1986–87*, Bureau of the Census, p. 1, Government Printing Office, 1988; and *Economic Report of the President*, Council of Economic Advisors, p. 248, Government Printing Office, 1988.

the Civil War, however, greater growth was recorded. In 1871 there were over 50,000 federal employees, and by 1881 this number had doubled to 100,000. The period of fastest growth was from the Depression through World War II. In 1931 there were still only 610,000 employees, but by 1945, the peak of the wartime economy, the federal civilian work force had climbed to nearly 4 million. Within a year, this was reduced to less than 3 million. Since then, only once, in 1950, has the federal work force dropped below 2 million. During the 1970s and 1980s, federal civilian personnel remained at about 3 million.

While the size of the federal bureaucracy is extraordinarily large, government personnel are geographically dispersed. In 1986 California had 314,000 federal civilian employees, a figure equivalent to about half of the total population of Delaware. These employees alone, not counting their families if located in the same area, would constitute a metropolitan area somewhat larger than Augusta, Georgia, or Corpus Christi, Texas. Comparable figures for federal employees in other states are Illinois, with 104,000; New York, with 156,000; and Texas with 172,000.[28]

At the state and local levels the number of employees has also increased. State employment grew from less than 1 million in 1947 to 4.1 million in 1986. In the same period, local employment increased from 2.9 million to 9.8 million. Overall, there was an average of 30 employees per local government in 1952 and 118 in 1986. Significantly, the growth at the local level has been accompanied by a decline in the number of local governments. In 1987 there were 83,166 local governments, 19,000 fewer than three decades earlier. This decline is largely attributable to school district consolidation.[29] Fewer and fewer governments are hiring more and more people who are spending more and more tax dollars.

SOURCES OF REVENUES AND PURPOSES OF GOVERNMENT EXPENDITURES

Government does not simply get money and spend it in general. Revenue is obtained from specific sources and spent for specific public goods and services. The following discussion considers the relationships between income and outgo, between the ways in which revenue is generated and the purpose of government expenditures.

Revenue Source

Tax structure always has been and always will be a greatly debated topic. This section is an overview of taxes and other revenues. Policy issues pertaining to the equitability of the tax system are covered in Chapter 4.

Table 2-3 displays the sources of revenue for the federal, state, and local governments in 1986–87. The first important item to understand from this table is that it covers the sources of revenue but not expenditures. Because of intergovernmental transfers of funds, governments may obtain revenue from many sources but not directly spend it. This is true for all levels of government, including local governments, which provide the states with some revenue (1 percent). As can be seen in the table, 20 percent of state government revenue and 33 percent of local government revenue come from other jurisdictions. Once again it is apparent that clear-cut distinctions among the three levels of government are nonexistent.

Three tax sources provide 80 percent of the federal government's revenue. The largest single share (41 percent) is obtained through the individual income tax; 30 percent through social insurance, including Social Security and unemployment compensation; and 9 percent through the corporate income

Table 2-3 Government Revenue by Source and Level of Government, 1986–87

Revenue Source	All Government Revenues (Millions of Dollars)	Distribution (Percent)			
		All	Federal	State	Local
General Revenue	1,235,685	73.7	70.0	81.2	87.4
Intergovernmental Revenue			0.3	19.8	33.3
From Federal Government				18.5	4.2
From States			0.3		29.1
From Local Government				1.3	
General Revenue from Own Sources	1,235,685	73.7	69.8	61.3	54.1
Taxes	944,549	56.3	56.6	47.8	33.7
Property	121,227	7.2		0.9	24.8
Sales, Gross Receipts, and Customs	192,716	11.5	5.1	23.2	5.2
Individual Income	476,238	28.4	41.2	14.7	1.6
Corporation Net Income	106,598	6.4	8.8	4.0	0.4
Other	47,771	2.8	1.5	5.0	1.6
Charges and Miscellaneous General Revenue	291,136	17.4	13.1	13.6	20.4
Utility and Liquor Store Revenue	49,810	3.0		1.1	9.4
Insurance Trust Revenue	392,242	23.4	30.0	17.7	3.2
Total Revenue*	1,677,737	100.0	100.0	100.0	100.0
			952,631	516,941	469,317

*Totals may not equal 100.0 percent due to rounding.

Source: Government Finances in 1986-87, Bureau of the Census, p. 2, Government Printing Office, 1988.

tax. Another 5 percent comes from sales and gross receipt taxes and customs duties. The latter accounted for 94 percent of all federal monies in 1792. Corporate income tax revenues also have declined in importance; they accounted for 30 percent of revenues in 1930.

As already indicated, one-fifth of state revenue comes from other governments, particularly the federal government.[30] Of the remainder, sales and gross receipts taxes are the largest revenue source, providing 23 percent of all state funds. Another 15 percent is obtained from individual income taxes.

Local governments obtain one-third of their money from other governments and the rest mainly through the property tax and other sources. Of all local revenue, 25 percent comes from the property tax. Approximately 30 percent is obtained from charges, miscellaneous general revenue, and utility fees.

Expenditures by Function

Expenditures are the product of a set of choices or decisions made as to what public goods and services should be produced. Total expenditures are the sum of decisions made at all levels of government. Each level of government, however, has discrete financial decision-making processes that are only partially dependent on the other levels. As the different levels depend on somewhat different sources for revenues, local, state, and federal governments also spend their funds for somewhat different functions.

The federal government provides financial assistance to state and local governments, the states to local governments, and, in some cases, local governments to states. Thus governments obviously do not spend directly all the money that flows through them. In 1986–87, direct federal expenditures were $1,037 billion, or 90 percent of all federal expenditures. State governments spent a smaller percentage of their funds—$314 billion or 69 percent of all state expenditures. Local governments spent directly virtually all their funds—$459 billion or 99 percent.

Government expenditures by function and by level of government are displayed in Table 2-4. Like Tables 2-2 and 2-3, it reports gross finances, including intergovernmental transfers. As the percentage distributions show, social insurance is the largest single function of government, accounting for 20 percent of all expenditures by the federal, state, and local governments. That number increases to 31 percent if social services and income maintenance (welfare) are added. Social insurance by itself, however, tied with defense for being the largest federal expenditure function in 1986–87; each constituted 28 percent of the federal budget.

Some of the financial costs of defense are not reflected in these figures. Veterans' benefits and services, which are obviously by-products of defense and which constituted 3 percent of the fiscal 1987 budget, are not included.

Table 2-4 Expenditures by Function and Level of Government, 1986–87

Function	All Government Revenues (Millions of Dollars)	Distribution (Percent)			
		All	Federal	State	Local
General Expenditure	1,374,297	75.9	72.4	88.6	85.4
National Defense and International Relations	319,084	17.6	27.8		
Postal Service	32,243	1.8	2.8		
Space Research and Technology	7,450	0.4	0.7		
Education and Libraries	244,325	13.5	2.8	33.0	36.3
Social Services and Income Maintenance	202,758	11.2	10.3	24.9	11.0
Transportation	66,237	3.7	1.8	9.2	6.1
Public Safety	61,611	3.4	0.4	4.1	8.5
Environment and Housing	147,910	8.2	9.3	2.9	9.3
Governmental Administration	44,126	2.4	0.8	3.0	4.7
Interest on General Debt	187,971	10.4	12.7	4.1	5.0
Other	60,584	3.3	3.1	7.5	4.6
Utility and Liquor Store	68,440	3.8		1.9	12.9
Insurance Trust	367,269	20.3	27.6	9.5	1.6
Total*		100.0	100.0	100.0	100.0
	1,810,006		1,148,584	455,696	463,826

*Totals may not equal 100.0 percent due to rounding.

Source: *Government Finances in 1986-87*, Bureau of the Census, p. 2, Government Printing Office, 1988.

A portion of the interest paid on the national debt can be ascribed to defense, given that major budgetary deficits have been incurred during wartime. Some aspects of the space program also could be charged to defense, because technological breakthroughs in space exploration are likely to have military applications.

Following defense and social insurance, all other federal program areas are comparatively small. The next largest "program" is interest paid on the national debt (13 percent). The remainder of federal expenditures are divided into small segments among education, postal service, transportation, the environment and housing, and other functions.

State and local expenditures follow different patterns. In the first place, neither the states nor local governments are responsible for defense, postal service, or space exploration. Education is the largest expense for both types of government, 33 percent for states and 36 percent for local governments, particularly school districts. Social services and income maintenance constitute the next largest state function (25 percent). "Traditional" local functions, such

as roads, public safety (police and fire), and housing each constitute only
6–9 percent of local spending.

Expenditures reported here cover intergovernmental transfers as well as
direct outlays. Because of double counting of funds, for example, federal
grants to states are reported under both federal and state expenditures. In
spite of this weakness, the table is useful in indicating the purposes for which
governments spend their resources. On the other hand, one should recognize
that in many cases governments do not actually spend these funds but rather
provide them to other governments. Also, these data do not reveal the relative
contributions of different levels of government to a given program area.

These points are clarified in Table 2-5, which displays federal, state, and
local expenditures as percentage contributions to functional areas. For instance, in Table 2-4 environment and housing expenditures constitute only
9 percent of the federal budget, but in Table 2-5 these expenditures account
for 64 percent of all outlays for this field.

SUMMARY

The preceding discussion has shown that government is indeed large, that
the growth pattern of the public sector has been an upward one, and that

Table 2-5 Direct Expenditures by Function and Level of Government

Function	Distribution (Percent)			
	All	Federal	State	Local
General Expenditure	100.0	57.3	17.4	25.3
National Defense and International Relations	100.0	100.0		
Postal Service	100.0	100.0		
Space Research and Technology	100.0	100.0		
Education and Libraries	100.0	5.9	25.3	68.8
Social Services and Income Maintenance	100.0	31.0	45.0	24.0
Transportation	100.0	9.7	49.2	41.1
Public Safety	100.0	8.1	28.1	63.9
Environment and Housing	100.0	63.6	7.4	29.0
Governmental Administration	100.0	20.9	30.2	48.9
Interest on General Debt	100.0	77.8	9.9	12.4
Other	100.0	39.3	27.4	33.2
Utility and Liquor Store	100.0		12.3	87.7
Insurance Trust	100.0	86.2	11.8	2.0

Note: Totals may not equal 100.0 percent due to rounding.

Source: Government Finances in 1986–87, Bureau of the Census, pp. 2, 13, Government Printing Office,
1988.

today drawing a definitive line between the public and private sectors is virtually impossible. If present trends continue, government can be expected to become even larger, although perhaps at a slower rate, providing more services directly, ensuring the provision of services by regulating the private sector, or both.

Governments in the United States specialize in both the types of revenue sources used and the functions for which revenues are expended. The federal government relies primarily upon personal and corporate income taxes and social insurance deductions; expenditures are concentrated in defense, international relations, and social insurance. States obtain a fifth of their revenue from the federal government and the remainder largely from sales and individual income taxes. State expenditures are concentrated in education, social services, and welfare. Local governments receive a third of their funds from other governments and a quarter from property taxes. The most expensive function of local government is education.

NOTES

1. Milton Friedman and Rose Friedman, *Freedom to Choose* (New York: Harcourt Brace Jovanovich, 1980).

2. Frederich A. Hayek, *The Road to Serfdom* (Chicago: University of Chicago Press, 1945).

3. Peter Drucker and Herman Finer, *The Road to Reaction* (Boston: Little, Brown, 1945).

4. John Kenneth Galbraith, *Economics and the Public Purpose* (Boston: Houghton Mifflin, 1973).

5. Richard A. Musgrave and Peggy B. Musgrave, *Public Finance in Theory and Practice* (New York: McGraw-Hill, 1984).

6. Harvey S. Rosen, *Public Finance*, 2nd ed. (Homewood, Ill.: Irwin, 1988).

7. William D. Berry and David Lowery, "Explaining the Size of the Public Sector," *Journal of Politics* 49 (1987): 401–40.

8. Patrick D. Larkey, Chandler Stolp, and Mark Winer, "Theorizing About the Growth of Government," *Journal of Public Policy* 1 (1981): 157–220.

9. Richard Bird, "Wagner's Law of Expanding State Activity," *Public Finance* 26 (1971): 1–26.

10. James M. Buchanan and Gordon Tullock, "The Expanding Public Sector: Wagner Squared," *Public Choice* 31 (Fall 1977): 147–50.

11. Morris Beck, *Government Spending: Trends and Issues* (New York: Praeger, 1981).

12. Michael S. Lewis-Beck and Tom W. Rice, "Government Growth in the United States," *Journal of Politics* 47 (1985): 2–30.

13. Nelson W. Polsby and Aaron Wildavsky, *Presidential Elections*, 7th ed. (New York: Free Press, 1988).

14. Francis M. Bator, *The Question of Government Spending* (New York: Harper and Brothers, 1960), pp. 9–39.

15. Charles J. Hitch and Roland N. McKean, *The Economics of Defense in the Nuclear Age* (Cambridge, Mass.: Harvard University Press, 1967).

16. David K. Henry and Richard P. Oliver, "The Defense Buildup, 1977–85," *Monthly Labor Review* 110 (August 1987): 8.

17. Henry and Oliver, "The Defense Buildup," p. 10.

18. Paul Koistinen, *The Military-Industrial Complex* (New York: Praeger, 1980).

19. Henry and Oliver, "The Defense Buildup," p. 6.

20. Roger E. Bolton, *Defense Purchases and Regional Growth* (Washington, D.C.: Brookings, 1966).

21. Bureau of the Census, *Statistical Abstract of the United States, 1988* (Washington, D.C.: Government Printing Office, 1988), p. 317.

22. Bureau of the Census, *Statistical Abstract*, p. 679.

23. Bureau of the Census, *Statistical Abstract*, p. 479.

24. The idea of comparing private and public organizations was suggested by Robert J. Mowitz, former Director, Institute of Public Administration, The Pennsylvania State University.

25. Bureau of the Census, *Statistical Abstract*, p. 806.

26. Bureau of the Census, *Government Finances in 1986–87* (Washington, D.C.: Government Printing Office, 1988), p. 1.

27. Bureau of the Census, *Government Finances in 1986–87*, p. 2.

28. Bureau of the Census, *Public Employment in 1986* (Washington, D.C.: Government Printing Office, 1988), p. 7.

29. Bureau of the Census, *Statistical Abstract*, p. 256.

30. J. Richard Aronson and John L. Hilley, *Financing State and Local Governments*, 4th ed. (Washington, D.C.: Brookings, 1986).

3

Budget Cycles

Public budgeting systems, which are devices for selecting societal ends and means, consist of numerous participants and various processes that bring the participants into interaction. As was seen in the preceding chapters, the purpose of budgeting is to allocate scarce resources among competing public demands and wants in order to attain societal goals and objectives. Those societal ends are expressed not by philosopher kings but by mortals who must operate within the context of some prescribed allocation process, namely, the budgetary system.

This chapter provides an overview of the participants and processes involved in budgetary decision making. First, the phases of the budget cycle are reviewed. Any system has some structure or form, and budgetary systems are not exceptions. As will be seen, there are steps in the decision-making process; more elaborate discussions of these steps are presented in subsequent chapters. The second topic is the extent to which budget cycles are intermingled within government and among governments.

THE BUDGET CYCLE

To provide for responsible government, budgeting is geared to a cycle. The cycle allows the system to absorb and respond to new information, and in doing so government is held accountable for its actions. While existing budget systems may be less than perfect in guaranteeing adherence to this principle of responsibility, the argument stands that periodicity contributes to achieving and maintaining limited government. The budget cycle consists of four phases: preparation and submission, approval, execution, and audit.

Preparation and Submission

The preparation and submission phase is the most difficult to describe because it has been subjected the most to reform efforts. Experiments in reformulating the preparation process abound. Although institutional units may exist over time, both procedures and substantive content vary from year to year.

Chief Executive Responsibilities. The responsibility for budget preparation varies greatly among jurisdictions. Budget reform efforts have pressed for executive budgeting, in which the chief executive has exclusive responsibility for preparing a proposed budget and submitting it to the legislative body. At the federal level, the president has such exclusive control, although it should be recognized that many factors curtail the extent to which the president can make major changes in the budget. Preparation authority, however, is not always available to governors and local chief executives. While a majority of governors have responsibility for preparation and submission, some share budget-making authority with other elected administrative officers, civil service appointees, legislative leaders, or some combination.

At the municipal level, the mayor may or may not have budget preparation powers. In cities where the mayor is strong—has administrative control over the executive branch—the mayor normally does have budget-making power. This is not necessarily the case in weak-mayor systems and in cities operating under the commission plan, where each councilor or commissioner administers a given department. Usually, city managers in council-manager systems have responsibility for budget preparation, although their ability to recommend may be tempered by their lack of independence. Managers are appointed by councils and commonly have no tenure. Even in cities in which the mayor or chief executive does not have budget preparation responsibility, it is still likely to be in the hands of an executive official such as a city finance director. Thus, a majority of cities follow the principle of executive budget preparation.[1]

Location of Budget Offices. Budget preparation at the federal level is primarily a function of a budget office that was established by the Budget and Accounting Act of 1921. That legislation established the Bureau of the Budget (BOB), which became a unit of the Treasury Department. With the passage of time, the role of the BOB increased in importance, and in 1939 it became part of the newly formed Executive Office of the President (EXOP). Given that the BOB was thought to be the "right arm of the president"—a common referent in early budget literature—the move out of the Treasury, a line department, into EXOP placed the BOB under direct presidential supervision. In 1970 President Richard M. Nixon reorganized the BOB, giving it a new title, the Office of Management and Budget (OMB). The intent of the reorganization was to bring "real business management into Government at the very highest level."[2,3]

Steps in Preparation Stage. In the federal government, budget preparation starts in the spring, or even earlier for large agencies. Agencies begin by assessing their programs and considering which programs require revision and whether new programs should be recommended. At approximately the same time, the president's staff makes estimates of anticipated economic trends to determine available revenue under existing tax legislation. The next step is for the president to issue general budget and fiscal policy guidelines, which agencies use to develop their respective budgets. These budget requests are submitted in late summer to OMB. Throughout the fall and into the later months of the year, agency requests are reviewed by OMB, and hearings are held between OMB and agency spokesmen. Not until the last months of the year, particularly November and December, does the president become deeply involved in the process, which culminates in January with the submission of a proposed budget to Congress.

At the state and local levels, a similar process is used where executive budgeting systems prevail. The central budget office issues budget request instructions, reviews the submitted requests, and makes recommendations to the chief executive, who decides which items to recommend to the legislative body. In jurisdictions not using executive budgeting, the chief executive and the budget office play minor roles; in this type of system, the line agencies direct their budget requests to the legislative body.

Political Factors. The preparation phase as well as the other three phases in the budget cycle are replete with political considerations, both bureaucratic and partisan. Each organizational unit is concerned with its own survival and advancement. Line agencies and their subunits attempt to protect against budget cuts and may strive for increased resources. Budget offices often play negative roles, attempting to limit agency growth or imposing agency budget cuts; budget offices always are fully conscious of the fact that whatever they propose can be overruled by the chief executive. All members of the executive branch are concerned with their relationships with the legislative branch and the general citizenry. The chief executive is especially concerned about partisan calculations: Which alternatives will be advantageous to my political party? Of course there is concern for developing programs for the common good, but this concern is played out in a complicated game of political maneuvering.[4]

Fragmentation. One complaint about the preparation phase is that it tends to be highly fragmented. Organizational units within line agencies tend to be concerned primarily with their own programs and frequently fail to take a broad perspective. Even the budget office may be myopic, although it will be forced into considering the budget as a whole. Only the chief executive is unquestionably committed to viewing the budget as a whole in the preparation phase.

Approval

Revenue and Appropriations Bills. The budget is approved by a legislative body, whether Congress, a state legislature, a county board of supervisors, a city council, or a school board. The fragmented approach to budgeting in the preparation phase is not characteristic of the approval phase at the local level. A city council may have a separate finance committee, but normally the council as a whole participates actively in the approval process. Local legislative bodies may take several preliminary votes on pieces of the budget but then adopt the budget as a whole by a single vote.

States, however, separate tax and other revenue measures from appropriations or spending bills. Some states place most or all of their spending provisions in a single appropriations bill, but others have hundreds of appropriations bills. Most state legislatures are free to augment or reduce the governor's budget, but some, such as those of Maryland and Nebraska, are restricted in their ability to increase the budget.

At the federal level, the revenue and appropriations processes have been fragmented greatly among committees and subcommittees. Not only have revenue raising and spending been treated as separate processes, but the expenditure side is handled in 13 major appropriations bills instead of being treated as a whole. Reforms introduced in 1974 attempted to integrate these divergent processes and pieces of legislation, but the system had numerous flaws, and additional problems of extraordinary magnitude developed in the 1980s. Gramm-Rudman-Hollings reforms were put into place to attempt to force reductions in budget deficits.

Executive Veto Powers. The final step of the approval stage is the signing of appropriations into law. The president, governors, and in some cases mayors have the power to veto. A veto sends the measure back to the legislative body for further consideration. Most governors, unlike the president, have item veto power, which allows them to veto specific portions of the bill but still sign it.[5] In no case can the executive augment parts of the budget beyond that provided by the legislature.

Execution

Apportionment Process. Execution is the third phase, commencing with the fiscal year—October 1 in the federal government. Some form of centralized control during this phase is common at all levels of government, and such control is usually maintained by the budget office. Following congressional passage of an appropriation bill and its signing by the president, agencies must submit to OMB a proposed plan for apportionment. This plan indicates the funds required for operations, typically on a quarterly basis. The apportionment process is used in part to ensure that agencies do not commit all their available funds in a period shorter than the 12-month fiscal year. The intent is to avoid the need for supplementary appropriations from Congress.

The apportionment process is substantively important in that program adjustments must be made to bring planned spending into balance with available revenue. Since it is likely that an agency did not obtain the funds requested, either from the president in the preparation phase or from Congress in the approval phase, plans for the coming fiscal year must be revised. To varying degrees, state and local governments also use the apportionment process.

Impoundment. Additionally, the chief executive may assert control in the apportionment process through an informal item veto known as "impoundment," or declining to release some funds to agencies. Thomas Jefferson often is considered the first president to have impounded funds. President Nixon impounded so extensively that it stimulated legislative action by Congress. The 1974 legislation in a sense was a treaty between Congress and the White House allowing limited impoundment powers for the president. As will be discussed later, the Supreme Court largely negated the agreed-upon procedures.

Allotments. Once funds are apportioned, agencies and departments make allotments. This process grants budgetary authority to subunits such as bureaus and divisions. Allotments are made on a monthly or quarterly basis and, like the apportionment process, the allotment process is used to control spending during the fiscal year. Control often may be extensive and detailed, requiring approval by the department budget office for any shift in available funds from one item to another, such as from travel to wages. Approval of such transfers may require clearance by the central budget office.

Pre-Audits. Before an expenditure is made, some form of pre-audit is conducted. Basically, the pre-audit is used to ensure that funds are being committed for approved purposes and that an agency has sufficient resources in its budget to meet the proposed expenditure. The responsibility for this function varies widely, with the budget and/or accounting office responsible in some jurisdictions and independently elected controllers or comptrollers responsible in others. Once approval is granted, the treasurer writes a check for the expenditure.

Execution Subsystems. During budget execution, several subsystems are in operation. Taxes and other debts to government are collected. Cash is managed in the sense that monies temporarily not needed are invested. Supplies, materials, and equipment are procured; strategies are developed to protect the government against loss or damage of property and against liability suits. Accounting and information systems are in operation. For state and local governments, bonds are sold and the proceeds used to finance construction of facilities and the acquisition of major equipment.

Audit

The final phase of the budgetary process is the audit. The purpose of the audit is undergoing considerable change, but initially the purpose was largely to guarantee executive compliance with the provisions of appropriations bills—particularly, to ensure honesty in dispensing public monies and to prevent needless waste. In accord with these purposes, accounting procedures are prescribed and auditors check the books maintained by agency personnel. In recent years, the scope of auditing has been broadened to encompass studies of whether governmental programs achieve desired results.

Location of Audit Function. In the federal government, considerable controversy was generated concerning the appropriate organizational location of the audit function. President Woodrow Wilson in 1920 vetoed legislation that would have established the federal budget system on the grounds that he opposed the creation of an auditing office answerable to Congress rather than the president. Nevertheless, the General Accounting Office (GAO) was established in 1921 by the Budget and Accounting Act and was made an arm of Congress, with the justification that an audit unit should be created outside of the executive branch so that it could provide objective assessments of expenditure practices.

GAO Functions. The GAO is headed by the comptroller general, who is appointed by the president for only one term of 15 years, upon the advice and consent of the Senate. Despite the GAO's title, the organization does not maintain accounts but rather audits the accounts of operating agencies and evaluates their auditing systems. In recent years the GAO has been given responsibility for assessing the results of government programs in addition to the traditional responsibility for financial audits.

State and Local Auditors. At the state and local levels, the issue over organizational responsibility for auditing has been resolved in different ways. The alternatives are to have the audit function performed by a unit answerable to the legislative body, the chief executive, directly to the citizenry, or some combination of these. The use of an elected auditor is defended on the grounds that objectivity can be achieved if the auditor is independent of the executive and legislative branches. The opposing arguments are that the electorate cannot suitably judge the qualifications of candidates for auditor and that the election process necessarily forces the auditor to become a biased rather than an objective analyst. States use primarily elected and legislative auditors.

SCRAMBLED BUDGET CYCLES

Although it is easy to speak of a budget cycle, there is no single such cycle in operation. Rather, a cycle exists for each budget period, and several cycles are in operation at any given time. The decision-making process is not one that simply moves from preparation and submission to approval, execution, and, finally, audit. Decision making is complicated by the existence of several budget cycles for which information is imperfect and incomplete.

Overlapping Cycles

A pattern of overlapping cycles can be seen in Figure 3-1, which shows the sequencing of five budgets typical of a large state. Only cycle 3 in the diagram displays the complete period covering 39 months. The preparation and submission phase requires at least 9 months, approval 6 months, execution 12 months, and audit 12 months. The same general pattern is found at the federal level, except that the execution phase begins on October 1, giving Congress approximately 9 months to consider the budget. As is indicated by the diagram, three or four budget periods are likely to be in progress at any point in time.

Budget preparation is complicated particularly by this scrambling or intermingling of cycles. In the first place, preparation begins perhaps 15 months or more before the budget is to go into effect. Moreover, much of the preparation phase is completed without knowledge of the legislature's actions in the preceding budget period.

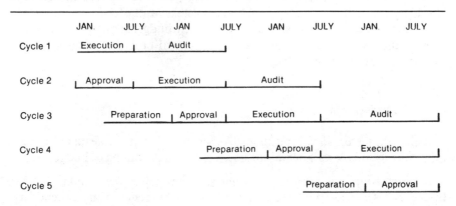

Figure 3-1 Scrambled Budget Cycles.

Federal Experience. At the federal level this problem has been especially difficult. Congress has been slow in passing appropriation bills, and the approval phase has rarely been completed by the start of the fiscal year when it began July 1. The usual procedure was to pass a continuation bill permitting agencies to spend at the rate of the previous year's budget while Congress continued to deliberate on the new year. Although the budget calendar adopted in the 1970s gave Congress an additional three months, which was expected to permit completion of the approval phase by October 1, agencies' preparation problems for the following year's budget request remained. In any given year, an agency prepares a budget request during the spring and summer, yet during this same period Congress deliberates on the agency's upcoming budget. Despite the additional time granted to Congress to act on the budget, work on the budget generally was not completed on schedule during the 1980s, thereby compounding the problem of scrambled budget cycles.

Links between Budget Phases. While a budget is being prepared, another one is being executed; this one may be for the immediately preceding budget year, but it can be for the one before. As can be seen in Figure 3-1, in the early stages of preparation for cycle 4 the execution phase is in operation for cycle 2. Under such conditions, the executive branch may not know the effects of ongoing programs yet is required to begin a new budget, recommending changes upward or downward. On occasion a new program may be created and an agency must recommend changes in the program for inclusion in the next budget without any time for assessing the merits of the program.

Length of Preparation Phase. The cycle, particularly in the preparation phase, may be even longer than that described so far, especially when agencies must rely upon other agencies or subunits for information. For example, in preparing the education component of a state budget, a department of education will require budget information and requests from state universities and colleges early to meet deadlines imposed by the governor's budget office. The reliability and validity of data undoubtedly decrease as the lead time increases. Therefore, the earlier these schools submit their budget requests to the state capital, the less likely it is that such requests will be based upon accurate assessments of future requirements.

Other Considerations

Besides the factors already mentioned, others further complicate budget cycles, most notably intergovernmental considerations and the timing of budget years.

Intergovernmental Factors. Another problem arises from intermingled budget cycles because the three main levels of government are interdependent. For the federal government, the main problem is assessing needs and finding resources to meet these needs. State government must assess its needs and those of local government, and then must search for funds by either raising state taxes, providing for new forms of taxation by local government, or obtaining federal revenues. In preparing budgets governors take into account whatever information is available on the likelihood of certain actions by the president and Congress. For instance, the president may have recommended a major reduction in medical health programs that would significantly decrease funds flowing to the states, but considerable doubt revolves around whether Congress will accept the recommendation. In such a case, should a governor set aside resources to compensate for federal resources that would be lost? The problem is still worse at the local level, which is dependent for funds upon both the state and federal governments.

Budget Years. Budget cycles are further complicated by a lack of uniformity in the budget period. While most state governments have budget years beginning July 1, four states do not—New York's begins April 1, Texas's begins September 1, and Alabama's and Michigan's correspond to the federal fiscal year of October 1. Consistency does not even exist within each state. It is common for a state to follow a July 1 fiscal year, while local governments operate under different years, such as January 1, April 1, and September 1.

A case can be made for staggering the budget year for different levels of government; this practice might assist decision makers at one level by providing information about action taken at other levels. For example, the federal government would complete action on its budget by October 1; states could then begin a budget year the following April 1 and local governments July 1. Under such an arrangement, states could base their budgetary decisions upon knowledge of available financial support from Washington. Local governments would know the aid available from both Washington and the state capital.

Rearranging the dates for fiscal years is no panacea. Information about financial support from other governments is only one of many items of information used in decision making. Also, any slippage by the legislature in completing its appropriations work by the time a fiscal year begins would void the advantages of staggered budget cycles. In addition, there is no direct translation from appropriations to aid to other governments. Money does not automatically flow to states and communities as soon as an appropriation bill is passed by Congress. Instead, these governments must apply for assistance, a process that typically requires many months.

Annual and Biennial Budgets. Not only is there inconsistency in the date budget years begin, but the length of the budget period is also inconsistent. While the federal government and most local governments operate under annual budgets, 21 states have biennial (two-year) budgets.[6] Under these systems, a governor typically submits the budget in January, and legislative action is supposed to be completed by June 30. The execution phase runs for 24 months beginning July 1. Such a system violates the once-standard principle of annuality.[7] The argument is that annual budgets allow for careful and frequent supervision of the executive by the legislature, and that this serves to guarantee responsibility in government. The problem with the annual budget, however, is that little "breathing time" is available; both the executive and legislative branches are continuously in the throes of budgeting. The biennial approach, on the other hand, relieves participants of many routine budget matters and may allow greater time for more thorough analysis of governmental activities.

One of the greatest dangers of a biennial system is that it may complicate, if not prohibit, prompt response to new conditions. The costs of not being able to adjust to changing conditions may far outweigh any benefits accruing from time saved with biennial budgeting. This consideration may explain why most of the more populous states are on annual budget systems.

Still another consideration is whether under "normal" conditions sufficient amounts of new information become available to warrant annual systems. If program analysis were a well-established part of the budgetary process, then conceivably new insights into the operations of programs would be a continuous input; in such instances, an annual process might be preferable. In other cases, in which decision makers operate one year with virtually the same information as was available the preceding year, there seems to be little need for annual budgets. Partially for this reason, there has been at least one proposal for abandoning the annual budget cycle for all programs. New programs or proposed changes in existing programs would be submitted in any given year for legislative review, while continuing programs would be reviewed only periodically.

SUMMARY

The four phases of the budget cycle are preparation and submission, approval, execution, and audit. In general, the first and third phases are the responsibility of the executive branch, and the second is controlled by the legislative branch. The fourth phase in the federal system is directed by the General Accounting Office, which is answerable to Congress and not the president. Auditing at the state and local levels often is the responsibility of independently elected officials.

A standard criticism of budgeting, especially at the federal level, is that the budget is seldom considered in its entirety. Within the executive branch, only the president and his immediate staff view the budget as a whole, while agencies are primarily concerned only with their own portions of the total.

The same disjointed approach has been characteristic of the approval phase at the federal level.

Budget cycles are intermingled. As many as four budget cycles may be in operation at any one time in a single government. This phenomenon complicates decision making; for example, budget preparation often is forced to proceed without knowledge as to what action the legislature will take on the previous year's budget. Moreover, the interdependent nature of the three levels of government contributes to a scrambling of cycles. One possibility would be conversion to biennial budgets, a practice that is common at the state level.

NOTES

1. Leonard I. Ruchelman, "The Finance Function in Local Government," in J. Richard Aronson and Eli Schwartz, eds., *Management Policies in Local Government Finance*, 3d ed. (Washington, D.C.: International City Management Association, 1987), pp. 3–29.

2. Richard M. Nixon as quoted in *The New York Times*, June 11, 1970.

3. Charles G. Dawes, *The First Year of the Budget of the United States* (New York: Harper and Brothers, 1923).

4. Aaron Wildavsky, *The New Politics of the Budgetary Process* (Glenview, Ill.: Scott, Foresman, 1988).

5. Calvin Bellamy, "Item Veto: Dangerous Constitutional Tinkering," *Public Administration Review* 49 (1989): 46–51.

6. *Book of the States, 1988–89* (Lexington, Ky.: Council of State Governments, 1988), p. 225.

7. J. Wilner Sundelson, "Budgetary Principles," *Political Science Quarterly* 50 (1935): 236–63.

4

Budget Preparation:
The Revenue Side

This chapter and the next two describe the budget preparation process. We draw attention first to revenues, then expenditures, and last the politics of budget preparation. Our discussion begins with the revenue side, for historically taxation has been a fundamental concern of the citizenry. Citizens may be less concerned about how government spends its money than how the money is raised to support programs. In developing a budget package political leaders are always mindful that program initiatives leading to higher expenditures and therefore higher taxes may have negative effects on the possibility of winning re-election to their offices.

This chapter has two sections. The first and longer details various revenue sources; tax equity and tax expenditures are included in the discussion. Second, we consider special concerns about taxation; the discussion concentrates on taxing limitations and revenue estimating.

REVENUE SOURCES

As was discussed in some detail in the preceding chapter, governments use a myriad of revenue sources to support their operations, with taxes usually the most important. In this section, we consider some of the overall concerns about revenue sources and then examine specific sources.

Tax Equity and Tax Expenditures

Besides the obvious concern that a tax source generate whatever is considered an adequate amount of revenue, another chief concern is that the system treat taxpayers fairly, equally, or equitably.[1] Equity generally is thought of as having horizontal and vertical dimensions. Horizontal equity refers to charging the same amount to different taxpayers whose income levels or ability to pay is the same. Vertical equity refers to the principle of charging differently those with different income levels or ability to pay. Confusion immediately develops as to whether it is fair for all taxpayers to pay equal amounts, an equal proportion of their incomes, or according to varying abilities to pay.

Ability to Pay. The concept of ability to pay reflects a concern for whether a tax or other revenue source is regressive, progressive, or proportional. In the latter instance, all taxpayers pay the same percentage, such as a 5 percent state tax on personal income. A progressive tax would charge a higher proportion to wealthier taxpayers than to poorer ones, while the regressive tax would do the opposite. A tax may seem proportional when it in fact is regressive. A sales tax on purchases seems to treat all taxpayers equally, but in fact is often regressive in that poorer families often spend a greater proportion of their incomes on taxed items than wealthier families do. Overall, the entire U.S. system of revenue falls in a range from slightly progressive to proportional.[2]

Benefit Received. Another concept to keep in mind is that of "benefit received," namely that some revenue sources are intended to have service recipients pay for those services. User charges or fees are noted examples, as in municipal parking garage fees, bus fares, and water and sewer charges. People who park in the garage, then, pay for the service.

However, if all government services were paid for by fees, some people would be unable to pay and necessarily would be excluded. With elementary and secondary education being the most expensive local government service, many parents would be unable to send their children to school, a situation that would lead to large segments of the society being uneducated and unable to secure employment that required the ability to read, write, and the like. Because of this important "spillover effect," namely that lack of education would affect others in the society, many government services cannot be appropriately supported solely through user fees. In addition, education is supported publicly for equity reasons. Similarly, public goods such as defense in which all citizens benefit cannot be funded through user fees in which some citizens chose to "purchase" defense while others did not. The benefit received concept simply cannot be applied uniformly throughout government.

Tax Expenditures. Revenues that could be but were not collected constitute "tax expenditures" and can aid or hinder the furtherance of equity.[3] According to federal law, tax expenditures are ". . . revenue losses . . . which allow a special exclusion, exemption, or deduction from gross income or which provide a special credit, a preferential rate of tax, or a deferral of tax liability."[4] Exemption of interest paid on home mortgages is a federal tax expenditure, as is exemption of taxation of food items for state sales taxes. The housing exemption may help make housing affordable to moderate-income families, but the exemption also benefits more affluent taxpayers and may be of no benefit to low-income families. Is the housing exemption, then, a factor that furthers or detracts from equity?

Since the 1970s, tax expenditures have become important aspects of debates over tax reform.[5] These measures reduce the revenue flowing into government treasuries and can be "loopholes" for the wealthy. The federal government routinely reports estimates of tax expenditures, as do some state governments (see Chapter 6).

Tax Efficiency. Another concept that needs to be considered is tax efficiency. An efficient tax is one that does not appreciably affect the allocation of resources within the private sector, such as between consumption and saving or among competing items for consumption. Taxes on cigarettes often are cited as efficient in that raising or lowering these taxes does not appreciably influence smokers' spending habits. However, tax provisions that exclude some items from taxation, such as selected tax deferrals on personal income saved for retirement, are designed to influence behavior and not be neutral or simply efficient. Tax systems that are progressive can be inefficient and have unintentional consequences. If tax rates are particularly high for wealthy persons, then the system may encourage them to spend more time on leisure and less on working and earning more income.

Personal Income Taxes

In the discussion of taxes, we will be concerned with three types of tax bases: income, wealth, and consumption. Taxes on income are applied to the amounts of different types of income earned during the defined tax period. Taxes on wealth are applied to accumulated value regardless of the time period; real property is considered wealth. Consumption taxes are applied to purchasing transactions, such as retail sales.

As is well known, all governments use personal income taxes, but the federal government's is by far the largest in terms of generating revenue; the income tax, as was seen in Chapter 2, is the largest revenue source for the federal government.

Tax Base. All taxes begin with identifying what is to be taxed, or the "base." For income taxes, not all income is taxable; local governments, for instance, tend to tax earned income as distinguished from other income. For a local government, salary and wages may be subject to an income tax while income from rents and stock investments are not. The federal government includes in the income tax base salaries, wages, commissions and tips, interest, rents, alimony, and unemployment compensation. Excluded are most fringe benefits (such as employer-provided health insurance), disability retirement, Workers' Compensation, food stamps, Social Security payments, and interest earned on some state and local bonds. These lists, of course, are only illustrative of what items are included and excluded.

Generally speaking, the more sources of income that are included within the tax base, the more equitable is the income tax. When the base excludes sizable segments of income, vigorous debates immediately arise over whether some interests are receiving undue favoritism as a result of legislative lobbying.[6]

Adjustments, Exemptions, and Deductions. Tax codes also provide for adjustments to gross income that typically have the effect of removing portions of income from the base. For example, some job-related educational expenses and moving expenses are excluded, as are some employer-paid business reimbursements.

The individual income tax base is reduced further by individual exemptions. The federal government allowed an exemption of $1,950 for each filer in 1988 and $2,000 in 1989. The purpose of these provisions is to equalize taxes among different family sizes.

A final set of adjustments is made in the tax base by allowing deductions. Taxpayers usually have a choice between using a standard deduction or itemizing deductions when they exceed the standard deduction. Deductions on the federal income tax include some medical expenses; casualty losses due to theft, fire, and the like; charitable contributions; home mortgage interest; and deductions for some taxes, such as property taxes. Taxes on gasoline and retail sales are not deductible.

The combination of these various exclusions, inclusions, adjustments, and deductions to the income base is intended to yield income figures for individuals and families that can further horizontal and vertical tax equity. These factors together are intended to recognize variations in total income and the circumstances involved in earning that income and meeting living expenses. Individuals earning the same income but having different numbers of family members and expenses will be treated differently, while others with unequal gross incomes may ultimately have the same ability to pay when adjustments and deductions are taken into account.

Rate Structure. The principle of equity is furthered at the federal level by the use of a progressive rate structure. Married taxpayers in 1988 having taxable incomes below $29,750 paid a 15 percent tax, while those with incomes between $29,750 and $71,900 paid at a 28 percent rate on income in that bracket. The next bracket was 33 percent on income up to $149,250. Above that level, the rate was 28 percent plus an adjustment that could be an additional 5 percent.[7]

Most personal income taxes levied by the states are modeled on the federal tax. The states sometimes use the federal base or a modification of it. Some state income taxes are simply a proportion of the federal tax owed. Other states use flat and graduated tax rates. When the federal government modifies its tax laws, changes inadvertently occur in state taxes. This was the case when Congress adopted the Tax Reform Act of 1986, resulting in would-be revenue windfalls for many states. Many state governments in response modified their laws to avoid collecting more revenue than needed and raising taxpayers' ire.[8] Local income taxes tend to be simple to calculate and involve flat rather than progressive tax rates.

Indexing. The federal government and some states use indexing in various forms to adjust income taxes in accordance with changes in price levels. If tax brackets are not altered and prices rise, then inflation will produce increases in tax revenue as citizens find their rising incomes place them in higher tax brackets without any real increase in income. Besides adjusting tax brackets, other indexing techniques include modifying the standard deduction or personal exemption.

Corporate Income Taxes

Taxes on corporate earnings have been defended as appropriate given the size of corporate economic power and the fact that some individuals might be able to escape taxation by "hiding" their income in corporations.[9] On the other hand, corporate income taxes may seem to result in double taxation in that first a corporation is taxed and then individuals are taxed on dividends paid on the stock of corporations.

Tax Base. Space does not permit detailed discussion of corporate income taxes. Briefly, they can be characterized as using net earnings as a base. Deductions are made for capital losses, operating losses, depreciation of capital investments, and expenditures for research and development. How these deductions are applied is often controversial, such as how rapidly capital investments can be depreciated. The federal tax rates after the 1986 tax reform are graduated from 15 percent to 34 percent.

Tax Incidence. The primary issue of corporate taxation is who actually pays the tax—the tax burden or incidence. Corporations may be able to increase prices and in turn have consumers pay the tax or may limit wage increases to workers and in effect have them pay the tax. The other option is to take taxes out of profits, thereby reducing dividends for investors. Corporations probably use some combination of these shifts.[10]

An issue involving state corporate taxes is whether they affect decisions to locate and expand operations in one state over another. Legislators and executives in a state government fear that any increase in their corporate income taxes will discourage corporations from locating in the state and encourage others to move out of the state.

Property Taxes

Taxes on wealth are based on accumulated value in some asset rather than on current earnings. Personal property, monetary or financial assets, and equipment are important types of wealth that are sometimes subject to taxation. The wealth tax that is most important in the eyes of taxpayers, however, is the real property or real estate tax. This tax is almost the exclusive domain of local governments, and despite forecasts of the demise of the tax, it remains the largest single generator of revenue for local governments.[11-13]

The philosophy behind the property tax as the major revenue source for local government is the increased economic value "earned" by one's property because of the services provided by local government. It is widely thought that people select their residences based on the quality of local schools and other public services. In high-quality service jurisdictions, housing costs are typically higher, reflecting higher costs for delivering services and higher expectations of home buyers for quality services.

The property tax, however, is regressive in its impact. Since higher-income taxpayers tend to have a larger proportion of their wealth in items not subject to the real property tax, these taxpayers tend to pay a disproportionately low tax in contrast with middle- and somewhat lower-income taxpayers whose only major assets may be their homes. In the latter case, basically all of their wealth is being taxed each year. This regressivity fuels the controversy over the property tax.

Tax Base. The base of the real property tax is the market value of land and improvements on it, such as homes, factories, and other structures. The value is what the property would sell for if placed on the market. Value for commercial and industrial property sometimes is reflected in the income earned by a corporation in a facility.

Property's use and value often do not coincide, with farmland in metropolitan areas being one of the prime examples. As metropolitan areas expand and encroach upon farming areas, the value of the land increases even though the use is unchanged. Situations emerge in which taxes rise beyond what farmers can afford and create a market incentive for the land to be sold and subdivided for homes and other development. Some states provide reduced tax assessments for farming and other undeveloped land as a means of preserving rural land and discouraging urban sprawl.

Considerable amounts of property are tax exempt in the United States. Since the "power to tax is the power to destroy," federal and state land is normally exempt from local property taxes, although these jurisdictions may make payments in lieu of taxation. Places of worship, such as churches and synagogues, are tax exempt, as are most parsonages and other related properties. Nonprofit hospitals, YMCAs and YWCAs, nonprofit cemeteries, and the like are usually tax exempt.

Keeping property market value assessments current is a continuous problem. When properties are sold, the opportunity exists for revising the assessment, but many properties do not go on sale for decades. Therefore assessments are revised by using market data and interpreting them to apply to properties that have not been sold. Such adjustments may be made annually or only once every several years.

Fractional Assessment. Property assessments usually are stated as a percentage or fraction of full market value. A home whose market value is $120,000 would be assessed at only $24,000 if the assessment ratio were 20 percent. In practice, it makes no difference whether full value or a fraction is used; fractional assessment simply requires a higher tax rate than market value assessment to produce the same revenue. Taxpayers may find some psychological satisfaction in fractional assessment, but the opportunity exists for some taxpayers to have their properties overassessed and therefore taxed more than their share.

Tax Rates. Property tax rates are a percentage of the assessed value. The rate is expressed in "mills," with one mill being one-tenth of a percent. As applied to property taxes, a one-mill rate yields $1 of revenue for every $1,000 of assessed value. A property tax rate of 68.5 mills as applied to a $120,000 property assessed at 20 percent of market value would yield $1,644 ($120 \times 0.2 \times 68.5 = 1,644$).

Local jurisdictions often determine the annual property tax rate by calculating backward from projected expenditures. Projected revenues are subtracted from expenditures, indicating the budget gap to be filled by increased taxes. The community's decision makers, then, can decide how many additional mills will be needed to close the gap. Of course, attempts are made to avoid such tax increases by keeping expenditures as low as considered possible. The process of adjusting the tax rate to match expenditure requirements probably accounts for the great popularity of the property tax among local officials. This tax is one over which officials have considerable control, unlike other taxes that depend on the economy (income and sales taxes) or intergovernmental aid.

Circuit Breakers. As taxes rise, some property owners may encounter considerable difficulty in paying their tax bills and may be forced to sell their homes and move into rental housing. To alleviate this problem, several states have initiated circuit breaker systems that set a cap on taxes, particularly for low-income elderly persons. A qualified homeowner pays an amount up to the cap and the state pays any additional amount that is owed.

Data Base. If one imagines a local government instituting the property tax for the first time, then the valuation process is almost overwhelming. Traditional valuation procedures involve an assessor's visiting each property, measuring the foundation to determine square footage, noting construction details, and recording information about the condition of the structure. Such is the case in many developing countries where property taxes are being newly applied or where existing records are incomplete and largely useless.

For most jurisdictions in the United States, properties have been built under building permits that require supplying information about construction details to the local jurisdiction. Periodic inspections of the property when under construction, conducted by a local code enforcement officer or building inspector, provide additional information. A data base, then, can be devised using existing building records and information about sales of properties when deeds are transferred. As new structures are built, they can be added to the data base.

Orange County, North Carolina, has what is considered a model property tax valuation system. It is fully computerized and includes diverse information about each property in the county (see Table 4-1). Besides information about the location of a lot, the size of a structure, and the number of baths in it, a drawing of the lot and the location of the structure on it is included in the computerized file and can be displayed on screen. Of course, hardcopy maps of properties also are available.

Table 4-1 Property Tax Registration Information Base, Orange County, North Carolina

---

Property address
Plot map and reference to deed register
Size of lot (square footage)
Size of dwelling (square footage of living space)
Number of structures
Number of stories of each structure
Basement, slab, or crawl space
Foundation construction method
Exterior construction material
Roof type and roofing materials
Number of bathrooms
Number of fireplaces
Special features (spas, etc.)
Landscaping
Paved or unpaved driveway
Last sale price and date

Source: Office of the Tax Assessor, Orange County, North Carolina, 1988.

Techniques such as those used in Orange County or paper-and-pencil systems used elsewhere help to foster a perception of fairness among taxpayers. Property owners conclude that they are paying their fair share and not being overcharged while other taxpayers are undercharged. If these equity considerations are met, then the likelihood of taxpayer revolts is minimized.

Personal Property. Besides taxing real property, some jurisdictions tax personal property. For individuals, such property includes furniture, vehicles, clothing, jewelry, and the like. Intangible personal property includes stocks, bonds, and other financial instruments such as mortgages. For corporations, personal property includes equipment, raw materials, and items in inventory. Taxes on personal property are unpopular and subject to considerable evasion.

Retail Sales and Other Consumption Taxes

Tax Base. While all three levels of government rely on some form of consumption tax, state governments are the most reliant, particularly on retail sales taxes. The base of any consumption tax is defined as a product or class of goods, and sometimes services, whose value is measured in terms of retail gross sales or receipts. The base is a function of what products and services are included and excluded. Almost all states exclude prescription medicines, and two-thirds exclude food, except for that sold in restaurants. Other commonly excluded items are clothing, household fuels, soaps, and some toiletries. Other items may be exempt from the general sales tax since they are subject to another sales tax; cigarettes, gasoline, and alcoholic beverages are examples. However, states generally are not precluded from levying two taxes on one sale, such as a general and specific sales tax being placed on cigarettes.

States currently have only limited authority to tax mail-order sales and have been lobbying for Congress to pass legislation allowing for such taxation. The reason is a simple one. Mail-order sales vastly increased during the 1980s and constitute a potentially lucrative source of revenue.

Sales taxes are regarded as regressive in that higher-income consumers typically have more discretionary income and may spend it on items not subject to sales taxes. The more the base of the sales tax includes luxury or nonessential goods and services, therefore, the less regressive the tax is likely to be.

Tax Rates. State sales tax rates vary from as low as 3 percent (Colorado, Georgia, North Carolina, and Wyoming) to 7.5 percent (Connecticut).[14] To avoid levies of a fraction of a cent, bracket systems are used in which a set amount is collected regardless of the specific sale. For example, a 5 percent tax might yield 5 cents on any purchase starting at 81 cents or 90 cents. With computers and electronic scanners at check-out stands in stores, determinations can be quickly made as to whether an item is taxable and, if it is, the amount can be calculated.

Other Consumption Taxes. Some taxes are considered to be "luxury excises."[15] At one time, federal excise taxes were levied on a wide range of luxury goods such as jewelry. The logic of the tax rests on the assumption that the purchase of such goods is prima facie evidence that the consumer can afford the tax.

Sumptuary excises are regulatory in nature. Taxes on alcohol and tobacco have been justified as deterring people from consuming these commodities. However, the evidence suggests that the demand for these products is relatively inelastic, casting doubt on whether taxes discourage usage.

Benefit-base excises are linked with the benefit received concept discussed earlier. Motor vehicle fuel taxes are the classic case. Taxes on gasoline and diesel fuels are dedicated for road and bridge construction and maintenance. Other such excises include taxes on airline tickets, with the revenues used to maintain airports and airport security.

User Charges

All governments have user charges, and almost all functional areas are partially supported by user charges. For example, admission is charged to national and some state parks and to local tennis courts, other recreational facilities, and exercise and athletic programs. Some elementary and secondary schools charge for textbooks, and higher education institutions charge tuition. Hospitals, transit systems, water and sewer operations, and refuse collection are supported with fees. Some jurisdictions operate electric and telephone facilities with user fees. Police departments charge fees for fingerprinting and special patrols, such as at stadiums.

Rationale for Fees. The principle behind user charges reflects the general belief that citizens ought to pay for the cost of public services as a control on the amount of a service produced. Economists' more technical argument for that principle holds that the amount of a service provided is closer to the optimal level of service, as determined by consumer preferences, when the cost of service is borne directly by the consumer.[16] If the cost of a service is part of general taxes, then citizens tend to demand more of that service than they are actually willing to pay.

In addition to any conceptual underpinning for user fees, practical considerations made these fees more popular during the 1970s and 1980s. One factor was that many state and local jurisdictions adopted measures that effectively limited the ability of these governments to raise revenues through taxes; increased use of fees became a logical alternative to taxes.[17] A second factor at the federal level was the Reagan administration's opposition to tax increases; with massive annual federal deficits and a president opposed to tax increases, federal agencies in need of additional revenues selectively considered fees as an alternative. Third, cutbacks in federal aid to state and local government created revenue gaps that resulted in these governments' placing increased reliance on fees.

Types of Charges. Fees vary regarding whether they are voluntary. Charges for entrance to museum exhibits and tennis lessons are clearly voluntary; other leisure options are available if citizens prefer not to pay for these public leisure services. On the other hand, charges for sewers and trash collection usually are mandatory; if a municipal sewer system exists, citizens normally have no choice but to use it and pay the requisite fee. Other services lie between these extremes. Paying a bus or subway fare may be voluntary, but for many people without other transit options the fees are required. Differentiating between a mandatory fee and a tax is difficult.

Some fees are continuous while others are for special occasions. Transit fares and sewer and water charges are examples of continuous fees. Other charges occur only on certain occasions, as in the case of issuing a building permit when a contractor plans to erect an office building. While many jurisdictions use general tax revenues to repave and improve streets, other communities levy special assessments on the property owners whose streets are to be improved. Similarly, when a community installs a sewer system for the first time, property owners are assessed fees. These charges are calculated on a front footage basis, namely the number of linear feet that a lot faces or fronts a street.

Special assessments are used in more general ways to support municipal services. Firms that construct new office buildings in a city may have an option to provide on-site parking or pay a fee that is used to construct municipal parking facilities. Raleigh, North Carolina, finances much of the cost of extending streets, extending water and sewer lines, and expanding parks in new developments through the imposition of "impact fees" on the developer. In addition, other communities use impact fees for low- and moderate-income housing and environmental programs.[18]

Charges and Tax Subsidies. Although user charges are extensive, they often fail to cover the costs of services they support. Entrance fees to a municipal swimming pool do not provide adequate funds to operate the pool; therefore tax revenues are used. An important example of such a subsidy is in the operation of municipal transit systems. If transit fares were set at a level to generate required revenue, the rates would be so high that poor commuters could not afford to use the system and higher-income commuters would shift to alternative modes of travel—private vehicles and taxicabs.

Subsidies, however, have the effect of aiding all who use a service. If transit fares are artificially low because of a tax subsidy, then both the wealthy and poor who use the system benefit. Alternative mechanisms include providing free service to the poor, such as free bus tokens, or setting fees on a sliding scale. In the latter situation, a government-operated mental health clinic might charge poor and moderate-income families little or nothing for service while higher-income families paid at a rate that covered costs.

Insurance Trusts

Contributions to insurance trusts stem from charges on salaries and wages, with the charges being paid by employees, employers, or both. These charges are not taxes in the sense of obtaining revenue in order to provide a service; instead, the programs provide insurance to people who are covered.

Social Security. A program of vast proportions is that of Social Security. Its complexities far exceed the scope of this book; all that can be done here is to sketch its overall structure. Three major programs are administered directly by the Social Security Administration, which is a unit within the Department of Health and Human Services. The first program, Old-Age and Survivors Insurance (OASI) is a benefits program for retired workers and their survivors. Chapter 13 discusses the program as it pertains to retired government employees. The second program, Disability Insurance (DI), provides benefits for covered workers who are disabled and cannot work. In 1988, 35.6 million people received benefits under the old-age and survivors program and 2.8 million under the disability program. Employers and employees pay into this system, and people earn benefit credits through their contributions over their working careers. Legislation in 1983 greatly modified the financing of OASI and allayed most concerns that the program would collapse financially.[19,20]

The third major program under Social Security provides monthly benefits to people who are aged, blind, and disabled; this program is known as Supplemental Security Income (SSI). SSI funds come from general tax revenues and not employer-employee contributions.]Unlike disability insurance, SSI does not require work credits for eligibility, but does require that recipients are needy, whereas DI does not. It is possible to qualify for both programs, although qualifying for DI has the effect of reducing SSI benefits. In 1988, 4.4 million people received benefits under the SSI program through the federal government and another 270,000 received benefits through their states.

In addition to these three main programs, a fourth one, Medicare, is overseen by Social Security but is administered by the Health Care Financing Administration, which also is in the Department of Health and Human Services. Medicare provides basic health insurance (HI) to the elderly, with a separately funded catastrophic coverage component, and is funded by contributions through Social Security, premiums paid by persons covered under the program, and general revenue.

A fifth program often mentioned in conjunction with these other programs is Medicaid, which is administered by the Health Care Financing Administration and funded with tax revenue. Medicaid provides medical care to the poor and the medically indigent (persons not classified as poor but who cannot afford medical care). Medicaid and SSI, then, are not trust programs as defined here.

Employee Retirement. The largest type of insurance trust fund at the state and local levels is for government employee retirement. These retirement programs as well as the federal government's are discussed at length in Chapter 13.

Unemployment Insurance. The second largest insurance trust for state governments is unemployment compensation.[21,22] The program is administered by the states within a framework imposed by the federal government. A floor on benefits is set nationally, while states have the option of exceeding the floor. The program is supported by payroll taxes paid mainly by employers but in a few states supplemented by employee payments. The program is expected to generate sufficient revenues during prosperous periods to cover payments to unemployed workers during recessionary periods. Sometimes state programs can be greatly out of balance. Louisiana, for instance, paid $123 in benefits for every $100 in revenue collected in 1985.[23] In such circumstances, the federal government loans money to the states but expects repayment with interest. As is obvious, a state that has a declining tax base can face severe problems with financing its unemployment insurance program.

Workers' Compensation. Another important insurance trust at the state level is Workers' Compensation, which provides cash benefits to persons who because of job-related injuries and illnesses are unable to work.[24,25] Accidents at work may disable people temporarily or permanently; working conditions can cause physical and mental health problems. In addition to cash benefits, the program pays for medical care and rehabilitation services.

Other Revenue

Besides all of these various revenue sources, there are still others that can only be mentioned here. Governments operate revolving loan programs that produce revenue as principal and interest payments are made. Licenses are issued that usually require fees; these fees may be used largely to cover costs, such as building permit fees used to pay the salaries of building inspectors, or may be intended to raise revenues beyond costs. Charitable contributions constitute another revenue source, as in gifts to municipal hospitals, county nursing homes, state universities, and the like.

Lotteries. Since 1963, when New Hampshire began the first modern state lottery, more than half of the states have launched lottery programs. Lotteries usually produce not much more than 2 percent of revenues for states. Revenues generated from the programs can vary considerably from year to year, depending upon lottery activity in adjacent states, the size of jackpots, and the extent to which a lottery has "matured" and lost interest among the public. Lotteries can be regressive in that lower-income individuals are more likely to participate than middle- and upper-income individuals.[26,27]

Borrowing. To complete the picture on revenue sources, borrowing must be mentioned. As will be seen later in discussions of congressional budgeting and budget execution, the federal government's budget is often out of balance and deficits are routinely financed through the issuance of debt instruments. State and local governments sometimes obtain revenues through borrowing to cover short-term cash-flow problems. These governments borrow on a long-term basis to fund capital projects such as highways and government buildings.

SPECIAL CONCERNS

Two topics of special interest are considered in this section. The first topic is the limitations that have been imposed on state and local taxes, and the second is the continuous problem of revenue estimating.

Taxing and Spending Limitations

Although it was long held that citizens had little opportunity to affect taxes and spending, other than through the process of selecting elected representatives, 1978 changed that viewpoint.[28] In that year, California voters approved Proposition 13, an initiative proposal that limited the property tax rate to 1 percent of market value. That provision by itself would have required a rollback in taxes, but an additional provision further cut taxes. Property assessments were to be set at their values in 1975, when property was considerably less expensive. While tax limitation measures were not new, Proposition 13 began a new era in forcing government to limit taxes and spending.[29]

Extent and Causes of Revolt. Many state and local governments followed California's lead during the late 1970s and early 1980s by passing statutory limits or in some cases adding restrictions to state constitutions. California voters approved Proposition 4 in 1979, which limited expenditures for the state government as well as local governments. In the ensuing years, restrictive measures were adopted in about half of the states. Massachusetts, which had come to be known as "Taxachusetts," gained notoriety in 1980 with passage of Proposition 2½. This measure required that local governments reduce taxes by 15 percent each year until they equaled 2.5 percent of market value.[30,31]

The original stimulus behind what came to be known as the "taxpayers revolt" was sharply rising property values and consequently tax bills, but a more generally negative attitude emerged, suggesting that government officials had an insatiable appetite for spending.[32] Besides government's taxing too much, the money was allegedly used to interfere needlessly in the lives of citizens and the operations of corporations.

Tax Revolt Impact. The effect of these limitations varied, but in most cases local governments made up for the revenue loss through other sources.[33] Overall, spending may have declined in some jurisdictions, but not enough to show up in aggregate figures for individual states. The main effects seem to have been four. First, state legislatures and local governments became conscious of citizen awareness of tax and expenditure decisions, and caution was exercised toward the rate of growth in taxes and expenditures.

Second, combined with major cutbacks in federal aid to states and localities in the 1980s, the limitation movement set these governments on an imaginative hunt for alternative finance measures.[34] The significantly greater use of impact fees, discussed above, and other direct charges to those benefiting from services was an outgrowth of the tax revolt.

Third, states provided increased financial assistance to hard-pressed local governments. That aid came at a price, namely that states were at liberty to attach strings to their aid. One simple example is that local governments could not give their employees salary increases greater than those given state employees.

Fourth, while overall expenditures may not have been cut, services were reduced, either in quality or quantity, as a means of curbing spending. Essential services such as police patrol and fire protection were maintained, but the services were less plentiful. Budget problems forced cutbacks in maintenance of buildings and purchase of new vehicles and equipment.

By the mid-1980s, enthusiasm for enactment of restrictive measures on government had waned, and by the close of the 1980s concern grew among citizens that the cuts imposed over the preceding decade had cut too severely into the level of services. At the same time, there was continued citizen consciousness about tax and expenditure matters.

During this period, proposals circulated for imposing limits on the federal budget. Gramm-Rudman-Hollings (GRH) was one measure that attempted to force the federal government to live within available revenue (see Chapter 9). GRH was adopted by Congress and could not be approved directly by the voters, since there is no mechanism for national initiatives. However, GRH must be considered a part of the same set of concerns exhibited in 1978 by the approval of Proposition 13.

Revenue Estimating

Little imagination is required to appreciate the importance of revenue estimating. If a government is required to have a balanced budget, as state and local governments are, then accurate revenue forecasts become critical. Estimates that are too high can create major crises during the execution phase, at which time expenditures must be cut in order not to exceed revenues. Low estimates also cause problems in that programs may be needlessly reduced at the beginning of the fiscal year, only for a surplus of funds to develop later.

Deterministic Models. Perhaps the easiest method of revenue forecasting involves deterministic models that manipulate the revenue base and tax rate to produce a desired level of revenue. Property tax forecasts are deterministic in that a government can adjust assessments and tax rates to meet desired revenue levels. The main problems to address in such forecasting are the extent that (1) property values overall will rise or possibly decline, (2) new properties will be added to the tax rolls, and (3) old and deteriorating properties will fall into default. Deterministic models are useful for revenue sources over which a jurisdiction has substantial control; the models are not useful for taxes on such items as personal income and retail sales.

Simple Trend Extrapolations. Both formal and informal trend extrapolations are used in revenue estimating. In an informal situation, an assumption may be made that a particular revenue source will increase by 5 percent since that is what has occurred for the last couple of years. In most cases, however, revenues do not increase or decrease by a set percentage or remain constant. Revenue growth may increase *on average* by 5 percent, but in some years the growth may be 10 percent and in others only 1 or 2 percent. Knowing this information, what percentage estimate should be used for the upcoming budgeting year?

One method of dealing with this problem is to use simple linear regression, a statistical technique that fits a straight line to a series of historical data. The formula used is $y = mx + b$.[35] In the equation, y, or the forecasted revenue, is a function of a coefficient m times a known value x plus a constant b. In the formula, m is the slope of the straight line, x is the actual revenue generated the previous year, and b is a scale factor that adjusts for orders of magnitude differences between values. Computer software is readily available for making the appropriate calculations, but such projections also can be made using simple calculators.

The straight-line calculation of linear regression, however, may not parallel the actual historical series; the fit of the regression can be gauged by calculating the correlation coefficient known as R. When the data are random, R is 0.00. The closer R is to 1.00, the more likely it is that the regression accurately forecasts revenue.

Besides linear regression, other techniques exist for smoothing out fluctuations in historical series into a straight line.[36] The method called "moving averages" calculates an average value for each point in the historical series. Starting with a series of, say, eight years, the revenues for years 1, 2, and 3 are averaged. This average becomes the new "smoothed" value for year 2. Then actual values for years 2, 3, and 4 are averaged for a new "smoothed" year 3. Similar averages are calculated for the remaining years.

Underlying these techniques is the premise that the future is modeled after the past. The purpose of any projection technique is to reduce historical information to a discernible pattern and then extend that pattern into the future. A test of how well the technique works is to "predict" several recent time periods and compare those predictions with what actually occurred.

Econometric Models. Several types of econometric models exist, with one of the most popular types being multiple regression. In multiple regression models, independent variables are sought that can serve as predictors of revenue yield. The assumption is that a linear relationship exists between each predictor and the dependent variable of forecasted revenue. Also assumed is that each independent variable is unrelated to the others. A model for sales tax receipts might include the independent variables of population, personal income, and the consumer price index.[37] As each of these variables increases, revenues increase.

Multiple predictor variables are used in simultaneous equation models, as distinguished from multiple regression models that rely on a single equation. In simultaneous equation models, individual equations relate each independent or predictor variable to the revenue to be forecast. These individual equations are solved simultaneously. The advantage of simultaneous equation models is that they do not assume that each predictor variable is independent of each other predictor variable, as does the multiple regression approach. Since many of the variables one would use to make a revenue forecast would in fact be expected to be related to each other, the simultaneous equation approach is both more realistic and computationally more valid.

Revenue forecasts can be made using microsimulation models that are dependent on large data bases manipulated by computers. Individual taxpayers and corporations are included in the models and exhibit behavior changes in response to projected changes in the economy, tax laws, price levels, personal income, and the like. Historical data are used for actual taxpayers in the jurisdiction.

All of these models necessarily use variables that are sensitive to changes in economic conditions. Sales and income tax receipts rise and fall according to economic trends. Many user charges are affected too; when people are unemployed, they curtail their use of public transit, parking facilities, and museums and zoos that have admission fees. Therefore, the Achilles' heel of these models is in the assumptions made about future economic trends. Projecting national trends is extremely difficult, and state and local trends are no easier, especially since each subnational jurisdiction has its own economic characteristics and is influenced by national trends.[38,39]

Politics. Revenue estimating has its political aspects. Presidents, governors, and mayors are loathe to forecast economic hard times and low revenue levels. Political executives tend to campaign for election in part on the promise that they will strive for economic growth. Presidents have the additional problem that the forecast of a recession may be a self-fulfilling prophesy. State and local executives must limit expenditures to available revenue; pessimistic estimates force executives to make difficult choices as to where to cut programs in order to reduce overall expenditures. Since revenue estimates can rarely if ever be certain, establishing contingency reserves may be a useful method of protecting against possible shortfalls and the political problems that ensue from such shortfalls.[40]

SUMMARY

Governments use numerous revenue sources to support their operations, with taxes obviously being one of the most important types. In devising a tax system, governments need to consider whether horizontal and vertical equity standards are met. Important considerations are whether to have persons pay based on the benefits received or the ability to pay. Taxes on personal and corporate income, property, and retail sales are the largest generators of tax revenue. Each tax has a base, and then a rate or rates are applied to it. Other important revenue sources include user charges; reliance on charges or fees has increased since the late 1970s. Insurance trusts constitute another important source of revenue; included here are Social Security, government employee retirement systems, unemployment insurance, and Workers' Compensation.

Two topics of special concern are limitations imposed on taxing and spending and the procedures used in revenue estimating. During the late 1970s and early 1980s, many state and local governments adopted limitations on tax rates and/or spending. While the tax revolt seemed to have subsided in the latter part of the 1980s, citizens and political leaders alike remained concerned that taxes and spending be kept to a minimum. Revenue estimating, on the other hand, is an ongoing process. Deterministic procedures, trend extrapolations, and econometric models are among the methods used to forecast future revenues.

NOTES

1. Carolyn Webber and Aaron Wildavsky, *A History of Taxation and Expenditures in the Western World* (New York: Simon & Schuster, 1986).

2. Joseph A. Pechman, *Federal Tax Policy*, 5th ed. (Washington: Brookings, 1987), pp. 5–6.

3. Ronald F. King, "Tax Expenditures and Systematic Public Policy: An Essay on the Political Economy of the Federal Revenue Code," *Public Budgeting and Finance* 4 (Spring 1984): 14–31.

4. Congressional Budget and Impoundment Control Act, P.L. 93-344, 88 Stat. 297, 299 (1974).

5. Allen Schick, "Controlling Nonconventional Expenditure: Tax Expenditures and Loans," *Public Budgeting and Finance* 6 (Spring 1986): 3–19.

6. Jeffrey H. Birnbaum and Alan S. Murray, *Showdown at Gucci Gulch: Lawmakers, Lobbyists, and the Unlikely Triumph of Tax Reform* (New York: Random House, 1987).

7. *Prentice-Hall Federal Tax Handbook* (Paramus, N.J.: Prentice-Hall, 1988), p. 17.

8. Robert Gleason, "Federalism 1986–87: Signals of a New Era," *Intergovernmental Perspective* 14 (Winter 1988): 9–14.

9. Pechman, *Federal Tax Policy*, p. 136.

10. Pechman, *Federal Tax Policy*, pp. 141–42.

11. David Lowery, "Public Opinion, Fiscal Illusion, and Tax Revolution: The Political Demise of the Property Tax," *Public Budgeting and Finance* 5 (Autumn 1985): 76–88.

12. H. Clyde Reeves, ed., *The Role of the State in Property Taxation* (Lexington, Mass.: Lexington Books, 1983).

13. C. Lowell Harriss, ed., *The Property Tax and Local Finance* (New York: Academy of Political Science, 1983).

14. Tax Foundation, *Facts and Figures on Government Finance*, 24th ed. (Baltimore: Johns Hopkins University Press, 1988), p. 257.

15. John L. Mikesell, *Fiscal Administration*, 2nd ed. (Chicago: Dorsey, 1986), pp. 294–96.

16. W. Patrick Beaton, "The Demand for Municipal Goods: A Review of the Literature from the Point of View of Expenditure Determination," in W. Patrick Beaton, ed., *Municipal Expenditures, Revenues and Services* (New Brunswick, N.J.: Center for Urban Policy Research, Rutgers University, 1983), pp. 144–79.

17. Robert Cervero, "Paying for Off-Site Road Improvements Through Fees, Assessments, and Negotiations: Lessons from California," *Public Administration Review* 48 (1988): 534–41.

18. Cynthia Angell and Charles A. Shorter, "Impact Fees: Private-Sector Participation in Infrastructure Financing," *Government Finance Review* 4 (October 1988): 19–21.

19. General Accounting Office, *Social Security: Past Projections and Future Financing Concerns* (Washington, D.C.: Government Printing Office, 1986).

20. Michael J. Boskin, *Future Social Security Financing Alternatives and National Savings* (Cambridge, Mass.: National Bureau of Economic Research, 1987).

21. *Unemployment Insurance: Trends and Issues* (Washington, D.C.: Tax Foundation, 1982).

22. General Accounting Office, *Unemployment Insurance: Trust Fund Reserves Inadequate* (Washington, D.C.: Government Printing Office, 1988).

23. Tax Foundation, *Facts and Figures on Government Finance*, p. 279.

24. Monroe Berkowitz and John F. Burton, Jr., *Permanent Disability Benefits in Workers' Compensation* (Kalamazoo, Mich.: Upjohn Institute, 1987).

25. John D. Worrall and David Appel, eds., *Workers' Compensation Benefits* (Ithaca, N.Y.: ILR Press, 1985).

26. John L. Mikesell and Kurt Zorn, "State Lotteries for Public Revenue," *Public Budgeting and Finance* 8 (Spring 1988): 38–47.

27. John L. Mikesell and Kurt Zorn, "State Lotteries as Fiscal Savior or Fiscal Fraud," *Public Administration Review* 46 (1986): 311–20.

28. Jerry McCaffery and John H. Bowman, "Participatory Democracy and Budgeting: The Effects of Proposition 13," *Public Administration Review* 38 (1978): 530–38.

29. David Merriman, *The Control of Municipal Budgets: Toward the Effective Design of Tax and Expenditure Limitations* (New York: Quorum, 1987).

30. Helen F. Ladd and Julie B. Wilson, "Who Supports Tax Limitations: Evidence from Massachusetts' Proposition 2 1/2," *Journal of Policy Analysis and Management* 2 (1983): 256–79.

31. Edward Moscovitch, "Proposition 2 1/2," *Government Finance Review* 1 (October 1985): 21–25.

32. David O. Sears and Jack Citrin, *Tax Revolt* (Cambridge, Mass.: Harvard University Press, 1982).

33. Gary J. Reid, "How Cities in California Have Responded to Fiscal Pressures Since Proposition 13," *Public Budgeting and Finance* 8 (Spring 1988): 20–37.

34. Elaine B. Sharp and David Elkins, "The Impact of Fiscal Limitation," *Public Administration Review* 7 (1987): 385–92.

35. Allen L. Edwards, *An Introduction to Linear Regression and Correlation* (San Francisco: W.H. Freeman, 1976), p. 4.

36. Llewellyn M. Toulmin and Glendal E. Wright, "Expenditure Forecasting," in Jack Rabin and Thomas D. Lynch, eds., *Handbook on Public Budgeting and Finance* (New York: Marcel Dekker, 1983), pp. 209–50.

37. Larry D. Schroeder, "Forecasting Local Revenues and Expenditures," in J. Richard Aronson and Eli Schwartz, *Management Policies in Local Government Finance*, 3rd ed. (Washington: International City Management Association, 1987), pp. 93–117.

38. Irene S. Rubin, "Estimated and Actual Urban Revenues," *Public Budgeting and Finance* 7 (Winter 1987): 83–94.

39. John L. Mikesell, "The Cyclical Sensitivity of State and Local Taxes," *Public Budgeting and Finance* 4 (Spring 1984): 32–39.

40. Jon D. Vasche and Brad Williams, "Optimal Governmental Budgeting Contingency Reserve Funds," *Public Budgeting and Finance* 7 (Spring 1987): 66–82.

5

Budget Preparation:
The Expenditure Side

In the budget preparation phase, important decisions about expenditures are made simultaneously with decisions concerning revenues. The two general types of information relevant for budgeting are program and resource information (see Chapter 1). The former refers to data on what government does and what those activities accomplish; the latter refers to the inputs necessary to perform those activities. The input side, which includes dollars, facilities, equipment, supplies, and personnel, has long been an established feature of budgetary systems. The use of program information, on the other hand, has been slow in developing as an integral part of budgeting.

The critical argument relating to these two types of information is that they must be considered in combination if budgeting is to be a rational process of allocating resources. The budget is expected to relate the accomplishments of government to the costs of resources. The history of budgetary reform can be viewed as a struggle to create such budget systems.

This chapter examines the varied approaches that have been used in assembling the expenditure side of budgets, with the following chapter considering the political concerns of budget preparation. The first section of this chapter discusses early reform efforts, and the next, the types of program information that are used to varying degrees in budget systems. The last section discusses the numerous budget systems that have been used, including performance, program, and zero-base budgeting.

EARLY DEVELOPMENTS

As noted in Chapter 1, budgeting can focus on expenditure control, management control, and planning control.[1] While there is some historical pattern to the development of these three emphases, they are not rigidly fixed to specific time periods, and both the management and planning phases have involved greater utilization of program information. Not only is there a blurring of distinctions among these stages in terms of the dates of their popularity, but the advocacy for using planning coupled with program information can be dated at least back to the early part of the century. Here we refer to planning as an effort to associate means with ends in order to attain goals and objectives in the future.

Program Information

1910–40. Before the establishment of the federal budgetary system, budgeting was often advocated as a means of allocating resources to obtain program results. Two of the most notable proponents were President William Howard Taft[2] and the 1912 Taft Commission on Economy and Efficiency. At one point in its report, the commission stated:

> In order that he [the administrator] may think intelligently about the subject of his responsibility he must have before him regularly statements which will reflect *results in terms of quality and quantity*; he must be able to measure quality and quantity of results by units of cost and units of efficiency. (Emphasis added.)[3]

Although there was an obvious interest in economizing—in saving dollars— a parallel interest was being able to obtain the best return in program terms for resources spent.

Other important spokesmen for program results in budgeting in the 1910s included Frederick A. Cleveland[4] and William F. Willoughby.[5] The 1920s and 1930s brought Lent D. Upson,[6] A.E. Buck,[7] Wylie Kilpatrick,[8] and the 1937 President's Committee on Administrative Management.[9] A.E. Buck's classic *Public Budgeting* (1929) admittedly was not strongly committed to a program information orientation, but Buck did express interest in reforms that would concentrate upon measuring the products of government activities.

1940-60. Although the use of program information and planning was advocated throughout the first four decades of the century, these ideas received far greater recognition beginning in the 1940s. V.O. Key, Jr., challenged previous budgetary literature as largely mechanical and criticized it for failing to focus upon the "basic budgeting problem" of comparing the merits of alternative programs: "On what basis shall it be decided to allocate X dollars to activity A instead of activity B?"[10] The 1949 Commission on Organization of the Executive Branch of the Government, known as the First Hoover Commission, recommended that the federal budget be "based upon functions, activities, and projects: this we designate as a performance budget." Budgeting should be in terms of "the work or the service to be accomplished."[11]

More proponents of the same viewpoint emerged in the 1950s. Noted scholars included Verne B. Lewis,[12] Frederick C. Mosher,[13] Catheryn Seckler-Hudson,[14] and Arthur Smithies.[15] The Second Hoover Commission supported the recommendations of its predecessor.[16] Arthur Smithies suggested the use of program information in budgeting as a primary means of improving both executive and legislative decision making. Jesse Burkhead's *Government Budgeting*, while basically descriptive rather than normative, devoted considerable discussion to performance and program budgeting.[17]

By the 1950s the use of program information in budgeting had become the mainstream of reform; at the same time, another school of thought, led by Charles E. Lindblom, Aaron Wildavsky, and others, challenged the budget reform movement on the grounds that political decision systems were not readily adaptable to program planning. Lindblom advanced the "muddling through" model of decision making (see Chapter 1), which ran counter to budgetary reform efforts. Wildavsky was to become the most outspoken skeptic of the feasibility of using program information in budgeting. In 1969 he concluded, *"No one knows how to do program budgeting."*[18]

Nonbudgetary Developments

An alternative school of thought led by David Novick, Charles J. Hitch, Roland McKean, and others was rooted in a series of technologies that were developed during and after World War II. These technologies were to be highly compatible with the budget reform movement and were to serve as the theoretical foundation for planning-programming-budgeting (PPB) systems attempted in the 1960s. At least six closely related fields were important.

1. Operations Research (OR)
2. Economic Analysis
3. General Systems Theory
4. Cybernetics
5. Computer Hardware
6. Systems Analysis

Budgeting per se was of limited interest to the leading theorists in each of these fields. The more important focus was using systems' resources to achieve desired systems' goals. Such a concern, however, obviously had budgetary implications, and in a sense, one can say that these six fields backed into budgeting.[19]

Operations Research. Like the other fields to be discussed, OR defies precise definition, but an acceptable one is ". . . the use of the scientific method to provide criteria for decisions concerning man-machine systems involving repeatable operations."[20] The focus is upon repetitive or recurrent operations.

Although the beginning of OR can be dated to 1972, when the British introduced the use of war games,[21] most observers date its actual beginning to the resolution of military problems before and during World War II.[22] OR involves the specifications of objectives, the design of a model representing the situation under investigation, and the collection and application of relevant data. The result is a set of highly quantitative techniques used in the analysis of data. These techniques include linear programming, queuing theory, game theory, and Monte Carlo techniques.

Following the war, the term "management science" entered the vocabulary and came to be equated with OR. By 1959, Stafford Beer, a noted leader in the field, was able to state that OR was not the application of the scientific method or a science but was science itself.[23]

Economic Analysis. The second related field is cost benefit, cost effectiveness, cost utility, or, the term used in this book, economic analysis.[24] The problems associated with analysis in general and economic analysis in particular are discussed in Chapter 7. Here it is important to note that such analysis is intended to determine whether the value of the benefits of a program or facility exceeds the costs. Analysis can be used in evaluating possible alternatives. The purpose is to improve choice capability through the use of instruments that predict the likely consequences of possible alternatives.

Like OR, economic analysis's beginning can be traced to the 1800s. A paper on public works by J. Dupuit is sometimes cited as the beginning of the field.[25] A more contemporary benchmark was the 1950 "Green Book" of the Subcommittee on Benefits and Costs of the Federal Inter-Agency River Basin Committee. This document attempted to codify and rank criteria for analysis.[26] Another major publication related to analysis of water resources was Roland N. McKean's 1958 book, *Efficiency in Government through Systems Analysis, with Emphasis on Water Resource Development.*[27]

General Systems Theory. The third field is general systems theory. As will be recalled from Chapter 1, a system is most simply defined as a set of units and the relationships among the units. Unlike OR, which was largely a by-product of war, systems theory was a product of the study of biological organisms. K. Ludwig von Bertalanffy, starting in the 1920s, broke from the popular biological emphasis upon the cell to concentrate upon organs in their relationships to one another.[28] Other leaders in the field included biomathematician Anatol Rapoport,[29] physiologist Ralph W. Gerard, and economist Kenneth E. Boulding.[30]

Cybernetics. The term "cybernetics" was derived from a Greek word meaning "steersman" by Norbert Wiener, a mathematician. Cybernetics, then, is the science of control and communication.[31] This field, like the others that have been discussed, can be traced to the turn of the century, but was not recognized as a discipline or subdiscipline until World War II. Cybernetics was used in the development of servomechanisms, self-regulating systems that adjusted in accord with new inputs of information. Radar, for example, was joined with antiaircraft artillery in such a way that the velocity, direction, and altitude of a target were related to the properties of antiaircraft weaponry.

Computer Hardware. The fifth field, the computer, is not a form of management technology but rather a machine or piece of hardware. Its importance is that it allows complex data manipulations that previously were impossible or impractical. Charles Babbage, an English mathematician, is usually recognized as the main forerunner in the development of the computer, having designed prototype machines in the 1920s and 1930s. Major breakthroughs were achieved by Vannevar Bush of the Massachusetts Institute of Technology in the 1920s and by Howard Aiken and IBM in the 1940s.[32]

Systems Analysis. The sixth and newest field is systems analysis. Its rise during the 1950s in many respects marked the breakdown in distinctions among the other fields that have been discussed. Systems analysis is eclectic in that it draws upon all of the above areas, and some observers today treat all of these as synonymous.[33] For some writers, systems analysis is the application of the scientific method, while for others it is "nothing more than quantitative or enlightened common sense aided by modern analytical methods."[34]

OR, or at least its early version, can be distinguished from systems analysis. The latter considers alternative values in conducting analysis whereas the former often operates within the limits of prescribed values. OR begins with the assumption that X is desired and then attempts to design or revise a system in order to produce X. Systems analysis is not so delimited.

Generally, one can say that systems analysis arose in connection with military problems following World War II and that persons associated with the RAND Corporation, a private consulting firm working mainly for the Air Force, were the major contributors to its development. One of the early works in this field was Hitch and McKean's *The Economics of Defense in the Nuclear Age* (1960 and 1967).[35]

Although this series of events was outside the mainstream of budget reform, it served as the basis for major efforts in budgetary reform during the 1960s. As work developed in OR, economic analysis, systems analysis, and the like, researchers almost backed into budgeting. By the mid-1960s, the systems approach, at least in theory, had gained wide acceptance. A landmark in the literature was the volume edited by David Novick of RAND, *Program Budgeting* (1965 and 1969). This was the first major publication to treat public budgeting within a systems framework.[36]

STRUCTURING THE REQUEST PROCESS

Except in the smallest organizations, a budget cannot be prepared by the central budget office alone. As noted in Chapter 3, budget preparation begins with the almost simultaneous amassing of supporting information in the operating agencies and the issuance of budget instructions from the central budget office. The information developed at this stage depends in part on how the agency chooses to make its case and in part on the way decisions are expected to be made. If only dollar requests are prepared, there obviously will be no information with which to make judgments on program effectiveness. On the other hand, there is no need to assume that central budget offices necessarily use program information in their deliberations even if they require its submission. Still another factor determining what information will be prepared is the known information demands from other budget participants, most notably the legislative body. Much data may be amassed not because the agency or the chief executive has any intention of using them for decision purposes but simply because each year the legislative body demands that information.

Preparation Instructions

Budget preparation practices vary considerably within agencies.[37] There will be varying degrees of participation by field office staff and other line personnel, but while such variation exists, the overall process is guided by a set of instructions issued by the central budget office of a government.

At the federal level, these instructions are contained in Office of Management and Budget (OMB) Circular A-11, "Preparation and Submission of Budget Estimates." Instructions such as these provide forms to be completed, reducing uncertainty among agencies as to what the budget office expects of them. Typically, a calendar will be provided explaining when requests are due for submission to the budget office and indicating a period when agencies may be called for hearings with the budget office. The instructions, then, tend to bound the amount of information that will be required of the agencies, although the budget office may request additional information from given agencies.

No matter what the jurisdiction, standard items can be found in virtually all budget instruction manuals. Where appropriate, agencies are asked to submit revenue data, such as an agency operating a loan program with a revolving fund. Most of the instructions, however, concentrate upon expenditures. The expenditures are keyed with the accounting system, using objects of expenditures such as personnel and supplies (see Chapter 11). There may also be detailed breakouts on the number of persons in a given unit, their job titles, and current salaries. The instructions usually allow for the agencies to provide narrative statements in order to justify the requests.

Separate sets of instructions may be provided for the operating and capital fund budgets. Instructions for the latter, used extensively at the state and local levels, are primarily for requests on major fixed assets such as buildings and equipment. (See Chapter 12.)

Program Information

Budget systems are making increased use of program information and therefore request instructions specify what types of program data are to be supplied. The measures typically will have been negotiated between the budget office and the agencies before budget preparation time. In other words, when the agencies receive the request instructions, they already know what program information is to be supplied.

Social Indicators. There are numerous types of program information, with social indicators being the broadest or most general type.[38,39] These measures of the physical, social, and economic environments are intended to reflect what sometimes is called the quality of life. In the area of employment, social indicators include job satisfaction broken out by age, sex, race, and income. Measures of this type are useful in assessing past and current trends and provide decision makers with some insight into the need for programs. Often absent, however, is any direct linkage between such indicators and a given government service, meaning that the indicators are of little use for yearly budget decisions.

Impacts. A measure of more direct relevance to budgeting is impacts, sometimes called outcomes. Measures of this type concentrate upon effectiveness, whether desired effects or consequences are being achieved. When a government service has affected "individuals, institutions [or] the environment," an impact has occurred.[40] In the employment case, an impact measure might be the average earnings of nonwhite men who completed a job training program or, even more focused, the average increase in hourly earnings after completion of the program compared with prior earnings. Such a measure needs to be assessed carefully, however, in that earnings may have increased in a given time period mainly because of an upturn in the economy or because of inflation and not because of training.

Sometimes myths or doctrines lead to problems in the selection of impact measures. In providing funds to police departments, the assumption is often made that crime will be controlled. This assumption leads to the selection of impact measures dealing with crime rates, despite the fact that police have only limited control over crime.

Outputs. In contrast with impacts, output measures reflect the immediate product or services being provided. Returning to the employment example, the number of graduates of the training program would be the output. The percentage of persons enrolled who graduate—the completion rate—or, conversely, the dropout rate can be calculated from year to year. Measures such as these are far easier to calculate than many impacts because data sources are within the organization. One needs only to keep accurate records of who enrolled and who graduated. Impacts, on the other hand, are external. In the case of earnings of graduates, a monitoring or follow-up system for the graduates would be necessary to obtain the appropriate data.

One drawback in using output measures without impacts is that an erroneous assumption can be made about causal relations. The employment example would suggest that training improves one's employability, but unless data are collected to verify such anticipated results, the system is operating strictly on faith or doctrine. Outputs, then, may encourage suboptimization, which is the improvement of operations for attaining subobjectives while risking the possibility of moving away from rather than toward larger values.

Activities and Work Load. Beyond outputs are activities. They constitute the work that is done to produce outputs. The total hours of instruction could be a measure for a job training program, or the measure might be more focused, such as hours of instruction in lathe operations. Activities are sometimes measured as work load. The number of classroom disruptions requiring special consultations could be a reflection of work load; other work load measures could include the number of enrollees or the number of applicants to a program. If the number of applicants increases, though enrollments are kept constant because of space limitations, the work load will have increased even though output has not.

Management by Objectives. Work load is often the focus of management by objectives (MBO) and other participative management techniques.[41,42] Although many diverse activities have been carried out in government under the rubric of MBO, a common theme tends to be prescribing objectives for organizational units, managers, and workers in terms of the work they are expected to accomplish. Participative management systems such as MBO emphasize involvement of all strata of the bureaucracy in the development of objectives.

Productivity. Another term having many different meanings is productivity.[43] The former National Center for Productivity and Quality of Working Life took a broad approach to the term, subsuming virtually all forms of program measurement.[44,45] Others take a different approach, limiting productivity to comparisons of resource inputs and work. Ratios are typically used for productivity measurement, such as the total cost of a job training program divided by the number of graduates, yielding an average cost per graduate. If average cost remains constant from one year to another, despite increases in salary rates and various supplies, then the assumption is made that the unit is more productive. Emphasis is placed on making government operations increasingly efficient. OMB Circular A-11 has provided for a productivity improvement plan,[46] as did President Ronald Reagan's Executive Order 12637, issued in 1988.

Productivity measures often require extensive record keeping. If a group of employees together perform several different activities, then a reporting system needs to account for the hours committed to each activity by each employee. This accounting is sometimes accomplished by daily report forms. State and local police often must submit daily reports on hours spent patrolling, investigating, testifying in court, and report writing itself. Less complicated systems may use weekly, monthly, or quarterly report forms. On the cost side, accounting systems need to capture nonpersonnel expenditures related to activities.

Need. A final type of measure gauges the need for a program. The need measure indicates the gap between the level of service and the need for it. Whereas the output measure may indicate the number of job training graduates, the need measure shows how many other persons are without adequate job skills and therefore in need of training.

In discussing need, we have come full circle back to social indicators, prompting a few words of caution. We have relied here mainly upon the employment example to show differences among types of measures, but it should be understood that the differences may not be so obvious in other programs. For example, the dollar value of fire damage in a city might be considered a social indicator, an impact of the fire department, and an indicator of fire service need.

SYSTEMS OF BUDGETING

If the central budget office simply instructed agencies to request budgets for the coming year, probably several different types of responses would result, based upon different assumptions about the coming budget year. One agency might respond by requesting what it felt was needed. Another might respond in light of what resources it thought were available, resulting in a much lower request. Others might use combinations of these and other approaches. The consequences would be budget requests based upon varied assumptions, and these requests would require different reactions by the budget office. To avoid such disparities in the assumptions made by requesting agencies, budget instructions often provide guidance to agencies.

Preparation Assumptions

Current Services. One type of guidance is to assume basically no change in programs. A department's current budget is considered its base and any increases are to be requested only to cover additional operating costs, such as increased costs for personnel, supplies, and the like. An assumption is made that the government is committed or obligated to continue existing programs. This base approach often has been used only implicitly, but since the 1960s and 1970s many governments have focused upon indicating explicitly the level of commitment. The federal budget has included current services estimates since the 1970s.

Explicitly determining what are current commitments is difficult because programs often are created without any such explicit statement of commitment. The easiest cases are those in which there is an obligation to serve all claimants on the system. School districts, for example, are obligated to serve all eligible children, and therefore budget requests from units within the school district would be determined by the expected number of enrolled children. In other cases, the commitment may be in terms of the level of service, specifically outputs and work load. Using job training again, the unit could have a commitment to maintain the same number of graduates or alternatively the same number of students. Budgeting, then, can be seen as adding increments to or subtracting them from the base.[47]

Fixed Ceiling. An alternative to the current commitment approach is fixed-ceiling budgeting. Under this system, a dollar limit is set governmentwide, then factored into limits for departments, bureaus, and other subunits. The advantage is a set of budget requests that, when totaled, come to the desired ceiling. The disadvantage is that some organizational units may receive inadequate funding and others may be overfunded in terms of program priorities; this results from inadequate information about program requirements being available when limits are set. This approach is most useful during periods of stability.

A weakness of both the base and fixed-ceiling approaches is that by themselves they offer no suggestions for program changes. If the budget office and chief executive have only these types of budget requests, they lack information about alternative resource allocations. In response to this lack of information, a variety of "what-if" approaches to budget requests has been devised. These approaches ask agencies to develop alternatives. The "what-ifs" may be expressed as, What if more or fewer dollars were available? What if program improvements were to be made in specific areas? and other ways.

Open-Ended. One of the most common what-if budget requests is open-ended or blue-sky budgeting. The question is asked, What if resources were available to meet all needs? Agencies are expected to ask for what they think they need to deal with problems assigned to them. This approach should not be confused with the absence of guidance, in which some agencies might request "needed" funds and others might ask for lesser amounts. The advantage of the open-ended approach is that it surfaces perceived needs for services in comparison with existing service levels. The "needed" budget, in contrast with the current budget, can serve as the basis for discussions of preferred funding levels. The disadvantage is that open-ended requests may exceed the economic and political capabilities of the jurisdiction, so that the requests seem like fanciful wish lists. Such has been the case in the Defense Department and its use of the Joint Strategic Objectives Plan (JSOP), which is based on the assumption that defense forces should be as strong as necessary to minimize the risk of being attacked by a potential aggressor.[48]

Performance Budgeting

A flurry of budget reform activity aimed at bringing greater program data into the budget decision-making process occurred in response to the First Hoover Commission (1949). The proposal was for what was called "performance budgeting." In response to the commission's recommendation, Congress specifically provided in the National Security Act Amendments of 1949 that performance budgeting be used in the military. The following year saw passage of the Budget and Accounting Procedures Act, which in essence required performance budgeting for the entire federal government. State and local governments followed suit.

Among federal, state, and local agencies, performance budgeting was geared mainly toward developing work load and unit cost measures of activities. For the Post Office, the number of letters that could be processed by one employee was identified. With this knowledge and an estimate of the number of letters to be processed, the Post Office department could calculate the personnel required for the coming budget year.[49] In the name of performance budgeting, the Defense Department in 1950 adopted a single set of budget categories that was applied to all services. These categories, most of which were still in use in the late 1980s, included personnel, maintenance and operation, and research and development.[50]

Inherent characteristics of defense complicate the use of performance budgeting; in particular, it is extraordinarily difficult to determine how much defense is enough. The problem is that defense is mainly a matter of deterrence and preparedness. The military is expected to have sufficient strength to deter an attack by a potential aggressor and to be sufficiently prepared for war if it does occur. The deterrent strategy is working when no attack has been launched. As for the preparedness argument, that can only be tested in real combat situations. When the nation is not fighting a war, it is difficult to prove conclusively that the nation is or is not sufficiently prepared.

While reconstructing the past is difficult, it seems that the efforts to install performance budgeting in the 1950s failed. There is little evidence that performance budgeting ever became the basis upon which decisions were made in federal, state, or local budget processes. But some lasting effect was evident. Performance budgeting did introduce on a wide scale the use of program information in budget documents, and that type of information gained increasing attention in the coming years.[51,52]

Planning-Programming-Budgeting and Program Budgeting

The origin of the phrase "planning-programming-budgeting" is uncertain. Mosher used the term in his 1954 book on Army program budgeting.[53] During the early 1960s in Defense, PPB stood for program package budgeting, because a package was presented in terms of the resource inputs (personnel, equipment, and so forth) and outputs.[54] By 1965, when President Lyndon B. Johnson extended the system to civilian agencies, PPB had come to mean planning-programming-budgeting. It should be recognized that planning and programming are not distinctly different functions but differ only in degree. The terms have been defined as follows: "*Planning* is the production of the range of meaningful potentials for selection of courses of action through a systematic consideration of alternatives. *Programming* is the more specific determination of the manpower, material, and facilities necessary for accomplishing a program."[55]

Today, PPB is generally used to refer to a series of budgetary reform efforts in the 1960s. The term "program budgeting" is a more generic one and refers to systems intended to link program costs with results.

Defense. There are several reasons why PPB started in Defense. Probably the most important one was that, despite having the authority to manage the military, the secretary did not have the management support necessary. Secretary Robert S. McNamara in 1961 had the determination to initiate change. In coming to the Pentagon, he brought with him several people from the RAND Corporation, a nonprofit "think tank" that earlier had done extensive work related to program budgeting. David Novick of RAND published reports in the 1950s recommending such a system for defense.[56] The McKean book on systems analysis (1958)[57] and the Hitch and McKean book on defense (first published in 1960) were also RAND products.[58] The key person for program budgeting under McNamara was Charles J. Hitch, who became assistant secretary of defense (comptroller). McNamara, Hitch, and others drew upon the experience discussed earlier, such as the development of operations research, computers, and systems analysis, all of which were complementary to the mainstream of budgetary reform.

The central component of the defense system is the Five-Year Defense Program (FYDP), which projects costs and personnel according to missions or programs. These form what is called the program structure, a classification system that begins with broad missions factored into subunits and activities. The structure groups like activities together, regardless of which branches of the service conduct them, thereby allowing for analyses across organizational lines. The major programs within the FYDP are

1. strategic forces
2. general purpose forces
3. intelligence and communications
4. airlift and sealift
5. guard and reserve
6. research and development
7. central supply and maintenance
8. training, medical, and other general purpose activities
9. administration and associated activities
10. support of other nations
11. special operations forces

Changes in terminology and process have occurred since the 1960s, but overall the main approach in Defense has remained constant. Changes in the FYDP are accomplished by the Office of the Secretary of Defense's issuing Defense Guidance to which the services respond by preparing Program Objective Memoranda (POMs) that contain budget proposals for modifying the FYDP.[59] The POMs are proposed programmatic and resource incremental changes to the base established in the FYDP.

The Defense PPB system has been in operation for approximately three decades, but the system clearly has not been a panacea for defense-related problems. During that period the department withstood extended and severe criticism regarding its conduct of the Vietnam War.[60] There have been major cost overruns and failures of various weapons systems during the period along with scandals involving alleged corruption in weapons contracting. The point is that budget systems may provide useful information for decision makers but do not constitute guarantees that wise decisions will be made.[61]

Federal Civilian Reforms. Turning to the civilian side of government, planning-programming-budgeting was announced for federal agencies in 1965 by President Johnson, who had been impressed with the Defense Department budget system.[62] This action sparked massive reform efforts throughout all levels of government in the United States.

The federal civilian system was intended to be similar to the Defense model. Multiyear plans, known as Program and Financial Plans (PFPs), were to be devised for each department. Changes were to be made through the submission of Program Memoranda (PMs). However, by 1969, when Richard M. Nixon became president, PPB had not been fully implemented among the civilian agencies, and in 1971 OMB relieved agencies of preparing PFPs and PMs. PPB as a major budget system and even as an acronym was allowed a quiet death.[63]

A study conducted by the then Bureau of the Budget, now OMB, found there were six factors that characterized the more successful efforts to introduce PPB.[64]

1. There were sufficient numbers of analysts.
2. Analysts were well qualified.
3. Analysts had formal access to agency heads and managers.
4. Analysts had informal access.
5. Agency heads and managers gave strong support for use of analysis.
6. Analysis was viewed as a valuable tool by agency heads and managers.

This study and others found that lack of the leadership's understanding of and commitment to using program budgeting tended to deter success, as did an agency's general "underdevelopment" in the use of analytic techniques. Agencies administering "soft" social programs had difficulty devising useful program measures. Bureaucratic infighting also reduced the chances of successful implementation.[65]

State and Local Reforms. Just as a revolution did not occur in federal decision making through the use of PPB, this approach did not revolutionize state and local decision making in the 1960s. Most of the states that experimented with PPB emphasized the development of program structure, multiyear plans, and program memoranda, while only a few concentrated upon analysis as their main thrust. By the mid-1970s, however, the emphasis had swung away from the structural features of PPB to the use of measures of effectiveness and efficiency and program analysis. In the 1960s many of the states and municipalities took only cautious first steps with no timetable for completion of the installation process. Others began the effort on a pilot basis, attempting PPB in one department with expectations to expand the coverage.

By the close of the 1960s it was difficult to identify many ongoing PPB systems at the state and local levels. The reasons for failure or lack of major success were similar to those already mentioned for federal agencies. State and local governments usually were not sufficiently developed in management practices to be able to undertake the transformation that was expected. Additionally, people simply expected too much to result from conversion to PPB and did not realize the financial and administrative costs associated with the conversion. Legislative bodies often showed little support for the new budget system, and this fact was interpreted by some as legislative hostility toward change.[66,67]

Change, however, did occur as a result of efforts to introduce PPB systems. Perhaps the biggest single achievement was that governments began to make greater use of program information in budgetary decision making, albeit largely of the output variety.[68]

Zero-Base Budgeting

Zero-base budgeting (ZBB) is another form of what-if budgeting. "Traditional" ZBB—that is, *not* the type used by the federal government during the Carter administration—asks, "What if a program were to be eliminated?" Rather than assuming that a base exists, the approach asks what would happen if a program were discontinued. Each program is challenged for its very existence in every budget cycle.

Early Use. The U.S. Department of Agriculture engaged in an experiment with ZBB in the early 1960s, and the results were disappointing.[69] Zero-base budgeting, it was found, wasted valuable administrative time by requiring the rehashing of old issues that had already been resolved. The system was unrealistic; many programs were mandatory within the political arena and could not be dismantled no matter how compelling the available data and analysis. The excessive paperwork that was generated could not be reviewed by decision makers within the agency.

The disadvantage of zero-base budgeting is analogous to that of open-ended budgeting. Both approaches make basically unrealistic assumptions. Whereas open-ended budgeting assumes unlimited resources, the zero-base approach makes the unrealistic assumption that decision makers have the capacity to eliminate programs. In reality, the political forces in any jurisdiction are such that few programs in any given year can be abandoned. For this reason, zero-base budgeting may be better applied to selective programs in any one year rather than governmentwide. A cycle of reviews can be established in which some programs are thoroughly reviewed each year using ZBB, and all programs are reviewed in any five-year period.

The 1970s. Zero-base budgeting gained new popularity in the 1970s.[70-72] Much attention focused on Georgia and its governor, Jimmy Carter, who subsequently brought a new version of ZBB to the federal government upon becoming president in 1977.[73] The Carter administration's version of zero-base budgeting had three major characteristics.[74-76]

1. Decision units were identified for which budget requests, called "decision packages," were to be prepared. Approximately 10,000 of these were prepared each year.
2. Alternative funding levels were used for each package.
   a. the minimum level that entailed providing services below present levels
   b. the current level that maintained existing service and reflected increased costs for personnel supplies and the like
   c. an enhancement level that provided for upgraded services
3. Alternative funding levels of decision packages were to be ranked by importance.

The ZBB experiment at the federal level was criticized on several counts. The most frequently heard complaint was the amount of time required to prepare requests and the corresponding amount of paperwork. The ZBB system, contrary to what President Carter had promised, did not require agencies to justify every tax dollar they received. Administrators puzzled over how there could be a minimum level below current operations when the statute under which an agency operated specified benefits, as in the case of Social Security.

ZBB rarely eliminated unnecessary programs, curtailed their growth, or resulted in reassigning priorities among programs.[77,78] In some isolated instances savings were achieved by funding programs at the minimum level, but that produced agency resentment. Administrators of a program saw themselves being punished by having their budget cut because they had identified how the program could operate with less than the current budget. More often, however, the system was seen as involving excessive paperwork that ultimately had little or no impact on policy making. Shortly after President Reagan took office in January 1981, the new administration announced that zero-base budgeting would no longer be practiced.

The experience at the state and local levels was comparable to that of the federal government. ZBB initially seemed to hold great promise but eventually was abandoned, although some governments continued to describe their budget systems as founded on the ZBB concept.

Strategic Planning and Guidance

Planning. Some governments, in part following the lead of private-sector organizations, have engaged in strategic planning efforts, which focus attention on fundamental missions, goals, and objectives.[79,80] In strategic planning, options are identified and chosen in regard to fundamental directions to be taken, such as favoring one set of problems and corresponding programs over another set. Annual budgeting, then, is used to allocate resources according to the established priorities.

Strategic planning can be an extraordinary and time-consuming process in which various plans, often entailing great detail, are drafted, reviewed, and then modified. Such processes usually involve developing an overall plan and then revising the plan annually to reflect new information and revised priorities. Comparisons can be drawn here with the Defense JSOP and FYDP mentioned earlier.

Policy and Program Guidance. A less ambitious but nevertheless useful approach is to provide broad policy guidance or more narrowly focused program guidance to departments and agencies before they begin to prepare their budget requests. At the federal level, OMB has instructed specific agencies as to what program funding proposals are likely to receive favorable review and instructed them to prepare issue papers on specific programs for which there is concern about the efficacy of resource utilization. Pennsylvania is one state that for numerous years has issued Program Policy Guidelines that indicate to agencies the concerns of the governor, namely the issues that have high priority for the coming budget year.

In response to such guidance, agencies prepare detailed program requests. There is likely to be a discussion of the range of available alternatives, possibly with detailed costing of each along with expected results of each. Where guidance is not directed at any one agency, two or more may submit competing requests, each attempting to show how its proposed alternative would deal with a problem. For example, both the city police and recreation departments might submit budget proposals for dealing with juvenile delinquency.

The advantage of such guidance is that agencies are spared many hours of needless work in preparing requests that are fated for rejection. The policy/program guidance, however, does not ensure executive approval of agency requests. The requests may be rejected simply because of inadequate funds or because the arguments for the proposed changes fail to be persuasive.

Multiyear Requests

All budget requests are multiyear in that they at least cover the current year plus the coming budget year and probably the past year as well. States with biennial budgets obviously have multiyear requests. An issue, however, is whether budget requests should extend beyond the budget year, and if yes, how this is to be accomplished. The argument for multiyear requests is simple: without looking beyond the budget year, commitments of resources may be made that were never intended. This argument applies particularly to proposed expansions and new programs.

Time Horizons. In theory, the time horizon should be geared to the life cycle of each program. This life cycle is clearest in specific projects or programs that have an obvious beginning and conclusion. A weapons system is one of the best examples. The system begins with research and concludes after it has become obsolete.

On the other hand, many governmental programs have no foreseeable conclusion. The need for education, roads, law enforcement, recreation, and the like will always exist. Each of these may have unique properties that suggest possible time horizons. Given the length of time required to design and construct schools, projections of several years are needed. Multiyear requests can reveal when roads will require major renovations.

Given that an appropriate life cycle for multiyear requests is often not obvious, an arbitrary set of years may be imposed. The most common is the budget year plus the four succeeding years, known as a five-year projection. The federal government, according to the 1974 Congressional Budget and Impoundment Control Act, makes such projections as do some state governments. Making projections beyond five years is difficult because there are many unknowns. Using the road example, it may be largely unknown what the typical commuting pattern will be ten or more years from now.

Cost and Program Projections. Assuming they can be made, however, projections can be limited to finances or can include program data projections. The state of the art tends to limit projections to finances, showing anticipated future financial requirements, but there is increasing use of program impact and output projections. The requests show what resources will be needed in future years along with the benefits that will be derived.

Multiyear projections using cost and program data can be helpful in coping with severe economic conditions. Where program reductions are necessary, agency requests can illustrate the consequences over a longer time period. Cuts in an agency's budget made this year may seem essential but may produce undesired future consequences. To live within available revenues, a city may reduce its road maintenance program with no noticeable reduction in road quality in the first year; however, by the second or third year following these cuts, the city may have a road network of substantially lower quality than before.

The Department of Defense has been authorized to experiment with the use of milestone budgeting for the development and acquisition of weapons systems.[81] Projects can be approved for multiple years and, depending upon stipulations, may not require additional congressional approval until particular phases are completed or milestones are reached. The approach has the potential to use resources more efficiently rather than constraining the funds available for a given budget year. Managers are encouraged to have a longer time horizon than the annual budget cycle.

Use of Budget Techniques

Many of the techniques discussed here can be used in combination with one another.[82] ZBB, for instance, can be used selectively for some agencies undergoing intensive review while others use a fixed-ceiling approach. Governments can use a current services budget in conjunction with priority listing of decision packages akin to the Carter administration's version of ZBB. The base approach can be combined with open-ended budgeting, in which agencies request funds for what they perceive to be their needs. Program guidance can be linked with priority listings.

Most governments probably have hybrids of the various systems that have been discussed. That is the case with the federal government, which uses a variety of program information for virtually all agencies but a version of PPB mainly for the Department of Defense.

A couple of surveys from the mid-1980s shed light on state budgetary practices. In a survey that was able to obtain responses from all 50 states, 37, or about 3 of 4, reported using program budgeting; that number included 14 states that said they used ZBB as well.[83] Another 6 states reported using only ZBB, while 7 reported use of neither system. In another study that was conducted in 1985 and twice before that, the use of effectiveness measures increased from 29 percent of the states in 1975 to 74 percent, and use of productivity measures increased from 45 percent to 74 percent.[84] However, the use of future-year projections has been limited. As of 1985, 13 percent of the states reported multiyear projections of effectiveness measures, 18 percent for productivity measures, and 35 percent for costs. Two out of 3 states (67 percent) reported using written policy guidance (up from 30 percent in 1970), but only 29 percent reported using written program guidance (up from 3 percent). About half of the states use a current services budget, and two-thirds use priority ranking.

Use of program information at the local level is more limited than at the state level. One study from the mid-1980s found that 58 percent used exclusively a line-item or object-of-expenditure budget.[85] However, 30 percent reported using performance budgeting, program budgeting, or a combination of these, sometimes in conjunction with line-item budgeting. Less than 3 percent reported using zero-base budgeting.

SUMMARY

One of the main threads running through budgetary literature has been the need to use the budgetary process as a vehicle for planning. In particular, this need has meant an attempt to incorporate program data into the system along with resource data, such as dollar and personnel costs.

During and after World War II, a series of concepts and techniques emerged that had great influence on budgetary reform. These included operations research, economic analysis, general systems theory, cybernetics, computer hardware, and systems analysis.

Budget requests are prepared by agencies in accordance with instructions provided by the central budget office. In addition to data on finances and personnel, request instructions increasingly require program data. These include social indicators, impacts, outputs, work loads and activities, and data on the need or demand for services. Productivity measures are used to relate resource consumption, as measured in dollars and personnel, to the work accomplished and the product of that work.

Budget request manuals take varied approaches to providing guidance on how agencies should request resources. These approaches include current commitment, fixed-ceiling, and open-ended budgeting. Reform efforts since the 1960s have focused on planning-programming-budgeting systems, or more generally program budgeting, and also on zero-base budgeting. Strategic planning and policy/program guidance have gained in popularity in recent years. Governments tend to use hybrids of these systems.

NOTES

1. Allen Schick, "The Road to PPB: The Stages of Budget Reform," *Public Administration Review* 26 (1966): 243–58.

2. William Howard Taft, *Economy and Efficiency in the Government Service*, House Doc. No. 458, January 1912: 16.

3. Commission on Economy and Efficiency, *The Need for a National Budget*, House Doc. No. 854, 1912: 4–5.

4. Frederick A. Cleveland, "Evolution of the Budget Ideas in the United States," *Annals* 62 (1915): 15–35.

5. William F. Willoughby, *The Problems of a National Budget* (New York: Appleton, 1918).

6. Lent D. Upson, "Half-time Budget Methods," *Annals* 113 (1924): 69–74.

7. A.E. Buck, *Public Budgeting* (New York: Harper and Brothers, 1929).

8. Wylie Kilpatrick, "Classification and Measurement of Public Expenditures," *Annals* 183 (1936): 19-26.

9. President's Committee on Administrative Management, *Report* (Washington, D.C.: Government Printing Office, 1937).

10. V.O. Key, Jr., "The Lack of a Budgetary Theory," *American Political Science Review* 34 (1940): 1138-44.

11. Commission on Organization of the Executive Branch of the Government, *Budgeting and Accounting* (Washington, D.C.: Government Printing Office, 1949), p. 8.

12. Verne B. Lewis, "Toward a Theory of Budgeting," *Public Administration Review* 12 (1952): 42-54.

13. Frederick C. Mosher, *Program Budgeting: Theory and Practice with Particular Reference to the U.S. Department of Army* (Chicago: Public Administration Service, 1954).

14. Catheryn Seckler-Hudson, "Performance Budgeting in the Government of the United States," *Public Finance* 7 (1954): 328.

15. Arthur Smithies, *The Budgetary Process in the United States* (New York: McGraw-Hill, 1955), pp. 198-225.

16. Commission on Organization of the Executive Branch of the Government, *Final Report to Congress* (Washington, D.C.: Government Printing Office, 1955); and Commission on Organization of the Executive Branch of the Government, *Budgeting and Accounting* (Washington, D.C.: Government Printing Office, 1955).

17. Jesse Burkhead, *Government Budgeting* (New York: Wiley, 1956), pp. 133-82.

18. Aaron Wildavsky, "Rescuing Policy Analysis from PPBS," *Public Administration Review* 29 (1969): 193.

19. The early thinking on this discussion was suggested by Robert J. Mowitz, Director of the Institute of Public Administration, The Pennsylvania State University, 1972.

20. David S. Stoller, *Operations Research: Process and Strategy* (Berkeley: University of California Press, 1964), p. 11.

21. Maurice F. Ronayne, "Operations Research Can Help Public Administrators in Decision-Making," *International Review of Administrative Sciences* 29 (1963): 227.

22. C. West Churchman, Russel L. Ackoff, and E. Leonard Arnoff, *Introduction to Operations Research* (New York: Wiley, 1957): 18.

23. Stafford Beer, "What Has Cybernetics to Do with Operational Research?" *Operational Research Quarterly* 10 (March 1959): 1-21.

24. For a survey of economic analysis, see A.R. Prest and R. Turvey, "Cost-Benefit Analysis: A Survey," *Economic Journal* 75 (1965): 683-735.

25. J. Dupuit, "On the Measurement of Utility of Public Works," *International Economic Papers* 2 (1844).

26. Inter-Agency River Basin Committee, *Proposed Practices for Economic Analysis of River Basin Projects* (Washington, D.C.: Government Printing Office, 1950).

27. This work overlaps greatly with other fields, especially operations research and systems analysis. Roland N. McKean, *Efficiency in Government through Systems Analysis, with Emphasis on Water Resource Development* (New York: Wiley, 1958).

28. Ludwig von Bertalanffy, "General System Theory: A New Approach to Unity of Science," *Human Biology* 23 (1951): 303-61.

29. Anatol Rapoport, *Strategy and Conscience* (New York: Harper & Row, 1964).

30. Kenneth Boulding, "General Systems Theory: The Skeleton of Science," *Management Science* 2 (1956): 198.

31. Norbert Wiener, *The Human Use of Human Beings* (Garden City, N.Y.: Doubleday, 1956), p. 16.

32. William G. Ouchi, "A Short History of the Development of Computer Hardware," in Thomas L. Whisler, *Information Technology and Organizational Change* (Belmont, Calif.: Wadsworth, 1970), pp. 129–34.

33. Gene H. Fisher, *The Analytical Bases of Systems Analysis* (Santa Monica, Calif.: The RAND Corporation, 1966).

34. Alain C. Enthoven, "The Systems Analysis Approach," in Harley H. Hinrichs and Graeme M. Taylor, eds., *Program Budgeting and Benefit-Cost Analysis* (Pacific Palisades, Calif.: Goodyear, 1969), p. 160.

35. Charles J. Hitch and Roland N. McKean, *The Economics of Defense in the Nuclear Age* (Cambridge, Mass.: Harvard University Press, 1967) (first published by the RAND Corporation in 1960).

36. David Novick, ed., *Program Budgeting: Program Analysis and the Federal Budget* (Cambridge, Mass.: Harvard University Press, 1965), 2nd ed. (New York: Holt, Rinehart & Winston, 1969).

37. General Accounting Office, *Budget Formulation: Many Approaches Work but Some Improvements Needed* (Washington, D.C.: Government Printing Office, 1980).

38. Fred Block and Gene A. Burns, "Productivity as a Social Problem: The Uses and Misuses of Social Indicators," *American Sociological Review* 51 (1986): 767–80.

39. Duncan MacRae, Jr., *Policy Indicators* (Chapel Hill: University of North Carolina Press, 1985).

40. Robert J. Mowitz, *The Design and Implementation of Pennsylvania's Planning, Programming, Budgeting System* (Harrisburg: Commonwealth of Pennsylvania, 1970), p. 17.

41. Robert D. Lee, Jr., *Public Personnel Systems*, 2nd ed. (Rockville, Md.: Aspen Publishers, Inc., 1987), pp. 311–13.

42. Harry P. Hatry and John Greiner, *Improving the Use of Management by Objectives in Police Departments* (Washington, D.C.: U.S. Department of Justice, 1986).

43. See current issues of *Public Productivity Review,* a quarterly journal.

44. *Improving Municipal Productivity: Work Measurement for Better Management* (Washington, D.C.: National Center for Productivity and Quality of Working Life, 1975).

45. See Robert P. McGowan and Theodore H. Poister, "Impact of Productivity Measurement Systems on Municipal Performance," *Policy Studies Review* 4 (1985): 532–40.

46. Carolyn Burstein and Donald M. Fisk, "The Federal Government Productivity Improvement Program," *Public Budgeting and Finance* 7 (Winter 1987): 36–47.

47. Rayston Greenwood, "Incremental Budgeting: Antecedents of Change," *Journal of Public Policy* 4 (1984): 277–306.

48. William A. Lucas and Raymond H. Dawson, *The Organizational Politics of Defense* (Pittsburgh: International Studies Association, University of Pittsburgh, 1974), p. 87.

49. Schick, "The Road to PPB," pp. 252–53.

50. Mosher, *Program Budgeting,* p. 87.

51. Thomas J. Cook, ed., "Symposium: Performance Measurement in Public Agencies," *Policy Studies Review* 6 (1986): 61–170.

52. Peter N. Dean, "Performance Budgeting in Sri Lanka," *Public Budgeting and Finance* (Summer 1986): 63–75.

53. Mosher, *Program Budgeting,* pp. 34–47.

54. Robert J. Massey, "Program Packages and the Program Budget in the Department of Defense," *Public Administration Review* 23 (1963): 30–34.

55. David Novick, "The Department of Defense," in Novick, ed., *Program Budgeting*, p. 91.

56. David Novick, *Efficiency and Economy in Government Through New Budgeting and Accounting Procedures* (Santa Monica, Calif.: The RAND Corporation, 1956).

57. McKean, *Efficiency and Economy in Government*.

58. Hitch and McKean, *Economics of Defense*.

59. "Program Objective Memoranda (POM) Preparation Instructions" (Washington, D.C.: Defense Resources Board, Department of Defense, 1987).

60. See William J. Weida and Frank L. Gertcher, *The Political Economy of National Defense* (Boulder, Colo.: Westview, 1987).

61. U.S. Congress, House Committee on the Budget, *Defense Budget Policy in a Constrained Environment: Hearings*, 100th Cong., 1st sess. (Washington, D.C.: Government Printing Office, 1987).

62. Lyndon B. Johnson, *Public Papers of the Presidents of the United States* 2 (Washington, D.C.: Government Printing Office, 1966).

63. Allen Schick, "A Death in the Bureaucracy: The Demise of Federal PPB," *Public Administration Review* 33 (1973): 146–56.

64. Edwin L. Harper, Fred A. Kramer, and Andrew M. Rouse, "Implementation and Use of PPB in Sixteen Federal Agencies," *Public Administration Review* 29 (1969): 634.

65. See Frederick Mosher and John E. Harr, *Programming Systems and Foreign Policy Leadership* (New York: Oxford University Press, 1970).

66. Robert C. Casselman, "Massachusetts Revisited: Chronology of a Failure," *Public Administration Review* 33 (1973): 129–35.

67. Robert L. Harlow, "On the Decline and Fall of PPBS," *Public Finance Quarterly* 1 (1973): 85–105.

68. David Sallack and David N. Allen, "From Impact to Output: Pennsylvania's Planning-Programming-Budgeting System in Transition," *Public Budgeting and Finance* 7 (Spring 1987): 38–50.

69. Aaron Wildavsky and Arthur Hammann, "Comprehensive Versus Incremental Budgeting in the Department of Agriculture," *Administrative Science Quarterly* 10 (1965): 321–46.

70. Peter A. Phyrr, *Zero-Base Budgeting: A Practical Management Tool for Evaluating Expenses* (New York: Wiley, 1973).

71. Peter C. Sarant, *Zero-Base Budgeting in the Public Sector: A Pragmatic Approach* (Reading, Mass.: Addison-Wesley, 1978).

72. Joseph S. Wholey, *Zero-Base Budgeting and Program Evaluation* (Lexington, Mass.: Lexington Books, 1978).

73. Thomas P. Lauth and Stephen C. Rieck, "Modifications in Georgia Zero-Base Budgeting Procedures: 1973–1981," *Midwest Review of Public Administration* 13 (1979): 225–38.

74. General Accounting Office, *Streamlining Zero-Base Budgeting Will Benefit Decision Making* (Washington, D.C.: Government Printing Office, 1979).

75. Lawrence A. Gordon and Donna M. Heivilin, "Zero-Base Budgeting in the Federal Government: An Historical Perspective," *GAO Review* 13 (Fall 1978): 57–64.

76. Donald F. Haider, "Zero-Base: Federal Style," *Public Administration Review* 37 (1977): 400–07.

77. Lawrence A. Gordon and Allen Schick, "Executive Policy-Making Authority and Using Zero-Base Budgeting for Allocating Resources," *Policy Studies Journal* 7 (1979): 554–68.

78. Allen Schick, "The Road from ZBB," *Public Administration Review* 38 (1978): 177–80.

79. John M. Bryson, *Strategic Planning for Public and Nonprofit Organizations* (San Francisco: Jossey-Bass, 1988).

80. John A. Pearce, II, Elizabeth B. Freeman, and Richard B. Robinson, Jr., "The Tenuous Link Between Formal Strategic Planning and Financial Performance," *Academy of Management Review* 12 (1987): 658–75.

81. G. Wayne Glass, *Assessing the Effectiveness of Milestone Budgeting* (Washington, D.C.: Congressional Budget Office, 1987).

82. Verne B. Lewis, "Reflections on Budget Systems," *Public Budgeting and Finance* 8 (Spring 1988): 4–14.

83. Stanley B. Botner, "The Use of Budgeting/Management Tools by State Governments," *Public Administration Review* 45 (1985): 616–20.

84. Unpublished data from surveys conducted by Department of Public Administration, The Pennsylvania State University in conjunction with the Budget Office, Commonwealth of Pennsylvania and in part with the National Association of State Budget Officers. Percentages based upon responses from 43 states that responded to all surveys.

85. Daniel E. O'Toole and James Marshall, "Budgeting Practices in Local Government." *Government Finance Review* (October 1987): 11–16.

6

Budget Preparation:
The Decision Process

Preparing a budget involves having agencies prepare requests and then assembling those requests, but the process also involves much more. Indeed, the request process may be considered simple compared with the difficult task that remains: making decisions as to the recommended levels for revenues and expenditures. Will a tax increase be recommended? What programs will be proposed for expansion and what ones will be scheduled for reduction?

This chapter has two sections. The first considers how a proposed budget is assembled; deliberations on the revenue and expenditure sides of the budget are examined. The second section reviews the products of budget preparation, namely the various types of budget documents and their formats.

DECISIONS ON BUDGET REQUESTS

Budget preparation involves participation by a variety of individuals and organizations along with a myriad of values associated with taxing and spending. In an executive budget system, the chief executive has the overall responsibility for the preparation process, but numerous other actors have roles including, of course, the central budget office along with other units such as the treasury office.

Legislators or their staffs may be involved in preparation. A survey in the mid-1980s found that one out of three states had legislative staff members attend executive budget hearings that reviewed the proposed budgets of line agencies.[1] In small local governments, budget preparation may be a relatively fluid process and may be characterized by close linkages between executive and legislative officials.[2] Even when legislative officers are not involved, their views on taxing and spending are taken into account.

Concerns of the Chief Executive

The chief executive—president, governor, mayor, county executive, and the like—may have official responsibility for preparation but usually will have limited direct involvement until the latter stages of preparation. In part, this approach is taken because of other demands on the executive's time. Having the budget office and other units, such as treasury, involved early in the process provides for the application of professional administrative talent in analyzing problems and options that will later come before the executive for review. The longer the chief executive waits to become involved in preparation, the better highlighted will be the strengths and weaknesses of various options, including the potential political ramifications.

Overall Concerns. On the other hand, the chief executive needs to convey to the units involved, and especially to the central budget office, a sense of priorities so that effort is not needlessly wasted on proposals that will be automatically rejected by the executive.[3] Several factors are of concern in this regard, one of which is an overall philosophy of the role of government in contemporary society.

Another concern for many chief executives is how the budget may positively affect the economic environment. School districts and special districts, such as water and sewer authorities, may have little or no role in economic development, but cities, counties, states, and the national government are concerned about budgetary influences on the economy. For local and state chief executives, the concern tends to focus on the economic climate, namely whether taxes deter business location and expansion. The national government has these same concerns coupled with other factors, including international implications and price stability (see Chapter 15).

The chief executive sets ground rules on program priorities. A president conveys an overall sense of priorities to the Office of Management and Budget (OMB) regarding defense and domestic spending and a sense of priorities within each of these categories, as in the case of health versus job training programs. Election campaign promises are important in that executives attempt to be consistent in pursuing objectives outlined in their bid for voter approval.

Program priorities also can be viewed in the broader sense of redistributing income among groups within the society. Funding one set of programs at a high level obviously will benefit the programs' clients, whether they are the elderly, poor, young, etc. Redistribution also occurs through tax measures, including tax expenditures in which potential tax revenues are not collected, as in the case of not taxing home mortgage interest payments (see Chapter 4).[4]

Tactical Concerns. In addition to a "philosophical" approach to taxation, the executive conveys a tactical view. An assessment must be made of political reactions to any possible proposed tax increase or cut. Of course, increases are more likely to have negative ramifications than tax cuts.

For governors and the president, intergovernmental relations will be an important component of budget preparation deliberations (see Chapter 14). Presidents may prefer where possible to carry out policies through state and local governments rather than through direct activities by federal agencies; the same type of preference may exist among governors working through local governments.

Governmental indebtedness and borrowing constitute another concern of the chief executive during budget preparation. For a president, indebtedness is a concern in regard to influencing the economy. For governors and local executives, indebtedness results from the sale of bonds that creates financial burdens for decades.

Another set of considerations involves relationships with the legislative body. Stated simply, the executive assesses the chances of various recommendations receiving the approval of Congress, the state legislature, or the city council. This does not mean that the executive recommends only that which is likely to be approved. The recommendation that is doomed to legislative rejection may be put forth by the executive as a means of preparing the legislature to approve the proposal in some future year, or the executive may be strongly committed to a proposal despite legislative opposition.

Perceived citizen preferences in terms of both service and tax levels constitute another area of consideration. Chief executives have a keen sense for what the general citizenry and interest groups desire. Results from national and state polls are watched for important trends. Some cities conduct surveys of citizens and/or hold public hearings at which citizens may testify as means of identifying prevailing attitudes about existing and desired services.[5,6]

Revenue Deliberations

Revenue Estimates. Central to deliberations on the revenue side of budget preparation are revenue estimates. Chapter 4 dealt with some of the technical problems associated with revenue estimating. Here it should be noted that there are important bureaucratic considerations. Sometimes revenue estimating is assigned to the organization responsible for collecting revenues, most often being a treasury or revenue department. Such an arrangement may place that unit in competition with the budget office in that the latter may differ on projected revenues. The budget office may be largely forced into developing a budget package that is perceived to be unnecessarily constrained because of an estimate that anticipates little or no growth in revenue or even a downturn. At the federal level, the revenue-estimating function is handled jointly by OMB, the Council of Economic Advisers, and the Treasury Department.

Taxing Limitations. Since the 1970s, taxing limitations have been popular at the state and local levels. California's Proposition 13 and Massachusetts's Proposition 2½ are particularly notable in their influence on local government budgeting.[7,8]

Balanced Budgets. For state and local governments, revenue estimating is particularly critical because of the standard requirement that they have balanced operating budgets. Indebtedness is possible but typically only for capital investments and other selected expenses. If a budget is built on revenue estimates that are too high, crises will ensue during execution as the government attempts to bring expenditures down in order to balance them against revenues.

While all but one state have requirements for a balanced budget, the requirements are not uniform among the states. In the first place, "balance" means that expenditures may not exceed revenues, but not all available revenues must be appropriated and spent. Coverage is not all-inclusive, with trust funds and capital expenditures often being excluded; as little as half of all state funds may be covered by the requirement for a balanced budget. The balancing requirements also vary by the stage of the budget process.[9]

Achieving balance in a state budget is a political process. There are the obvious alternatives of seeking revenue increases and/or spending decreases, but balance also is achieved through other means.[10] Budget reserves, "rainy day" funds, or savings from previous years may be drawn upon to increase available revenues.[11] It sometimes is possible to shift some payments from one fiscal year to the next, even though resources are actually used in the earlier year.

The concept of requiring a balanced budget for the federal government has been an enduring one and yet has not been adopted.[12,13] One procedure would be to enact such a requirement into law; Chapter 9 discusses the experience in regard to Gramm-Rudman-Hollings legislation. Another procedure would be to impose such a requirement by adoption of a constitutional amendment. Many state legislatures have endorsed forming a constitutional convention that presumably would adopt a balanced budget amendment for the federal government.[14]

Spending Deliberations

Organizational Competition. Just as there are central administrative organizations that compete to some extent to influence revenue decisions, there are competitors on the spending side of the budget. At the top level of a government, personalities become important. The roles of various participants at the federal level depend upon a president's administrative style, his confidence in the abilities of key figures, and the roles these figures seek for themselves. A president is not obligated to rely on the advice of any individual and may at his discretion rely on anyone both inside and out of government.

In the international policy arena there are many participants, each of which can be expected to be sensitive to any major exercise of control by the central budget office. OMB control is likely to be resisted by the State Department, the Defense Department, and the Central Intelligence Agency (CIA). In addition, the National Security Council (NSC) exists to advise the president on "domestic, foreign, and military policies relating to national security."[15] The NSC is headed by the president and includes as members the vice-president and secretaries of state and defense; the director of the CIA and the chair of the Joint Chiefs of Staff serve as statutory advisers to the council. Also included is the president's national security adviser.

OMB is notably not part of the National Security Council, although it can be invited to meetings at the president's discretion. The point is that OMB can be eclipsed in this area, performing a largely routine function of assembling budget materials rather than having much influence on how much money is to be allocated to defense and foreign affairs and for what purposes.

In the domestic arena, the competition is also fierce. Cabinet officers seek to gain acceptance and financial support for their agencies' programs. Central advisers to the president are other contenders for attention. In addition to the White House Office staff, there is an Office of Policy Development that advises on domestic matters.[16]

Budget Office Roles. The central budget office has numerous roles to perform.[17-19] Not only does the budget office recommend policies on spending, but it participates in review of legislative proposals, economic policy, administrative regulations, evaluation of programs, and agency management studies and management improvement efforts.[20] OMB during the 1980s gained increased responsibility in advocating legislative changes before Congress.[21] When OMB examines an agency's budget request, all of these other forces come into play. Agency budget proposals will be seen in the context of what legislative changes will be necessary, what regulatory actions will be required by the agency, and whether the agency is perceived as well managed.

Agency Expectations and Deliberations. In approaching the budget process, including the preparation phase, agencies have expectations about what constitutes success. Until the latter half of the 1970s, success often was measured in terms of budget increases approved by the executive and ultimately by the legislative body. This approach of adding increments to a base has been discarded in many locales. Where taxing and spending limits have been imposed at the state and local levels, agencies have had to take the strategy of defending their bases and attempting to minimize the extensiveness of cuts imposed on their budgets. This period has been dubbed the "decremental age."[22,23] A survey of state officials found that program expansion was ranked seventh, rather than first, as an indicator of success in budgeting; higher-ranked measures involved maintaining good relations with the legislature and governor and protecting against budget cuts and personnel layoffs.[24]

By the time a budget request reaches the budget office, an extensive series of discussions has been completed within the line agency. In large agencies having several layers of organizational units, those at the bottom will have attempted to persuade their superiors to approve requests for additional funding. The forces from the top downward tend to be negative in the sense that there is pressure to limit the growth of programs and the corresponding rise in expenditures. Yet this does not mean that there is simply a set of no-men and yes-men who do battle within each agency or department. Middle managers up through departmental heads are required to take both positions, rejecting many of the proposals brought to them by subordinates and, in negotiating with their superiors, advocating those proposals that they accept.

Part of the negative influence within an agency is a function of superior levels attempting to determine what is likely to be salable to the budget office and the chief executive. Agencies are aware that they are unlikely to get more than they request and are likely to get less. Therefore, they will avoid requesting too little but will not ask for exorbitant sums unless an open-ended budget system is in use.

Budget Office and Agency Relations. Just as the interplay is extensive and vociferous within an agency in preparing a budget, so considerable tension exists between the central budget office and the agencies.[25] The central office, as the agency of the chief executive, must assert a centralizing influence over the diverse interests of administrative units; these, on the other hand, can be expected to favor greater autonomy. Operating departments and agencies can be presumed to favor the advancement of their respective programs (seeking greater funds or defending programs against cuts), while the budget office is forced to take the unpopular position of having to say no to program growth and often yes to cutbacks.

When the budget office receives agency budget submittals, examiners are assigned to review these documents. The examiners are the main link between the budget office and line units. With the passage of time, examiners gain considerable knowledge about their agencies, providing a substantive expertise within the budget office. It is not uncommon for examiners eventually to become advocates for the agencies they review and frequently even to shift their employment to an operating agency. Still, the accusation is commonly made by agency officials that budget examiners, not being program oriented, are insensitive to the needs of operating units.

The nature of the dialogue between the budget office and agencies hinges in large measure upon the extent to which the latter consider the former an important ally or an opponent. Only minimal information can be expected from the agency that is suspicious of the central budget office. A common concern is that the agency not release data that could be used to its detriment. On the other hand, if an agency can win the confidence and support of the examiner, then the agency in effect has gained a spokesperson for its program within the chief executive's staff.

At the same time, winning budget office approval is no guarantee of success for the agency. The resistant or recalcitrant agency, indeed, may be able to increase the caution with which the examiner makes recommendations to reduce the agency's budget. At the federal level, the significance of OMB action may be mitigated, considering that Congress has the power to pass appropriations. It has been suggested that opposition by the budget office to any agency's request for funds may be helpful in winning legislative support.

The agencies and not OMB have had major responsibility for defending their budget requests before Congress, and therefore the office's utility to the agencies has been more important in the preparation phase than in the approval phase of the budget cycle. Some organizational units, such as the Federal Bureau of Investigation in the 1950s and 1960s, were able to secure extensive support within Congress, thereby providing the agencies with some autonomy vis-à-vis their respective departments and OMB. During the 1980s, OMB gained greater responsibility for explaining and defending the president's budget before Congress; this role, however, often was negative in the sense of explaining how and why reductions should be made in agencies' budgets.[26,27]

The budget office holds hearings with agency representatives. Whereas earlier in the process the examiners may have contacted agencies by phone or in person to clarify detailed items included in requests, hearings tend to focus upon broader concerns. The budget office must decide whether agencies can accomplish what they propose and whether the anticipated accomplishments are worth seeking. The burden of proof rests with the agencies. The operating agency that has a reputation for requesting excessive sums and for overpromising on results will be suspect.[28,29]

Budget Office Recommendations. The response of the budget office to agency requests is in part a function of the office's assessment of its own powers and responsibilities in relation to the operating agencies and other central units. Few would deny to a budget office the ministerial or bookkeeping functions of assembling requests and carrying out the mechanical duties of designing, tabulating, and seeing to the printing of the budget. However, how many additional responsibilities the budget office has depends largely upon competition from other units and the management style of the chief executive.[30,31]

Because in an executive budgeting system the chief executive has the final say on what to recommend to the legislative body, the budget office attempts to formulate recommendations thought to be in keeping with the executive's priorities. As part of the calculation of what to recommend, the budget office assesses the chances of agencies' making direct appeals to the chief executive and thereby overturning the budget office's recommendations. If this strategy, sometimes known as making an end-run around the budget office, is successful, it can severely weaken the budget office's role. If an agency knows it can get what it wants by making direct appeals to the chief executive, the agency is likely to consider the budget office as only a bookkeeper that can be largely ignored.

As a staff unit of the chief executive, the budget office is expected to develop recommendations that are compatible with executive priorities. On the other hand, budgeters as professionals are said to have a responsibility to report to the executive their views on the worthiness of programs. To report that a given program is operating well, simply because the executive wants to hear that, does a disservice. Similarly, to recommend severe budget cuts to the executive when the budget office knows these cuts could have devastating results on the affected programs would disserve the executive. A role of "neutral competence" has been proposed in which the budget office retains its professional approach to budget recommendations but simultaneously seeks to develop recommendations in tune with executive priorities.[32]

Spending Cutbacks

For many governmental programs, the 1980s represented hard times as spending increases changed to reductions or cutbacks. So-called "uncontrollable" segments of the budget were not immune from these reductions. The financial problems that materialized were due to several factors. For the federal government, deficits in the total budget during the 1980s attained new magnitude—often in the range of $200 billion each year. The deficits resulted in part from the massive tax reduction measures initiated in 1981 when Ronald Reagan became president and expected tax cuts to stimulate the economy, which then would produce increased tax revenues. That bonanza of revenues never materialized.

Fiscal Stress. State and local governments encountered fiscal stress or distress.[33,34] Some of their problems were due to economic downturns in the economy, most notably during the first half of the 1980s. When the economy slumps, state and local sales and income tax revenues fall. So-called "rust belt" states and communities faced a different set of economic woes, namely a long-term erosion in their tax bases. Fiscal stress was encountered by state and local governments, also because of major reductions in aid from the federal government. During the 1980s, the national government reduced funding of many grant programs and totally eliminated general revenue sharing (see Chapter 14).

The tax revolt movement discussed in Chapter 4 imposed additional constraints on spending. In some instances, a jurisdiction's economy may have been vibrant, but the government was precluded from taxing that economic base to the extent it perceived was needed to fund governmental programs.

Cutback Management. The result of these pressures was what has been called "cutback management" or "retrenchment."[35,36] It should be noted that governments in other countries have experienced similar problems.[37] Also, sometimes retrenchment programs are undertaken not because of fiscal stress but because of the preferences of the political leadership, namely a desire on the part of officials to reduce the size of government.

Dealing with budget shortages depends in part upon the perceived duration of the problem. If it is considered to be short range, perhaps only for the current year, then modest adjustments can be made such as imposing temporary cuts on programs and drawing upon budget reserves or "rainy day" funds.

When budget retrenchment is seen as long range in nature, then decision makers must manage the immediate problems of the current and upcoming budget years and anticipate problems in future years. Where budget cuts must be imposed several years in a row, as was the case for many communities in Massachusetts because of Proposition 2½, then decision makers must be prepared for making extraordinarily difficult choices.

Budget cuts ultimately hinge on the issue of who or what groups in society will suffer the most from loss or reduction of programs. The answer to that question is partially political. Budget cuts are less likely to be imposed on groups that are politically organized and vocal than on other groups. Applying the budget knife to programs for the elderly often may seem to be politically dangerous whereas cutting programs for the poor, since they tend to be politically less active, may seem "safer" for decision makers.[38] In relatively homogeneous communities, budget cutback procedures do not pit one segment of the community against another.[39]

Budget Office Roles. When jurisdictions confront fiscal stress, the decision process initially tends to be centralized, for without central instructions to begin a process of cutting agencies might well submit budget requests based upon unrealistic assumptions. The central budget office, working with the chief executive, attempts to instruct departments as to priorities for funding. Effort is made to avoid across-the-board cuts in all programs, since such an approach can cause severe harm to essential services.

If some programs are set aside as immune from budget cuts, there may be few incentives, then, for these programs to be efficient in their spending of funds. Moreover, achieving the level of budget reductions needed to balance a budget may be impossible if many key programs are immune from cuts. This problem has existed at the federal level, where Social Security and the Defense Department often have been protected from cuts. The same problem materializes at the local level if fire protection, police services, and roads are immune from cuts. Major savings in spending simply cannot be achieved by reducing funding for perceived "luxuries" such as zoos, libraries, and recreational programs. On the other hand, these "luxuries" are often the first to be cut in any jurisdiction and sometimes suffer for long periods of time with gross underfunding.

In a retrenchment environment, agencies normally can expect budget office approval of no more than their projected current services budgets. As explained in the preceding chapter, this type of request indicates what funds would be needed to keep a department's programs operating without any improvements being introduced.[40]

In other situations, the central budget office may provide specific budget ceilings to each department.[41] These figures, which most likely are below the current services levels, are used in preparing budget requests. The process has all of the strengths and weaknesses of fixed-ceiling budgeting. Where such approaches are taken, the process of cutting often starts earlier in the calendar than in a budget situation where growth, rather than reduction, is predominant.[42] More time is needed to plan for what programs will be cut than to introduce new programs or expand existing ones.

Legislative Role. If legislative preferences can be identified at the beginning of budget preparation, then cuts can be planned that later are likely to meet with legislative approval. Some communities have used confidential questionnaires and other techniques for soliciting legislative input when budget cuts must be part of the preparation phase. Members of local legislative bodies, however, may prefer not to reveal their preferences until later, when more is known about the options for cutting and citizens' attitudes.

Items to Cut. When reductions must be made in expenditures, there are standard areas that are considered, one of them being personnel costs. Since much of any government's operating budget is in personnel, it is difficult to make any appreciable reduction in expenditures without reducing personnel. Usual techniques are to delay filling vacant positions, not to fill other positions as they become vacant, and if necessary, to lay off workers. Holding down general pay increases for workers is a common practice, although this technique can make compensation for government jobs noncompetitive with that for private sector jobs.

Equipment and facilities are other areas for cutting.[43] Deliberate decisions may be made to delay purchase of major equipment and to defer maintenance, such as postponing repairing city-owned sidewalks, roofs on government buildings, and potholes in city and state roads. The savings here can be short-lived, as in the failure to repair a roof that results in many thousands of dollars in water damage. There may be a tendency to use the deferred maintenance approach on less visible facilities, most notably water and sewer lines.[44]

In so-called "tight" budget periods, major emphasis is given to making operations as efficient as possible. The expectation is that organizational units should be able to operate with fewer resources while maintaining existing service levels.[45] On the other hand, no single agency is eager to relinquish resources through increased efficiency if other agencies are not compelled to take the same route. A "you-go-first" attitude may develop in which each agency is fearful of being the first to show how savings can be accomplished in its operations. This same attitude prevails in the approval phase among legislators, who are not eager to agree to budget cuts in their favored programs even though it is well understood that major cuts will be necessary.[46]

Budget cutting creates havoc, low morale, and some inefficiencies in agencies.[47] Personnel rightfully become concerned that their positions will be eliminated in the agency's budget request. Political appointees in an agency may be at odds with career personnel over which activities are considered essential and which expendable. Some budget cuts necessitate agency reorganization, which causes disruptions in operations. Uncertainty in funding can require stretching the completion of projects. Defense is a major example of this problem, where changes in project schedules can result in billions of dollars of increased costs.[48]

Budget Systems and Cutbacks. A final consideration regarding cutback budgeting is how the various budget systems discussed in the preceding chapter assist in retrenchment efforts. As already noted, central budget offices use variations on fixed-ceiling budgeting to indicate to agencies what funding levels are acceptable in the budget preparation process. It may be that most other budget systems have been developed on the stated or unstated premise that budgets will increase from year to year and therefore that these budget systems are less central to decision making when budget cuts must be imposed. At the same time, program budgeting and various forms of zero-base budgeting in theory should be highly useful in budget-cutting situations.

Final Preparation Deliberations

The chief executive becomes most active in the preparation phase during its final weeks, a frustrating period for the budget office. Decisions are seemingly reached and then may be reversed. The executive may instruct the budget office that an agency's proposed change will be included in the budget, but reject the proposal after considering revenue estimates. Proposals for funding program improvements may be approved initially and then rejected as the executive has second thoughts about recommending tax increases. Materials prepared evenings and weekends by the budget office may find their way to the paper shredder as decisions are changed. The approach may seem haphazard and probably is in many respects, but it is this way because of the numerous factors being evaluated simultaneously.

A common complaint about the preparation phase is that only the chief executive considers the budget as a whole. An organizational unit within a department or agency is concerned primarily with its own piece of the budget, and the same is true of a department vis-à-vis other departments and the rest of the budget. Even within the central budget office, budget examiners focus mainly on one or a few segments of the budget and not on the total package. The executive, however, must pull together the pieces of information and intelligence provided by various sources into a set of decisions that can be defended as a whole. The budget that is to be submitted to the legislative body is the chief executive's.

BUDGET DOCUMENTS

The final product of the preparation phase of budgeting is a budget document or documents that contain the decisions reached in the months of agency requests and executive reviews. The budget at this point is only a proposal, a set of recommended policies and programs set forth by the chief executive in an executive budgeting system. The budget remains a proposal until the legislative body acts on it.

Number and Types of Documents

The budget for any government may consist of one or several documents. Small jurisdictions often have only one volume to their budgets whereas larger governments have several. The size of a jurisdiction's budget does not always determine the size of its documents; Kentucky, which is a medium-sized state, produces five major volumes while New York State has one main volume. Documents are printed on different sizes of paper and vary considerably in their graphics. Some volumes have mainly text and tables while others include charts, graphs, and photographs of citizens and government buildings. Massachusetts has used themes for various budget years, such as "Expanding Opportunities" for 1988–89. Since 1984 the Government Finance Officers Association has given its Award for Distinguished Budget Presentation to hundreds of jurisdictions.

Federal Documents. At the federal level, the following documents are prepared by OMB and released by the president in January of each year:

1. The *Budget of the United States* consists of several hundred pages and provides substantial narrative discussions of programs along with supporting tables covering financial data but little program data.
2. The *Budget in Brief* is a budget synopsis intended for general public use. Similar summary documents are prepared by state governments and some local governments.
3. The *Budget Appendix*, which is the size of a major metropolitan telephone directory, is the main federal document providing extensive detail on the expenditure side of the budget.
4. The volume *Special Analyses* provides selected discussions and tables on items such as borrowing and debt, aid to state and local governments, federal civilian employment, and investment expenditures. The volume includes current services estimates and calculations for Gramm-Rudman-Hollings (see Chapter 9).
5. *Historical Tables* selectively reports data back to the 1960s, 1950s, and 1940s.
6. *Management of the United States Government* reports on various efforts to improve cash management, procurement, productivity, and related areas.
7. *Major Policy Initiatives* contains discussions of the president's recommendations for changing programs or creating new ones.
8. Another document, the *Information Collection Budget*, is not part of the above series but is prepared by OMB and issued each spring. Known as the "paperwork budget," the document reports OMB efforts to control the burden imposed by federal agencies in collecting information from private individuals and corporations and from state and local governments.

The *Economic Report of the President* is prepared by the Council of Economic Advisers and is released at about the same time as the other main budget documents. The *Economic Report* discusses expected economic trends for the coming fiscal year and is the basis upon which the president's economic policy is formulated.

Other Specialized Documents. Governments sometimes publish specialized budget-related documents in addition to those already mentioned. Some states and many local governments publish capital budgets, showing planned construction projects and major pieces of equipment to be purchased (see Chapter 12). Illinois publishes a separate volume on personnel as part of its series of budget documents (see Chapter 13).

The federal government and some states publish discussions of tax expenditures, which are losses in government revenue due to tax provisions that exempt some items from taxation or provide favorable tax rates.[49] One of the best examples at the federal level is the exclusion from taxation of interest paid on home mortgages. Massachusetts publishes a separate volume on tax expenditures; Table 6-1 illustrates benefits to human services resulting from provisions in state tax laws.

Budget Messages. Another aspect of budget documents is the budget message, in which the chief executive highlights the major recommendations in the budget. The message sometimes is presented orally to the legislature. The president's budget message is included in the *Budget* itself. New York State uses the same format, with the budget message extending over more than 100 pages. State and local jurisdictions sometimes publish their budget messages as separate documents.

Approved Budgets. Some jurisdictions publish their approved budgets, namely ones that reflect action taken by the legislative bodies. North Carolina, for example, publishes a *Post-legislative Budget Summary*. The federal government does not produce such a volume.

Coverage

An issue concerning budget documents at all levels of government is the extent of their coverage. All report information about government receipts and expenditures. Intergovernmental transactions also are reported. A state budget highlights funds it receives from the federal government and funds it provides to local governments within the state. Issues arise over how much detail to provide on these items.

General and Special Funds. Confusion is common in the handling of funds in budget documents. State and local governments are major users of special funds, which basically are financial accounts for special revenue sources and from which expenditures can be made only for specific purposes. A jurisdiction's general fund consists of revenue that can be used for all functions of the government. These different types of funds are discussed elsewhere in conjunction with accounting problems (Chapter 11), but here it should be noted that many jurisdictions have a general fund budget document and then one or more documents covering special funds. The result of these separate budgets is confusion over the size of the total budget and the amount spent by any given agency, because the agency may be receiving support from several funds.

Federal Coverage Prior to 1969. The coverage issue at the federal level is similar.[50,51] Until the late 1960s, there were really three forms of federal budgets: the administrative budget, the consolidated cash statement, and the federal sector of the national income accounts. The main difference between the administrative budget and the consolidated cash statement was that the

Table 6-1 Human Services Tax Expenditures, Commonwealth of Massachusetts, 1989 (Millions of Dollars)

		Tax			
Budget Function	All	Personal Income	Corporate Excise	Sales	Estate
Charitable Deductions			6.0		
Deduction of Charitable Bequests					24.4
Exemption for Sales to Tax-Exempt Organizations				132.0	
Exemption for Publication of Tax-Exempt Organizations				0.8	
Exemption of Employer Contributions for Medical Insurance Premiums and Medical Care		178.9			
Deduction for Medical Expenses		20.3			
Exemption for Medical and Dental Supplies and Devices				26.8	
Exemption for Cigarettes				40.9	
Exemption for Alcoholic Beverages				32.0	
Exemption for Funeral Items				3.0	
Exemption for Certain Meals				0.7	
Total	465.8	199.2	6.0	236.2	24.4

Note: Table excludes items in the original table for which tax expenditure costs were not reported.

Source: Expanding Opportunity, Vol. 4, No. 1, pp. 2–3, Commonwealth of Massachusetts, 1989.

former did not include trust funds, particularly for Social Security and highways, and the latter did. These funds were excluded on the grounds that they were earmarked for specific purposes and therefore were not subject to annual budget decision processes. The disadvantage of their exclusion was that the magnitude of federal revenues and expenditures was greatly understated. The third type of budget, national income accounts, shows the economic character of federal transactions such as the government's purchase of goods and services in the economy. This budget statement, however, excludes governmental lending and borrowing.

Unified Budget. These three types of budgets resulted in much confusion, which eventually led to the development of a new concept in budget coverage. Because each of the three approaches had different coverages, total revenues and expenditures varied from one to another, leading to different statements of budget surpluses and deficits. Different pictures of federal finances—gloomy or bright—could be painted by choosing to discuss one budget statement and ignoring the other two. In response to this problem, in 1967 Lyndon Johnson appointed the President's Commission on Budget Concepts, whose eventual recommendation for a "unified budget" was incorporated in the 1969 budget.[52]

In the new format, four types of information were presented.

1. The amount of appropriations requested was shown.
2. Receipts, expenditures, and loans were tabulated along with the budget surplus or deficit. Trust funds were included in these figures.
3. The means of financing showed how the total deficit was to be financed or the surplus was to be spent.
4. The outstanding federal debt section showed total indebtedness and the total amount of federal credit programs, both direct loans and guaranteed or insured loans.

Off Budget. Since adoption of the unified budget, important changes have been made. One trend was toward greater use of what is known as the "off budget."[53,54] Congress determined what was included in this budget, which varied somewhat from year to year. The Postal Service, for example, was placed off budget, because it was expected to operate like a business, largely independent of the government. Other federal entities were removed from the budget because they operated largely with revolving funds rather than annual appropriations and made direct loans to the public. For example, the Rural Telephone Bank, the Federal Financing Bank, and the U.S. Synthetic Fuels Corporation were off budget. The Gramm-Rudman-Hollings Act of 1985, however, required that all federal entities be placed on-budget, with one set of important exceptions. The Old-Age and Survivors Insurance (OASI), Disability Insurance (DI), and Hospital Insurance (HI) trust funds are outside of the budget.[55]

Information Displays

Receipts. Turning to other aspects of the budget document, both revenue and expenditure data are presented. The coverage of receipts or revenues usually is substantially less extensive than expenditures. Budgets show receipts from taxes, such as individual and corporate income taxes; from user charges, such as water service; and from other governments, such as state grants to local government. Budget documents usually discuss proposed changes in tax laws and particularly proposed tax-rate changes.

Expenditures. The bulk of the budget document is devoted to the expenditure side of government finance, with the main classification usually by organizational unit. Each department presents a budget within which subunits are given separate treatment. A generally uniform format is used for each subunit, including a brief narrative description of the subunit's responsibilities and functions. Narratives contained in the federal *Budget Appendix* also contain proposed appropriation language that may be quite specific: for the Commodity Futures Trading Commission's budget of $35.5 million, not more than $700 was to be used for "official reception and representation expenses."[56]

In addition to the narrative are various tabular displays. Expenditures are reported by object classes, such as personnel, equipment, and travel (see Chapter 11). These financial tables may be primarily for information purposes or may later be incorporated in the legislative appropriation. When this practice is used, the legislative body is said to have adopted a line-item budget, a practice that reduces the president's, governor's, or mayor's flexibility in executing the budget.

Program Information. Since World War II, program data have been increasingly common in budget documents of most governments. Federal program data are presented in the federal *Budget Appendix*, but only for selected agencies, and the information tends to be in terms of work load or outputs rather than impacts. Table 6-2 illustrates U.S. Coast Guard work load data for the control of ice in shipping channels. The table indicates days and hours of operations but provides no clues to the effectiveness of this activity.

Program Structure. An alternative to arranging the budget document by organizational unit is to arrange it by program structure. The structure at its highest level consists of a number of broad programs that are subdivided into more narrowly focused subprograms and then are further subdivided. Terminology varies, but one approach is to have programs divided into program categories, which are divided into subcategories and then into elements.

The federal government does not have a program budget but does use broad functional classifications to summarize the budget: national defense, natural resources and environment, agriculture, transportation, and the like. The functional classifications are useful for highlighting the changing character of governmental expenditures over time, such as changes in the proportion of

---

Table 6-2 Work Load Data for Ice Operations, U.S. Coast Guard, Fiscal 1989

	1987	1988*	1999*
Polar Ice Operations: Icebreaker Deployment Days	551	435	335
Domestic Ice Operations			
Cutter Operating Hours	2,413	3,400	3,400
Aircraft Reconnaissance Operating Hours	115	155	155
Vessels Assisted	115	690	690
International Ice Patrol			
Aircraft Hours	429	500	500

*Estimated.

Source: *Budget of the United States Government, 1989: Appendix,* Office of Management and Budget, p. I-R37, Government Printing Office, 1988.

the budget committed to social services, but these categories are not linked explicitly to program descriptions or specific agency activities.

Using a program structure for the main outline of a budget has both strengths and weaknesses. On the positive side, the budget shows how the various activities of different programs relate to each other, since they are juxtaposed with one another in the document. By having two or more agencies in the same program, these organizations are forced to recognize their dependence on each other and the need for cooperation. For example, a city transportation department and police department are forced to recognize that they both influence traffic safety.

On the negative side, the "pure" program structure type of budget disperses parts of agencies throughout the budget, making it difficult to determine what the budget is for any one agency. One solution to this problem is known as "crosswalking," in which information organized by program is reconfigured into an organizational format. Crosswalking, while a successful technique, is cumbersome and often forces a government to produce two budgets—a program budget and an agency budget.

The state of Vermont has used a budget format that is a compromise between program structure and a format based on organizational units. The budget is divided into major programs first, such as protection of persons and property, human services, employment and training services, and general education. These are then subdivided into organizational units. The protection program includes such units as the Office of the Attorney General, the Military Department, and the Department of Labor and Industry. The latter department has its operations divided into such activities as fire prevention and occupational safety and health.[57]

Program Revisions. Exhibit 6-1 displays the programmatic format used by Lakewood, Colorado. The table shows the city's standards of performance for traffic patrol, assesses compliance with the standards, proposes program improvements, and provides data on traffic accidents and related matters.

Table 6-3 illustrates another type of information display provided in budget documents. The table is for a proposed revision in Pennsylvania's program for students requiring special services—dropouts, pregnant teenagers, and students with reading problems. Note that the table compares existing state support and the proposed level of support along with projections of state commitment for several years into the future. Multiyear costs also are provided as part of the recommendation but are not included in the table.

Space Limitations. Not all available program and resource information can be presented in budget documents unless one is willing to have a totally unwieldy document. The budget formats of some jurisdictions are rigid in prescribing space limitations—perhaps one page set aside for each bureau, program, or activity. Such a format may increase the readability of the docu-

Exhibit 6-1 Program Data for Traffic Patrol Services, City of Lakewood, Colorado, 1988

Service Standards: Services are standard when
1. 80 percent of available sworn man-hours is being devoted to operational activities versus nonoperational activities such as court time, administrative time, vehicle maintenance, etc.
2. citizen satisfaction with police services reflects a greater number of commendations than complaints

Current Service Evaluation:
The Patrol Division is currently functioning at a service level of 8.8 percent below the ideal 80 percent goal of available sworn man-hours being devoted to operational activities versus nonoperational activities. The division, through differential police response tactics and the expansion of the telephone reporting function, is attempting to increase operational times to meet service standards. A goal has been set for 1988 to raise the operational time to at least 75 percent of available man-hours. The Patrol Division is currently meeting its standard of commendations outnumbering complaints in citizen satisfaction.

Program Objectives for the Coming Year:
1. Computer-aided dispatch to become fully operational and provide timely, accurate management reports, thus increasing the division's ability to more effectively deploy and utilize existing resources.
2. Seek and obtain funding for a second year on the two existing traffic enforcement grants.
3. Critically evaluate, expand, and modify as needed the telephone reporting unit to increase effectiveness and efficiency.
4. Continue to provide enforcement services in Lakewood parks through the use of the police officer program.
5. Provide police service to the community in a timely and professional manner resulting in citizen satisfaction with police service.

Statistics:	1986 (Actual)	1987 (Estimated)	1988 (Budget)
Traffic Accidents Reported	6,144	6,469	6,344
Traffic Summonses Issued	22,035	19,592	20,907
Driving under the Influence (DUI) Arrests	1,486	1,651	1,672
Total Arrests	10,630	9,761	9,436
DUI Accidents	447	328	325
Percent of Time Spent on Operational Activities	70%	N/A	75%
Commendations/Complaints Received	313/173	363/189	338/181

Source: Lakewood Annual Budget, 1988, p. 164, Lakewood, Colorado.

Table 6-3 Program Revision Data for Special Services for Students, Commonwealth of Pennsylvania, 1986–1993

Program Measures	1986–87	1987–88	1988–89	1989–90	1990–91	1991–92	1992–93
Schools with Dropout Programs							
Current		13	13	13	13	13	13
Program Revision			26	26	26	26	26
Pregnant and Parenting Teens Receiving On-Site Services							
Current	1,410	1,420	1,420	1,420	1,420	1,420	1,420
Program Revision			1,656	1,656	1,656	1,656	1,656
School Districts Participating in the Comprehensive Reading Program							
Current							
Program Revision			20	50	90	150	300

Program Revision Recommendations

This budget recommends the following changes (dollar amounts in thousands):

General Government Operations

44 —to provide support for expanded services to students.

Comprehensive Reading

300 —to create a program for improving literacy and encouraging school students to read.

Teen Pregnancy and Parenting

118 —to expand program grants for school-based education and health care programs.

Schools for Excellence

205 —to provide for the continuation of five schools for excellence and to transfer the Governor's School for Business from the Economic Development Partnership to the Department of Education.

Dropout Prevention

500 —to double the number of state-supported program grants, from 13 to 26, for school-based programs to reach high-risk students.

1,167　Total Program Revision

Source: Governor's Executive Budget, 1988–89, p. E147, Commonwealth of Pennsylvania, 1988.

ment, so that each subdivision, for example, begins a new page. The disadvantage is that not all subunits are of equal importance, either in terms of budget size or political interest. Therefore, many jurisdictions use more flexible formats, providing more information on some agencies and programs and less information on others. Under these formats, larger agencies commonly receive more extensive coverage because they are more complex and have more varied activities. However, agencies that are particularly popular or unpopular may receive more extensive coverage regardless of their sizes.

SUMMARY

In beginning the preparation phase, the chief executive conveys to agencies some sense of priorities, either formally in writing or by more subtle means. The executive's perception of the role of government in society is indicated to agencies as well as more specific priorities.

The revenue side of the budget is examined carefully, especially in that state and local governments are not permitted to have operating budgets that exceed available revenues. Requiring the federal government to balance its budget is a proposal that has gained considerable acceptance (see Chapter 9 on Congress).

Budget preparation begins in agencies and involves extensive debate; similar debate and tension develops between agencies and the central budget office, which in turn must compete with other central staff units. Since little formal authority is granted to a central budget office, it must always be concerned with being overruled by the chief executive.

The 1980s ushered in a new era in budgeting, namely one that concentrates upon budget cutbacks rather than program expansion. Fiscal stress, taxing and spending limitations, and a conservative attitude on the part of political leaders have resulted in retrenchment efforts.

The product of the preparation phase is a budget or set of budget documents that reflect executive decisions on policies and programs. The federal government has what is a called a "unified budget." Revenue and expenditure data are treated in all budgets, but the latter receive much more extensive treatment. A budget format is used, often structured by organizational unit with supporting narratives and tabular displays on costs, personnel, and program data.

NOTES

1. Unpublished data from survey conducted by the Department of Public Administration, The Pennsylvania State University and the Pennsylvania Office of the Budget and in conjunction with the National Association of State Budget Officers.

2. Alvin D. Sokolow and Beth Walter Honadle, "How Rural Local Governments Budget," *Public Administration Review* 44 (1984): 373–83.

3. See Charles Brecher, "Management Strategies and Budgetary Politics," *Public Budgeting and Finance* 5 (Autumn 1985): 58–75.

4. Ronald F. King, "Tax Expenditures and Systematic Public Policy," *Public Budgeting and Finance* 4 (Spring 1984): 14–31.

5. Daniel E. O'Toole and James Marshall, "Budgeting Practices in Local Government," *Government Finance Review* 3 (October 1987): 11–16.

6. Robert F. Pecorella, "Community Input and the City Budget," *Journal of Urban Affairs* 8 (1986): 57–70.

7. Terry Schwadron, ed., *California and the American Tax Revolt* (Berkeley: University of California Press, 1984).

8. David Merriman, *The Control of Municipal Budgets* (Westport, Conn.: Quorum, 1987).

9. General Accounting Office, *Budget Issues: State Balanced Budget Practices* (Washington, D.C.: Government Printing Office, 1985).

10. See Robert B. Albritton and Ellen M. Dran, "Balanced Budgets and State Surpluses: The Politics of Budgeting in Illinois," *Public Administration Review* 47 (1987): 143–52.

11. Michael Wolkoff, "An Evaluation of Municipal Rainy Day Funds," *Public Budgeting and Finance* 7 (Summer 1987): 52–63.

12. U.S. Congress, Joint Economic Committee, *The Balanced Budget Amendment: Hearing*, 99th Cong., 1st sess. (Washington, D.C.: Government Printing Office, 1986).

13. John P. Hagan, "Judicial Enforcement of a Balanced-Budget Amendment," *Policy Studies Journal* 15 (1986): 247–67.

14. David C. Nice, "State Support for Constitutional Balanced Budget Requirements," *Journal of Politics* 48 (1986): 134–42.

15. See National Archives and Records Administration, *1987/88, The United States Government Manual* (Washington, D.C.: Government Printing Office, annual).

16. Raymond J. Waldmann, "The Domestic Council: Innovation in Presidential Government," *Public Administration Review* 36 (1976): 260–68.

17. Frederick C. Mosher, *A Tale of Two Agencies: A Comparative Analysis of the General Accounting Office and the Office of Management and Budget* (Baton Rouge: Louisiana State University Press, 1984).

18. David G. Mathiasen, "The Evolution of the Office of Management and Budget Under President Reagan," *Public Budgeting and Finance* 8 (Autumn 1988): 3–14.

19. Bruce Johnson, "OMB and the Budget Examiner," *Public Budgeting and Finance* 8 (Winter 1988): 3–21.

20. James J. Gosling, "The State Budget Office and Policy Making," *Public Budgeting and Finance* 7 (Spring 1987): 51–65.

21. Bruce E. Johnson, "From Analyst to Negotiator: The OMB's New Role," *Journal of Policy Analysis and Management* 3 (1984): 501–15.

22. Allen Schick, "Incremental Budgeting in a Decremental Age," *Policy Sciences* 16 (1983): 1–25.

23. Lee Sigelman, "The Bureaucrat as Budget Maximizer: An Assumption Examined," *Public Budgeting and Finance* 6 (Spring 1986): 50–59.

24. Sydney Duncombe and Richard Kinney, "Agency Budget Success," *Public Budgeting and Finance* 7 (Spring 1987): 29.

25. James W. Davis and Randall B. Ripley, "The Bureau of the Budget and Executive Branch Agencies: Notes on Their Interaction," *Journal of Politics 29* (1967): 751–53.

26. David A. Stockman, *The Triumph of Politics: How the Reagan Revolution Failed* (New York: Harper & Row, 1986).

27. Aaron Wildavsky, *The New Politics of the Budgetary Process* (Boston: Little, Brown, 1988).

28. L.L. Wade, "The U.S. Bureau of the Budget as Agency Evaluator: Orientations to Action," *American Journal of Economics and Sociology* 27 (1968): 55–62.

29. Raymond D. Horton, "Expenditures, Services, and Public Management," *Public Administration Review* 47 (1987): 378–84.

30. Larry Bermon, *The Office of Management and Budget and the Presidency, 1921–1979* (Princeton, N.J.: Princeton University Press, 1979).

31. Philip Bromley and John P. Crecine, "Budget Development in OMB: Aggregate Influences of the Problem and Information Environment," *Journal of Politics* 42 (1980): 1031–64.

32. Hugh Heclo, "OMB and the Presidency—The Problem of 'Neutral Competence,'" *Public Interest* 38 (1975): 80–98.

33. Brian Stipak, Robert P. McGowan, and John M. Stevens, "Effect of Fiscal Stress on Attitudes of Local Executives," *State and Local Government Review* 17 (1985): 188–92.

34. John M. Stevens and Josephine M. LaPlante, "Shaping State-Based Financial Policy in an Era of Change," *Policy Studies Review* (1987): 61–76.

35. Charles H. Levine, ed., *Managing Fiscal Stress* (Chatham, N.J.: Chatham House, 1980).

36. James Mingle and associates, *Challenges of Retrenchment* (San Francisco: Jossey-Bass, 1981).

37. George G. Wynne, ed., *Cutback Management: A Trinational Perspective* (New Brunswick, N.J.: Transaction Books, 1983).

38. Sheldon Danziger and Peter Gottschalk, "The Impact of Budget Cuts and Economic Conditions of Poverty," *Journal of Policy Analysis and Management* 4 (1985): 587–93.

39. Mark Weinberg, "Budget Retrenchment in Small Cities," *Public Budgeting and Finance* 4 (Autumn 1984): 46–57.

40. Thomas P. Lauth, "Exploring the Budgetary Base in Georgia," *Public Budgeting and Finance* 7 (Winter 1987): 72–82.

41. Sydney Duncombe and Richard Kinney, "Cutbacks—Idaho Style," *Public Budgeting and Finance* 4 (Summer 1984): 87–98.

42. Allen Schick, "Macro-Budgetary Adaptations to Fiscal Stress in Industrialized Democracies," *Public Administration Review* 46 (1986): 124–34.

43. George M. Guess, "Budgetary Cutback and Transit System Performance: The Case of MARTA," *Public Budgeting and Finance* 8 (Spring 1988): 58–68.

44. General Accounting Office, *Effective Planning and Budgeting Practices Can Help Arrest the Nation's Deteriorating Public Infrastructure* (Washington, D.C.: Government Printing Office, 1982).

45. Charles Brecher and Raymond D. Horton, "Retrenchment and Recovery: American Cities and the New York Experience," *Public Administration Review* 45 (1985): 267–74.

46. Robert D. Behn, "Cutback Budgeting," *Journal of Policy Analysis and Management* 4, (1985): 155–77.

47. Irene S. Rubin, *Shrinking the Federal Government* (New York: Longman, 1985).

48. Rolf Clark, "Defense Budget Instability and Weapon System Acquisition," *Public Budgeting and Finance* 7 (Summer 1987): 24–36.

49. Kimberly K. Edwards, "Reporting for Tax Expenditures and Tax Abatement," *Government Finance Review* 4 (August 1988): 13–17.

50. "Budgetary Concepts: A Symposium," *Review of Economics and Statistics* 45 (1963): 113–47.

51. Ronald W. Johnson, "Evolution of Budget Concepts in the President's Message: 1923–1968," in President's Commission on Budget Concepts, *Staff Papers and Other Materials Reviewed* (Washington, D.C.: Government Printing Office, 1967), pp. 93–103.

52. President's Commission on Budget Concepts, *Report* (Washington, D.C.: Government Printing Office, 1967).

53. General Accounting Office, *Federal Budget Concepts and Procedures Can Be Further Strengthened* (Washington, D.C.: Government Printing Office, 1981).

54. General Accounting Office, *Federal Budget Totals Are Understated Because of Current Budget Practices* (Washington, D.C.: Government Printing Office, 1980).

55. Office of Management and Budget, *Budget of the United States Government, 1989* (Washington, D.C.: Government Printing Office, 1988).

56. Office of Management and Budget, *The Budget of the United States Government, 1989: Appendix* (Washington, D.C.: Government Printing Office, 1988), p. I-Z10.

57. *Executive Budget, Fiscal Year 1989* (Montpelier: State of Vermont, 1988).

7

Policy and Program Analysis

The use of policy and program analysis is part of the long-standing trend toward developing linkages between financial and program decision making. As preceding chapters have indicated, reformists since the early 1900s have advocated decision systems that focus upon the results of public expenditures. Analysis, though in no sense a new development, has gained in recognition as a means of relating information about what government does and costs to what is accomplished.[1] Today, there is little issue over whether analysis should be conducted. The issue is: how is analysis to be conducted and used in the decision-making system?

We discuss three main topics in this chapter. The first section considers the purposes or roles of analysis—what analysis is; the second section reviews techniques of conducting analysis; the third discusses the limitations of analysis within a political framework.

FOCUS OF ANALYSIS

There seem to be as many types of analysis as there are potential subjects for analysis and persons to conduct the analyses. In the field of budgeting and finance, financial analyses can be conducted regarding revenue projections, the expected costs of proposed program changes, alternative methods for financing debt, and the like.[2] The concern in this chapter, however, is less with financial matters and more with serving public policy and program goals and objectives. The main emphasis here is on the expenditure side of government, but the revenue side should be kept in mind. Important policy goals, such as redistributing income among groups in society, can be achieved through tax measures, such as increasing rates of taxation as personal income rises.

Intellectual Roots

Policy Sciences. Analysis has many intellectual roots. Chapter 5 noted some of these as they related to the emergence of program budgeting in the 1960s. Knowledge utilization or the sociology of knowledge is one central concern.³ How can information/knowledge be used to improve the quality of decision making? This broad area can be labeled as "policy sciences" or "policy studies," terms that allow the inclusion of a wide range of intellectual inquiry.⁴ "Public choice" is another possible unifying term that encapsulates numerous forms of analysis.⁵ Generally, public choice refers to collective decisions being made through decision structures on behalf of societal interests as distinguished from individual choices being made in market situations.

Social Sciences. Political science, sociology, and economics are relevant social science disciplines. Political science studies governmental institutions and processes, including policy formulation and implementation. Sociology examines group behavior, including decision making in governments and related bodies. One major branch of economics is welfare economics, which is an outgrowth of microeconomics that focuses upon rational choice making; welfare economics is particularly concerned with identifying and evaluating alternative decisions.⁶

Public administration/management, of course, is deeply committed to analysis, but how this field relates to other social sciences is difficult to discern. Also, left begging is whether distinctions can be made between a public management approach to analysis and a public administration approach. Whatever the case, public administration/management is committed to analysis that has practical application, whereas political science, for example, may be less concerned with how analytic results can be utilized. Public administrators are involved in a wide range of analyses that often are intended to have impact on policy and program deliberations.

Policy Analysis. Another elusive field of study is policy analysis; it is elusive in the sense of defying simple definition.⁷⁻⁹ One author defined it as "the painstaking investigation of matters of public concern."¹⁰ Such a definition, to say the least, is rather all-encompassing. The field's main root perhaps is economics, but other social sciences have contributed to its origins. Policy analysis, like public administration, is an applied field, often concentrating upon options available in policy formulation. The field is sometimes differentiated from systems analysis, with policy analysis focusing upon the broadest concerns of government and systems analysis more on the concerns of a particular government department or agency.

Scholars have attempted to sort out these various approaches but with little success in devising a paradigm that is accepted widely. Clear-cut definitions of these fields and how they relate to each other simply do not exist.¹¹

Uses and Types of Analysis

Policy Formulation. One way of cutting through this morass is to think of analysis in terms of its use. There are at least three types of uses, the first being policy formulation. Sometimes analysis is initiated when a problem is identified. One useful form of analysis here might focus largely on the causes of the problem while other analyses would identify options for handling the problem and the probable consequences of the options. These types of analyses are prospective in that they look to possible events in the future.

A broad policy type of problem might be the illegal use of narcotics, and alternatives could include a variety of law enforcement options and preventive options, such as public education programs aimed at increasing general awareness of the hazards to health associated with drug use. Other analyses might be more narrowly focused, such as examining only options that relate to law enforcement. The analysis also can be limited by the costs of options, as in the case of examining only options in drug law enforcement that cost no more than X million dollars.

Program Monitoring. A second general type of analysis measures or monitors program results; another term used is that of "program audit."[12] Program monitoring, especially when used in conjunction with a budget system, is intended to keep agencies honest in the sense that promised results are indeed produced with the resources provided. Lent D. Upson in 1924 wrote, "The budget should be supplemented by an operation audit that will measure the effectiveness of expenditures as thoroughly as the financial audits measure the legality of expenditures."[13] Another term used is "accountability," in the sense that agencies should be held answerable for promised results. Monitoring can deal with the implementation of a program as well as with established, ongoing programs.[14]

Program Evaluation. A third type of analysis deals with evaluation of ongoing programs.[15,16] A host of research questions can be included in this type of research. One area of inquiry may deal with the intended goals and objectives of a program, since sometimes they are not readily available and little attempt has been made at specifying them. A governmental program is created in response to a perceived problem, yet there may be no clear understanding as to how the new program will eliminate or alleviate the problem.[17] Former Director of the Budget Charles Schultze has suggested:

> Systematic analysis does not simply accept objectives as immutably given and then proceed to seek the most effective or efficient means of achieving these objectives. One of its major contributions to the complex decision making process lies precisely in its consideration of both objectives and means, allowing analysis of each to influence the other.[18]

In making the argument, however, Schultze warns that he does not mean that analysts determine objectives for persons in decision-making positions. Analysis may suggest objectives previously not considered, and a good analyst may argue for their importance, but decision makers still have the final choice.

In dealing with goals and objectives, analysts by definition are immersed in values and cannot be objective, or value free. At the same time, analysts are "scientific" in their pursuit of knowledge even though they are not value free; social scientists sometimes expect greater objectivity of themselves than is possible even in the physical and biological sciences.[19]

When objectives of a program are unknown or not clearly delineated, the nature of the analysis is more qualitative and less quantitative. This type of research has been called "social evaluation" as distinguished from "technical evaluation," which, for example, might examine an air pollution control program's impact on the environment given the agreed-upon objective of reducing pollutants.[20] Social evaluation, in contrast, might include interviewing policy makers and administrators in regard to their perceived objectives of a pollution program.

Effectiveness and Efficiency. Evaluations commonly deal with issues of effectiveness and efficiency. "Effectiveness" means the use of resources to obtain desired program results that impact upon persons or the environment. Such impacts might be a reduction in infant mortality produced by a prenatal health care program. Efficiency analysis, on the other hand, focuses upon alternative uses of resources in reaching desired ends. Whereas effectiveness analysis might disregard the costs of a program and focus exclusively upon the results or impact, efficiency analysis considers the costs of producing a given unit or set of results and might include consideration of whether alternative approaches could produce more results at the same cost or the same results at reduced costs.

Productivity. The terms productivity analysis and performance measurement also have received much publicity in recent years. Sometimes the terms are used interchangeably and encompass effectiveness and efficiency concerns.[21] On other occasions, the term productivity is restricted to the efficient use of resources in conducting work with little or no emphasis on results or impacts.

Equity and Delivery. Another concern of evaluation is equity, namely whether program benefits are distributed according to some concept of fairness. Analysis of special low-interest mortgages subsidized by government might consider how various income groups benefit. City services can be examined in terms of delivery to poor, middle-income, and upper-income neighborhoods.[22]

Analysis also can consider the delivery mechanism for meeting objectives. Obvious choices are the direct delivery of services, delivery in conjunction with another organization (called "coproduction"), and policy setting through regulation. Executive Order 12291, issued by President Ronald Reagan, has required an evaluation of major regulations in terms of their costs imposed on the federal government, state and local governments, individuals, and corporations along with the benefits derived.[23]

METHODS AND TECHNIQUES OF ANALYSIS

Policy and program analysis techniques range from simple to complex.[24,25] Depending upon the precision of policy definition, the susceptibility of the problem to quantification, and the skills of the analyst, analysis ranges from primarily qualitative research to highly quantitative studies.

Approaches to Analysis

Harry Hatry and others have described the basic methodology of program analysis as consisting of eight steps.

1. define problem
2. identify relevant objectives
3. select evaluation criteria
4. specify client groups
5. identify alternatives
6. estimate costs of each alternative
7. determine effectiveness of each alternative
8. present findings[26]

This description is useful in calling attention to the several phases of the research process that should not be overlooked.

Operations Research. Most techniques of analysis predate program budgeting, being derived in large part from such antecedent fields as systems analysis and operations research (OR). Although OR is sometimes considered synonymous with the application of the scientific method to problem solving,[27] in the narrower sense in which it was described in Chapter 5 OR refers to a set of algorithms for solving recurrent problems that can be expressed quantitatively. Several types of problems recur with such frequency in private business organizations that prototype solutions have been developed to handle them. These prototype models involve problems of allocation, inventory, replacement, queuing, sequencing and coordination, routing, and search.[28] Specific techniques for solving these problems include linear programming, queuing theory, Monte Carlo or randomizing methods, and gaming theory.[29]

When government programs involve similar problems, such as transportation scheduling, warehousing, inventory, or other routinized tasks, OR techniques are readily applicable. Problems associated with postal service, for example, are susceptible to such analytic techniques. The basic requirement for applying them is that a single objective be stated in a quantifiable form. The usual form is that some specific measure of production (output) is maximized or a measure of cost (input) is minimized.

Systems Analysis. The techniques of OR as well as techniques associated with economics may be used by systems analysis, but a distinguishing feature of systems analysis is that it may deal with issues that go beyond these techniques. For example, OR may aid in deriving means for logistical support for combat troops, but systems analysis might go beyond this question to ask: Are there other means of handling a situation that would reduce the need for logistical support? Systems analysis is intended to minimize the danger of myopic vision in which techniques are emphasized over purpose.[30,31]

Cost-Benefit and Cost-Effectiveness Analysis. Within economics, distinctions can be drawn between cost-benefit and cost-effectiveness analysis.[32,33] Both attempt to relate costs of programs to performance and to quantify costs in monetary terms, but they differ in the methods of measuring the outcomes of programs. Cost-effectiveness analysis measures outcomes in quantitative but nonmonetary form. For example, program results might be in terms of the number of lives saved through a highway traffic control program or the time a new supersonic passenger aircraft saves for travelers.

Cost-benefit analysis, on the other hand, measures program outcomes in monetary form, thereby allowing for the development of ratios or other measures of the extent to which returns exceed costs or vice versa.[34] In the above examples of effectiveness analysis, the dollar value of the outcomes cited would be derived. In the case of travel time, the analysis would estimate the worth of time to travelers, assuming that travel time is wasted and that any savings in time would make people more productive.

The potential merit of cost-benefit analysis over cost-effectiveness analysis is that the former allows for analysis across subject areas. When the expressed ratio of benefits to costs of a program is 1.0, costs are equal to benefits. As the ratio increases, the benefits accruing have increased. In theory, then, if a supersonic transport program yielded a ratio of 1.7 and a traffic control program had a ratio of 2.5, then using the standard of economic efficiency and adjusting for differences in program magnitude, government would be advised to favor traffic control over air transportation. Cost-effectiveness analysis, in contrast, would not allow such direct comparisons because the effects would be expressed in time and lives saved.

Problems in Conducting Analysis

Despite the variations in the approaches to analysis, several problems are common to most or all analyses.

Causal Relationships. The first problem is estimating the causal relationships operative in the problem under analysis. In examining alternative programs, the analysis is required to make some assumptions about causation in order to proceed. Some reliance can be placed upon earlier experiences or evaluations of existing programs of similar character. For example, if one is analyzing a possible advertising program to persuade smokers to stop their habit, some reliance might be placed upon available research on advertising programs aimed at reducing drunk driving.

In some cases, there may be little available material from which to make an assessment of causal relationships. This is the case particularly when new technologies and materials must be developed as part of the project being analyzed. The analysis of a new fighter aircraft might require an assessment of person-hours, materials, and equipment needed to develop new lightweight metals and to design new instrumentation. Estimates must be made of the relationships between resource inputs and technological breakthroughs.

Identifying Costs and Benefits. Then there is the issue of what is counted as a cost and a benefit.[35] Determining the financial costs of existing programs is often difficult because accounting systems are designed to produce information by organizational units and not by program. Even when this matter is resolved, all that is produced are the direct financial costs to government. Indeed, analyses often can be criticized as considering only the costs to government and overlooking the costs imposed upon others. Failure to consider all costs tends to weight the analysis in favor of the proposed project under review.

Externalities. Indirect costs as well as benefits imposed or granted to others are referred to as externalities, or spillover, secondary, and tertiary effects. These are costs and benefits that affect parties other than the ones directly involved. In the private sector, air and water pollution from industrial plants are externalities. The main concern of a private enterprise is making a profit, but part of the cost of production may be imposed upon persons living in the area. Residents of the area downstream and downwind of the plant pay a cost in terms of discomfort, poor health, and loss of water recreation opportunities. If a municipality downstream is required to treat water that has been polluted by the plant, the costs imposed are relatively easy to identify.

Most government expenditure decisions involve similar spillover effects. The costs of an urban renewal program may be assessed in terms of the outlays required for purchasing and clearing land to the exclusion of spillover costs imposed upon families, businesses, and industries that must be relocated.[36] One government's decision can affect thousands of individuals, businesses, nonprofit organizations, and other governments, including national governments throughout the world.

The conclusion can be drawn that there are no such things as secondary or spillover effects, that anyone or anything affected by a program should be part of the explicitly considered benefits and costs of that program. The concept of "standing" is used to suggest that an individual or organization should be taken into account in the analysis if affected by the governmental decision or program.[37] Affected parties are said to be "stakeholders" in that they have interests regarding the outcomes of a program and any decisions that would change the program.

Redistributive Effects. Related to spillover costs and benefits are redistributive effects, a matter that analyses tended to ignore until the 1980s. Involved here is the matter of whether some groups in the society will benefit more than other groups. In the example of travel time mentioned above, the program presumably would benefit middle- and upper-income groups. Other criteria for judging redistribution include race, educational level, and occupational class.[38]

Subjective Information. Analyses often must rely on subjective, attitudinal data as distinguished from data that gauge behavior. One objective measure of a city road program might be the miles of roads resurfaced while an attitudinal measure might be citizen satisfaction with road conditions. It is indeed possible for citizens (stakeholders) to exhibit no increase in satisfaction even though road conditions may have been increased markedly. The same type of situation can develop regarding police protection. Citizens' fear of being burglarized may not decrease despite a decline in the burglary rate.[39]

Internal Validity. When costs, benefits, and expected relationships among them are defined, analysis must consider whether other possible variables may influence outcomes. This influence is known as a threat to "internal validity."[40] For example, a school program working to increase employment among disadvantaged teenagers may seem to be effective when in fact the program may be having little influence on employment; any increase in employment might be attributable not to school district efforts but to some other program, such as one operated by a nonprofit agency or church. This type of problem is common in the area of social services, where several agencies may overlap in working with clients or may be engaged in the "coproduction" of services.[41]

Problems of Quantification

Even if an ideal model is designed displaying all of the relevant types of costs and benefits or effects of a program, the problem of quantifying them remains. What are the monetary costs imposed upon families relocated by urban redevelopment activities? Part of the costs will be moving expenses, perhaps higher rents, and greater costs for commuting to work. While these can be measured, it is much more difficult to set a dollar value on the mental anguish of having to move and leave friends behind.

Shadow Pricing. Much of the problem of setting dollar values in the analysis stems from the fact that governmental programs do not entail market prices. Despite various limitations, the private market does provide some standard for measuring the value of goods and services by the prices set for these. Much of analysis in the public sector, however, must impute the prices or values of programs. This practice is known as shadow pricing.[42,43]

The use of shadow pricing can be seen in an example of predicting the benefits of a proposed outdoor recreation project.[44] The average hourly value to a person attending the proposed new facility (the shadow price) can be assumed to be what an individual on the average spends per hour for other forms of outdoor recreation. This figure times the number attending will yield an approximate value of the recreational opportunities to be provided by the facility under study.

More detailed approaches can examine each form of outdoor recreation—hiking, swimming, tennis, golfing, picnicking, and so forth. In the case of swimming, one can derive the average spent per person for one hour of swimming at a private beach and impute that to be the value of swimming at a public beach. One danger of such an assumption, however, is that it ignores the possibility that the quality of swimming may be different between the public and private beaches. Therefore, the shadow price needs to be adjusted accordingly.

Shadow pricing becomes increasingly difficult and the analysis more tenuous when the subject matter for study involves functions that are primarily governmental. There is no apparent method by which a dollar value can be set for a defense capability of killing via intercontinental missiles x million people of an aggressor nation within one hour. Similarly, it is difficult to calculate the dollar value of avoiding one traffic fatality. The calculations employed require assessing what kinds of people are killed in automobile accidents, how old they are, and what income they would have earned in their lifetimes.

Given the questionable assumptions that must be made in estimating the dollar value of saving a life, the argument can be made that cost-effectiveness analysis is preferable to cost-benefit analysis. The former does not attempt to place a dollar value on life, but that calculation is left to decision makers. The disadvantage is that cost-effectiveness analysis, unlike cost-benefit analysis, seldom will yield a single measure of effectiveness. A traffic safety program might be measured by the number of lives saved and by the dollar value of property damage caused by crashes. Because these are like apples and oranges, they cannot be added together.

Discount Rates. Another problem for analysis involves the diversion of resources from the private to the public sector and from current consumption to investment in future returns. Investment in a public project or program is warranted only if the returns are greater than they would be if the same funds were left to the private sector and if the future returns are worth the current sacrifice. Thus, the relevant concept of the cost of a public expenditure is the value of the benefits forgone by not leaving the money in the private sector where it would be consumed or invested.

A dollar diverted from the private to the public sector is not just an equivalent dollar cost or dollar benefit forgone. "Part of the money taken from the private sector decreases consumption immediately, while the rest decreases investment and therefore future consumption." Thus, the value of a dollar removed by government expenditure is worth the "discounted value of the future consumption that would have occurred if the investment [in the private economy] had been made."[45] Some charge must be made against that dollar removed from consumption to arrive at the current value of future consumption forgone. This charge is known as the discount or interest rate.[46,47]

The discount rate must in some way serve two purposes. First, it should be similar to an interest charge that reflects the costs of removing a dollar from private-sector use and diverting it to the public sector. If a dollar could earn 8 percent in the private sector, investment in the public sector would be warranted (in an economic sense) only if the rate of return from the public investment would be at least 8 percent. Second, the discount rate must take into consideration the time pattern of expenditures and returns. In general, people prefer present consumption to future consumption. A dollar that might be spent for current consumption is worth more than a dollar that might be consumed ten years from now. Normally people do not willingly save unless they receive interest in compensation for the temporary loss of consumption. A discount rate, then, must provide a means of showing the present value of dollars to be spent or returned in the future.

The relationships among costs, returns, and time are depicted graphically in Figure 7-1. Most investment projects involve an early expenditure of heavy capital costs followed by a tapering off to operating costs. Returns are nonexistent or minimal for the first few years and then increase rapidly. The shape of the return curve after that point depends on the nature of the particular investment and is arbitrarily drawn for illustrative purposes in the figure. The comparison of costs to benefits over time makes the necessity for discounting obvious. Higher costs occur earlier in most projects. The higher benefits that occur later are valued less because of the time factor.

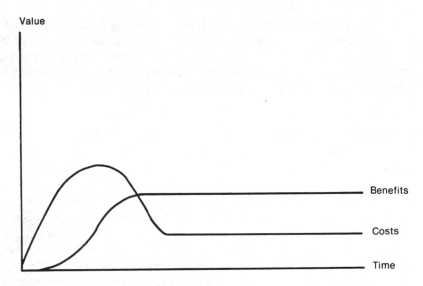

Note: The value scale is expressed in common units, usually dollars. The time scale goes from one unit, such as one year, through the expected life span of the project.

Figure 7-1 Relationship of Costs and Benefits to Time.

Costs and benefits must therefore be compared for each time period (usually each year), and the differences summed over the life span of the project. That is in essence what a discount rate accomplishes. The longer it takes for returns to occur, the more their value is discounted. In effect, it is compound interest in reverse. Costs occurring earlier are subject to less discounting. Thus, for a project to be economically feasible, total discounted benefits must exceed total discounted costs.

It is obvious that the choice of a discount rate has an important influence on investment decisions. Too low a rate understates the value of current consumption or of leaving the money to the private sector. Too high a rate uneconomically favors current consumption over future benefits and results in less investment than is worthwhile. The choice of a discount rate may thus determine the outcome of the analysis.

Selecting appropriate discount rates is difficult. Private market rates are inappropriate because they include calculations of the risks of loss involved in making loans. On the other hand, interest rates charged governments often are artificially low because of various guarantees against defaults and sometimes the loans' tax-exempt status. The appropriate discount rate lies between these extremes.

Several discount rates may be applied to program alternatives to determine the sensitivity of the analysis to discounting. If the cost-benefit ratios of a project are well above 1.0 regardless of the discount rate used, there is little problem, but a different situation arises if some plausible discount rates yield results well below 1.0. In other situations, one discount rate might result in a favorable cost-benefit ratio for alternative A and another rate for alternative B. The point is that an arbitrary choice of a discount rate without consideration of other ranges can produce misleading results.

ORGANIZATIONAL LOCUS AND USE OF ANALYSIS

Analytic Units

With the increasing interest in analysis has come a proliferation of analytic units. Central budget offices, other central units such as planning departments, and line agencies have developed analytic capabilities. Legislative analytic units have been established.[48] The 1974 Congressional Budget and Impoundment Control Act specifically empowered standing committees and the comptroller general to "review and evaluate the results of Government programs and activities." The Congressional Budget Office, which initially restricted its work to economic trend analysis, has broadened its scope to include policy and program analysis. State legislative staff units, such as the Virginia Legislative Audit and Review Commission, have gained national prominence in the field of program evaluation.

Analysis has become widespread at the state level, as revealed by surveys of state budget offices.[49,50] Whereas in 1970 only 8 state budget offices were conducting effectiveness analysis and 14 efficiency analysis, by 1985 there were 27 and 35 states, respectively, engaged in these types of analysis. Major line agencies in approximately 20 states were conducting analysis. Also about 20 state legislatures were reported to be engaged in effectiveness and efficiency analysis. The survey results seem to show that where analysis is prominent in the executive branch, it tends also to be prominent in the legislature, although no cause-and-effect relationships should be assumed.

Local governments are also engaged in analysis, but a problem that many face is that they are too small to be able to afford large analytic staffs. Greater dissemination of analyses may be of help in allowing more than one community to benefit from the findings of a given study. One possible drawback is that communities may be reluctant to apply the findings of another city's study on the grounds that the communities are dissimilar in important respects.

Universities are another locale for analysis.[51] Faculty and staff in a wide range of research and academic units conduct research that is of direct relevance to policy deliberations in government.

Regardless of the location of the analytic unit, it has limited resources and must choose carefully the targets of analysis. If an analytic unit in a government commits all of its resources to one study each year, that means many programs will go unreviewed. At the opposite extreme, numerous "quick-and-dirty" studies can be conducted in a year, but at the risk of excessive superficiality. Central analytic units may take a mixed strategy of conducting both short and long analyses and diversifying them over a wide range of programs and departments. Criteria used in selecting targets for analysis include the dollar magnitude of programs and the political feasibility of changing them.

Analysis in Decision Making

Producing reports and studies is not the same as using them in policy deliberations. In the 1985 state budget office survey mentioned above, only 9 states reported that executive budget decisions were based substantially on effectiveness analyses and 12 states on efficiency analyses. Another 27 and 28 states respectively reported analyses being used somewhat in executive decision making. State budget offices reported that only 5 state legislatures use analysis substantially in decision making, but another 30 legislatures were reported to use analysis somewhat. The complaint from analysts that their findings and recommendations are often unheeded is common.[52]

One reason for the limited use of analyses may be the analyses themselves. Any decision maker needs to examine an analysis before using it. Of course, analysis is subjective from the standpoint of selecting possible causal relationships to consider and determining which benefits and costs to count.[53] The decision maker needs to maintain a healthy skepticism and be aware of the technical difficulties, discussed in the preceding section, that might influence or determine the outcome of a study.

Some analyses may serve the purpose of a "fund-raising prospectus."[54] A state department of transportation study that concludes that the department needs more funds may be the product of overzealous analysts eager to serve the needs of their department. Analysts face serious ethical conflicts over loyalty to their agencies and loyalty to some degree of objectivity.

There are many other factors that can make an analysis of limited use. The topic may be too politically hot or excessively trivial for decision makers to act upon. If research reports are not relevant to decision makers, the reports will not be used.[55] Sometimes "windows" open on program areas in which major decisions can be made, at which time analyses can be influential. At other times, these same program areas are unlikely to be influenced greatly by analyses because of political conditions.[56,57]

Windows on decisions also are influenced by matters of timing as well as politics. An analysis that concluded that a bridge was unnecessary but that was not completed until after construction was under way probably would have little impact. Decisions of this type, once made, are largely irreversible.

Other limitations pertain to the technical nature of reports. The data base of a study may have been weak, resulting in highly qualified and tentative conclusions; in such a case the decision makers will probably rely on their hunches more than on those of the analysts. "Too many studies are becoming so complex that they are almost impossible for anyone except (and sometimes including) the authors to understand. Many analyses simply are too technical, too detailed, and too encumbered with extraneous information for ready understanding by would-be users. The studies simply lack credibility."[58]

Beyond the analyses is the nature of the decision system. It may be that a program budget system, for instance, is more likely to use available analyses because the decision structure is specifically geared to that effect. However, most budget systems may be biased largely in favor of maintaining existing programs and organizations.[59] It is possible that analyses often are directed toward revising and perhaps salvaging existing operations rather than toward exploring alternative opportunities for dealing with society's problems.[60]

The political and administrative cultures of a government and agencies within it influence the use of analysis. Some units operate in an environment where analysis and the use of information is taken as a given, whereas other organizations find analysis to be a new commodity.[61]

The organizational location of analytic units can be critical in ensuring visibility or obscurity for their products. An analytic unit that is buried in an agency is unlikely to have much influence upon decision making. Having an analytic unit within a budget office can give it visibility but, on the other hand, can result in analysts being regularly assigned to deal with brush fires so that no time is left for analysis.[62]

The use of analysis is related to the incentives for conducting it. Analysis can be used to identify means to reduce costs, but if such studies are used to cut agency budgets, then there is little incentive for agencies to engage in cost-saving studies.[63] Evaluations may be mandated by legislatures, but executive agencies may be reluctant to conduct these with vigor, since most—if not all—analyses are regarded as threats.[64] Negative findings are seen as indicators of administrators' failures and can be used as the rationale for budget cuts.

Implementation of analysis is further complicated by interagency and intergovernmental relations. The benefits of an improved municipal law enforcement program may not be gained if courts are unable to cope with increased numbers of arrests and prosecutions (assuming that increased arrests yield reductions in crime). Moreover, societal problems do not respect political boundaries, and problems do not coincide with each other. One mix of governmental units may be appropriate for dealing with air pollution problems and another with physical health.

Finally, one must consider the increasing maturity in the conduct and use of analysis. Over the long run, how many analytic units can a government afford to maintain, in what locations in the bureaucracy, and at what staffing levels? How can rigor in the conduct of analysis be maintained on an extended basis? How can analysis be incorporated as an integral part of the ongoing process of public policy making? How can analysts retain some degree of objectivity when over time they will be examining and re-examining the same problems and programs?

SUMMARY

There are related but divergent fields of study that impinge upon analysis. Included are the sociology of knowledge, policy science, and public choice and the disciplines of political science, sociology, economics, and public administration/management. Operations research and systems analysis are also included. Much of this chapter has focused upon cost-benefit and cost-effectiveness analysis. These two are similar, except that cost-benefit analysis quantifies program outcomes in monetary terms whereas cost-effectiveness analysis quantifies outcomes in programmatic terms, such as the number of lives saved. Many of the problems associated with analysis relate to the assumptions that must be made in terms of deriving cost and benefit data, particularly through the use of shadow prices and discount rates.

Numerous political and institutional factors limit the use of analysis. Because analysis is part of the political process, one can expect analysis on occasion to be designed to produce the desired conclusions. Even when studies conclude that existing programs are not yielding the intended impacts, these studies can serve as justification for expanding rather than shrinking these programs. Beyond the politics of the situation are institutional constraints that deter the translation of analytic findings into program decisions for the coming budget year. Analysis is now a maturing field; gone is the era in which analysis was viewed as a novel activity.

NOTES

1. Prest and Turvey in their survey of cost-benefit analysis date program analysis in the United States back to the River and Harbor Act of 1902, which required analysis of the costs of river and harbor projects undertaken by the Army Corps of Engineers in comparison with the amount of commerce benefited by these projects. A.R. Prest and R. Turvey, "Cost-Benefit Analysis: A Survey," *The Economic Journal* 75 (1965): 683–735.

2. Robert Berne and Richard Schramm, *The Financial Analysis of Governments* (Englewood Cliffs, N.J.: Prentice-Hall, 1986).

3. James M. Rogers, *The Impact of Policy Analysis* (Pittsburgh: University of Pittsburgh Press, 1988).

4. Anne L. Schneider, "The Evolution of a Policy Orientation for Evaluation Research: A Guide to Practice," *Public Administration Review* 46 (1986): 356–63.

5. Davis B. Bobrow and John S. Dryzek, *Policy Analysis by Design* (Pittsburgh: University of Pittsburgh Press, 1987), pp. 44–61.

6. Bobrow and Dryzek, *Policy Analysis by Design*, pp. 27–43.

7. Randall B. Bovbjerg and James W. Vaupel, eds., "Symposium: What Is Policy Analysis," *Journal of Policy Analysis and Management* 4 (1985): 419–32.

8. William N. Dunn, ed., *Policy Analysis: Perspectives, Concepts and Methods* (Greenwich, Conn.: JAI Press, 1986).

9. Stuart S. Nagel, ed., *Research in Public Policy Analysis and Management* (Greenwich, Conn.: JAI Press, 1986).

10. Alexander M. Mood, *Introduction to Policy Analysis* (New York: North-Holland, 1983), p. 1.

11. Dennis J. Palumbo, "Politics and Evaluation," in Dennis J. Palumbo, ed., *The Politics of Program Evaluation* (Newbury Park, Calif.: Sage, 1987), pp. 12–46.

12. Thomas J. Cook, ed., "Symposium: Performance Measurement in Public Agencies," *Policy Studies Review* 6 (1986): 61–170.

13. Lent D. Upson, "Half-Time Budget Methods," *Annals* 113 (1924): 74.

14. George C. Edwards III, ed., *Public Policy Implementation* (Greenwich, Conn.: JAI Press, 1984).

15. Terry Busson and Philip Coulter, eds., *Policy Evaluation for Local Government* (Westport, Conn.: Greenwood, 1987).

16. Elmer L. Struening and Marilynn B. Brewer, eds., *University Edition of the Handbook of Evaluation Research* (Beverly Hills, Calif.: Sage, 1983).

17. Elmer B. Staats, "Evaluating the Effectiveness of Federal Social Programs," *The GAO Review* 8 (1973): 1–7.

18. Charles L. Schultze, *The Politics and Economics of Public Spending* (Washington, D.C.: Brookings, 1968), p. 65.

19. Barry Bozeman, "The Credibility of Policy Analysis: Between Method and Use," *Policy Studies Journal* 14 (1986): 519–39.

20. Brian M. Gardner and Patricia S. Florestano, "The Necessity of Utilizing Social Measurement Techniques in Program Evaluation," *Policy Studies Journal* 12 (1983): 295–304.

21. Frank P. Scioli, Jr., "Problems of Controlling the Efficiency of Bureaucratic Behavior," *Policy Studies Review* 6 (1986): 71–89.

22. Philip B. Coulter, Inferring the Distributional Effects of Bureaucratic Decision Rules," *Policy Studies Journal* 12 (1983): 347–55.

23. Policy Research Project on Federal Regulatory Impact Analysis, *Federal Regulatory Reform Programs and the Use of Cost-Benefit Analysis* (Austin: Lyndon B. Johnson School of Public Affairs, The University of Texas, 1984).

24. Robert H. Haveman and Julius Margolis, eds., *Public Expenditure and Policy Analysis*, 3rd ed. (Boston: Houghton Mifflin, 1983).

25. Theodore H. Poister, *Public Program Analysis* (Baltimore: University Park Press, 1978).

26. Harry Hatry et al., *Program Analysis for State and Local Governments*, 2nd ed. (Washington, D.C.: Urban Institute, 1987), p. 4.

27. Russell L. Ackoff and Maurice W. Sasieni, *Fundamentals of Operations Research* (New York: Wiley, 1968).

28. Ibid., p. 13.

29. Joseph G. Ecker and Michael Kupferschmid, *Introduction to Operations Research* (New York: Wiley, 1988).

30. C. West Churchman, *The Systems Approach and Its Enemies* (New York: Basic Books, 1979).

31. Jerry FitzGerald et al., *Fundamentals of Systems Analysis*, 3rd ed. (New York: Wiley, 1987).

32. Edward M. Gramlich, *Benefit-Cost Analysis of Government Programs* (Englewood Cliffs, N.J.: Prentice-Hall, 1981).

33. E.J. Mishan, *Cost-Benefit Analysis*, 3rd ed. (London: Allen and Unwin, 1982).

34. Kirk C. Harlow and Duane Windsor, "Integration of Cost-Benefit and Financial Analysis in Project Evaluation," *Public Administration Review* 48 (1988): 918–28.

35. Robert H. Haveman and Burton A. Weisbrod, "Defining Benefits of Public Programs: Some Guidance for Policy Analysts," *Policy Analysis* 1 (1975): 169–96.

36. Anthony Downs, *Urban Problems and Prospects* (Chicago: Markham, 1970), pp. 192–227.

37. Dale Whittington and Duncan MacRae, Jr., "The Issue of Standing in Cost-Benefit Analysis," *Journal of Policy Analysis and Management* 5 (1986): 665–82.

38. Ronald W. Johnson and John M. Pierce, "The Economic Evaluation of Policy Impacts: Cost-Benefit and Cost-Effectiveness Analysis," in Frank P. Scioli, Jr., and Thomas J. Cook, eds., *Methodologies for Analyzing Public Policies* (Lexington, Mass.: Lexington Books, 1975), pp. 131–54.

39. Jennifer G. Greene, "Stakeholder Participation and Utilization in Program Evaluation," *Evaluation Review* 12 (1988): 91–116.

40. Emil J. Posavac and Raymond G. Carey, *Program Evaluation*, 2nd ed. (Englewood Cliffs, N.J.: Prentice-Hall, 1985), pp. 183–89.

41. Jeffrey L. Brudney, "The Evaluation of Coproduction Programs," *Policy Studies Journal* 12 (1983): 376–85.

42. Roland N. McKean, "The Use of Shadow Prices," in Samuel B. Chase, Jr., ed., *Problems in Public Expenditure Analysis* (Washington, D.C.: Brookings, 1968), pp. 33–65.

43. Joseph E. Stiglitz, *Economics of the Public Sector* (New York: Norton, 1986), pp. 225–26.

44. Ruth P. Mack and Sumner Myers, "Outdoor Recreation," in Robert Dorfman, ed., *Measuring Benefits of Government Investments* (Washington, D.C.: Brookings, 1965), pp. 71–101.

45. M.S. Feldstein, quoted in Prest and Turvey, "Cost Benefit Analysis," pp. 686–87.

46. Robert L. Banks and Arnold Kotz, "The Program Budget and the Interest Rate for Public Investment," *Public Administration Review* 26 (1986): 283–92.

47. Mood, *Introduction to Policy Analysis*, pp. 85–91.

48. Judith R. Brown, ed., "Mini-Symposium on Legislative Program Evaluation," *Public Administration Review* 44 (1984): 257–67.

49. Data are from surveys conducted by the Department of Public Administration, The Pennsylvania State University, in conjunction with the Pennsylvania Budget Office and with the endorsement of the National Association of State Budget Officers.

50. John M. Stevens and Robert D. Lee, Jr., "Patterns of Policy Analysis Use for State Governments," *Public Administration Review* 41 (1981): 636–44.

51. Irwin Feller, *Universities and State Governments: A Study in Policy Analysis* (New York: Praeger, 1986).

52. Richard E. Brown, ed., *The Effectiveness of Legislative Program Review* (New Brunswick, N.J.: Transaction Books, 1979).

53. Fred A. Kramer, "Policy Analysis as Ideology," *Public Administration Review* 35 (1975): 509–17.

54. Robert N. Anthony, "Closing the Loop Between Planning and Performance," *Public Administration Review* 31 (1971): 389.

55. Anne L. Schneider, "The Evolution of a Policy Orientation for Evaluation Research," *Public Administration Review* 46 (1986): 356–63.

56. Peter J. May, "Politics and Policy Analysis," *Political Science Quarterly* 101 (1986): 109–25.

57. Chimezie A.B. Osigweh, "Program Evaluation and Its 'Political' Context," *Policy Studies Review* 6 (1986): 90–98.

58. Bozeman, "The Credibility of Policy Analysis."

59. Thomas P. Lauth, "Performance Evaluation in the Georgia Budgetary Process," *Public Budgeting and Finance* 5 (Spring 1985): 67–82.

60. William T. Gormely, Jr., "Institutional Policy Analysis: A Critical Review," *Journal of Policy Analysis and Management* 6 (1987): 153–69.

61. Jean-Louis Quermonne and Luc Rouban, "French Public Administration and Policy Evaluation," *Public Administration Review* 46 (1986): 397–406.

62. J. Fred Springer, "Policy Analysis and Organizational Decisions," *Administration and Society* 16 (1985): 475–508.

63. Herbert J. Rubin et al., "Evaluation for Cutback Management in Small Cities," *Policy Studies Journal* 12 (1983): 356–64.

64. Robert G. St. Pierre, "Congressional Input to Program Evaluation," *Evaluation Review* 7 (1983): 411–36.

8

Budget Approval:
The Role of the Legislature

The struggle over the budget has only begun when the budget document is presented to the legislative body. Budget preparation at the state and federal levels will have consumed months, but the product of the process is only a proposal. The distinction between preparation and approval is sometimes phrased as "the executive proposes and the legislature disposes." The process is distinctly different from that used in parliamentary governments such as the British one, in which the executive and legislative functions are controlled by the same political party. In such systems, the approval phase is largely pro forma. In the United States, however, the legislative body typically may approve a budget that differs greatly from what has been proposed.

In this chapter, major emphasis is given to the similarities in the approval phase across levels of government—local, state, and federal. The next chapter, in contrast, focuses exclusively on Congress, because that body is unique in the American political system and has unique budgetary procedures.

This chapter has two main sections. The first discusses the parameters that constrain how legislative bodies operate and the processes used in approving government budgets. The second section examines the relationships between the legislative and executive branches and the changing role of the legislature as an overseer of the executive branch.

PARAMETERS

Legislative Characteristics

Legislative bodies—city councils, school boards, state legislatures, and Congress—sometimes have had a reputation for being relatively weak, ineffective bodies, but that perception has been changing, especially since the 1970s. Legislative bodies at all levels of government are seen as reasserting their authority to set policy.[1]

Economic Environment. As with all human enterprise, legislative bodies must operate within a set of parameters; these greatly constrain how the budget approval process will be conducted. One of the most important constraints is the economic environment, both short- and long-term. How a legislative body approaches the task of passing a budget is influenced greatly by whether there is a projected surplus of revenues or whether sizable cuts must be made to bring expenditures down to meet anticipated reductions in revenues.

Previous Decisions. Before a local legislative body commences considering the budget, many decisions already will have been made. As explained in previous chapters, the state will have imposed a variety of mandates. A school district will be told how many days it must operate in a school year, possibly what the starting salary should be for new teachers, and what courses must be taught.[2] Over half of a school district's budget typically comes from state aid, thereby greatly reducing what the school district can decide on its own. The state also will have imposed limits on taxation for each type of local government and may deny taxing power to some jurisdictions, as is sometimes the case with special districts.

Just as many decisions will have already been made before a local legislative body begins its deliberations, so will many decisions have been made for state legislatures and Congress. Legislation that provides open-ended benefits to individuals, such as guaranteed payments to all persons qualifying for disability benefits under Social Security, greatly curtails what Congress can do in a given year. Similarly, some federal grant programs to state and local governments have been on a permanent appropriation basis, providing for no input from Congress over a period of several years. State legislatures face this same situation, most notably in the case of aid to local school districts.

Representation of Interests. Socioeconomic-political diversity influences legislative behavior. At the national level, Congress must deal with a broad range of issues and associated interest groups. States tend to be less diverse and therefore tend to have fewer interest groups that press their preferences upon legislatures; this situation can allow for a relatively few number of interest lobbyists influencing legislation.[3] This concentration of influence can be even greater at the local level, as in the case of a town that is dominated by a single employer.

Citizen initiatives, allowable in many states, constitute another set of parameters that can have major impacts on the legislative bodies responsible for approving budgets.[4] Under the initiative process, citizens have the power to legislate changes, often by making amendments to state constitutions; if citizens are dissatisfied with tax rates, as was frequently the case in the 1970s, voters may approve new limits on taxes that force jurisdictions to cut tax rates and spending.

It is understood that a chief responsibility—if not *the* chief responsibility—of legislators is to represent their constituents. How that duty is met is influenced by another parameter, namely the method by which legislators are elected to their jobs. The Supreme Court ruled in the 1960s that state legislatures must have district lines drawn that are proportional to population; the effect has been to reduce substantially what was over-representation of rural interests and increase representation of urban and suburban areas in states.[5,6] Local governments are undergoing similar changes. City councils are changing from using at-large seats, because this procedure tends to result in under-representation of minority interests. The movement is toward what is called "single-member districts" based upon neighborhood populations or a combination of these and at-large seats.[7]

Fragmentation. An overriding characteristic of state legislatures and Congress is fragmentation in budgeting. Constitutionally imposed bicameralism divides the legislature into two chambers, a house and a senate, which seek to establish their own identities and powers but which must be coordinated if a budget is to be approved. Local governing bodies, in contrast, usually are unicameral and do not face this fragmentation problem.

Fragmentation also is apparent in relations between the executive and legislative branches. This topic will be discussed at length later in this chapter. It should be noted here that political parties can serve as a unifying force between branches and between legislative chambers. Conventional practice provides that whichever party wins a majority of seats in a chamber will control the leadership positions, have a majority of its members on each committee, and have each committee chaired by a member of the party. In theory, if the Democrats hold a majority of the seats in a state senate, then the party has control of that chamber in handling all legislative matters.

However, political parties are weak and unable to control their own party members. On any given issue there may be no guarantee that all or even a majority of the party's members will vote as a block. The problem is further complicated in that the two chambers can be controlled by different parties, or both may be controlled by one party while the chief executive is of another party. Many members of the legislative body and especially persons in leadership positions have served long tenures and are not always amenable to changes proposed by the executive, regardless of party affiliation.

Parties attempt to exert influence on their legislators through caucuses. Republicans in a state house of representatives, for example, meet periodically to develop party positions on issues and then attempt to exert influence to have party members in the house vote accordingly. The positions approved in caucus meetings do not always coincide with the views of the party's leadership.

Legislative Committees. The extensive use of legislative committees is essential in that acting as a committee of the whole is untenable, but committee structures add to fragmentation. Committees become little legislatures in their own right.[8] Given that the U.S. House of Representatives has 435 members and the Senate 100, and given the major problems Congress must address each year, a committee structure becomes inevitable. Among the states, New Hampshire has the largest legislature, with 424 members, and Nebraska the smallest, with 49 members in one chamber. Most states have more than 100 legislators.[9]

In a bicameral legislative body, legislation is handled by parallel committees in each chamber. These committees report out bills that are acted upon by the full membership of the house and senate. When differences exist in the two bills, a conference committee is usually appointed, which reports a revised bill that again is acted upon by both houses; the conference committee consists of members from the two committees that prepared the legislation.[10] Once the chambers have passed identical bills, the legislation is ready for signing or vetoing by the governor or president.

At the local level, where unicameralism prevails, a budget committee often has main responsibility for reviewing and amending the executive's proposed budget and for submitting a set of recommendations to the full legislative body, such as a city council or school board.

Committees that continue on a permanent basis are regarded as standing committees, as distinguished from ad hoc committees that may be created to deal with a problem and then disband.[11] Most standing committees consist of selected members of one house of a legislature but can be joint in nature, namely consisting of selected members from both chambers. State legislatures usually have 15 to 20 standing committees in each chamber.[12]

To summarize, legislative policy is influenced by some combination of party leadership, caucuses, and committees. According to one scholar, nearly a third of the state chambers are characterized by party leaders and committees having the greatest effect on policy making.[13] The remaining two-thirds of the chambers are divided among the other possible permutations. In general, partisan leadership has greater influence over legislators in the state chambers than in Congress, where power is more diffuse.

Availability of Time. How a legislative body operates is greatly influenced by whether it continues in session throughout the year. City councils usually hold meetings once, twice, or even more times per month throughout the year. Congress is in session much of each year except for holidays and recesses during election periods. State legislatures vary widely. While about a dozen states have no limits on the length of legislative sessions, the rest control whether the legislature can meet each year, for how many days, and whether the legislature may call itself back into session after adjournment. The legislatures in California, Illinois, Massachusetts, Michigan, New Jersey, New York, Ohio, Pennsylvania, and Wisconsin hold sessions that run during much of the year.[14] When legislatures have time limitations, such as meeting for a maximum of 60 days, procedural limits are used to "budget" the available time. For example, a common practice is to set a cutoff date as to when bills may be introduced, since late submission would carry deliberations beyond the required adjournment.

A major problem facing Congress is not that it has limits on the time that it may be in session, but rather that it has difficulty approving the budget within the available time. Until legislation was adopted in 1974, Congress faced a situation in which the president's budget was delivered to it shortly after the first of the calendar year and work was to be completed by July 1, then the beginning of the fiscal year. Part of the problem was that every two years Congress had to reorganize itself and in the process lost valuable time. In January and February of odd-numbered years, Congress must reorganize since all members of the House of Representatives and one-third of the members of the Senate had been elected the previous November. New memberships result in new committee assignments, new chairs of some committees, some new leadership, and a reassignment of offices. Under these conditions, Congress simply could not complete its work within the allotted five to six months. However, the track record since the beginning of the fiscal year was shifted to October 1 is not much better.

Compensation and Staff. Closely associated with time limits on legislatures is compensation for their members. If compensation is low, then most legislators will be forced to have some other source of income and will regard their legislative tasks as part time in nature. Members of Congress earn incomes and receive other benefits, such as travel expenses, that allow the legislative job to be a full-time occupation. Several states pay their legislators less than $10,000 annually, which more or less forces them to seek other income or to be financially independent.

Staffing is another factor that influences legislative behavior. Staff dedicated to assist legislators presumably can help them perform more effectively and reduce their reliance on the executive branch and lobbyists for information. Although local bodies, such as county commissioners or city council members, rarely have sizable staffs at their disposal, Congress does and so do many state legislatures. Staffs serve individual members, committees, and persons holding leadership positions, as in the case of the speaker of a state house of representatives. In addition, there are some legislative staff units that serve a variety of individuals and committees in both chambers; the Congressional Budget Office is a noted example. Since the 1960s, staffs in state legislatures and Congress have greatly increased their professional training; staff members often have graduate degrees, including doctorates.

The Legislative Process

Members of the legislature or their staff members often participate in preparation deliberations by the executive branch. When the budget reaches the legislature, therefore, there may be relatively few surprises in terms of proposals being advanced; that is, many of the key legislators already will be familiar with the budget's main proposals. Legislative involvement during preparation can help build support for executive budget recommendations.

Committee Responsibilities. When a budget reaches a state legislature or Congress, the document is divided into numerous pieces and sent to committee.[15,16] Proposals that require new substantive legislation to implement them will be sent to substantive standing committees; these committees exist for such topics as environmental protection, education, recreation, and welfare and at the federal level also for defense and international relations. For programs to be implemented, these committees must report bills that eventually will be approved by the two chambers of the legislature.

While deliberations proceed on these substantive matters, other committees deal with the financial aspects of the budget. A regular practice is to assign taxing and other revenue matters to one group of committees and spending or appropriations to another.[17] In Congress, taxation is handled by the Ways and Means Committee in the House of Representatives and by Finance in the Senate; spending is dealt with by the chambers' respective Appropriations Committees. These committees actually conduct much of their work in subcommittees rather than in the whole committees (see Chapter 9).

Coordination problems and terrain battles among committees are common. A person achieves the position of chair of a committee by serving a long tenure, and once having achieved that position, is unlikely to look favorably upon threats to the committee's powers. Nevertheless, some coordinating mechanisms are essential if realistic budgets are to be adopted. For example, if separate revenue and expenditure committees are free to act independently, then the situation is analogous to a couple with one member earning income and the other spending with only occasional references to how much is earned.

Fiscal Notes. One important mechanism that has been adopted is the requirement that fiscal notes be developed for most draft legislation. A fiscal note, a report that addresses the current and future costs of implementing a proposed bill, may include analysis of the purpose of the legislation, the proposed sources of funding, and the impact on other governments, as in the case of a state law affecting local government budgets.

The fiscal note is intended to help decision makers be better informed about the implications of draft legislation. For example, if a proposal provides for revising a state program for teenagers to include 13-year-olds, whereas only those 14 and above were included, the revision could greatly increase the number of clients served and the demand on resources. Fiscal notes also are prepared for revenue proposals, as in the case of forecasting the extra income that would be generated by increasing a state sales tax by 1 percentage point. Congress prepares fiscal notes to estimate the impact on state and local governments; the process is required under the State and Local Government Cost Estimate Act of 1981.[18]

Fiscal notes are typically prepared by legislative staff. At the state level, appropriations committees often have this responsibility. At the federal level, the Congressional Budget Office prepares fiscal notes regarding impacts on state and local governments.

Fiscal notes are particularly important at the state and local levels, where balanced budgets are required, that is, budgets in which projected expenditures do not exceed revenues. Indeed, the revenue estimates prepared by the executive coupled with any fiscal note on proposed revenue increases will greatly influence what spending programs the legislature will be able to approve.

In addition to fiscal notes, other mechanisms are devised to link together the work of committees and ensure that "reasonable" budgets are developed. Some states have used a system by which lump-sum amounts are assigned to program areas, and these funds then are distributed among programs within each area by standing committees and reported back to the appropriations committee for inclusion in their budget bills. Congress, as Chapter 9 shows, uses a variation of this approach. Local governments generally have less of a coordination problem, since most of the budget work will be handled by a single committee.

LEGISLATIVE ROLES

Legislative-Executive Interactions

In this section, we turn to how the executive relates to the legislative body.[19] Having seen that legislatures are not integrated wholes but rather consist of numerous subunits, this section considers how the executive relates to those subunits, especially to the two legislative chambers and their committees.

Authority. The executive and legislative branches of government in the United States are typically said to be coequal. Therefore the two branches tend to be wary of possible diminution of their powers and may seek strategies for demonstrating their independence. Confrontations between the two are sometimes akin to tests of strength, with each branch showing it is not subservient to the other.

The legislature is responsible for setting policy and the executive for executing policy. Conflicts arise as to the extent to which the executive becomes involved in policy making and the legislature in policy execution. The movement toward executive budget systems has placed the executive in the policy-making process, because the preparation of budget proposals by the executive is, in effect, the drafting of proposed policies. Congress, state legislatures, and city councils have found themselves in the position of reactors to executive recommendations and often not the formulators of policy.[20] To demonstrate their independence, then, legislatures may feel a compulsion to alter the proposed budget, no matter how compatible its recommendations may be with their own preferences.

Constitutional and legal constraints greatly affect the extent of executive and legislative powers in budgeting. The Budget and Accounting Act of 1921 and comparable legislation at the state level have granted substantial budgetary powers to the president and governors. Yet, in some states, the governor must share budget-making authority with other relatively independent executive officers and/or legislative bodies. In most states the legislature is free to adjust the governor's budget either upward or downward, but in a few states (Maryland, Nebraska, New York, and West Virginia) the legislature has limited or no authority to appropriate above what was recommended by the governor.

Constituency Differences. The legislative and executive branches have different constituencies and as a result have different perspectives on the budget. One common interpretation has been that the chief executive, being elected by the jurisdiction's entire constituency, has a broader perspective on the budget; a governor will attempt to satisfy the diverse needs of citizens throughout the state. Legislative bodies, on the other hand, have been seen as consisting of parochial individuals, who may be less impressed with governmentwide problems and therefore more likely to cut budgets. The legislature, then is seen as a protector of the treasury and as a budget cutter.

A competing view of legislative bodies is that in their desire to represent constituents they tend to be eager to spend resources far beyond what is financially sound, and that while the requirement for a balanced budget keeps that desire to spend in check at the state and local level, few constraints are evident at the national level. "Pork barrel" is a basic term of U.S. politics, referring to legislatively approved government projects that are aimed at helping home districts and states.[21] A standard complaint of "pork barrel" projects is that they have limited utility other than possibly winning votes for legislators seeking re-election.

Recent presidents have simultaneously attempted to advance their own legislative programs while minimizing the gap between high spending and lower revenues. For example, budgets submitted during the Reagan administration were intended to support a buildup in defense, and in order to minimize deficits sizable reductions in domestic programs were proposed. In such situations, almost regardless of political party positions, legislatures tend to be supportive of efforts to restore budget cuts proposed by the executive. Selective cuts may cost the executive few votes in a bid for re-election, whereas those same cuts can have dire effects on the political futures of many legislators.

Executive Fragmentation. An executive budget system provides the chief executive with control over budget preparation, but there is no guarantee that all units within the executive branch will subscribe fully to the budget's recommendations. The chief executive will not be uniformly in support of all portions of the budget; some recommendations will have been approved because of perceived political considerations. Typically, the chief executive will single out a few major recommendations for which approval is sought, with other recommendations being considered of low priority. The budget office will be expected to make general presentations on the overall recommendations contained in the budget, although the budget office may be lukewarm to many of those recommendations.[22]

Detailed defense of specific recommendations is normally the responsibility of the operating agencies. Because the heads of the agencies in a strong executive system are the appointees of the chief executive, they have an obligation to defend the budget recommendations, even though higher funding levels may be preferred. Agency representatives, however, may have little enthusiasm for defending budget proposals that call for deep cuts in programs. As a result, agencies attempt to calculate the extent to which they reveal their preferences for greater resources to the spending committees in the legislature while being "faithful" to the executive.

Influence of Bicameralism. One set of calculations from both the executive and legislative branch perspectives involves the relative roles of the two chambers. At the federal level, the Constitution requires that revenue or tax bills begin in the House of Representatives, namely with the Ways and Means Committee (Article I, Section 7). Until the 1974 reform legislation, the normal procedure was for the Senate Finance Committee to wait until the House completed action before taking up the tax bill. Appropriations were handled in a similar manner, although the practice was based on custom and not the

Constitution; appropriations bills began in the House and later were referred to the Senate. Under that system, strategists were able to concentrate their attentions on first one committee and then another as the legislation found its way through Congress. Since 1974, the House and Senate have simultaneously commenced work on the budget.

Where appropriations are handled sequentially, namely, beginning in the lower chamber and then moving to the upper chamber, the two chambers tend to take on different roles. Since a house of representatives tends to have more members than a senate, a house appropriations committee tends to have more members than its counterpart in the senate. This factor results in house committee members being able to specialize more in segments of the budget whereas senators must attempt to become informed on a large number of areas within the budget, and consequently may be viewed as amateurs. Members of the senate committee, in contrast, might consider themselves to have a broader awareness of total budget needs while house members are seen as excessively parochial. Also, given the step-by-step approach of appropriations from one chamber to another, the house appropriations committee tends to focus on the proposed budget whereas the senate committee focuses on what the house did to the proposed budget.[23,24]

Federal Aid to States. Turning specifically to state governments, one particular area of executive-legislative contention has been control over federal assistance.[25] Historically, legislative bodies did not appropriate federal funds coming into state treasuries. Governors contended that they acted as custodians over federal dollars and were bound by federal regulations that established how and for what purposes monies were to be spent; the conclusion followed that the legislature had no role in deciding about the use of these funds. However, governors on occasion were able to use federal grants to finance services that state legislatures opposed. The legislative view of this situation was and is that, once received, federal dollars become state dollars and can be spent only when approved by an appropriations bill adopted by the legislature. Although the Supreme Court has not ruled on this issue, the Court in 1979 let stand a lower court's ruling in favor of the legislature.[26]

The situation involving state appropriation of federal funds became more important starting in 1981 when Congress passed legislation creating large block grants to be administered by the states (see Chapter 14). Under these grant programs, the states were given increased flexibility in how they spend some of the grant monies and how they distribute the remainder to local governments.

The response has been for state legislatures to require that appropriations be passed before federal dollars can be spent. Florida, Ohio, and Washington, for example, appropriate specific amounts to programs and subprograms in considerable detail.[27]

Strategies. Regardless of what level of government is considered, executive-legislative relationships inevitably can be characterized as cat-and-mouse games, although it is not always clear who is the cat and who is the mouse. Strategies are devised in each branch to deal with the other. On the executive side a general posture that is almost ubiquitous is to cultivate clientele who will support requests for increased funding. Agencies are sensitive to where they locate various facilities; a new facility in a key legislator's district may gain the support of that legislator. Agencies pursue these strategies continuously as a matter of general posture.[28]

Contingent strategies, on the other hand, are limited to particular situations. No comprehensive cataloging of them is possible, because they vary from agency to agency and from circumstance to circumstance. However, they arise out of perceptions of what is possible in a given budget period. In growth periods, when revenue surplus or slack is evident, agencies may seek to expand existing programs or gain approval for the creation of new ones. Even when revenues are scarce, agencies may seek expansion, given that their areas are favored by the chief executive, as was the case of defense during the Reagan years. Sometimes obtaining approval for a new program may be easier than obtaining approval for expansion of an existing one; executives and legislators alike prefer being able to take credit for creation of a new program over simply enriching an existing one. A ploy that may be used is to start a new project with a small appropriation, getting the legislature accustomed to the program, and then seeking much greater appropriations in subsequent years.

When funds are less plentiful or "tight," the strategy may be to defend programs against cuts and to maintain what is called the "base." An agency's existing budget is often regarded as the base, with the budget process adding or subtracting increments to the base. Agencies have been known to warn that the slightest of budget cuts would necessarily diminish popular programs and thereby erode electoral support of legislators.

When cuts are perceived as inevitable, often because of a declining tax base and/or tax limitations, the strategy taken by an agency is to minimize cuts in the base and to obtain "fair share" funding. An agency will argue, on the one hand, that its programs are essential and should not be cut at all but, on the other hand, will insist that, if cuts must be made, they be no greater than cuts imposed on programs in other agencies.

While various strategies may be influential, there are limits to their effectiveness. Legislatures are influenced by personal values and committee role expectations as well as agency budget strategies and presentations. Agency strategies may influence the behavior of members of the appropriations committees, but perhaps the influence is limited in the sense of exploiting rather than creating favorable predispositions.

In response, legislators also devise a number of strategies for dealing with their budgetary responsibilities and agency strategies. A major problem is dealing with the capacity of agencies to produce vast amounts of information in support of their requests relative to the more limited capacity of a legislature to process all that information. Legislative strategies, then, may be seen as methods by which complex choices are simplified.

An appropriations committee or subcommittee finds it difficult, if not impossible, for example, to decide rationally if $83.6 million is the exact amount that should be granted to an agency.[29] Thus, legislators in appropriations committees look for other ways to determine what should be granted an agency. They place much of the burden for calculation upon the executive and demand that an agency justify its need for certain funds in response to probing questions. Detailed questions, which to outsiders may seem petty and trivial, are designed to determine how much confidence the subcommittee can place in the executive's testimony.

How the various strategies affect the outcomes of appropriations is uncertain and no doubt varies among jurisdictions and over time. One study of five western states that surveyed legislative staff, budget office staff, and agency officials found that the most important factor influencing appropriations was revenue availability.[30] The second factor was the legislature itself, followed by the governor and the budget staff. Agency influence was ranked fourth.

Item Veto. Once appropriations and revenue bills are adopted by the legislature, the approval phase is not necessarily completed. In over 40 states, governors have item-veto power, which permits reductions in amounts that have been appropriated.[31] State legislatures may seek to override these vetoes; usually a two-thirds vote is required to override. The item veto has three uses.[32,33]

1. It allows governors to keep total expenditures within what is anticipated to be available revenue.
2. The executive can reduce or even eliminate funds for projects or programs considered to be unworthy. The item veto can help curtail the excesses of pork barrel projects mentioned earlier.
3. The veto is used for partisan purposes, often in situations where the governor is of one political party and one or both chambers of the legislature are of another party.

From a practical standpoint, the item veto allows action by the governor without forcing the legislature to react unless it chooses to do so. Indeed, legislators may be privately pleased to have the governor item-veto some projects that were included in an appropriations bill to satisfy strong lobbying pressure.

At the federal level, the president does not have the item veto, although the last several presidents have endorsed the idea.[34,35] Instead, the president can veto only an entire appropriations bill. When this power is exercised, the House and Senate may override the veto by a two-thirds vote, but should the veto be sustained, the legislation is referred back to committee for further review. The disadvantage of the veto power for both Congress and the president is that much time and energy may be consumed in redrafting the legislation and negotiating an agreement between the two branches.

Congress, however, has been reluctant to provide the item-veto power to the president. The reason is obvious. After fighting hard to win the necessary votes to fund a program, members of the House and Senate could see all of that effort wasted by the stroke of the president's pen in reducing or eliminating the expenditure. Instead, a procedure known as "impounding" has been used, and that is explained in the next chapter.

Legislative Oversight

Not only are the executive and legislative branches typically separated in U.S. governments, but each branch is provided with powers that can be used to limit the powers of the other. The basic structure of this checks-and-balances system is set forth in the U.S. Constitution, state constitutions, and city charters. However, constitutional and statutory provisions must be implemented on a daily basis, and the extent to which one branch limits the other may fluctuate over time. In this section, we consider the increasing interest being given to the legislative body's overseeing of executive operations.[36,37]

Influences on Oversight. When revenues are limited and the demands for expenditures are seemingly limitless, legislators perceive a need for greater efficiency and effectiveness in government operations. Such perceptions increase the interest in oversight operations, which in turn increase pressure on administrative agencies to improve their operations while curtailing or even reducing expenditures.

There are, of course, other reasons for the current legislative oversight movement. Watergate during the Nixon administration and subsequent scandals and abuses of government funds have stimulated interest in greater legislative oversight. Financial crises in major cities have contributed to the interest in oversight.

Moreover, legislators are sincerely interested in using government to alleviate societal problems. Frustrated by what is perceived as inept administration, legislators are attracted to expanding their roles in the hope of improving government operations.

Methods. Legislative oversight can be performed using numerous methods. Providing authorization, revenue, and appropriations legislation constitutes one set of methods. Other familiar devices are laws that prescribe the structure of executive agencies and personnel policies involving hiring, promotion, and dismissal procedures. An informal type of oversight is the practice of a legislator contacting an agency about specific day-to-day operations; although legislators may have no official power to command any action of an agency, their wishes will not be treated casually by agency personnel.[38]

Legislative investigations or the simple threat of investigations are other instruments of oversight. A legislative committee chair may greatly influence an agency by suggesting that investigative hearings will be scheduled unless certain practices are changed within the agency.

Greater specificity of legislative intent is being used to reduce executive discretion. In the past, ambiguous language was used as a deliberate tool for delegating responsibilities to the executive and increasing executive flexibility in carrying out policies. The opposite is common today. State legislatures use several methods for establishing legislative intent: by wording contained in line items, footnotes, and concluding sections to appropriations bills; by committee reports; and by letters of intent delivered to the governor.

A problem of legislatures is enforcing legislative intent. What if an agency stays within the legal prescriptions of legislative intent but violates its spirit? The punitive action of cutting the agency's budget often is not possible; citizens benefiting from agency programs would be harmed as well as the agency itself. Therefore, the main punitive alternative may be to impose more restrictions on the agency, such as making legislative intent more explicit, specifically prohibiting various practices, and perhaps increasing the line items in the agency's budget in order to hamstring flexibility.

As part of legislative intent, there is increasing specificity of information that agencies are expected to collect and provide to the legislature. This practice denies agencies the tactic of confessing ignorance about their own programs; if legislation indicates an agency is to collect specific data, the agency will be expected to deliver it.

Sunset and Zero-Base. Another type of oversight mechanism is sunset legislation and zero-base legislative budgets. Programs are authorized to exist for a given period, after which they expire, or the sun sets on them. Before the sunset date, an agency may be required to present a zero-base budget, indicating the achievements of the agency's programs and the results if the programs were not renewed. Depending on how these proposals are implemented, they can provide greater leverage for the legislature. Sunset legislation has been used widely by state legislatures.[39,40]

Information and Analysis. Program budgeting and analysis constitute another approach to legislative oversight. Legislatures are increasingly demanding impact and output data from agencies; such demands have reinforcing effects on chief executives' efforts to install program budgeting.

A multiyear study of two state legislatures found that the nature of legislative review was related to budget format.[41] When line-item budgets were presented, about half of the questioning focused on the control orientation, which emphasizes keeping officials accountable for staying within spending ceilings, and 40 percent on the management orientation, which emphasizes efficiency. Budgets framed in terms of programs or organizational units resulted in legislators' devoting about 70 percent of their remarks to management-type questions and 15 percent or less to control-type questions.

Legislatures are developing their own capabilities to conduct analysis.[42] New York State's Legislative Commission on Expenditure Review and Virginia's Joint Legislative Audit and Review Commission are examples of state legislative analysis units.[43] At the federal level, the General Accounting Office has an extensive ongoing research agenda that examines the full gamut of governmental programs.[44,45]

Information technology also makes possible greater legislative oversight. Congress and state legislatures have developed their own information systems that allow them to tap into a variety of data bases, including those maintained by agencies. However, the application of this technology is limited by the quality of data being maintained; computer hardware and software cannot compensate for agency neglect in collecting important information.[46,47]

Legislative Veto. Legislatures are making increased use of the veto of proposed executive actions. For instance, an agency may be granted authority to issue regulations but a stipulation in the legislation can require the agency to obtain legislative approval prior to implementation of the regulations.[48,49] Depending on the governing legislation, a proposed action can be vetoed by a vote in either house or both houses of a legislature, or can be implemented only with a vote of approval from both houses. Sometimes legislative committees have veto powers.

The legislative veto is used as a means of furthering policy. Legislative intent is served presumably by allowing the full legislature or designated committees to oversee executive implementation. The veto process can steer executive agencies away from actions that are contrary to what the legislature wishes to see implemented.

Executives have a less positive view of legislative vetoes. The process often delays implementation of actions because the legislature is assured a given number of weeks to consider whether to support or veto a proposal. These vetoes are seen as giving authority to legislatures to meddle needlessly in the details of administration and, more significantly, to infringe upon the constitutional administrative powers of the executive.

A crisis seemed to develop in 1983 when the Supreme Court handed down one of its most controversial decisions in *Immigration and Naturalization Service v. Chadha*.[50,51] The case dealt with congressional veto power involving the deportation of aliens, but what was significant was not that the Court struck down that legislative veto but that it struck down most if not all such vetoes. The Court's reasoning was simple, namely that the Constitution provided for the House and Senate to set policy subject to veto by the president and did not allow for the opposite procedure.

Following the *Chadha* decision, Congress did not rush to adopt statutory measures or seek constitutional revisions that would reinstate the legislative veto. Instead, Congress dealt with matters as they arose and, in some instances, largely ignored the Court's ruling. For example, subsequent appropriations bills have included legislative vetoes.[52] The next chapter considers the veto power in regard to what are called "impoundments."

Oversight Limitations. While numerous methods of oversight are available, the organizational locus of oversight remains a problem because of the fragmentation discussed earlier. A coherent approach to oversight is not possible when committee powers overlap.[53] Every federal agency must deal with at least one substantive committee, the Appropriations Committee, and the Budget Committee (to be discussed in the next chapter) in each chamber of Congress. These committees may differ with each other and not have the backing of the full legislative body.

One approach to overcoming fragmentation might be to center oversight in a staff unit of the legislature. The General Accounting Office at the federal level could be given greater oversight responsibilities; other options would be to give committee staffs oversight duties. The problem with these suggestions is that they tend to conflict with legislators' keen sensitivity to having staffs act in subordinate and inferior capacities. For a staff unit to evaluate a program enacted by the legislative body, to find the program inadequate, and to suggest means of improving it is likely to be viewed by many legislators as an affront to their responsibility for setting policy. For this reason, legislative analytic units tend to be cautious in program analysis and tentative in reaching conclusions and recommendations.

A final limitation on oversight is the priorities legislators set for themselves.[54] Re-election is always paramount, and legislators often regard oversight activities as not contributing appreciably to their prospects for winning voter approval. Voters are seen as more supportive of legislators who initiate new programs than of those who serve as watchdogs over the executive branch.

SUMMARY

A variety of factors constrain the budgetary role of legislatures. The availability of revenue greatly influences how the legislature approaches budget approval. Previously reached decisions, such as established entitlement programs, limit action along with numerous socioeconomic-political considerations, such as the influential roles of interest groups. Fragmentation that results from bicameralism and the use of committees complicates the approval phase of budgeting, although political parties can help to overcome some of the fragmentation problems.

The budget is approved through the work of substantive standing committees, appropriations committees, and revenue or finance committees. Fiscal notes have become an important factor in tracking the financial implications of proposed legislation.

At least since the 1970s, a movement has existed to revitalize the role of legislatures vis-à-vis executives in the budgetary process. While in years past legislatures sometimes had a reputation for being budget cutters, more recently their role has been to represent constituents who would be harmed if proposed budget cuts were implemented. Governors, unlike presidents, have the power to item-veto appropriations that seem excessive.

Agencies use numerous strategies in seeking approval of their budgets. Administrators' objectives may be to obtain increased funding for new or expanded programs, but if that is not possible, then the objective becomes protecting the base and suffering no more than one's "fair share" of budget cuts.

Legislative oversight is increasingly popular. Prior legislative approval of some administrative decisions may be required. Legislative investigative hearings serve the oversight function along with detailed specification of legislative intent. Sunset legislation and zero-base budgeting are other techniques for oversight.

NOTES

1. William T. Pound, "Reinventing the Legislature," *State Legislatures* 12 (July 1986): 16–20.

2. William T. Hartman, *School District Budgeting* (Englewood Cliffs, N.J.: Prentice-Hall, 1988).

3. William J. Keefe and Morris S. Ogul, *The American Legislative Process: Congress and the States*, 6th ed. (Englewood Cliffs, N.J.: Prentice-Hall, 1985), pp. 267–304.

4. David B. Magleby, "Legislatures and the Initiative: The Politics of Direct Democracy," *State Government* 59 (1986): 31–39.

5. *Baker v. Carr*, 369 U.S. 186 (1962), and *Reynolds v. Sims*, 377 U.S. 533 (1964).

6. Malcolm E. Jewell, *Representation in State Legislatures* (Lexington: University Press of Kentucky, 1982).

7. Susan A. MacManus, "Mixed Electoral Systems: The Newest Reform Structure," *National Civic Review* 74 (1985): 484–92.

8. George Goodwin, Jr., *The Little Legislatures: Committees of Congress* (Amherst: University of Massachusetts Press, 1970).

9. *Book of the States, 1988–89* (Lexington, Ky.: Council of State Governments, 1988), p. 90.

10. David J. Vogler, *The Third House: Conference Committees in the United States Congress* (Evanston, Ill.: Northwestern University Press, 1971).

11. Heinz Eulau and Vera McCluggage, "Standing Committees in Legislatures: Three Decades of Research," *Legislative Studies Quarterly* 9 (1984): 195–270.

12. *Book of the States*, pp. 124–25.

13. Wayne L. Francis, "Leadership, Party Caucuses, and Committees in U.S. State Legislatures," *Legislative Studies Quarterly* 10 (1985): 243–57.

14. William T. Pound, "The State Legislatures," in *Book of the States*, pp. 76–83.

15. Keith E. Hamm, "The Role of 'Subgovernments' in U.S. State Policy Making," *Legislative Studies Quarterly* 11 (1986): 321–51.

16. Alan Rosenthal, *Legislative Life: Process and Performance in the States* (New York: Harper & Row, 1981).

17. James H. Bowhay and Virginia D. Thrall, *State Legislative Appropriations Process* (Lexington, Ky.: Council of State Governments, 1975).

18. Catherine H. Lovell and Hanria R. Egan, "Fiscal Notes and Mandate Reimbursement in the Fifty States," *Public Budgeting and Finance* 3 (Autumn 1983): 3–18.

19. Thomas P. Lauth, ed., "Symposium: Executive and Legislative Budgeting in Three States," *State and Local Government Review* 18 (1986): 47–70.

20. James J. Gosling, "Patterns of Influence and Choice in the Wisconsin Budgeting Process," *Legislative Studies Quarterly* 10 (1985): 457–82.

21. Joel A. Thompson, "Bringing Home the Bacon: The Politics of Pork Barrel in the North Carolina Legislature," *Legislative Studies Quarterly* 11 (1986): 91–108.

22. James J. Gosling, "The State Budget Office and Policy Making," *Public Budgeting and Finance* 7 (Spring 1987): 51–65.

23. Richard F. Fenno, Jr., *Power of the Purse: Appropriations Politics in Congress* (Boston: Little, Brown, 1966).

24. Stephen Horn, *Unused Power: The Work of the Senate Committee on Appropriations* (Washington, D.C.: Brookings, 1970).

25. Fred C. Doolittle, ed., "Mini-Symposium: State Legislatures and Federal Grants," *Public Budgeting and Finance* 4 (Summer 1984): 3–115.

26. *Shapp v. Sloan*, 480 Pa. 449, 391 A.2d 595 (1978); *Thornburgh v. Casey*, 440 U.S. 942 (1979).

27. Fred C. Doolittle, "State Legislatures and Federal Grants: An Overview," *Public Budgeting and Finance* 4 (Summer 1984): 7–23.

28. Aaron Wildavsky, *The New Politics of the Budgetary Process* (Glenview, Ill.: Scott, Foresman, 1988), pp. 70–119.

29. James E. Jernberg, "Information Change and Congressional Behavior: A Caveat for PPB Reformers," *Journal of Politics* 31 (1969): 736.

30. Sydney Duncombe and Richard Kinney, "The Politics of State Appropriation Increases: The Perspectives of Budget Officers in Five Western States," *State Government* 59 (1986): 113–23.

31. *Book of the States*, pp. 113–15.

32. Glenn Abney and Thomas P. Lauth, "The Line-Item Veto in the States," *Public Administration Review* 45 (1985): 372–77.

33. James J. Gosling, "Wisconsin Item-Veto Lessons," *Public Administration Review* 46 (1986): 292–300.

34. Thomas E. Cronin and Jeffrey J. Weill, "An Item Veto for the President?" *Congress and the Presidency* 12 (1985): 127–51.

35. Calvin Bellamy, "Item Veto: Dangerous Constitutional Tinkering," *Public Administration Review* 49 (1989): 46–51.

36. General Accounting Office, *Observations on Oversight Reform* (Washington, D.C.: Government Printing Office, 1981).

37. Bert A. Rockman, "Legislative-Executive Relations and Legislative Oversight," *Legislative Studies Quarterly* 9 (1984): 387–440.

38. Alan Rosenthal, "Legislative Behavior and Legislative Oversight," *Legislative Studies Quarterly* 6 (1980): 115–31.

39. William Lyons and Patricia K. Freeman, "Sunset Legislation and the Legislative Process in Tennessee," *Legislative Studies Quarterly* 9 (1984): 151–59.

40. Marcy Stephens, *The Status of Sunset in the States* (Washington, D.C.: Common Cause, 1982).

41. Gloria A. Grizzle, "Does Budget Format Really Govern the Actions of Budgetmakers?," *Public Budgeting and Finance* 6 (Spring 1986): 60–70.

42. Judith R. Brown, ed., "Mini-Symposium on Legislative Program Evaluation," *Public Administration Review* 44 (1984): 457–67.

43. Richard E. Brown, "Legislative Performance Auditing," *State Government* 52 (1979): 31–34.

44. Frederick C. Mosher, *The General Accounting Office: The Quest for Accountability in American Government* (Boulder, Colo.: Westview, 1978).

45. Frederick C. Mosher, *A Tale of Two Agencies: A Comparative Analysis of the General Accounting Office and the Office of Management and Budget* (Baton Rouge: Louisiana State University Press, 1984).

46. Robert D. Miewald and Keith J. Mueller, "The Use of Information Technology in Oversight by State Legislatures," *State and Local Government Review* 19 (1987): 22–28.

47. Robert D. Miewald, Keith Mueller, and Robert Sittig, *State Legislative Use of Information Technology in Oversight* (Washington, D.C.: Office of Technology Assessment, U.S. Congress, 1985).

48. Barbara H. Craig, *The Legislative Veto: Congressional Control of Regulation* (Boulder, Colo.: Westview, 1983).

49. James A. Gazell and Darrell L. Pugh, "The Legislative Veto and the Administrative State," *American Review of Public Administration* 17 (December 1987): 17–37.

50. *Immigration and Naturalization Service v. Chadha*, 462 U.S. 919 (1983).

51. Jonathan B. Fellows, "Congressional Oversight through Legislative Veto after *INS v. Chadha*," *Cornell Law Review* 6 (1984): 1244–66.

52. Daniel P. Franklin, "Why the Legislative Veto Isn't Dead," *Presidential Studies Quarterly* 16 (1986): 491–502.

53. William M. Pearson and Van A. Wigginton, "Effectiveness of Administrative Controls: Some Perceptions of State Legislators," *Public Administration Review* 46 (1986): 328–31.

54. Michael J. Scicchitano, "Congressional Oversight: The Case of the Clean Air Act," *Legislative Studies Quarterly* 11 (1986): 393–407.

9

Budget Approval: The U.S. Congress

The preceding chapter examined the budget approval process across levels and types of governments. This chapter, then, examines the special case of Congress, which is of unique importance in the U.S. governmental system and has unique procedures. Whereas the preceding chapter emphasized similarities among governments in how they adopt their budgets, this chapter considers the special processes used by Congress and the problems it faces.

The chapter has three parts, with the first reviewing developments in Congress until passage of the Congressional Budget and Impoundment Control Act of 1974. The next section examines experience under the law and notes differences in the period before 1981 and after, when Ronald Reagan became president. The third section discusses efforts to reduce deficits in the budget, most notably the reforms under Gramm-Rudman-Hollings. The section concludes by considering a variety of reform proposals.

EXPERIENCE PRIOR TO THE 1974 REFORMS

Authorizations, Revenues, and Appropriations

An axiom about Congress is that it conducts its work in committees. One group of committees, as explained in the preceding chapter, has responsibility for substantive legislation. The committees' job is to develop authorizing legislation, which establishes departments and agencies and the programs they operate. Beginning about 1950, committees turned increasingly to annual authorizations.[1,2] The advantage of this was that departments were required to testify annually before the committees to win approval for continuing departmental programs, thereby keeping departments "on a short leash" and increasing the oversight function of the committees.

Authorizations eventually came to include dollar ceilings, whether annual or multiyear. A department might be authorized to operate a given program for a maximum of $10 billion for one year or possibly four. The dollar ceiling often was well above what Congress was willing to appropriate for a program. The dollar authorization, in effect, gave an agency permission to spend money provided it could be obtained from the appropriations process.

Another set of committees has provided the wherewithal for the government to operate.[3] The Ways and Means Committee in the House and the Finance Committee in the Senate provide legislation that generates revenue for the government. In addition to being responsible for tax legislation, the committees are responsible for some substantive measures such as Social Security and Medicare. To handle these tasks, each committee has several subcommittees. In the case of the subcommittees dealing with Social Security, decisions must be made not only about what taxes are to be imposed but also about how those funds will be distributed among beneficiaries.

One of the most sensitive responsibilities of these committees is to recommend legislation permitting increases in the federal debt; such legislation has been necessary in that historically the government has spent more money than was available. The issue is sensitive because members of Congress fear that their voting for debt increases can be used by political rivals as evidence of fiscal irresponsibility. As a result, annual rituals occur over whether to increase the debt, but the outcome is always certain—approval of an increase is essential to allow the government to borrow funds and continue operating.

To handle these revenue-related duties, the Ways and Means Committee has about 35 members of the 435 members of the House, and the Finance Committee has 20 of the 100 members of the Senate. The number of seats held by each party on the committees is generally proportional to total party membership in the chambers.

Spending is under the aegis of the Appropriations Committee in each house.[4-7] There are nearly 60 members on the House committee and 30 on the Senate committee. The spending side of the government, in effect, is divided into 13 segments assigned to parallel subcommittees in the House and Senate that report out appropriations bills.

In addition to the 13 regular appropriations bills, Congress each year adopts one or more supplemental appropriations bills. These are necessary to correct situations in which an agency has insufficient funds to meet its legal responsibilities. Supplemental appropriations often are omnibus in scope, providing funding for numerous agencies.

Another matter to note about the Appropriations Committees is that they provide agencies with the authority to commit or obligate the government to spend money and historically have not exercised control over outlays or the expenditure of funds. An agency might receive an appropriation for $1.2 billion to provide a health program, but much of that money will not be expended during the current fiscal year. The funds will be obligated through grants or contracts, with expenditures occurring in subsequent fiscal years.

Two major problems became abundantly apparent with this process, starting in the 1940s. Since Congress dealt with the budget through a variety of bills, the budget was handled piecemeal, making the setting of overall comprehensive policy difficult. Second, the piecemeal approach meant that various subcommittees, committees, and the two chambers as a whole had to exercise discipline over themselves to complete their work in time for the beginning of the fiscal year.

When appropriations bills are not passed on time, agencies no longer have the funds to operate and are forced to close. In order to avoid this situation, Congress passes a continuing appropriations bill that basically permits the affected agencies to operate for a specified time period and to spend at the same level as they did in the just-completed fiscal year. When the federal government's fiscal year began on July 1, it was common for many or most appropriations bills not to have cleared Congress by the deadline, and agencies often operated for an entire fiscal year with continuing rather than regular appropriations.

Early Reforms and Emergence of Backdoor Spending

In an attempt to deal with these problems, Congress in 1946 passed the Legislative Reorganization Act, which provided for a fixed-ceiling or legislative budget. A maximum ceiling on the amount to be appropriated each year was to be prepared by a joint committee consisting of members from House Ways and Means, Senate Finance, and the two Appropriations Committees. A concurrent resolution was to be passed, with all agreeing not to appropriate above estimated revenues unless the public debt was increased in the same resolution. Therefore, as with the case of fixed-ceiling budgeting in the executive branch, Congress would determine in advance the resources to be allocated before considering program needs.

The legislative budget process failed. In 1947, the House and Senate could not reach agreement, and in 1948, the chambers reached agreement but ignored it. The following year the process collapsed. Congress simply was unprepared to implement this change. The essential political ramifications of budget making were not sufficiently taken into account.[8]

The failure of the legislative budget was followed by an attempt to appropriate all funds in a single omnibus bill rather than in the numerous separate appropriations bills. A feature that the omnibus appropriation shared with the legislative budget was the attempt to look at the budget as a whole. The profusion of appropriations bills makes it difficult to hold total spending in line; thus a single appropriation bill presumably would focus more attention on the question of total spending. The omnibus appropriation approved for fiscal year 1951 did leave Congress two months sooner than the last of the previous year's appropriations bills.

Despite the praise the omnibus approach received from some reformers, the House Appropriations Committee voted the following year to return to the traditional method of separate bills. The Senate Appropriations Committee was equally opposed to the omnibus approach.[9] The Budget Bureau (now the Office of Management and Budget [OMB]) also was critical of the approach, unless the president was given the item veto. Critics of the approach charged that it led to casual consideration of important details.

As Congress moved into the 1960s and 1970s, the situation became more complicated by what became known as backdoor spending, in which spending authority is provided outside of the appropriations process.[10,11] Backdoor spending may take several forms, including direct actions by substantive committees, such as approving contract authorizations and extending borrowing authority, and indirect actions, such as the relatively open-ended commitments authorized for various entitlement programs. Contract authority provided by substantive committees sometimes has allowed agencies to enter into contracts that obligate the government to spend even though funds are not made available to cover these obligations. Later, an agency that has made such contracts must obtain the needed appropriations from the Appropriations Committees.

Borrowing authority or authority to spend debt receipts allows an agency to borrow from the Treasury, incur obligations, and spend debt receipts, all of which are beyond the control of the Appropriations Committees. Farm price supports and public housing have been funded in this way.

A permanent appropriation may be considered still another form of backdoor spending. The appropriation may be for an indefinite period of time, such as an appropriation to cover interest to be paid on the national debt or trust fund expenditures, as in the case of Social Security and federal employee retirements.

Entitlement programs, starting in the 1960s, came to constitute one of the most rapidly growing forms of backdoor spending. These programs provide a virtually open-ended level of benefits to all qualifying applicants. For example, persons with black lung disease are entitled to benefits; therefore expenditures are a function of the number of persons qualifying for assistance.

The effect of backdoor spending was that virtually all committees in Congress came to play an important role in financial decisions, with no mechanism existing to coordinate these diverse activities. The result was that during the early years of the Nixon administration, Congress provided for spending well beyond what the president wanted and often beyond what Congress itself wanted. The president exercised his constitutionally granted veto power over various appropriations, but the disadvantages of that action were that Congress had to commit more energies to devising new bills that would be acceptable to President Richard M. Nixon and that agencies were forced to operate indefinitely with continuing rather than regular appropriations.

A deadlock between Congress and the president developed when Nixon began using an alternative mechanism known as impoundment. Instead of vetoing a bill, the president signed it but then refused to spend some or most of the money that had been provided, much to the uproar of Congress. The outcome was passage of the Congressional Budget and Impoundment Control Act of 1974 (PL 93-344), the topic of the next section.

BUDGET REFORMS, 1974–85

Many objectives underlie the 1974 reform legislation.[12] There was concern for providing Congress with a means for controlling the budget as a whole, namely linking appropriations bills with each other and linking these with revenue measures. Controlling the budget as a whole was seen as essential if Congress was to influence economic policy. Resolving conflict between Congress and the president was important and would require dealing with the impoundment problem. Members of Congress wished to reassert their policy-making role vis-à-vis the presidency. A process was needed by which Congress could complete its work on the budget by the beginning of the fiscal year.

It is important to recall the era in which these budget reforms were attempted. The Budget and Impoundment Control Act was signed into law in July 1974 by President Nixon. It was the time of the energy crisis, inflation, and economic stagnation. One month after the law's signing, Nixon was out of office, having been forced to resign as a result of the Watergate scandal involving his bid for re-election in 1972. Gerald R. Ford assumed the presidency.

The Nixon-Ford-Carter Era

Committees and Staff. To provide for coordination among the various components of Congress, the new law established House and Senate Budget Committees, whose members are representatives from the chambers' leadership and relevant committees—the four major money committees and the substantive committees that provide authorizations. There are 34 members on the House Budget Committee (HBC) and 24 on the Senate Budget Committee (SBC).

The new process provided Congress with additional staff support to handle the budget. Left in place were the staffs of the four money committees, the other standing committees, the leadership, and the individual members of Congress; staff was added to the new Budget Committees. In addition, a new congressional agency, the Congressional Budget Office (CBO), was created to serve as overall staff to the Budget Committees, the other four money committees, and any other committees or individuals in Congress that needed assistance in the area of budgeting; the CBO has a staff of between 200 and 250.

Timetable. The discussion here begins by explaining what was prescribed in the law and later turns to analysis of experience under the law. The timetable that the 1974 legislation created can be seen in Exhibit 9-1.[13] The new process was to begin with the president's submission of a current services budget to Congress no later than November 10; this budget was intended to show future financial requirements that would arise due to existing legislation. In January, the president would submit a proposed budget that showed how he would diverge from the current services budget. Substantive committees would review the proposed budget and make recommendations on their portions of the budget to the newly created House and Senate Budget Committees.

The instrument created to coordinate the various portions of the budget was a concurrent budget resolution setting forth the overall outline of the budget; the resolution requires approval of each chamber but not presidential approval. The resolution was to be prepared by April 15 and adopted by Congress no later than May 15. Five major parts were included in the resolution.

1. total outlays and new budget authority
2. outlays and authority by major function
3. the expected deficit or surplus
4. total revenues, indicating increases and decreases
5. the appropriate level of debt

According to the schedule, Congress then reverted to its old procedures. Subcommittees of the Appropriations Committees considered specific appropriations bills and the revenue committees considered their portion of the budget. One important difference, however, was that appropriations subcommittees were expected to stay within the functional ceilings contained within

Exhibit 9-1 Congressional Budget Process Timetable, Fiscal Years 1977–85

November	
10	President submits current services budget.
January	
14th day after Congress meets	President submits his budget.
March	
15	Committees and joint committees submit reports to Budget Committees.
April	
1	Congressional Budget Office submits report to Budget Committees.
15	Budget Committees report first concurrent resolution on the budget to their Houses.
May	
15	Committees report bills and resolutions authorizing new budget authority.
15	Congress completes action on first concurrent resolution on the budget.
September	
7th day after Labor Day	Congress completes action on bills and resolutions providing new budget authority and new spending authority.
15	Congress completes action on second required concurrent resolution on the budget.
25	Congress completes action on reconciliation bill or resolution, or both, implementing second required concurrent resolution.
October	
1	Fiscal year begins.

Source: Congressional Budget and Impoundment Control Act, Title III, section 300 (1974).

the concurrent resolution. Another difference was that the Budget Committees served as watchdogs, seeing that legislation was not substantially at variance with the resolution. The Budget Committees' powers in this respect were mainly persuasive, since the HBC and SBC could not require compliance with the functional ceilings in the concurrent resolution.

To allow for no changes in revenues, total outlays, and functional outlays after passage of the May resolution would be inadvisable. Therefore, a second resolution was to be adopted by September 15. The second resolution allowed for considering possible changes in the economy and various program needs that might require adjusting revenues or expenditures either upward or downward.

The second resolution contained information similar to that of the first and allowed Congress to direct the relevant committees to adjust spending and revenue measures upward or downward. This process of instructing committees of action to take, known as "reconciliation," is discussed later. Work on the budget was to be completed before October 1, the beginning of the new fiscal year; Congress gave itself three additional months—July, August, and September—to complete its budgetary work.

Adherence to the Timetable. The effort to improve the timing of congressional actions on appropriations bills was moderately successful in the early years of experience under the law. Congress used 1975 as a "trial run" for experimenting with implementation of the law, with 1976 being the first real test of the new process. Action in 1976 for the fiscal 1977 budget resulted in eight bills being passed by the beginning of the fiscal year, with the remainder clearing Congress by December 1. Fiscal 1978 and 1979 also were successes, with most bills passing Congress by October 15. In these early years, the memory of the deadlock between Congress and the president was vivid and both the House and Senate Budget Committees were able to cajole their colleagues into helping ensure that the new timetable was followed.

By the end of the Carter administration in January 1981, Congress had slipped badly in adhering to the schedule it had set for itself; for fiscal 1981, six appropriations bills were late in clearing Congress by two months or more and three bills never were passed, forcing the affected agencies to operate with continuing appropriations. Under the 1974 law, Congress had given itself three additional months to act on appropriations, but by 1981 it was experiencing as much difficulty acting on time as when the fiscal year began on July 1.

New Relationships. The new budget process altered significantly relationships between the House and the Senate. Since a concurrent budget resolution was expected of them in the early spring of each year, the bodies were forced into coordinating their activities early in the approval cycle rather than waiting until conference committees were convened for particular tax and spending bills. This change in timing also meant that the Senate began its budget work earlier than before and no longer served as an "appeals court" to which agencies brought their complaints over the action taken earlier by the House and its Appropriations Committee.[14,15]

The law necessitated the development of a set of relationships among the CBO, other congressional staffs, and OMB. Staffs of long-established committees were not necessarily eager for the CBO to play a prominent role in budgeting. OMB, from the outset, had to be concerned with the CBO's calculations on what revenues and expenditures would result from different economic forecasts.

Impoundments. In addition to the new Budget Committees, the CBO, and the new timetable, the 1974 law established a procedure for impoundments. These executive decisions simply halt selectively the spending of appropriated funds. Since Thomas Jefferson's administration probably most presidents have impounded monies, often at the outrage of major segments of Congress.[16]

As noted earlier, the issue came to a head during the early 1970s when Nixon extended the use of impoundments over a wide range of appropriations. The argument was made that the president had a constitutionally implied power to impound, given the constitutional requirement that he faithfully execute the laws. Because the Employment Act of 1946 assigned to the president responsibility for economic policy and because Congress had no means of coordinating revenue and spending legislation, the president supposedly had the responsibility of limiting expenditures to achieve desired economic objectives.

The impoundment power also was defended on the grounds that cutbacks were necessary to keep within the public debt ceiling set by Congress. Also, the Anti-Deficiency Act of 1950, allowing the executive to establish agency reserves in the apportionment process (see Chapters 3 and 10), was used as further support.

Impoundments were used prior to the 1974 reforms not only for economic reasons but also as political tools. The Nixon administration refused to release some grant monies to state and local governments in the hope that such action would force Congress into approving special revenue sharing or block grants (see Chapter 14).

Several court suits developed, which generally were decided in favor of releasing funds. *Train v. New York City* (1975) was the only case decided by the Supreme Court; the Court ruled that grant funds for sewers and sewage treatment plants should be released in that Congress had specified in the governing legislation that the funds were urgently needed.[17] The Court did not address the issue of whether the president has a constitutional power to impound monies.

The Congressional Budget and Impoundment Control Act represented a compromise between the legislative and executive branches, albeit a compromise that the Nixon administration was forced to accept. Two forms of impoundments were permitted—rescissions and deferrals. When in the judgment of the president part of or all funds of a given appropriation are not needed, a rescission proposal was to be made to Congress; the rescission would not take effect unless approved by Congress within 45 working days. The other type of impoundment, deferral, was a proposal to delay obligations or expenditures. As with rescissions, deferral proposals must be submitted to Congress, but these became effective unless either the House or Senate passed a resolution disapproving the proposal.

During the early years under the 1974 law, proposed rescissions and deferrals competed for the attention of Congress with the need to approve the budget for the upcoming fiscal year. The president could propose a series of extensive rescissions, which Congress might take many weeks to handle. Even when Congress rejected a rescission, the issue was not necessarily settled, since the president could then propose a related deferral.[18]

The impoundment process was dealt a major blow by the Supreme Court in *INS v. Chadha* (1983), which prohibited most uses of the legislative veto (see Chapter 8).[19,20] In effect, the 1974 law had given the president a form of item veto coupled with a legislative veto, but those were nullified by the *Chadha* decision. Lower courts ruled in 1986–87 that, since Congress would not have granted the impoundment power without retaining for itself the veto power, the two were inseparable and therefore the president was denied the impoundment power under the law.[21] The president, then, has been forced to request congressional action on policy rescissions and deferrals, and Congress has not amended the 1974 legislation to bring it into conformance with the *Chadha* decision. One approach might be to have Congress act on impoundments through joint resolutions, since these require presidential signatures and presumably would pass muster with the Supreme Court.[22]

Congress Reoriented. Before turning to the experience during the first part of the Reagan administration, there are two major trends that should be noted. First, Congress dramatically changed its mode of operations during this period. In an earlier time, committee chairs were held by the most senior members of Congress. They had become senior by coming from districts and states where re-election was routine. The chairs of committees tended to be southern conservatives, commonly seeing their job as protecting the treasury from the excessive spending tendencies of presidents. During the Nixon and Ford years, roles were reversed on spending proclivities, and less senior members were able to gain seats on important committees, such as the Appropriations Committees, and to become chairs of these committees.

There were other important changes in the congressional political environment.[23,24] Members of the House and Senate asserted greater independence in speaking their views on issues, despite the views held by their parties' leadership. There was a greater tendency to allow amendments to bills in floor debate, amendments that might well be opposed by the sponsoring committees.[25] The Ways and Means Committee's membership was enlarged, allowing less senior members to be added without removing more senior ones, and subcommittees were established that diluted the power of the committee's chair. Both the House and the Senate became more democratic institutions in regard to the roles played by their members. However, that meant that the leadership of the two parties exercised less discipline, making more difficult any coordinated, comprehensive approach to congressional budgeting.

The Controllability Problem. The other change to note is that the budget was becoming increasingly uncontrollable, meaning that, barring any major readjustment in commitments to programs, much of the budget could not be controlled in a given year. Contributing to this situation are multiyear contracts with government suppliers, such as defense contractors, multiyear grants to state and local governments, and entitlement programs that guarantee benefits to eligible clients. Interest due on the national debt must be paid and therefore is uncontrollable. As debt has become a larger portion of the budget, the budget's controllability has decreased. OMB estimated that 73 percent of the 1981 budget was relatively uncontrollable, compared with only 63 percent for the 1970 budget.[26,27] (That percentage was to climb further during the Reagan years.)

Another aspect of controllability emerged in the late 1970s pertaining to what came to be called the "federal credit budget," involving direct and guaranteed loans by the government to individuals, corporations, state and local governments, and foreign governments. The segment of the federal credit budget that grew substantially in size and therefore grew in importance were loans from so-called government-sponsored enterprises (GSEs), which operate with government endorsement but are largely independent of daily government control. Included are the Federal Home Loan Bank System, the Financing Corporation (FICO) of the Federal Savings and Loan Insurance Corporation, and the Federal National Mortgage Association (Fannie Mae). These GSEs were to become of even greater importance during the Reagan administration.

As the federal credit budget grew along with other so-called "uncontrollables," Congress was left with a smaller portion of total federal operations to act upon each year.

The Reagan Era, 1981–85

Ronald W. Reagan was swept into office in January 1981 following a major victory at the polls the previous November. The 1980 election created a phenomenon not seen since the 83rd Congress of 1953—the Senate dominated by a Republican majority, the House remaining under the control of the Democrats, and a Republican president.

According to law, outgoing President Jimmy Carter submitted his budget to Congress just five days before Reagan became president. The new president submitted a set of budget proposals in March that provided for severe budget cuts in domestic programs, a shift toward the use of block grants to state and local governments (see Chapter 14), and a buildup in defense spending. The administration recommended a massive set of cuts in the personal income tax that became law in the Economic Recovery Tax Act of August 1981. Although the House of Representatives was under the control of the Democrats, there was little "loyal opposition" to the president's recommendations. Reagan's popularity was of such magnitude that few political leaders dared to speak out against his recommended policies.

The early Reagan years ushered in an increasingly important role for OMB.[28,29] In earlier times, OMB had had the job of making overall presentations on the budget before congressional committees, but the defense of specific recommended appropriations was left to the affected departments. During the Reagan years, in contrast, major realignments in policies were being recommended on both the revenue and expenditure sides of the budget, and the defense of these recommendations became the job of OMB. Director David A. Stockman, a former congressman himself, demonstrated an ability to deal with congressional committees on the details of a host of administration-recommended policies.[30,31]

The Deficit Milieu. A cloud soon developed over the euphoria of early 1981 as one item came to dominate budget considerations and dominate Congress itself. The budget's deficit began to grow at an alarming rate.[32,33] A national economic recession—the worst since the Depression of the 1930s—forced federal expenditures upward while revenues declined, but once the economy came out of the recession, the outlook was no better for reducing the budget's deficit. The administration had championed the 1981 massive tax cuts as a means of stimulating the economy, which in turn would increase revenues. That desired pattern simply did not materialize sufficiently to avoid large deficits. Forecasts indicated that the budget would be considerably out of balance for the foreseeable future.

Members of Congress exhibited more concern for avoiding blame for the situation than for gaining credit for bold new directions.[34] One of the first victims of the situation was what was supposed to be the annual adoption of the second concurrent budget resolution. These were adopted each year by Congress through 1981. In that year the resolution was not adopted until mid-December, even though the 1974 law required its adoption by September 15. The reason for the delay was that an "honest" resolution would depict the budget grossly out of balance; Congress avoided admitting to the situation by basing the December resolution on a set of fanciful assumptions that had the effect of reducing the projected deficit. That year, 1981, was the last in which Congress adopted a second budget resolution. In later years, the first resolution was made binding either at the time of adoption or by the beginning of the fiscal year.

Another consequence of the deficit milieu was that Congress more than ever before did not want to vote to increase the total national debt. Yet debt ceiling increases were essential; the limit had to be raised to $1.1 trillion in 1981 and $2.1 trillion in 1985. One practice developed in the House was to include the debt increase in the budget resolution, allowing members to approve raising the ceiling while voting on a more general budget package.

Timetable Problems. Congress has always been prone to letting schedules slide until crises develop, but during the 1980s this pattern became pervasive. Essential bills were often passed at the last moment, such as when appropriations bills expired at the end of the fiscal year, when the debt limit was about to be reached forcing a halt to government borrowing and government operations, and when Congress wanted to adjourn so that members could campaign for their own re-election.

The use of stopgap continuing appropriations resolutions became characteristic. For example, only one appropriations bill cleared Congress by October 1, 1981, the start of fiscal year 1982. A stopgap appropriations bill was passed to keep the government operating, but the bill expired in November. Another temporary bill was passed, with its expiration set for a month later. That bill expired before Congress could act, forcing the president to send workers home. Another continuing appropriations bill was passed that expired in March, followed by still another that carried the affected departments through the remainder of the fiscal year.

The same type of record was set from 1982 through 1985. Congress adopted stopgap appropriations bills and then completed its work each year by passing a continuing appropriations bill that covered many or most agencies through the remainder of the entire fiscal year.

Stalemate. Substantive problems were to blame for the congressional debacle in adhering to the prescribed timetable. President Reagan during these years took a firm stand on priorities; he wanted the tax cuts that had been approved in the 1981 law, wanted a buildup in defense expenditures, insisted that programs such as Social Security be protected from budget cuts, *and* at the same time wanted a balanced budget.

Those objectives simply could not be met simultaneously. In fiscal 1983, for example, total outlays were $728 billion, including $210 billion for defense, $203 billion for Social Security and Medicare, and $90 billion for interest on the national debt.[35] In that year, the deficit was $128 billion. If the budget was to be brought into balance by reducing the unprotected areas of the budget, which included an array of social programs, including Aid to Families with Dependent Children, the remaining part of the federal government would have been decimated.

The result was a stalemate between the president and Congress, with the two occasionally reaching agreement on actions that only marginally improved the situation.[36] Cuts in programs, of course, were one avenue.[37] Other options included having beneficiaries of programs pay a greater share of the services they received, as in the case of Medicare patients. Some increases in taxes were possible, as in customs duties and business taxes, but the president was prepared to veto any personal income tax increase and Congress was not inclined to provide such a political opportunity for him.

Congress adopted extraordinarily large pieces of financial legislation during this period. The Omnibus Budget Reconciliation Act of 1981 had 577 pages, the Economic Recovery Tax Act, also of 1981, had 185 pages. The Tax Equity and Fiscal Responsibility Act (TEFRA) of 1982 had 384 pages, and that year's second continuing appropriations bill had 95 pages. The use of massive continuing appropriations bills was the result of congressional failure to pass separately the 13 regular bills in time for the beginning of the fiscal year. Some of the large bills involved reconciliation.

Reconciliation. As noted above, reconciliation was intended to provide in one resolution directed guidance to committees on how they should alter authorizing, taxing, and spending legislation. The process was envisioned as coming at the end of the budget approval phase. However, in the early years of experience under the 1974 reforms, the House and Senate Budget Committees were reluctant to use reconciliation in that it would have been seen as infringing upon the domains of powerful committees and as personal affronts to the committee chairs.

The reconciliation process was used for the first time in 1980, the last year of the Carter administration; starting in 1981, reconciliation became a prominent feature of congressional budgeting.[38] Significantly, reconciliation was used early in the 1981 approval process, with the bill clearing Congress in July rather than in September as originally intended. Early action was needed in order to give affected committees sufficient time to adhere to the reconciliation instructions, such as reducing amounts in a given appropriations bill.

There are at least four major observations to be made about the use of reconciliation and other large financial bills. First, the size and complexity of these bills defy individual comprehension. When these bills are assembled, even the members of the originating committees may not be familiar with all of the detail. Large bills are open invitations to pork barrel politics, in which some members are successful in adding pet projects or programs that, if required to stand by themselves for approval, might not be accepted by Congress.

Second, large bills place the president at a distinct disadvantage in that he must either accept or reject the bills in their entirety. If a bill is rejected and the veto is sustained in the Congress, then Congress must devote energy to reworking the bill in order to avoid another veto.

Third, large bills are compatible with congressional interests in avoiding blame. Members of the House or Senate simply cannot be held accountable for their votes supporting any one aspect of a bill. Senators can fend off any rebukes by indicating that they felt compelled to vote for the bill even though it admittedly was flawed in numerous respects.

Fourth, the use of large bills and Congress's preoccupation with budgeting in the 1980s has contributed to centralization of decision making at a time when Congress has been democratized.[39] Power seems to have been redirected to those most closely associated with the budget process.

Shifts in Power. The trend toward annual authorizations noted earlier has been reversed to the point that the only important authorization dealt with each year is that of defense, which is reported out by the House and Senate

Armed Services Committees. Serving on other standing committees, then, has become less attractive to members of Congress.[40] The reconciliation process has diminished the roles of these committees, since those bills often provide instructions on how much funding may be authorized.[41]

Power, then, has shifted away from substantive committees toward some combination of the four long-established money committees and the two relatively new Budget Committees. What the balance of power is among these committees varies from year to year and from chamber to chamber.

Members of both Appropriations Committees express concern that their powers are diminished through the reconciliation process that is under the direction of the Budget Committees. Reconciliation admittedly involves far more members of Congress than those who serve on the HBC and the SBC. In working out a conference bill between the two chambers, the numerous subconference committees created include conferees who are not members of either the HBC or the SBC.[42] Nevertheless, the Appropriations Committees see the situation as centralizing power in the hands of the Budget Committees.

Controllability and Policy Making. An additional woe of the Appropriations Committees is that much of the budget increasingly is outside of their annual control.[43] As noted earlier, entitlements, which do not require annual appropriations, have come to dominate much of domestic spending, leaving only a comparatively minor role for appropriators.

The deficit situation during the 1980s imposed constraints on Congress in regard to what it could and could not fund. The Reagan administration proposed numerous cuts in programs that were not popular in Congress. While Congress has every right to reject the recommendations of a president, the problem arose that in rejecting these proposed savings and not wanting to adopt a budget more out of balance than recommended by the president, Congress was forced to find offsetting measures to raise revenues, cut expenditures, or both.

There was a tendency to impose across-the-board budget cuts on programs. This meant that programs became smaller and smaller; advocates of programs struggled to maintain the existence of programs, no matter how small they might become. "Staying alive" became an objective, since it would be extremely difficult to revive a program once cut out of the budget.

Whether Congress made substantive policy during this period is difficult to determine.[44,45] While what Congress approved is different from what the president recommended, that does not necessarily mean Congress had a great influence on policy. It should be understood, of course, that both branches take each other into account when advocating policy. The president's budget is based in part on an assessment of what he thinks Congress will approve; similarly, congressional actions always take into account possible presidential reactions.[46]

Impact on Departments. The uncertainty of a department's programs, given recommended cuts by the president, is unsettling; the uncertainty is compounded when Congress delays taking action and resorts to continuing appropriations bills. Congressional budgeting problems resulted in workers being briefly sent home in November 1981 and October 1986. There were numerous other cliffhangers in which Congress narrowly met a deadline before workers were sent home for lack of government funding. Crises such as these are administratively disruptive.

There have been sharp criticisms of congressional requirements that departments testify; this activity often is considered a waste of executives' time in both preparing for and giving testimony. The defense area is particularly redundant with congressional involvement. On average in the first half of the 1980s, Defense Department representatives testified annually before 84 committees and subcommittees.[47]

The Blue Ribbon Packard Commission in 1986 was highly critical of how Congress had become involved in the details of defense management.[48] Interestingly, a scandal in defense procurement developed two years later. All of the congressional involvement in defense decision making apparently had little effect in keeping corruption out of the defense industry.

As congressional committees are eager to find places to cut departmental budgets, there is little incentive for departments to offer suggestions in this area. Indeed, there may be a tendency for agencies to avoid most initiatives, because they draw attention and could inadvertently result in budget cuts. Where program changes are recommended, there is an emphasis on suggesting methods of self-financing those changes, such as introducing or increasing user fees.

1985 AND AFTER

The situation came to a crisis in the latter part of 1985. Democrats agreed with Republicans and House members agreed with senators that the deficit situation had become intolerable. The White House did not exhibit the same level of concern but concurred that something should be done to remedy the situation.

Gramm-Rudman-Hollings

By October 1, 1985, the beginning of the fiscal year, not a single appropriations bill had cleared Congress; a stopgap continuing appropriations bill was passed to keep the government operating. The budget resolution had been adopted on August 1, despite the official deadline of May 15. By November the stopgap appropriations bill was expiring, the debt-limit ceiling was expiring, and the president was scheduled to leave for Geneva, Switzerland, to meet with Soviet leader Mikhail Gorbachev. Another stopgap appropriations bill was rushed through Congress along with an increase in the debt ceiling in mid-November.

Law's Enactment. It was in this politically charged atmosphere that Congress adopted the Balanced Budget and Emergency Deficit Control Act of 1985 (PL 99-177).[49-51] The chief authors were Senators W. Philip Gramm (Republican of Texas), Warren B. Rudman (Republican of New Hampshire), and Ernest F. Hollings (Democrat of South Carolina). As an indication of how Congress had changed (see earlier discussion), both Gramm and Rudman were serving their first terms in the Senate; in an earlier time, only more senior senators would have authored legislation of such importance.

The main objective of Gramm-Rudman-Hollings (GRH) was simple: to reduce annually the size of the budget deficit until expenditures were in balance with revenues. Target figures were set, and if the president and Congress could not reach agreement on a budget package that met the target figure for a given fiscal year, then automatic across-the-board reductions in expenditures were to occur. Senator Rudman described the law as "a bad idea whose time has come."[52]

Legal Challenge and Revision. As soon as the law was enacted, it was challenged in court. The case was swiftly acted upon by a special lower court and then appealed to the Supreme Court, which ruled in July 1986 that one key provision violated the Constitution (*Bowsher v. Synar*).[53,54] The Court ruled that the comptroller general, being an officer of Congress, had been unconstitutionally assigned executive powers. In anticipation of such a ruling, the 1985 law included a fallback procedure, but it was one that did not have sufficient restrictions to force compliance with the deficit targets that had been established.

After much debate, Congress in September 1987 adopted the Balanced Budget and Emergency Deficit Control Reaffirmation Act (PL 100-119).[55] In the interim between the *Bowsher v. Synar* decision and the 1987 revisions, the Republicans lost control of the Senate in the November 1986 elections; when Congress convened in January 1987, the Democrats controlled both chambers while the White House was still controlled by Republican President Ronald Reagan.

Timetable. Exhibit 9-2 illustrates the schedule established by the 1985 law as revised in 1987; the schedule in the table applies to fiscal 1989 through 1993, while a phase-in schedule was provided for fiscal 1988.[56] The annual allowable deficits, in billions of dollars, are as follows:

FY 1988	144	FY 1991	64
FY 1989	136	FY 1992	28
FY 1990	100	FY 1993	0

Exhibit 9-2 Congressional Budget Process Timetable, Fiscal Years 1989–93

January	
1	Date from which deficit reduction is measured.
First Monday after	
January 3	President submits budget to Congress.
February	
15	Congressional Budget Office (CBO) issues annual report to Budget Committees.
25	Committees submit views and estimates to Budget Committees.
April	
1	Senate Budget Committee reports budget resolution.
15	Congress completes budget resolution.
May	
15	Appropriations bills may be considered in the House.
June	
10	House Appropriations Committee reports last annual appropriations bill.
15	Congress completes reconciliation.
30	House completes action on annual appropriations bills.
July	
15	President submits mid-session budget.
August	
15	Office of Management and Budget (OMB) and CBO estimate deficit for upcoming fiscal year; presidential notification regarding military personnel.
20	CBO issues its initial report to OMB and Congress.
25	OMB issues its initial report to president and Congress; president issues initial sequester order.
September	
6	Deadline for president's explanatory message on initial order.
October	
1	Fiscal year begins.
10	CBO submits revised report to OMB and Congress.
15	OMB issues its revised report to president and Congress; president issues final sequester order, effective immediately.
	Congressional alternative to presidential order, if any, developed and adopted.
30	Deadline for president's explanatory message on final order.
November	
15	Comptroller general compliance report issued.

Source: The Congressional Budget Process: An Explanation, 100th Congress, 2nd session, Senate Committee on the Budget, p. 26, Government Printing Office, 1988.

The GRH process begins with the president's submitting his budget in early January. The president must provide a current services budget taking into account projected changes in the economy involving employment rates and prices (inflation) and changes in clients to be served under entitlement programs (the greater the number of eligible clients, the greater the resource requirement).

Provisions are made for calculating a "baseline," which is analogous to but not identical to current services calculations. The baseline projects revenues, expenditures, and the resulting deficit or balance. For these calculations, the off-budget is included with the on-budget (see Chapter 6). Government-sponsored enterprises (see above), however, are not part of the baseline, nor are tax expenditures.

In response to the president's submission of the budget, the various substantive and money committees prepare reports that are submitted to the House and Senate Budget Committees for consideration. The deadline for this is February 25, whereas under the procedure adopted in 1974 the deadline was March 15. The intent here is to accelerate this early step in budget approval in order to reserve time for later deliberations and to help ensure that the budget work is completed by the beginning of the fiscal year.

The deadline for adoption of a budget resolution is April 15, after which the House begins deliberations on specific appropriations bills. The previous deadline was May 15. Reconciliation follows, to be completed by June 15, after which the president prepares a mid-session budget due July 15.

Sequestration. The forced procedure for reducing the deficit, known as sequestration, begins in August. The CBO and OMB prepare separate reports estimating the deficit in the budget package that has been approved by Congress. It is at this point that baseline calculations become critical, since the results indicate how much spending must be eliminated from the budget unless revenues are to be increased through higher taxes and the like.

On August 25, the president issues his initial sequester order, indicating cuts to be made in programs, projects, and activities (PPAs), and that order becomes effective on October 1, the beginning of the fiscal year. In the next two weeks, Congress and the president can attempt to develop an alternative plan, but barring the approval of such a plan, the president is required to issue a final sequester order by October 15. These rigid provisions are waived only when specific conditions of economic recession exist or when war is declared.

Budget reductions are handled by formula, leaving little room for presidential discretion. Baseline calculations determine what amount must be cut from projected spending. Half of the cuts occur in defense and the other half in domestic programs. Congress insisted upon this division in that it did not want to attempt to balance the budget with defense activities exempt. A percentage is derived as to how much each PPA will be cut, so that the president does not have authority to impose more severe cuts on some programs and less severe ones on others.

Special rules apply to some domestic programs, such as Medicare and guaranteed student loans; the rules generally limit the severity of sequestration. Other PPAs are totally protected from sequestration. These include the basic retirement program under Social Security, Aid to Families with Dependent Children, civil service retirement funds, and the like. The budgets of Congress and the courts are *not* exempt from sequestration.

It should be stressed that sequestration is a procedure of last resort. The process is used only in the event that Congress fails to develop a budget that stays within the deficit limit specified in the law *and* that meets with the approval of the president, since he could veto whatever Congress developed. Sequestration is thought to be so unpalatable to both Congress and the president that it forces the two sides to work together in order to avoid triggering the process.

1987 Budget Accord. Less than a month after Congress passed the Reaffirmation Act of 1987, the stock market crashed; on Tuesday, October 19, the Dow Jones Industrial Average dropped 508 points or 22.6 percent. That drop compared with one of only 12.8 percent on October 28, 1929.[57]

The crash, as would be expected, had a startling effect on both private and public sector leaders. There was concern that unless the government's budget deficit situation was brought under control, there would be a depression of vast proportions. Although the depression did not materialize, the situation served as a catalyst to force an agreement on budget deficit reduction. A summit meeting was called between the president and the leadership in Congress, and in November a two-year agreement was reached on cutting the deficit. This accord was outside of the Gramm-Rudman-Hollings law but was implemented using it. After four stopgap measures, Congress on December 22 passed a huge continuing appropriations bill for the remainder of the fiscal year along with a reconciliation bill. Exhibit 9-3 provides a chronological account of the major budgetary events pertaining to adoption of the fiscal 1988 budget.

GRH and the 1987 budget accord have contributed to the trend toward centralization mentioned earlier. Both have provided for decision making to be handled by central players, with lesser figures being told what the parameters of the budget will be. Meanwhile, the trend toward uncontrollability has continued. Reagan's budget for fiscal 1989 envisioned that 77 percent of the budget was relatively uncontrollable.[58] The budget states: "The outlays from permanent appropriations, together with the outlays from obligations incurred in prior years from both permanent and current authority, comprise most of the outlay total for any year in the budget."[59]

Whether Congress will be able to make the revised Gramm-Rudman-Hollings process work is uncertain, especially in light of past reform experiments. At the same time, the problem remains whether in making the

Exhibit 9-3 U.S. Budget Approval Process, Fiscal Year 1988*

January 1987

5   Democratic Party regains control of Senate after six years of Republican control.

5   Budget submitted by President Reagan to Congress.

May

14   First debt ceiling clears Congress (PL 100-40); signed May 15.

June

24   Budget resolution clears Congress (H. Con. Res. 93). Budget totals are binding.

July

29   Second debt ceiling clears Congress (PL 100-80); signed July 30.

August

7   Third debt ceiling clears Congress (PL 100-84); signed August 10.

September

23   Balanced Budget and Emergency Deficit Control Reaffirmation Act clears Congress (PL 100-119); signed September 20. Includes fourth debt ceiling increase.

25   First continuing appropriations resolution clears Congress (PL 100-120); signed September 30. Expires November 10.

October

1   No appropriations bill passed by beginning of fiscal year.

19   Stock Market crash.

November

6   Second continuing appropriations resolution clears Congress (PL 100-162); signed November 10. Expires December 16.

20   Budget Summit Accord reached between Congress and president.

December

16   Third continuing appropriations resolution clears Congress (PL 100-193); signed December 16. Expires December 18.

20   Fourth continuing appropriations resolution clears Congress (PL 100-197); signed December 20. Expires December 20.

21   Fifth continuing appropriations resolution clears Congress (PL 100-202); signed December 22. 450 pages. Covers all 13 appropriations bills.

21   Omnibus Budget Reconciliation Act clears Congress (PL 100-203); signed December 22. 473 pages.

*Exhibit excludes some items for clarity and brevity reasons. Not listed are actions on individual authorization and appropriations bills or actions taken by House and Senate committees, conference committees, and each chamber.

Source: Congressional Quarterly Weekly Report, Congressional Quarterly, 1987; and *U.S. Code: Congressional and Administrative News*, West Publishing Company, 1987.

---

process work Congress is able to set policy, given that so much of the budget is outside of its annual control.

Reforms and the Future

There is always a plethora of proposals in circulation for reforming how Congress conducts its business. Of course, many proposals have been adopted, most notably in the case of budgeting with the 1974 reforms and Gramm-Rudman-Hollings as contained in the 1985 and 1987 legislation.

There also are a host of substantive proposals for how to reduce the deficit. In 1988, the National Economic Commission (NEC) was appointed to examine how the budget could be brought into balance. The commission consisted of appointees from the White House and Congress.[60] While the commission considered a host of possible reforms, its members divided sharply along political party lines and failed in 1989 to reach a consensus position.

This section, rather than focusing on the substantive problems associated with the deficit, highlights some of the proposals that pertain to congressional budgeting.[61-63] First there is a set of technical problems that need to be addressed; the possible solutions, while technical in nature, have policy and political implications.

Technical Corrections. Confusion exists over the calculation of a variety of baselines developed by OMB and the CBO. OMB, for instance, presents current-year budgets along with current services and GRH baseline estimates. OMB and the CBO make different assumptions in calculating baselines so that the two produce different projections. One option would be for Congress to specify baseline calculations and assumptions, although that would greatly curtail the independent analysis of both OMB and the CBO.

Other technical corrections pertain to the credit budget and to the treatment of trust funds (particularly Social Security and the Highway Trust Fund). Associated with these matters is the extent to which agencies and programs should be in the off-budget.

Procedural Corrections. There are numerous possible procedural corrections, all of which have implications for the powers of Congress and its committees. One such proposal is to avoid the ritual associated with increasing the public debt limit by using an automatic procedure. When the House approves a budget resolution that includes a debt ceiling increase, a separate bill approving the debt ceiling increase is automatically drafted and forwarded to the Senate as though the bill had been formally acted upon by the House.[64] The Senate could adopt a similar rule. The advantage is that "cliffhanger" decisions would be less common, but the disadvantage is that the debt increase would be approved without as much focused attention as under the current procedure. The proposal also does not deal with temporary debt ceiling increases in which an increase must be approved prior to approval of a budget resolution.

Automatic continuing resolutions for appropriations is another proposal; when Congress failed to pass an appropriations bill, the agencies affected would operate with a continuing appropriation without Congress's having to act.[65] Not acting on the budget in a timely fashion has almost become the norm. In 1988 there was cause for celebration when Congress did complete passage of all appropriations bills one minute before the start of the new fiscal year. The obvious advantage of an automatic continuing resolution is that it would eliminate the crisis handling of appropriations bills. The disadvantage of the proposal is that incentives for Congress to adopt regular appropriations bills would be reduced.

Reconciliation bills are often massive in size, and according to one proposal, a rule should be adopted prohibiting the addition of extraneous matters to these bills. The Senate generally has such a rule, but the House does not. The advantage is that the rule would limit the scope of a bill and therefore would prevent its becoming a tangled mess of diverse pieces.

The budget resolutions as provided under the 1974 legislation are "concurrent" in nature and do not require the signature of the president. One proposal would have the resolutions become "joint," which would require presidential signature. The main advantage of this proposal is that the resolution would be binding on committees and would disallow, for instance, one of the Appropriations Committees from assigning a figure to domestic programs higher than that in the resolution and making up the difference with corresponding cuts in defense appropriations. A disadvantage of the proposal is that it could be overly restrictive on the Appropriations Committees.

Proposals for reorganizing congressional committees and the relationships among them are always in abundance. One proposal would link together the authorizing and appropriating processes. The House Armed Services Committee and the Defense Subcommittee of the Appropriations Committee might hold joint hearings and report out one bill that provided authorizations and appropriations. Other proposals in circulation suggest that the House and Senate Budget Committees, rather than resolving the problems of congressional budgeting, instead have contributed to the confusion and therefore should be disbanded. These proposals dealing with committees threaten the power bases of the individuals involved and face steep opposition. While the HBC and the SBC have been convenient whipping boys for critics of congressional budgeting, the elimination of these committees would not necessarily solve any problems.

Far-Reaching Corrections. There is a set of more far-reaching proposals. One frequently mentioned is a biennial budget.[66] Since Congress has such great difficulty acting on a budget, why not simplify the problem by requiring action only every other year? Whether Congress would be willing to relinquish annual control is highly questionable. Biennial budgets might be routinely reopened in their second years and completely revised. The proposal would need to be coordinated with the election of Congress and the president. No Congress would want the government operating on a budget adopted by the previous Congress; the same concern would exist for a president.

Adoption of a capital budgeting system is another proposal. It is advocated as helping to put the deficit into perspective, namely that much of federal spending is of an investment nature and not simply annual consumption. Capital budgeting presumably would encourage better planning of expenditures. On the negative side, capital budgets could be used to downplay the true magnitude of federal budget deficits and total debt (see Chapter 12).

Giving the president rescission authority or the item veto is another frequently heard proposal. The strengths and weaknesses of this proposal pertaining to state legislatures were discussed in the preceding chapter and need not be recounted here. The main stumbling block for this proposal is that it is seen as strengthening the hand of the president vis-à-vis Congress.[67]

A constitutional amendment requiring a balanced budget has been recommended repeatedly.[68-70] The main advantage of this proposal is that the requirement for balancing the budget could not be ignored by Congress and the president. Critics contend that this could be a dangerous straitjacket that could prevent Congress from taking appropriate action in times of crises— both economic and national security crises. Depending on the specific proposal for reform, the power of the presidency might well be increased at the expense of Congress.

A final proposal calls for an omnibus budget bill that would include all spending and revenue measures in one package. The virtue of the proposal is that it provides for a comprehensive overview of the total budget with the prospect of Congress's developing a coherent set of policies pertaining to programs and the financing of government. The disadvantages have been mentioned earlier. Large bills tend to include extraneous materials that go unexamined. Without the item veto, the president would be forced either to accept or reject the entire package.

SUMMARY

Prior to reforms in the 1970s and 1980s, Congress already had an elaborate system for approving the budget. An authorization process exists independent of appropriations. Meanwhile, the House Ways and Means Committee and the Senate Finance Committee have power to deal not only with tax measures but also with some spending. The Appropriations Committees in the two houses operate by developing a series of bills through subcommittees. Following World War II, Congress experimented unsuccessfully with the use of a legislative budget and an omnibus appropriation bill.

The Congressional Budget and Impoundment Control Act of 1974 attempted to deal with several problems, including congressional tardiness in adopting the budget, impoundments, and piecemeal handling of the budget. New Budget Committees were established along with the Congressional Budget Office. Congress generally adhered to the timetable in the law for the first several years but then slipped badly. The Supreme Court, in a sweeping decision, voided the rescission and deferral process because of its inclusion of a legislative veto.

The budget process was drastically altered by practice during the first several years of the Reagan administration. Budget resolutions were not passed in a timely fashion. Reconciliation was used in budget approval but early in the process rather than at the end as originally envisioned. Appropriations bills rarely were passed on time, and Congress resorted instead to massive continuing appropriations.

The mounting federal debt alarmed Republicans and Democrats alike in Congress, and the result was the Balanced Budget and Emergency Deficit Control Act of 1985—Gramm-Rudman-Hollings. The procedure in the law was revised by the 1987 Reaffirmation Act, after the Supreme Court declared unconstitutional a provision pertaining to the role of the comptroller general. GRH sets target figures for reducing the budget deficit to zero by 1993. In the event Congress, working with the president, cannot develop a budget that stays within the established limit for a given year, an automatic sequestration process is triggered which imposes budget cuts of equal amounts on defense and domestic programs.

Numerous proposals exist for further revising how Congress acts on the budget. These include technical and procedural proposals as well as more far-reaching ones. One proposal would amend the Constitution to require the government to adopt a balanced budget.

NOTES

1. Louis Fisher, "Annual Authorizations: Durable Roadblocks to Biennial Budgeting," *Public Budgeting and Finance* 3 (Spring 1983): 27.

2. Louis Fisher, *The Politics of Shared Power: Congress and the Executive*, 2nd ed. (Washington, D.C.: Congressional Quarterly Press, 1987), pp. 91–217.

3. John F. Manley, *The Politics of Finance: The House Committee on Ways and Means* (Boston: Little, Brown, 1970).

4. Richard F. Fenno, Jr., *The Power of the Purse: Appropriations Politics in Congress* (Boston: Little, Brown, 1966).

5. Lance T. LeLoup, *Budgetary Politics*, 4th ed. (Brunswick, Ohio: King's Court, 1988).

6. Howard E. Shuman, *Politics and the Budget: The Struggle between the President and the Congress*, 2nd ed. (Englewood Cliffs, N.J.: Prentice-Hall, 1988).

7. Aaron Wildavsky, *The New Politics of the Budgetary Process* (Boston: Little, Brown, 1988).

8. Louis Fisher, "Experience with a Legislative Budget (1947-1949)," in Senate Committee on Government Operations, *Improving Congressional Control of the Budget: Hearings, Part 2,* 93rd Cong., 1st sess. (Washington, D.C.: Government Printing Office, 1973), pp. 237-39.

9. Robert A. Wallace, "Congressional Control of the Budget," *Midwest Journal of Political Science* 3 (1959): 161.

10. Sun K. Kim, "The Politics of a Congressional Budgetary Process: 'Backdoor Spending,'" *Western Political Quarterly* 21 (1968): 606-23.

11. Allen Schick, "Backdoor Spending Authority," in Senate Committee on Government Operations, *Improving Congressional Control Over the Budget: A Compendium of Materials*, 93rd Cong., 1st sess. (Washington, D.C.: Government Printing Office, 1973), pp. 293-302.

12. Louis Fisher, "Ten Years of the Budget Act: Still Searching for Controls," *Public Budgeting and Finance* 5 (Autumn 1985): 3-28.

13. Allen Schick, *Congress and Money* (Washington, D.C.: Urban Institute, 1980), pp. 17-81.

14. John W. Ellwood, "Budget Reforms and Interchamber Relations," in W. Thomas Wander, F. Ted Hebert, and Gary W. Copeland, eds., *Congressional Budgeting* (Baltimore: Johns Hopkins University Press, 1984), pp. 100-32.

15. James Malachowski, Samuel Bookheimer, and David Lowery, "The Theory of the Budgeting Process in an Era of Changing Budgetary Roles," *American Politics Quarterly* 15 (1987): 325-54.

16. Louis Fisher, "The Politics of Impounded Funds," *Administrative Science Quarterly* 15 (1970): 361-77.

17. *Train v. New York City*, 420 U.S. 35 (1975).

18. General Accounting Office, *Review of the Impoundment Control Act of 1974 After Two Years* (Washington, D.C.: Government Printing Office, 1977).

19. *Immigration and Naturalization Service v. Chadha*, 462 U.S. 919 (1983).

20. Also see *Alaska Airlines v. Brock*, 480 U.S. 678 (1987).

21. *City of New Haven v. United States*, 634 F.Supp. 1449 (1986) and 809 F.2d 900 (1987).

22. "High Court Weighs New Legislative Veto Issue," *Congressional Quarterly Almanac, 1986* 42 (Washington, D.C.: Congressional Quarterly Press, 1987), pp. 49-53.

23. Randall Strahan, "Agenda Change and Committee Politics in the Postreforms House," *Legislative Studies Quarterly* 13 (1988): 177-97.

24. Heinz Eulau and Vera McCluggage, "Standing Committees in Legislatures: Three Decades of Research," *Legislative Studies Quarterly* 9 (1984): 195-270.

25. Stanley Bach, "Representatives and Committees on the Floor," *Congress and the Presidency* 13 (1986): 41-48.

26. Office of Management and Budget, *Budget of the United States Government* (Washington, D.C.: Government Printing Office, selected years).

27. F. Ted Hebert, "Congressional Budgeting, 1977-1983," in Wander, Hebert, and Copeland, eds., *Congressional Budgeting*, pp. 31-48.

28. Joseph A. Davis, "Budget Office Evolves into Key Policy Maker," *Congressional Quarterly Weekly Report* 43 (1985): 1809-17.

29. Bruce E. Johnson, "From Analyst to Negotiator: The OMB's New Role," *Journal of Policy Analysis and Management* 3 (1984): 501-15.

30. David S. Stockman, *The Triumph of Politics* (New York: Harper & Row, 1986).

31. Aaron Wildavsky, *The New Politics of the Budgetary Process* (Glenview, Ill.: Scott, Foresman, 1988), pp. 165–79.

32. Lawrence J. Haas, "The Deficit Culture," *National Journal* 20 (1988): 1460–67.

33. Lance T. LeLoup and John Hancock, "Congress and the Reagan Budgets," *Public Budgeting and Finance* 8 (Autumn 1988): 30–54.

34. R. Kent Weaver, "The Politics of Blame Avoidance," *Journal of Public Policy* 6 (1986): 371–98.

35. Bureau of the Census, *Statistical Abstract of the United States* (Washington, D.C.: Government Printing Office, 1984), pp. 309, 311.

36. Congressional Budget Office, *Reducing the Deficit: Spending and Revenue Options* (Washington, D.C.: Government Printing Office, 1988).

37. Paul N. Courant and Edward M. Gramlich, *Federal Budget Deficits* (Englewood Cliffs, N.J.: Prentice-Hall, 1986).

38. Robert A. Keith, "Budget Reconciliation in 1981," *Public Budgeting and Finance* 1 (Winter 1981): 37–47.

39. Barry Bozeman and Jeffrey D. Straussman, "Shrinking Budgets and the Shrinkage of Budget Theory," *Public Administration Review* 42 (1982): 509–15.

40. Barbara Sinclair, "The Role of Committees in Agenda Setting in the U.S. Congress," *Legislative Studies Quarterly* 11 (1986): 35–45.

41. Lawrence J. Haas, "Unauthorized Action," *National Journal* 20 (1988): 17–21.

42. Allen Schick for the House Committee on the Budget, *The Whole and the Parts: Piecemeal and Integrated Approaches to Congressional Budgeting*, 100th Cong., 1st sess. (Washington, D.C.: Government Printing Office, 1987), pp. 25–33.

43. Lawrence J. Haas, "Blame the Appropriators," *National Journal* 19 (1987): 2025–29.

44. Michael L. Mezey, "The Legislature, the Executive and Public Policy: The Futile Quest for Congressional Power," *Congress and the Presidency* 13 (1986): 1–20.

45. Joseph Cooper, "Assessing Legislative Performance: A Reply to the Critics of Congress," *Congress and the Presidency* 13 (1986): 21–40.

46. D. Roderick Kiewiet and Mathew D. McCubbins, "Appropriations Decisions as a Bilateral Bargaining Game between President and Congress," *Legislative Studies Quarterly* 10 (1985): 181–201.

47. David C. Morrison, "Chaos on Capitol Hill," *National Journal* 18 (1986): 2302–07.

48. President's Blue Ribbon Commission on Defense Management, *A Quest for Excellence: Final Report* (Washington, D.C.: The Commission, 1986). The Commission was chaired by David Packard.

49. Harry S. Havens, "Gramm-Rudman-Hollings: Origins and Implementation," *Public Budgeting and Finance* 6 (August 1986): 4–24.

50. House Committee on the Budget, *A Summary: The Balanced Budget and Emergency Deficit Control Act of 1985*, 99th Cong., 2nd sess. (Washington, D.C.: Government Printing Office, 1986).

51. Lance T. LeLoup, Barbara L. Graham, and Stacey Barwick, "Deficit Politics and Constitutional Government: The Impact of Gramm-Rudman-Hollings," *Public Budgeting and Finance* 7 (Spring 1987): 83–103.

52. W. Philip Gramm as quoted in Elizabeth Wehr, "Congress Enacts Far-Reaching Budget Measure," *Congressional Quarterly Weekly Report* 43 (1985): 2604.

53. *Bowsher v. Synar*, 478 U.S. 714 (1986).

54. "Symposium: *Bowsher v. Synar*," *Cornell Law Review* 72 (1987): 421–597.

55. House Committee on Government Operations, *Reform of the Federal Budget Process: Hearings*, 100th Cong., 1st sess. (Washington, D.C.: Government Printing Office, 1987).

56. Senate Committee on the Budget, *The Congressional Budget Process: An Explanation*, 100th Cong., 2nd sess. (Washington, D.C.: Government Printing Office, 1988).

57. Tim Metz et al., "Stocks Plunge 508 Amid Panicky Selling," *Wall Street Journal* 210 (October 20, 1987): 1+.

58. Office of Management and Budget, *Budget of the United States* (Washington, D.C.: Government Printing Office, 1988), p. 6g-29.

59. Office of Management and Budget, *Budget*, p. 6e-3.

60. Macon Morehouse, "Critics Take Aim at New Deficit Commission," *Congressional Quarterly Weekly Report* 46 (1988): 340–41.

61. *Budget Reform Proposals* (Washington, D.C.: American Enterprise Institute for Public Policy Research, 1985).

62. House Committee on Government Operations, *Reform of the Federal Budget Process: An Analysis of Major Proposals*, 100th Cong., 1st sess. (Washington, D.C.: Government Printing Office, 1987).

63. Mark S. Kamlet and David C. Mowery, "The First Decade of the Congressional Budget Act," *Policy Sciences* 18 (1985): 313–34.

64. "Automatic Debt-Limit Vote," *Congressional Quarterly Almanac* 42 (1987): 458.

65. General Accounting Office, *Appropriations: Continuing Resolutions and an Assessment of Automatic Funding Approaches* (Washington, D.C.: Government Printing Office, 1986).

66. Roy T. Meyers, "Biennial Budgeting by the U.S. Congress," *Public Budgeting and Finance* 8 (Summer 1988): 21–32.

67. Richard E. Cohen, "Congress Plays Election-Year Politics with Line-Item Veto Proposal," *National Journal* 16 (1984): 274–76.

68. Advisory Commission on Intergovernmental Relations, *Fiscal Discipline in the Federal System: National Reform and the Experience of the States* (Washington, D.C.: Government Printing Office, 1987).

69. John P. Hagan, "Judicial Enforcement of a Balanced-Budget Amendment: Legal and Institutional Constraints," *Policy Studies Journal* 15 (1986): 247–67.

70. Richard E. Wagner et al., *Balanced Budgets, Fiscal Responsibility, and the Constitution* (Washington, D.C.: Cato Institute, 1982).

10

Budget Execution

Once the budget has been approved, the execution phase of the cycle begins. Of course, one should recognize that at the federal level it is common for many agencies to enter the execution phase only with a continuing resolution to spend at the previous year's rate rather than spend under a new appropriation. This same practice sometimes occurs at the state level, while local governments usually are required by state law to complete the budget approval phase by the beginning of the new fiscal year.

This chapter has two sections. The first deals with interactions between the central budget office and line agencies. The second covers subsystems of the execution phase. Included in that section are tax administration, cash management, procurement, and risk management.

BUDGET OFFICE AND AGENCY RELATIONS

As would be expected, relationships—both direct and indirect—are extensive between the central budget office and line agencies during the execution phase of the budget. In this section, we first examine these relationships as they pertain specifically to the budget and then turn to broader concerns for fostering economy and efficiency.

Interactions on Budgeting

Execution is the action phase of budgeting, in which the plans contained in the budget are put into operation. Every budget either explicitly or implicitly contains plans for the work to be done and the achievements to be gained. Execution, then, involves converting those plans into operations.

Legislative Intent. In acting on the budget, the legislature provides some indication of what is called "legislative intent." Such intent may be expressed in terms of the dollars to be available for an organizational unit. The greater the specificity of these appropriations, the less flexibility afforded agencies and the budget office in how funds will be spent.[1]

Some flexibility seems essential if for no other reason than the legislative body cannot readily specify all aspects of all operations of all agencies. Most legislative action, therefore, leaves the door open to further decision making; the process of decision making is not completed once the legislative body has acted on the budget.

Apportionment and Allotments. At the state and federal levels an apportionment process is used in which line agencies submit plans to the central budget office for how appropriated funds will be used; the plans often indicate proposed expenditures for each month or quarter of the fiscal year. Office of Management and Budget (OMB) Circular A-34 governs this process at the federal level. The budget office may require modification of these proposals and eventually approves apportionments for each agency. Following the approval of apportionments by the budget office, allotments are made within departments. This process grants expenditure authority to subunits. At the local level this process may be relatively informal.

The chief executive, operating through the budget office, has greater denial powers than initiating authority in the apportionment process. The executive cannot approve apportionments for projects prohibited in the appropriation but may be able to reduce or eliminate some appropriated items. As was seen in Chapter 9, presidents have impounded appropriated funds. At the state level and sometimes the local level, the line-item veto serves the same denial role.

Initial Planning. Agencies at the outset of the fiscal year must accommodate changes that have been adopted. One common problem that local governments confront is meeting state-imposed requirements or mandates, such as new standards for disposal of solid waste in landfills and possibly requirements for recycling aluminum and glass.[2] Cutbacks in funding, such as those resulting from tax limitation measures at the state and local levels, must be accommodated through cutbacks in programs.[3] Gramm-Rudman-Hollings stipulations at the federal level have forced agencies to make difficult choices on how to operate with reduced funding.[4]

For agencies that were fortunate in obtaining increased funds for improving or expanding existing programs or for new programs, the budget office plays a key role. Mindful that the legislature will expect a detailed reporting of how these funds were used, the budget office exercises oversight in implementing the program revisions or new programs.[5]

Control of Agencies. From the perspective of the central administration, agencies must be required to live within their budgets; otherwise the budget process becomes an empty exercise. Therefore, various controls are imposed upon agencies, with one control being the pre-audit. After having an approved apportionment plan and receiving an allotment, the agency is still not free to spend but must submit a request to obligate the government to spend resources. The request is matched against the unit's budget to determine whether the proposed expenditure is authorized and whether sufficient funds are available in the agency's budget.

The pre-audit function may be carried out by several different units. Not only the budget office but also an accounting department may be involved. Often at the state and local levels, independent comptrollers, controllers, or auditor generals have pre-audit responsibilities. These elected officials have the duty of providing another, presumably independent, check upon financial transactions.

In the case of an agency proposing to hire new staff, not only will the usual pre-audit procedure be used, but in addition a central personnel office may have authority to review the request. This procedure, known as personnel complement control, is used in part to avoid increasing personnel commitments and corresponding increases in budget requirements.

Midyear Changes. As the year progresses, the budget office conducts reviews of agency operations. One problem that often emerges is that resources in some agencies' budgets are not sufficient to meet the demands for services. One alternative is for the budget office to approve requesting supplemental appropriations to meet those demands. However, in other circumstances, the budget office will work with agencies to stay within funding ceilings.[6]

Midyear crises also may emerge because of an unfavorable revenue situation. A downturn in the economy can have devastating effects on sales tax and income tax receipts, forcing across-the-board cutbacks in spending at the state and local levels. Since personnel costs usually are the largest single item in operating budgets, these costs must be curtailed when revenue receipts are below projected levels; personnel hiring freezes are common in government. Another, more extreme technique is to furlough employees. Some governments have expected all employees to share in the problem by each working a four-day week, thereby creating a 20 percent saving.

As the fiscal year approaches its end, agencies will attempt to zero out their budgets; an agency having unexpended funds at the end of the fiscal year may be considered a prime candidate for cuts in the upcoming budget.[7,8] Also, unexpended or unencumbered funds often lapse at the end of the budget year. From the agency's perspective, it is a now-or-never situation for spending the available money. Another factor is that an agency may have delayed some expenditures, saving a portion of its budget for contingencies. This delay results in a spurt in expenditures at the end of the year, with some spending being highly appropriate and other spending utterly wasteful. Congress has reduced this last-minute spurt by limiting the proportion of an agency's funds that may be spent in the final quarter of the fiscal year.

An alternative is to allow surplus funds to be transferred to the agency's new budget without requiring a reappropriation. Some jurisdictions allow this within limits, such as a small percentage of each unit's total budget.

Revival of Economy and Efficiency

The Taft Commission on Economy and Efficiency is best known for its 1912 report recommending the establishment of a federal budget process under the direction of the president. The title of the commission is significant in that a primary thrust was to better utilize governmental resources (see Chapter 1). Nearly eight decades later, the same concerns of the Taft Commission are prevalent at all levels of government.

This swing toward economy and efficiency, of course, is closely related to cutback management, discussed earlier. Incentives for economy and efficiency were created by taxing and spending limitation measures, by fiscal stress or distress resulting from the erosion of tax bases of many jurisdictions, and by the increased popularity of conservatism that was aimed at reducing the role of government in society.[9]

Reagan Administration Initiatives. Pursuing this theme of economy and efficiency, the Reagan administration undertook several major initiatives. The President's Private Sector Survey on Cost Control, better known as the Grace Commission, issued its final report in 1984, making about 2,500 recommendations.[10] The commission, consisting of top-level private-sector executives, claimed that if the recommendations were adopted, a saving of nearly a half billion dollars would be achieved over a three-year period. OMB was assigned the task of implementing the report.

Paralleling the Grace reforms was Reform 88, also under the control of OMB.[11] Named after the target completion date, Reform 88 included such activities as reducing the number of government publications, reducing the size of the bureaucracy, and improving cash management.

The Reagan administration also had a Productivity Improvement Program, under the direction of OMB, that required the largest federal agencies to target each year functions to be improved.[12] An example is the Federal Bureau of Investigation's effort to improve the accuracy and timeliness of fingerprint identification.

Several criticisms of these efforts have been made.[13] One is that the Grace Commission greatly overestimated the savings to be achieved by its recommendations. Some savings were to be achieved at the expense of government employees, such as reducing retirement benefits and raising the retirement age. There tended to be a lack of clarity regarding how the Grace Commission, Reform 88, and the Productivity Improvement Program were related.

Privatization of Services. While definitions vary, the core of any definition of "privatization" is that government activities are turned over to the private sector. A common mechanism used for this is contracting, in which a private firm provides a product or service at agreed-upon quantity, quality, and price.

While the procedures used in contracting are reviewed later in this chapter, it should be noted here that OMB Circular A-76, "Performance of Commercial Activities," provides for a review process to determine when activities of the government should be contracted out. There are two main criteria—that the activity be a "commercial" one and not "governmental" and that the cost be lower in the private sector than in government. Commercial activities include such services as guarding public buildings and providing cafeterias for employees. Policy-making activities are not to be contracted out. Use of Circular A-76 was increased extensively during the Carter and Reagan administrations.[14]

Contracting out differs from the privatization movement in that the former focuses primarily on an efficiency standard while the latter has a policy orientation.[15,16] Circular A-76 uses an efficiency standard, namely that contracting out should be used when the unit cost for a service is lower outside of government than inside. The privatization movement endorses that view but adds to it the idea that the population is better served if service delivery is left, where possible, to the private sector. The advocates of privatization contend that government should be proactive in seeking opportunities for turning over functions to the private sector.

During the Reagan administration, privatization was endorsed by the Grace Commission, included in various budget proposals, and reinforced by the 1988 report of the President's Commission on Privatization. That commission recommended privatization activities in such diverse areas as low-income housing, air traffic control, passenger train service, and health care for the elderly.[17] Critics contend that sometimes too much faith is placed in private enterprise and that privatization leads to supporting nonunionized firms that pay low wages.[18]

Management Controls. Budget offices have been assigned a variety of management-related duties beyond the core activities of assembling proposed budgets and overseeing their execution. Budget offices may be partially responsible for establishing standards to be used in accounting systems (OMB Circular A-127); of course, other units such as the General Accounting Office at the federal level also play major roles in this area. Information systems and procurement are other important areas in which budget offices have key roles. Procurement is discussed later in this chapter.

Some budget offices have responsibility for studying agency procedures and for recommending or prescribing new procedures. These organization-and-management (O and M) studies can recommend changes in the department's structure, such as realignments of bureaus and their responsibilities.

Budget offices set ground rules for many of the routine activities of line organizations. Limitations are set for paying employee travel costs. Another example of centrally imposed standards is in the use of consulting services; for the federal government, OMB Circular A-120 sets the rules in this area.

A legislative clearinghouse function is the responsibility of some budget offices. Before an agency may endorse proposals for new or revised legislation, the proposal must be cleared through the budget office. This practice helps ensure that what is proposed is consistent with the views of the chief executive, both substantively and financially (see OMB Circular A-19).

Since corruption in government often involves finance, budget offices sometimes have major responsibility for protecting the government against fraud, waste, and abuse of governmental resources. The Inspector General Act of 1978 created relatively independent inspector general (IG) offices in major federal departments and gave these offices responsibility for investigating possible cases of fraud and other wrongdoing. The IGs meet as the President's Council on Integrity and Efficiency, which is chaired by OMB.

OMB also oversees agency compliance with the Federal Managers' Financial Integrity Act of 1984, which requires safeguarding financial systems, particularly accounting and payroll, from fraud (OMB Circular A-123).[19] The budget office is involved in dealing with alleged instances of postemployment conflicts of interest in which former government employees may be illegally benefiting from their previous experience in government.

Of course, OMB is not the sole central agency responsible for handling problems in this area. Other important offices include the Office of Personnel Management, the Merit Systems Protection Board, the Department of Justice, and the General Accounting Office.

Government collection of information has constituted another problem area in which budget offices are involved. The concern is the burden imposed on individuals, corporations, and state and local governments in supplying information to the government. OMB and many state budget offices have long had responsibility for approving agency forms to be used outside of the government; forms used exclusively within an agency do not require central clearance.

The Paperwork Reduction Act of 1980, as its title suggests, set as an objective the reduction of paperwork demanded of individuals, corporations, and other governments. OMB prepares an annual *Information Collection Budget*, which indicates increases and decreases in the amount of information collected by the major agencies of the government. The paperwork burden is measured in terms of thousands of hours required of respondents in complying with government's demands for information (OMB Circular A-130).[20]

In addition to relief from paperwork, budget offices also may be responsible for regulatory relief of businesses and governments. The Regulatory Flexibility Act of 1980 encourages the use of flexible regulations that require lesser amounts of information from smaller entities, including small businesses and local governments. Executive Order 12291, issued by President Reagan in 1981, gives OMB responsibility for overseeing agencies in their review of regulations.

Executive Order 12498, issued by Reagan in 1985, goes even further in assigning powers to OMB. The order created a regulatory planning process that requires agencies to plan each year regarding what regulations to revise, issue, or rescind. These plans must be submitted to OMB for approval.[21] While OMB does not have statutory authority to approve or reject agency regulations, the budget office greatly influences the issuance of regulations.[22]

Besides these areas mentioned, there are other management controls over agencies for which budget offices may have some responsibility. Budget offices may be involved in implementing governmentwide affirmative action plans. Some states have right-to-know laws that require employers—public and private—to inform their employees whether they are working with hazardous materials; measures aimed at reducing dangerous conditions obviously have budgetary implications.[23] Budget offices may have some responsibilities in implementing freedom-of-information laws.

Given all of the items discussed here, some observers have suggested that the tasks are too great to be left to budget offices. One suggestion is to create a separate office of management that would have wide-ranging duties other than budgeting. The argument against this proposal hinges mainly on the fact that the topics covered have budgetary implications, and to assign them to a different agency would automatically create coordination problems between it and the budget office.[24,25] In response to these concerns, the position of chief financial officer was created in OMB in 1987; that position, however, is responsible largely for accounting matters and not the broader concern of management practices in the government.

EXECUTION SUBSYSTEMS

In addition to relations between the central budget office and line agencies, several other subsystems are in operation during budget execution. Taxes and other debts must be collected, the cash needs of the government must be met, items must be purchased, and the vulnerability of the government to loss of property and other problems must be managed.

Tax Administration and Debt Collection

The next topics to be discussed are tax administration and cash management, two functions that are usually under the same administrative officer, namely a secretary of treasury or revenue. Having the two linked together administratively facilitates their sharing of information. Information generated by the tax administrator is used by the cash manager. At the federal level, the Treasury Department handles these tasks.

Main Steps. Tax administration has four main steps.

1. Determining the objects or services to be taxed. Using the local property tax as an example, parcels of land and structures must be identified along with their owners.
2. Applying the tax. In the case of the property tax, this is an annual process, while sales tax calculations are made each time a sale occurs. Property tax calculations are made by governments and bills sent to property owners, in contrast with income taxes, for which individuals initially calculate what they owe.
3. Collecting the revenues. Funds are paid either directly to the government, as in the case of a corporation paying income tax, or through a third party, as in the case of employers remitting individual income tax withholdings to the government.
4. Enforcing the law. Audits are conducted selectively of taxpayers to verify compliance and some taxpayers are prosecuted for tax evasion.

Tax administration is not concerned with the policy issue of tax equity. Instead, the objectives of tax administration are to generate the revenue that is expected and to gain compliance from the vast majority of taxpayers.

Enforcement. Numerous tax enforcement measures are used, and a persistent question is how many resources should be committed to each activity.[26]

1. The Internal Revenue Service verifies mathematical accuracy through the use of optic scanning.
2. Tax return information supplied by individuals is compared with information supplied by banks and employers.[27]
3. Governments share computer tapes to compare information on income being reported (or not reported).[28]
4. Taxpayer services are provided to help in preparing tax returns.[29]
5. Governments draw samples of taxpayer returns to audit. Regression models are designed to identify cases that are most likely to involve noncompliance with the tax laws.[30]

6. One of the most common groups singled out for tax auditing are individuals and corporations for which "leads" have been given.[31]
7. Delinquent accounts are investigated along with accounts in which taxpayers have stopped complying altogether.
8. Some taxpayers are prosecuted in court, depending upon the "seriousness" of the cases and the availability of resources to pursue the cases in court.
9. Special enforcement is reserved for sources of illegal income, such as gambling, prostitution, narcotics, and more generally, organized crime.[32]

Tax Amnesty. During the 1980s, tax amnesty became a popular practice for about half of the state governments. Taxpayers who were delinquent in their income taxes could file returns during a specified time period in a state without fear of prosecution; the taxpayers, however, were expected to pay all back taxes and interest. The amnesty programs have been successful in getting many taxpayers back on the tax rolls.[33]

Computer Usage. It should come as no surprise that computers are playing increasingly important roles in tax administration.[34] Besides routine record keeping, computers are used in drawing samples for tax auditing and for cross-checking information between different sources. Portable computers are used by auditors on field assignments. Computers can be used to manage cases, providing on any one case a variety of information displays and prompting the case manager with reminders about the status of the case. The conversion of various aspects of tax administration from paper files to computer systems or from one computer system to a more advanced one can result in problems for both tax administrators and taxpayers.[35]

Intergovernmental Relations. There are intergovernmental aspects to tax administration. As already noted, some governments share information with each other to help detect noncompliance with tax laws. Local governments sometimes work together in joint billing, such as a county, city, and school district preparing a single bill for property taxes. Tax provisions of governments are sometimes related to each other, which can unintentionally create policy and administrative problems. Changes in the federal income tax can affect provisions in state taxes, necessitating adjustments in those laws. This was the case with passage of the Federal Tax Reform Act in 1986.

Other Revenue. Besides taxes, there are of course numerous other revenue sources that must be administered. User charges are common at the local level. State lotteries have become important sources of revenue. Administrative strategies involving lotteries focus upon marketing to increase sales; as the dollar value of sales increases, the unit cost of administration declines.[36]

Debt Collection. One of the biggest debts owed government is taxes, but beyond those are several other situations that lead to individuals' and corporations' owing government. Loans, both direct and guaranteed, result in some defaults. Federal loan programs exist for college students, low-income housing, ship construction, development in other nations, and small businesses recovering from disasters, to name only a few. Various business transactions with government result in debts, such as farmers owing on crop insurance payments and foreign countries owing on purchases of agricultural commodities. Fines are another form of debt, as in the case of a corporation's being fined for not meeting environmental standards for the mines that it operates.[37]

The federal government has attempted to deal with its debt collection problem. OMB publishes a "credit budget" that covers direct and guaranteed loans; that budget provides information about the financing of these operations through appropriations and revolving funds.

OMB Circular A-70, "Policies and Guidelines for Federal Credit Programs," requires that agencies review their credit programs in terms of the costs and benefits to society. The circular establishes requirements for "sound" credit programs. The Debt Collection Act of 1982 and OMB Circular A-129 further require that agencies take steps to improve their credit programs. Loan applications must be examined regarding the risks that government would take in approving loans. Delinquent cases can be turned over to collection agencies and can be reported to consumer credit agencies. Salary offsets can be used against federal employees owing the government. Individuals may have income tax refunds withheld from them up to the amount owed government; state governments also have used this technique.[38]

Cash Management

Cash management is the process of administering monies to ensure that they are available over time to meet expenditure needs and that monies, when temporarily not needed, are invested at a minimum risk and a maximum yield. Cash management involves both short- and long-term investments; the latter is used mainly in the case of pension funds where investments are made for future years when employees retire.

Forecasting. Cash management requires forecasting cash needs over the length of the fiscal year and beyond. Essential to the process is forecasting when revenues will be received and in what amounts (see Chapter 4). Expenditures also must be planned, and that is one of the reasons agencies are required to submit apportionment plans to the central budget office. Agencies may be instructed to shift expenditures in apportionment plans from one quarter to another.

Borrowing. Another option in dealing with revenue shortfalls is to use short-term borrowing. State and local governments borrow from banks for up to one year in cases where expenditures are considered essential and funds are unavailable to cover the expenses. The backing of these bank notes is future receipt of revenues, and the instruments are known as RANs and TANs for revenue and tax anticipation notes.

Governments also may borrow from themselves. Some governments have established "rainy day funds" or reserves that can be used during periods when revenues decline.[39] Short-term borrowing from one fund to meet the cash needs of another is used, as in the case of a local government borrowing from its pension funds. State laws, however, may greatly restrict such borrowing as a protection against depleting the funds.

Investment Planning. When forecasts show periods during the year when revenues will exceed expenditures, plans are made for investments. Virtually all governments encounter this situation. Often there are spurts in revenue receipts, such as when property taxes are due at the local level or when state sales tax receipts are due following the Christmas shopping period.

We turn now to investment practices at the state and local levels of government, returning later to the federal government and then more generally to cash management practices common to all levels of government.[40]

Numerous factors must be taken into account when devising an investment strategy.

1. Security. Financial institutions insure some deposits up to only $100,000.
2. Maturity date. Some instruments mature in a few months while others mature in 30 years.
3. Marketability or liquidity. If cash is needed before the maturity date, may an instrument be sold to a third party or will the issuer convert the instrument to cash?
4. Call provisions. May the issuer repay the investor before the date of maturity?
5. Denominations. Minimum amounts for investing range from $1,000 to $100,000 and more.
6. Yield or return on investment. Yield is measured in terms of a percentage of the investment and often expressed as an interest rate.[41]

Federal Securities. The instruments available for state and local investments consist of three general types: federal government securities, corporate securities, and money market instruments. Fully guaranteed federal securities include treasury bills (T-bills), notes, and bonds. T-bills mature in 13, 26, and 52 weeks. They are sold at a discount by auction and consequently have no set percentage return. Treasury notes and bonds, which range in maturity from

1 to 30 years, have coupons that mature every 6 months. Other securities issued by the federal government may or may not be guaranteed. Ginnie Maes, based on federally backed home mortgages, are guaranteed, unlike bonds issued by the Tennessee Valley Authority.

Corporate Securities. Corporations are a source for investing state and local monies. Corporate bonds constitute loans being made to the issuers. Stocks, in comparison, represent ownership of the corporation. In the event that a corporation goes into bankruptcy, creditors such as bondholders are paid first, and whatever assets remain, if any, are then distributed among stockholders.

Money Market Instruments. Banks and savings and loan institutions provide numerous investment opportunities.[42] Interest is paid on negotiable order of withdrawal (NOW) checking accounts and on savings accounts. Other investment opportunities are money market instruments, with certificates of deposit (CDs) being one of the most popular. Issuers include banks, savings and loan associations, off-shore subsidiaries of U.S. banks, and U.S. branches of foreign banks. The latter two issue what are known as Eurodollars and Yankee CDs, respectively, which are not guaranteed by the federal government. Some, but not all, CDs are negotiable. Issuers may charge interest penalties for early withdrawal of monies.

Other instruments include bankers' acceptances, commercial paper, and repurchase agreements. Bankers' acceptances are agreements to purchase a bank's agreement to loan money on a short-term basis to a corporation, usually involved in international trade; these instruments are issued by the largest banks in the nation. Commercial paper, also available through banks, is a corporate promissory note. A repurchase agreement (repo) is a pool of U.S. government securities held by a financial institution and sold temporarily to state and local governments and other purchasers; the institution agrees to repurchase the securities at a later date.

Repurchase agreements have constituted a controversial topic because a few major firms specializing in repos went bankrupt in the mid-1980s. Some governments, including Beaumont, Texas, and Toledo, Ohio, lost many millions of dollars.[43] Congress passed the Government Securities Act of 1986, which brought these securities dealers under the regulation of the Treasury Department and the Securities and Exchange Commission.

State and local governments may purchase combinations of various money market instruments. One technique is to invest in a money market fund, which is a pool of securities. Many governments, however, are precluded by law from investing in these funds because they often include higher risk investments such as Eurodollars.

Investment Pools. Another technique that has become popular is for jurisdictions to combine their investments into a state-authorized investment pool. By pooling resources, smaller jurisdictions can take advantage of higher-yield investments that require larger investments than passbook savings or certificates of deposit. Liquidity is improved in that jurisdictions often can withdraw some of their monies from these pools without the financial loss that would be involved if they held securities themselves and had to liquidate them.[44]

Yield Rates. Table 10-1 is a snapshot of yield rates for some of the instruments that have been discussed. Rates increase with risk and time. Banker's acceptances, which involve risks, pay a higher return than generally risk-free T-bills. Bonds usually pay a higher rate than notes, and notes a higher rate than bills, because of the time factor involved.

Use of Investment Instruments. Table 10-2 indicates state and local governments' use of investments. Insurance trust funds, such as employee retirement systems and Workers' Compensation, invest the vast bulk of their monies (92 percent), whereas the rest of government keeps about one-third of its money in cash and deposits and invests the remaining two-thirds. Retirement systems invest mainly in federal securities (27 percent) and corporate stocks and bonds (52 percent).[45]

Federal Cash Management. The federal government's cash management system is considerably different from those of state and local governments.[46-48] Federal monies are kept with the Federal Reserve System (see Chapter 15), which pays a form of interest for deposits. Transactions are handled by the Financial Management Service of the Treasury Department. Other departments and agencies, however, handle many transactions in accordance with instructions issued by Treasury.

Table 10-1 Yield Rates of Selected Investments Instruments, February 1989

Instrument	Yield (Percent)
Federal Securities	
13-Week Treasury Bills	8.49%
26-Week Treasury Bills	8.54
52-Week Treasury Bills	9.23
10-Year Treasury Notes	9.20
30-Year Treasury Bonds	9.05
Ginnie Maes	10.45
Other Securities	
1-Month Certificates of Deposit	8.69%
6-Month Certificates of Deposit	9.07
30-Day Bankers' Acceptances	9.20
30-Day Commercial Paper	9.30
1-Month Eurodollars	9.44

Source: *Wall Street Journal*, Vol. 213, pp. C13 and C17, February 17, 1989.

Table 10-2 Cash and Security Holdings of State and Local Governments, by Type of Holding, 1986–87 (Percent)

Type of Holding	Insurance Trust Funds	Noninsurance Trust Funds	Total
Cash and Deposits	4.3%	34.6%	8.8%
Deposits with U.S. Treasury	4.1	0	2.1
Securities	91.5	65.4	79.0
Federal	28.5	22.4	25.6
State and Local	0.2	2.0	1.1
Nongovernmental	62.8	40.9	52.4
Total*	100.0	100.0	100.0

*May not add to 100.0 percent due to rounding.
Source: *Government Finances in 1986–87*, Bureau of the Census, p. 17, Government Printing Office, 1988.

The inflow of federal receipts comes from taxes and other payments and from the sale of T-bills and other instruments discussed earlier. These sales are handled through the Federal Reserve and are limited according to the total debt ceiling set by Congress (Chapter 9). T-bills are auctioned off weekly and other instruments less frequently; there is, of course, a secondary market for these securities.[49]

Maximizing the inflow of monies is a key activity of federal cash management as well as of state and local governments. Enforcement of tax laws is viewed as one means for maximizing inflow. Other techniques involve depositing government receipts as soon as possible into interest-bearing accounts. For example, when tax payments accompany tax returns, the checks can be deposited immediately in banks while processing of the returns occurs later.

Lock-Boxes. Another technique used selectively by the federal government and some state governments is the lock-box system, which uses post office boxes that are under the control of banks.[50] Taxpayers send their payments to designated post office boxes that are opened by banking officials, and the receipts are deposited promptly. The process reduces the amount of float time between when a check is written and when government deposits it and begins earning interest.

Prompt Payment. In addition to inflow techniques, some deal with outflow; here the concern is to keep money in interest-bearing accounts until it is needed to cover expenses. One rule is that of "prompt payment," that is, paying bills when due and not before or later. This procedure is mandated at the federal level by the Prompt Payment Act of 1982, as amended, and OMB Circular A-125.[51]

Letters of Credit and EFTs. Another technique is the use of letters of credit. These are provided to governments that are awarded grants. The letters allow governments to establish credit at banks without the federal government having to provide money until the governments need it to cover expenses under the grants.

Electronic fund transfers (EFTs) are used in conjunction with letters of credit but also more generally in handling receipts and expenditures. Through the use of EFTs, monies are moved via computer communication from one bank to another.

Monies received at one bank through a lock-box system, for instance, can be moved to other accounts in distant banks. Another advantage of EFTs is that they can be used for recurring payments, such as making direct deposits of Social Security payments into retirees' bank accounts. The cost of using EFTs is much lower than that of checks.

Computer Usage. New computer technology has greatly altered how financial institutions operate and how cash is handled for government. During the 1980s, the federal government changed from its decades-old green, computer-card checks to new ones that are more secure from forgery and that can be magnetically "read." The Treasury Department also moved to a new high-speed system for reconciling cleared checks. Off-the-shelf computer software is available for state and local cash management functions, reducing the need for expensive, individually designed systems.[52]

Intergovernmental Relations. Cash management has important intergovernmental aspects. States, as noted, have set standards for their respective local governments; these laws often are viewed by local governments as unnecessarily restrictive. Several states have established investment pools. Some states provide assistance to local governments in developing cash management plans.[53] Issues have existed over the timing of grant payments the federal government makes to state and local governments; the former, for cash management reasons, attempts to provide grant installments at the last possible moment.

Procurement

Procurement entails the acquisition of resources required in providing governmental services. While this function is not at the core of budgeting, it has major budgetary implications.

Organizational Configurations. While procurement can be handled on a centralized or decentralized basis, most jurisdictions have systems that lie between these two extremes. There may be a central purchasing agency that is responsible for acquiring commonly used materials, such as office furniture and supplies, while line agencies have authority to purchase items used primarily by themselves.

At the federal level, there are several major organizational units responsible for procurement. The General Services Administration provides overall support to departments by procuring buildings, equipment, motor vehicles, computer systems, telephone systems, supplies, and the like. The Department of Defense, as might be expected, has its own procurement operations; the Defense Logistics Agency purchases many items centrally for the department, while the individual services also have purchasing authority.[54] Besides these agencies, procurement is carried out by other line departments and agencies, including Energy, Transportation, and the National Aeronautics and Space Administration.

Having many procurement offices can result in a hodgepodge of operations, each with its own peculiar set of regulations. Congress in 1974 dealt with this problem by creating the Office of Federal Procurement Policy (OFPP) within OMB. President Reagan strengthened the OFPP's role in 1982 by issuing Executive Order 12352.[55] The OFPP, while not conducting purchasing activities, is responsible for coordinating the activities of purchasing offices.

Objectives. A procurement program has several objectives. One chief concern is having the materials and supplies available when needed. Keeping unit costs as low as possible is another objective; often the lowest costs for acquiring items are obtained by ordering large quantities, whether large amounts of office stationery or entire fleets of automobiles. Ordering large quantities, however, conflicts with another concern, namely keeping stocked items to a minimum. Procurement specialists strive to determine "economic ordering quantities" for when to purchase particular types of items.

Choices also must be made between purchasing or leasing.[56] In some instances, there may be financial and other advantages to leasing a building rather than purchasing it. A wide range of equipment can be leased, including photocopying machines, computers, and dump trucks.

Competition in procurement is considered one of the best means of ensuring quality products or services at minimum cost. The Competition in Contracting Act of 1984 requires the use of competitive bidding whenever possible in federal procurement and includes a provision authorizing the comptroller general of the General Accounting Office to nullify contract awards that violate competition requirements. At the state and local levels, corporations have become more aggressive in challenging contract awards when they seem to violate state legal requirements for competition.[57]

Reforms. There have been numerous efforts to improve procurement practices. OMB in 1982 issued a report recommending a uniform federal procurement system.[58] The Grace Commission issued several reports dealing with procurement. The 1986 Packard Commission's report on defense management included numerous recommendations on defense procurement.[59] The Advisory Commission on Intergovernmental Relations, the Council of State Governments, the Government Finance Officers Association, the International City Management Association, and the American Bar Association have all encouraged improvement in procurement procedures used by state and local governments.[60]

Despite sustained efforts to improve procurement practices, the field has been plagued with scandals involving waste, as in the case of toilet seats costing the military hundreds of dollars, and charges of bribery and other forms of collusion between government contractors and purchasing offices. During summer 1988, a major scandal developed over Pentagon spending. Defense, of course, has not been the only area subject to such scandals. Unethical and illegal practices in purchasing arise with some degree of frequency in federal domestic agencies and throughout state and local governments.

Intergovernmental Relations. There are important aspects of procurement that involve intergovernmental relations. States, through laws and regulations, set standards for purchasing conducted by their respective local governments. Cooperative purchasing is used to increase the "buying power" of governments. These agreements are among local governments or sometimes local governments and their state government.

Risk Management

Exposures. To provide services, governments must have property and personnel. Arising from this simple fact are a series of exposures or risks, such as the risk of property being damaged or lost owing to natural disasters and employee error and fraud. Property damage can lead to major repair or replacement costs and to loss of income, as in the case of having to close a municipal stadium because of unsafe conditions arising from structural problems. The destruction of the space shuttle, Challenger, in 1986 is a dramatic example of how one accident can disable a program for months or even years.

Liability. Exposures also exist regarding liability in which government is sued by its own employees or by corporations and private citizens. Negligence is often the basis of suits in which government is alleged not to have acted the way a "reasonable" person would and therefore to have inflicted harm. During the 1980s, there were many suits against local governments based on harmful chemicals leaking from landfills into privately owned water wells. Governments also may be sued for violating antitrust legislation, as in the instance of a city favoring one cable television operator over another.

Liability cases, of course, are governed by laws. The federal government may be sued only in federal court. One of the most important federal laws is the Tort Claims Act, which selectively permits suits against the government in cases not arising out of contract. State and local governments sometimes may be sued in federal courts as well as in their respective state courts. Antitrust cases against local governments, for example, are the domain of federal courts. Discrimination cases can be filed in federal and state courts.

Managing Risks. Governments need a management strategy for dealing with such exposures.[61] Risk management planning begins by identifying exposures and, where possible, eliminating them. A faulty woodworking machine in a school shop should be repaired; the repair will improve the safety of the machine, thereby eliminating some risk when students use it. A road intersection widely known to be dangerous can be redesigned as a means of eliminating liability risk.

Having eliminated or reduced risks, governments must be prepared to deal with remaining exposures. In self-insurance, governments expend from current budgets to cover small to moderate expenses. Examples are the costs of repairing police cars damaged in the line of duty. For larger cases, commercial insurance is used, or in some instances governments cover each others' risks through self-insurance pooling.

Insurance premiums for liability coverage have become extremely expensive, sometimes being beyond the reach of governments—if available at all. Costs are a function of the nature of a policy. Factors include the number of employees and officials of a government, the services covered, the deductibles included, and the loss experience. The latter is not just the experience of a particular government. A given city might have had no major suits filed against it, but because some cities have had major legal problems, as in cases involving landfills, all cities pay heavily for coverage.

SUMMARY

Execution is the conversion of plans embodied in the budget into day-to-day operations. At stake are factors such as devising means of observing legislative intent as prescribed in appropriations and providing the services that have been authorized. Control over line agencies is exercised through apportionment planning and pre-auditing of expenditures.

During the 1980s there was a resurgence of interest in economy and efficiency. This trend was embodied in the Grace Commission at the national level. Privatization of services has been sought as a means of increasing efficiency of operations.

Tax administration and cash management, which usually are under the direction of a secretary of treasury, are processes aimed at maximizing revenues and minimizing costs. Numerous mechanisms are used to enforce tax laws, ranging from offering taxpayer assistance in preparing tax returns to prosecuting delinquent taxpayers.

Cash management is the process of administering monies to ensure that they are available over time to meet expenditure needs and that monies, when temporarily not needed, are invested at a minimum risk and a maximum yield. Many instruments exist for investing state and local funds. Federal cash management is handled by the Treasury Department through the Federal Reserve System.

Procurement entails the acquisition of resources required in providing governmental services, and risk management, then, is concerned with protecting those resources. Governments often have a central purchasing office but allow individual departments some independence to purchase products and services. A procurement program attempts to purchase only that which is needed, avoid stock outages, and keep unit costs low. Risk management attempts to eliminate or reduce exposures and to prepare for such events as damage to government property and liability suits arising out of government operations.

NOTES

1. Bernard T. Pitsvada, "Flexibility in Federal Budget Execution," *Public Budgeting and Finance* 3 (Summer 1983): 83–101.

2. Shawna Grosskopf and Kathy Hayes, "Reimbursement of State Mandates," *State and Local Government Review* 15 (1983): 102–105.

3. Irene S. Rubin, *Shrinking the Federal Government* (New York: Longman, 1985).

4. General Accounting Office, *Implementing FY1986 Reductions: Balanced Budget and Emergency Deficit Control Act of 1985* (Washington, D.C.: Government Printing Office, 1986).

5. Daniel Mazmanian and Paul Sabatier, eds., "Symposium on Successful Policy Implementation," *Policy Studies Journal* 8 (1980): 531–653.

6. Thomas A. Reiner and Julian Wolpert, "Funding Caps," *Public Administration Review* 45 (1985): 391–97.

7. General Accounting Office, *Budget Issues: Governmentwide Analysis of the Growth in Unexpended Balances* (Washington, D.C.: Government Printing Office, 1986).

8. General Accounting Office, *Federal Year-End Spending Patterns for Fiscal Years 1982, 1983, and 1984* (Washington, D.C.: Government Printing Office, 1985).

9. Allen Schick, "Micro-Budgetary Adaptations to Fiscal Stress in Industrialized Democracies," *Public Administration Review* 48 (1988): 523–33.

10. President's Private Sector Survey on Cost Control, *War on Waste* (New York: Macmillan, 1984).

11. Mark A. McBriarty, "REFORM 88: A Sense of Deja Vu," *American Review of Public Administration* 18 (March 1988): 47–61.

12. Larry Hubbell and C. Morgan Kinghorn, "President Reagan's Productivity Improvement Program: A Prescription for Success?" *Public Productivity Review* 11 (Summer 1988): 1–9.

13. General Accounting Office, *Compendium of GAO's Views on the Cost Saving Proposals of the Grace Commission* (Washington, D.C.: Government Printing Office, 1985).

14. General Accounting Office, *Synopsis of GAO Reports Involving Contracting Out Under OMB Circular A-76* (Washington, D.C.: Government Printing Office, 1983).

15. Steve H. Hanke, ed., *Prospects for Privatization* (New York: Academy of Political Science, 1987).

16. E.S. Savas, *Privatizing the Public Sector* (Chatham, N.J.: Chatham House, 1982).

17. President's Commission on Privatization, *Privatization* (Washington, D.C.: Government Printing Office, 1988).

18. Douglas W. Dunham, "Inmates' Rights and the Privatization of Prisons," *Columbia Law Review* 86 (1986): 1475–1504.

19. President's Council on Management Improvement, *Streamlining Internal Control Processes and Strengthening Management Control with Less Effort* (Washington, D.C.: Government Printing Office, 1985).

20. William F. Funk, "The Paperwork Reduction Act: Paperwork Reduction Meets Administrative Law," *Harvard Journal of Legislation* 24 (1987): 1–116.

21. Office of Management and Budget, *Regulatory Program of the United States Government* (Washington, D.C.: Government Printing Office, annual).

22. Barbara Coleman, *Through the Corridors of Power: A Citizen's Guide to Federal Rulemaking* (Washington, D.C.: OMB Watch, 1987).

23. Caron Chess, "Looking Behind the Factory Gates," *Technology Review* (August–September, 1986): 42–47+.

24. Peter M. Benda and Charles H. Levine, "OMB and the Central Management Problem: Is Another Reorganization the Answer?" *Public Administration Review* 46 (1986): 379–91.

25. General Accounting Office, *Financial Management: Progress of OMB's Chief Financial Officer* (Washington, D.C.: Government Printing Office, 1988).

26. General Accounting Office, *Further Research into Noncompliance Is Needed to Reduce Growing Tax Losses* (Washington, D.C.: Government Printing Office, 1982).

27. Keith Snavely, "Innovations in State Tax Administration," *Public Administration Review* 48 (1988): 903–10.

28. General Accounting Office, *Tax Administration: The Federal/State Tax Information Exchange Program* (Washington, D.C.: Government Printing Office, 1985).

29. General Accounting Office, *Tax Administration: Accessibility, Timeliness, and Accuracy of IRS' Telephone Assistance Program* (Washington, D.C.: Government Printing Office, 1987).

30. General Accounting Office, *Tax Administration: Difficulties in Accurately Estimating Tax Examination Yield* (Washington, D.C.: Government Printing Office, 1988).

31. John F. Due, "Trends in State Sales Tax Audit Selection since 1960," *National Tax Journal* 38 (1985): 235–40.

32. General Accounting Office, *Tax Administration: Investigating Illegal Income—Success Uncertain, Improvements Needed* (Washington, D.C.: Government Printing Office, 1988).

33. Linda L. Spencer, "More States Conduct Tax Amnesty Programs," *Tax Administrators News* 52 (1988): 13–14+.

34. General Accounting Office, *ADP Modernization: IRS' Redesign of Its Tax Administration System* (Washington, D.C.: Government Printing Office, 1987).

35. General Accounting Office, *Tax Administration: Replacement of Service Center Computers Provides Lessons for the Future* (Washington, D.C.: Government Printing Office, 1987).

36. Larry Deboer, "Administrative Costs of State Lotteries," *National Tax Journal* 38 (1985): 479–87.

37. General Accounting Office, *Debt Collection: Information on the Amount of Debts Owed the Federal Government* (Washington, D.C.: Government Printing Office, 1985).

38. William M. Parle and Robert E. England, "Tax Refund Offset Policies in the American States," *State and Local Government Review* 20 (1988): 32–37.

39. Richard Pollock and Jack P. Suyderhoud, "The Role of Rainy Day Funds in Achieving Fiscal Stability," *National Tax Journal* 39 (1986): 485–97.

40. Julian Walmsley, *The New Financial Instruments* (Somerset, N.J.: Wiley, 1988).

41. Girard Miller, *Investing Public Funds* (Chicago: Government Finance Officers Association, 1986), pp. 183–206.

42. Rhett D. Harrell, *Banking Relations*, rev. ed. (Chicago: Government Finance Officers Association, 1986).

43. Girard Miller and Michelle R. Saddler, "Collateralization: Protecting Public Deposits," *Government Finance Review* 3 (October 1987): 23–26.

44. Fred Thompson, "Taking Full Advantage of State Investment Pools," *Journal of Policy Analysis and Management* 7 (1988): 353–56.

45. Bureau of the Census, *Finances of Employee-Retirement Systems of State and Local Governments in 1985–86* (Washington, D.C.: Government Printing Office, 1987), p. vii.

46. Office of Management and Budget, *Report on Strengthening Federal Cash Management* (Washington, D.C.: Government Printing Office, 1980).

47. President's Private Sector Survey on Cost Control, *Report on Financial Asset Management* (Washington, D.C.: Government Printing Office, 1983).

48. President's Private Sector Survey on Cost Control, *Report on Financial Management in the Federal Government* (Washington, D.C.: Government Printing Office, 1983).

49. General Accounting Office, *U.S. Government Securities: An Examination of Views Expressed about Access to Brokers' Services* (Washington, D.C.: Government Printing Office, 1987).

50. President's Private Sector Survey on Cost Control, *Report on Financial Asset Management*, pp. 38–40.

51. General Accounting Office, *Prompt Payment Act: Military Exchanges Had Problems in Paying on Time* (Washington, D.C.: Government Printing Office, 1988).

52. Paul Zorn, "The Functional Requirements of Cash Management Software," *Government Finance Review* 12 (October 1986): 13–17.

53. Charles K. Coe, "The Effects of Cash Management Assistance by States to Local Governments," *Public Budgeting and Finance* 8 (Summer 1988): 80–90.

54. Department of Defense, *Selling to the Military* (Washington, D.C.: Government Printing Office, 1987).

55. General Accounting Office, *Progress of Federal Procurement Reform Under Executive Order 12352* (Washington, D.C.: Government Printing Office, 1983).

56. A. John Vogt and Lisa A. Cole, eds., *A Guide to Municipal Leasing*, 2nd ed. (Chicago: Municipal Finance Officers Association, 1985).

57. Georgina Fiordalisi, "Vendors Challenge Contracts as Bidding Wars Get Hotter," *City and State* 5 (August 1, 1988): 1, 28.

58. Office of Management and Budget, *Proposal for a Uniform Federal Procurement System* (Washington, D.C.: Government Printing Office, 1982).

59. President's Blue Ribbon Commission on Defense Management, *A Formula for Action: A Report to the President on Defense Acquisition* (Washington, D.C.: Government Printing Office, 1986).

60. *State and Local Government Purchasing*, 2nd ed. (Lexington, Ky.: Council of State Governments, 1983).

61. Natalie Wasserman and Dean G. Phelus, eds., *Risk Management Today* (Washington, D.C.: International City Management Association, 1985).

11

Financial Management: Accounting, Auditing, and Information Systems

An important component of budget execution is accounting systems that track projected and actual expenditures during the budget year. Accounting, as will be seen in the following sections, serves a variety of purposes, but one of the most important has always been maintaining honesty or integrity. Accounting also is important to the functions of the preceding chapter, namely tax administration, cash management, procurement, and risk management.

This chapter has three sections, with the first and largest being devoted to accounting systems. The second section discusses the role of auditing of accounting systems. The third considers information systems used in accounting and, more broadly, information systems used in budgeting and finance.

GOVERNMENTAL ACCOUNTING

"An accounting system accumulates and measures financial data and converts those data to information that is then communicated and applied by various groups."[1] Accounting, then, is one type of information system and usually contains mostly financial information on the receipt of funds and their expenditure.

In this section, we explore several aspects of accounting systems, beginning with the purposes and standards of accounting and the organizations that shape accounting systems. Fund accounting, the structure of accounting systems, the classification of expenditures, and the bases for accounting are considered. The section concludes with a discussion of the types of reports that are generated by accounting systems.

Organizational Responsibilities and Standards

Purposes. Accounting systems have been devised for a variety of purposes, with the maintenance of honesty being one of the most prominent ones.[2] Through accounting, people who have wrongly intercepted monies being paid to government or channeled expenditures to their own advantage can be detected. Accounting, then, serves as a deterrent to theft and corruption.

A related purpose is that of restricting expenditures to stay within legal parameters. Illegal expenditures can occur that do not involve graft, as in the case of agency expenditures exceeding an appropriation or being used for purposes other than those permitted in authorizing legislation.

Another important purpose is reporting on the management of funds that are held in custody or trust. One major example is accounting systems devised to handle contributions to employee retirement funds and outlays to beneficiaries.

Decision making is facilitated by accounting systems, which report past revenues and expenditures and can be used in forecasting financial transactions. Without accurate information from an accounting system, decision makers are unable to determine whether a gap exists between proposed spending for the budget year and available revenue.

Accounting is used internally to help managers increase efficiency and effectiveness in delivering services. Managerial accounting focuses upon calculating the costs associated with providing services to citizens.[3] These derived costs also can be used for setting schedules for service charges.

Accounting Organizations. Numerous, somewhat competing, organizations establish the ground rules for accounting. As has been noted throughout this volume, the General Accounting Office (GAO) sets guidelines for federal agencies.[4] The Federal Managers' Financial Integrity Act of 1982, amending the Accounting and Auditing Act of 1950, requires that each executive agency establish internal accounting and administrative controls in accordance with standards prescribed by the GAO and conduct annual reviews to determine the extent of compliance with those standards. As of late 1986, the GAO reported that of the 323 accounting systems in use in the major agencies, fully one-fourth were not in conformance with the established standards.[5]

The Office of Management and Budget (OMB) also influences federal agencies and, as noted in the preceding chapter, established the position of chief financial officer in 1987.[6] Proposals have circulated for Congress to establish a financial office that would be independent of OMB.

State and local accounting systems are influenced by several sources. State auditors and comptroller generals set standards for their respective state and local systems. These systems also are influenced by the GAO and OMB, which determine how federal grant monies are handled.

A variety of professional organizations have periodically attempted to establish standards of accounting in the public sector. The former National Council on Governmental Accounting consisted of representatives of such bodies as the Government Finance Officers Association, the American Institute of Certified Public Accountants, and the American Accounting Association and produced what was known as the "blue book" or *GAAFR—Governmental Accounting, Auditing, and Financial Reporting. GAAFR* currently is published by the Government Finance Officers Association and is designed to assist governments at all levels achieve what are considered the standards in the field.[7] The Council of State Governments publishes materials suggesting appropriate accounting systems for its membership.[8]

The private sector has long had a well-established standard-setting organization; the Financial Accounting Standards Board (FASB) issues authoritative pronouncements on accounting for profit and nonprofit organizations.

In 1984, a governmental counterpart to FASB was established. The Governmental Accounting Standards Board (GASB) is a fledgling organization that attempts to speak for governmental bodies.[9] GASB and FASB have some territorial issues, such as which organization should speak for higher educational institutions. Both FASB and GASB are under the umbrella of the Financial Accounting Foundation.

Principles of Accounting. GASB and its predecessors have recognized what are considered generally accepted accounting principles, or GAAP.[10] While space limitations do not allow a thorough discussion of each of the 12 principles, it should be noted that they are intended as guides to establishing and modifying accounting systems. The first principle provides the foundation for the other 11 by requiring that accounting principles should be followed *and* that the legal requirements of a government should be met. Adhering to this first principle can be difficult in that laws can require accounting practices that are contrary to GAAP.

Fund Accounting

One of the main differences between public and private sector accounting is what is called the accounting "entity." For the typical private sector institution, the entity is the organization itself, since accounts are designed to reflect the resource position of the entire corporation. Governments, in contrast, separate financial resources into distinct accounting entities called funds. Each fund is set up to record and account for the uses of a specific group of assets or sources of revenue. There are three general classes of public sector funds, with different types of funds within each class for a total of seven types.[11]

Governmental Funds. The first class, known as Governmental Funds, consists of four types. The most important one is (1) the *General fund.* Several revenue sources may flow into a government's general fund, such as property tax and income tax receipts at the local level. The resources in the fund are available for expenditure on virtually any purpose that the jurisdiction is legally empowered to pursue. Most municipalities, for instance, may use general fund receipts for police and road services but not schools, since the latter are the domain of independent school districts.

The other fund types within the governmental class are available for what are thought of as normal government operations, but these types have restrictions for receipts and/or expenditures. (2) *Special revenue funds* account for resources from special sources and are earmarked for special purposes. Gasoline taxes are typically accounted for in a special revenue fund, with expenditures limited to transportation, especially roads and highways.

(3) *Capital project funds* account for receipts and expenditures related to projects, such as construction of a new park or city hall, or for major pieces of equipment, such as vehicles for a city fire department. Monies may come into these funds from bond sales that will be paid for with general fund tax receipts.

(4) *Debt service funds* are used to account for interest and principal on general-purpose long-term debt. The revenue received by this type of fund usually is from the general fund.

Proprietary Funds. The second class of funds consists of those that are proprietary or businesslike in nature. (5) *Enterprise funds* operate as businesses with the customers external to government. Such funds are established for toll roads, bridges, and local water systems. The other type of proprietary fund is (6) *Internal service funds* for governmental businesses in which the customers are internal to government. A central purchasing office or a vehicle maintenance garage may operate as an internal service fund, with revenues coming from other departments as services are rendered. When bonds are sold to support the activities of proprietary funds, as in the case of bond proceeds being used to renovate a city sewerage system, capital expenditures and payment of debt are handled through the proprietary fund, not through capital project and debt service funds.

Fiduciary Funds. The third class consists of fiduciary funds. Within it is one type known as (7) *Trust and agency funds.* Employee pension funds are one of the most important types of trust funds in government. Agency funds include revolving funds, such as government loan programs, and funds arising from contributions or donations, as in the case of a benefactor establishing a scholarship program at a university. In some instances, a county government may collect all property taxes within its boundaries on behalf of the county, municipalities, and school districts. Monies for these other governments, then, are placed in separate trust funds.

Structure and Rules of Accounting Systems

Ledgers. Accounting systems use ledgers as a means of organization or structure. Each fund has a general ledger and then subsidiary ledgers. The general ledger records the overall status of revenues and expenditures, while subsidiary ledgers are established for each revenue source and type of expenditure. In a general fund having several tax sources of revenue, a subsidiary revenue ledger is used for each source.

Expenditure subsidiary ledgers control expenditures by appropriation, organizational unit, object of expenditure, and sometimes purpose or activity. Accounting systems are used to track expenditures according to provisions in appropriations; often these appropriations are specific to organizations, as in the case of $2 million appropriated to a city recreation department. The appropriation also may contain limitations on how funds will be spent, such as on personnel or equipment expenditures; this aspect of accounting is explained later. Some jurisdictions track expenditures by program or activity, as in governments having program budget structures that do not match organizational structure.

Accounting Formula. Accounting systems use equations that allow systematic recording of transactions and double-checking that the transactions have been properly recorded. The basic equation that is used is

$$\text{Assets} = \text{Liabilities} + \text{Fund Balance}$$

In the formula, assets can be the revenue in a fund, liabilities are the monies owed others, such as suppliers of office equipment and tires for police cars, and the fund balance comprises the residual, uncommitted monies. Specific accounts are established for each of these three components of the formula. Asset accounts, for example, can include those showing cash on hand as well as monies owed by taxpayers.

Double-entry accounting is used as a cross-check in which any single transaction is recorded twice (at a minimum). If taxes are received and no additional obligations are incurred, then assets are increased and so is fund balance. Double entry can be used within one portion of the overall formula. If taxes are received but were already noted in an asset account called "taxes receivable," then that account would be reduced while another asset account for cash would be increased; that particular set of transactions would not affect liabilities or fund balance.

Transactions are recorded according to a "T" in which the left side of the T constitutes debits and the right, credits. The terms "debits" and "credits" refer only to the left and right sides of the T and have no connotation of negative and positive as is customary in common language. Rules exist as to when an account should be debited and when credited. In any transaction, the amount debited to one or more accounts must equal the amount credited to other accounts.

Classification of Expenditures

Fund and Appropriation. Expenditures are accounted for in a variety of ways. One set of characteristics is the fund and appropriation. An appropriation is legislative approval to spend from a specific fund. Since several bills may be passed that appropriate out of the general fund, the dollar stipulations in each of these bills must be observed vis-à-vis the total assets available in the general fund. Even if a jurisdiction uses only one appropriation bill, each of the expenditure limits in the bill must be observed and consequently must be monitored by the accounting system. When an expenditure is made, it is charged against the appropriated amount and the remaining available balance is shown. In this way, an accounting system can be used to keep agency expenditures within budgeted figures.

If the legislative body earmarks expenditures in detail, then the accounting system becomes increasingly complex. For example, Congress in its annual foreign assistance appropriations bill typically imposes detailed figures on the level of funding for programs within the Agency for International Development *and* amounts to be available in each country receiving aid. The accounting system, therefore, must monitor expenditures by program (e.g., infant mortality prevention) and by country to adhere to the stipulations in the appropriations bill.

Organizational Unit. Expenditures are made by organizational units, and accounting systems must track expenditures accordingly. Appropriations bills usually are specific to agencies so that, rather than the government simply being authorized to spend an amount on forest preservation, a specific unit within a department is granted that money. Large governments, then, account for expenditures not only at the departmental level but also at the bureau, office, division, or regional unit level.

Objects of Expenditure. Accounting systems invariably account in terms of the objects acquired or the objects of expenditure. Broad groupings of objects are called major objects, and their subdivisions are called minor objects. Exhibit 11-1 illustrates the object classes used by the federal government. The object series beginning with the number "1," or the "10" series, covers all personnel-related expenditures. Within that series are the three subclasses of direct compensation, benefits for employees, and benefits for former employees.

Accounting systems can become unwieldy in their use of minor objects. Travel as a major object can be subdivided in numerous ways.

1. mode (personal automobile, government automobile, commercial airline, and the like)

Exhibit 11-1 Federal Object of Expenditure Classification

Code	Title
Personal Services and Benefits	
11	Personnel Compensation
11.1	Full-Time Permanent
11.3	Other than Full-Time Permanent
11.5	Other Personnel Compensation
11.7	Military Personnel
11.8	Special Personal Services Payments
12	Personnel Benefits
12.1	Civilian Personnel Benefits
12.2	Military Personnel Benefits
13	Benefits for Former Personnel
Contractual Services and Supplies	
21	Travel and Transportation of Persons
22	Transportation of Things
23	Rent, Communications, and Utilities
24	Printing and Reproduction
25	Other Services
26	Supplies and Materials
Acquisition of Capital Assets	
31	Equipment
32	Land and Structures
33	Investments and Loans
Grants and Fixed Charges	
41	Grants, Subsidies, and Contributions
42	Insurance Claims and Indemnities
43	Interest and Dividends
44	Refunds
Other	
91	Unvouchered
92	Undistributed
93	Limitation on Expenses

Source: "Preparation and Submission of Budget Estimates," Office of Management and Budget, Circular A-11, pp. 109–116, Government Printing Office, 1988.

2. type of person traveling (elected official, political or career executive, employee, and client)
3. purpose (meeting, conference, training, and inspection)
4. location (in state, out of state, and out of nation)
5. type of expense (lodging, meals, and transportation)

The number of possible permutations is great. When an accounting system uses such detail, the entry of many transactions may be delayed due to uncertainties about classifications.

Despite the administrative problems of detailed minor objects, legislative bodies often incorporate such details in appropriations bills. These "line items" in an appropriation allow control when there is concern that funds may be abused. Restrictions may be inserted on the purchase of newspaper subscriptions, the number of automobiles, and government employee travel. When minor object restrictions are embedded in appropriations, the limits are by definition the law and the accounting system must assure compliance.

Purpose and Activities. Program-oriented budgets that focus decision-making attention on specific program goals and objectives also require accounting-based information on how much each program costs. If a budget based on program classifications cuts across agency lines, then the accounting system needs to cut across agency lines to accumulate the costs according to program. Similarly, preparing a budget that allocates funds according to detailed work activities requires an accounting system that tracks expenditures by those activities. In a 1985 survey of state budget offices, about two-thirds reported that their states' accounting systems recorded expenditures at the specific program level.[12] The problem of accounting by program or activity is discussed more fully in the next section in regard to cost accounting.

Basis of Accounting

The "basis of accounting" refers to the timing of transactions, or when a revenue item is recorded as received by the government and when an expenditure is recorded as having occurred.[13] There are several methods for determining when a revenue or expenditure item is recorded, and each has a different purpose.

Cash Accounting. The oldest system is cash accounting, which is still used today, particularly in small governments, but more generally all governments must have a cash aspect to their accounting systems. In a cash accounting system, tax receipts are recorded when actually received by the government and expenditures are recorded when payments are made. Minor variations exist; some systems record expenditures when checks are written, but others record expenditures when checks clear the banking system. The major advantages of the cash system are that it is simple in comparison with alternatives and that it presents an accurate picture of cash on hand at any point in time.

The major disadvantage of the cash system is that it does not provide information about the future, namely anticipated receipts and expenditures. The cash on hand may seem to suggest that one's financial situation is reasonably secure, but a different picture may emerge when considering future obligations, such as payrolls.

Encumbrance Accounting. A step in the direction of anticipating future transactions is encumbrance accounting. Expenditures are recorded when purchase orders are written or contracts are signed; some of the cash on hand, then, is said to be encumbered and not available for covering other expenditures. In the case of a multiyear contract, all of the expenditures for a year may be encumbered at the outset of the fiscal year, or amounts may be encumbered each month as work is completed by the contractor. An encumbrance system helps ensure that a governmental unit will not overspend its appropriation.

Accrual Accounting. In accrual systems, financial transactions are recognized when the activities that generate them occur. Revenues are recorded when the government earns the income, as when a local government sends tax bills to property owners. Expenditures are recognized when the liabilities are incurred, regardless of when payment for those goods or services might actually be made during the year.

The accrual basis has been required of federal agencies for over 30 years, but virtually no federal agency accounting system actually uses accrual accounting.[14] The obstacle has been the diversity of accounting systems, with large departments such as Defense having many different accounting systems.[15]

Despite the obstacles to implementation, the accounting profession continues to endorse strongly the accrual basis of accounting. GASB recommends the accrual basis.

Cost Accounting. While the cash, encumbrance, and accrual bases of accounting focus attention on resources coming into government and being expended, cost accounting is concerned with when resources are used in the production of goods and services.[16] For example, gasoline purchased for a state highway department could be accounted for when the order is made (encumbrance), when the goods are received (modified accrual method), or when the vendor is paid (cash method). The cost approach, in contrast, records the transaction when the gasoline is consumed.

The concepts of inventory and depreciation are critical to cost accounting. If an agency builds up its inventory in a given year, the expenditures for that inventory are not considered part of the costs of providing services in that year. Similarly, the purchase of capital goods should not be considered costs in the year of purchase but should be depreciated over the life span of the goods. From a cost standpoint, the cost of police patrol cars might be spread over three years, but from a cash standpoint, the purchase will be recorded in the first year. Buildings and vehicles then are depreciated over time, showing a truer picture of the cost of services than the cash method does.

Cost accounting improves management capabilities in several ways. The costs of delivering services can be monitored over time, thereby giving an impetus for increased efficiency of operations. This accounting method facilitates improved inventory control, since what is held in inventory is monitored carefully. The method is useful for internal service funds, allowing a more equitable fee structure for services, such as a printing services unit charging departments for printing their reports, brochures, and the like.

Cost accounting can be useful for program budgeting in that it can identify the costs of producing impacts, outputs, and activities. For example, cost accounting can track the costs of municipal street lighting. If activity-type accounting is used, then the cost of repairing and replacing lights can be recorded separately.

Any jurisdiction must decide to what extent it wishes to pursue the identification of costs. One option is to devise a cost accounting system that records costs by program and activity; the costs may not necessarily follow organizational configurations. Any given bureau might have responsibility for conducting two or more activities on which all bureau personnel work from time to time. These activities become "cost centers" for which both program and financial information is collected. To determine costs for the centers, records must be maintained regarding the amount of time each worker spends on each activity. Other bureau costs, such as those for supplies, telephones, and furniture, must be distributed among the cost centers. This form of accounting obviously is complicated and requires some degree of sophistication to be able to collect, enter, and manipulate data.

Project-Based Accounting. Another option that is not as elaborate as cost accounting is project-based accounting. Accounts can be established on a temporary basis to track costs for selected activities. Private firms, both for-profit and nonprofit, keep detailed accounting records for contracts, including costs at the task or subtask levels. If a consulting firm has been awarded a government contract, a separate set of accounts is established and costs are accumulated showing what personnel worked on what tasks for what length of time within a given reporting period (weekly, biweekly, or monthly). Accounts of this type are important for reimbursement purposes.

Project-based accounting also is used for monitoring internal operations. If a corporation is developing a new product or group of products, separate accounts can be established to gauge the developmental costs of the project. In the quasi-governmental arena, the World Bank uses account codes and employee time report systems to account for project costs, enabling management to evaluate the cost of preparing, negotiating, and supervising a specific loan to a country.

Cost Finding. In some instances, governments may be satisfied with something less than a complete cost accounting system or even project-based accounting.[17] Rather than having an ongoing system of collecting cost information, governments sometimes selectively study costs of specific activities that may be contained within a single organization or spread across several units. The cost of delivering family planning services to teenagers might be derived through analysis of expenditure records and sampling of employee time commitments. A far more elaborate cost-finding endeavor would be deriving the costs of AIDS to a state government; the analysis would attempt to determine the costs of prevention and treatment activities that are not encoded in the accounting system. For example, AIDS may well increase health care costs for prisoners, but such costs would not routinely be segregated in the accounting system.

The analysis of cost data can be useful in identifying base costs and differential costs. There may be a minimum cost for providing any level of service—the base—after which costs increase as units of service increase. For example, a preschool program for disadvantaged children begins with a base cost for essentials such as a school room, teacher, and some supportive services independent of whether one or perhaps ten children are taught. As the number of children in the class increases, differential costs increase, such as those for teacher aides, another teacher, and possibly another classroom.

Need for Different Bases. These different approaches to the basis of accounting are not substitutes for each other. Rather, each satisfies a different type of need. From the standpoint of a treasury department, a cash basis for recording receipts and expenditures is necessary because the department has the legal responsibility to receive revenue and issue checks to cover expenditures. This responsibility extends to determining that there are sufficient funds to cover checks to be issued. The encumbrance basis is important to ensure that appropriations are not exceeded. An accrual basis is important in showing the current status of assets and liabilities, including liabilities that will place a demand on cash in the future. Cost accounting is valuable in identifying the resources consumed as distinguished from resources acquired and placed in inventory.

Reporting

Accounting systems generate reports used by managers, policy makers, and people outside of government. Principle 12 of GAAP provides that jurisdictions prepare interim and annual reports. Interim reports, such as daily and weekly reports, are used for internal purposes, as in the case of checking on appropriated funds that are neither spent nor encumbered. These interim reports are useful in monitoring budget execution and anticipating situations in which agencies will not have sufficient funds to operate their programs throughout the fiscal year.

Annual reports are particularly useful to people and organizations outside of government. Such reports can show taxpayers how revenues have been used to support services. Annual reports of local governments are helpful for businesses that are considering locating, relocating, or expanding existing facilities. The reports are used in understanding the financial condition of governments and deciding whether to purchase their bonds.

Financial Reports. GASB recommends a comprehensive annual financial report (CAFR) that has three sections—introduction, finances, and statistics.[18,19] The first section includes a letter of transmittal and general information about the government. The section lists the principal officials and provides an organization chart indicating lines of authority and responsibility.

The second section contains a variety of financial statements. Since governments make great use of funds, several different types of statements may be provided on each fund. These statements by themselves can be confusing in that they do not provide an overall perspective on the finances of the government. One particularly troubling aspect of these statements is the use of transfers among funds. Monies can be moved from one fund to another without affecting the overall assets of a jurisdiction, but if transfers are not carefully noted, they appear as expenditures in one fund and as new assets or receipts in another fund. For this reason, GASB and other professional accounting organizations prescribe the use of condensed statements that provide a comprehensive picture of a jurisdiction without some of the confusing detail.

The third section of a financial report provides statistical data. Some tables present trend data assembled from earlier financial reports, such as general revenues by source over the most recent ten-year period. Other tables provide demographic data and indicate the principal taxpayers in the jurisdiction.

Balance Sheets and Operating Statements. Of the numerous types of financial statements, balance sheets and operating statements are the most common. A balance sheet can be thought of as a snapshot of a government's finances at a point in time, such as at the end of a quarter or fiscal year, while an operating statement shows financial transactions over a period of time, such as an entire fiscal year.

A balance sheet is organized according to the accounting formula discussed earlier. Assets are first listed, showing cash on hand (bank deposits) and taxes receivable. For proprietary funds and fiduciary funds, fixed assets (buildings, land, etc.) also are reported as assets. The balance sheet then indicates liabilities, namely accounts that are payable and bonds outstanding, followed by fund balance, showing items such as monies that are encumbered.

Operating statements cover a specified time period and indicate the revenues received and the monies expended during that time. Revenues can be reported by source—sales tax and income tax. Expenditures can be reported by major objects, organizational units, or other means.

As would be expected, practice varies widely among jurisdictions as to how they present financial reports. Some governments provide a wealth of financial information, while others provide only basic data.[20] How these reports are structured greatly influences the "bottom line." For instance, a jurisdiction can present a favorable view of its financial situation by adjusting reporting periods on revenues received and by ignoring some liabilities, an example being accumulated sick leave of employees.[21]

GOVERNMENTAL AUDITING

Auditing serves a variety of functions and consequently exists in many different forms. One distinction made is between pre- and post-audits, namely between reviewing transactions before and after they occur. The pre-audit occurs before the government commits itself to a purchase and is used to verify, for example, that the police department has sufficient funds to purchase a piece of equipment and that the department is authorized to have that equipment. Not only the budget office but also an accounting department may be involved in pre-audits; if personnel are to be hired, a personnel office may have some pre-audit responsibility. Often at the state and local levels, independent comptrollers, controllers, or auditors general have pre-audit responsibilities.

Post-audits generally involve more extensive procedures and often more participants. The following discussion considers the function of post-audits in government budgeting and finance. This form of auditing has been defined as ". . . a systematic collection of the sufficient, competent evidential matter needed to attest to the fairness of management's assertions in the financial statements, or to evaluate management's efficiency and effectiveness in carrying out its responsibilities."[22]

Audit Objectives and Organizational Responsibilities

Purposes. Auditing in the private sector is used largely to ensure that the financial statements issued by a firm fairly reflect its financial status, and this same concern exists in government. Auditing is used to protect investors in both the private and public sectors; stockholders of businesses and bond-holders of businesses and governments gain some assurance through auditing that their investments are being well managed.

Auditing in government also is used for compliance purposes. As has been noted, accounting systems track receipts and expenditures to ensure that they are handled in conformance with restrictions contained in revenue and appropriations bills. Auditing helps ensure that an agency does not spend funds on an activity that, while beneficial to society, simply has not been authorized. Compliance auditing can include ensuring that an agency has accomplished programmatically what it was instructed to do.

Auditing Organizations. Nationally, several organizations influence the practice of governmental auditing. The American Institute of Certified Public Accountants (AICPA) issues generally accepted auditing standards (GAAS). GASB, in the process of identifying standards for accounting, inevitably becomes involved in auditing. GAO issues generally accepted government auditing standards (GAGAS) that are applied to federal agencies and may be applied to state and local governments that receive federal financial assistance.

Auditing within a government often is performed by several organizations. Audits are conducted periodically by officers within an agency to provide information to management; these internal audits help maintain managerial control over operations. Other audits are conducted by external officers, who can be from a unit answerable to the legislative body (GAO), a unit headed by an independently elected officer, or an independent private corporation that has a contract to conduct an audit.[23] After audit reports are prepared, these are sometimes formally reviewed by designated audit committees that usually consist of legislators.[24]

The federal government augmented the auditing function during the 1970s and 1980s by creating inspectors general (IGs) in major federal agencies.[25,26] Appointed by the president with the advice and consent of the Senate, IGs are located within agencies but can only be removed by the president. According to the Inspector General Act of 1978, IGs are responsible for conducting audits and for investigating possible cases of fraud, waste, and abuse of government resources.

Types of Audits and Standards

Audit Types. As already noted, there are pre- and post-audits and internal and external audits. Another means of categorizing audits is to consider the purposes to be served. The definition of auditing provided above suggests that audits can be directed toward finance and performance. According to

GAGAS, issued by GAO, financial audits focus upon whether financial statements prepared by a government accurately reflect financial transactions and the government's or agency's status.

Financial audits also review how financial matters are handled. Auditors are concerned with the vulnerability of a financial management system to potential fraud. Are organizational lines of responsibility clearly established to ensure that whoever is in charge has the authority to protect the government's or agency's finances? Are policies and procedures established for maintaining records, and are those policies and procedures adhered to in practice? Are computer systems that handle financial transactions protected against potential fraud? Guidelines in this area are established at the federal level by the Federal Managers' Financial Integrity Act of 1982 and OMB Circular A-123.[27]

The other major function served is performance auditing, which deals with whether resources are being used efficiently and whether results or objectives are being achieved.[28] This subject is discussed in Chapter 7. All that is necessary here is to note that some audit agencies, most notably GAO, have had their traditional financial duties expanded to include performance audits. Any audit agency faces the difficult choice of deciding how much effort and therefore resources should be devoted to the competing functions of financial and performance auditing. If major emphasis is given to performance auditing, fraud and other abuses may become more prevalent; conversely, emphasis on financial auditing may keep government honest but contribute little to encouraging agencies to fulfill their missions.

Auditing Standards. GAAS provides overall guidelines as well as standards for conducting fieldwork and preparing audit reports.[29] Overall standards call for auditors to be independent of the agencies under review and to be fully trained in the audit function. Fieldwork is to be adequately planned in advance and sufficiently staffed to meet the requirements of the work plan. Auditors must keep accurate records of their fieldwork to answer questions that may arise at a later time.

Field auditing involves verifying sample transactions to ensure that transactions did occur as recorded. For example, an expense report of a trip taken by a city employee to a national conference, among numerous expense reports, might be selected for review. The auditor may (1) call the travel agent or airline to verify the ticket price, (2) check that the trip was an authorized budget expenditure, (3) interview the employee to verify unreceipted miscellaneous expenses, and (4) review other receipts and documents to determine the accuracy of the report. The purpose of this fieldwork is not particularly to find cases of fraud, waste, and abuse but to verify that the jurisdiction has procedures to protect against them.

Both GAAS and GAGAS (of GAO) set standards for audit reporting. Of course, one of the chief concerns of any report is whether financial statements are in accordance with GAAP. Audit reports are expected to indicate deficiencies, such as accounting procedures not being consistently followed. Reports indicate whether internal controls exist to protect against fraud, waste, and abuse.

The Single Audit Act. A concern of the federal government for many years has been the large volume of federal financial transfers to state and local governments and to nongovernmental organizations. Individual audits of grants and contracts were conducted each year, but given the volume, many such transfers could not be audited by either the funding departments or GAO.

The Single Audit Act of 1984 (PL 98-502) is intended to deal with the problem.[30] The law requires that recipients of federal assistance of $100,000 or more in a fiscal year must undergo a single audit of their accounting systems and the way federal funds are handled. Governments receiving $25,000 to $100,000 may use a single audit or a series of individual audits of grants. Governments receiving under $25,000 are not required to have an audit but must maintain records that could be audited. The law has had the effect of requiring tens of thousands of audits annually.[31] The audit is intended to help ensure that recipients use federal resources in accordance with federal laws and regulations. The act is implemented through OMB Circular A-128.

INFORMATION SYSTEMS

Contemporary approaches to budgeting and accounting, as we have shown, require considerable amounts of information for decision making and evaluation. Information systems, then, constitute an effort to bring about greater coordination of organizational units in the collection, storage, manipulation, retrieval, and analysis of information. The following discussion addresses the design of information systems, the use of computers, and problems and issues that are endemic to information systems.

Management Information Systems

The term management information system (MIS) is most commonly used to describe an effort in which "management" refers to planning, administration, and control functions and "system" suggests a categorizing or ordering of information processing.[32] A distinction is made between data and information; data refer to facts and information to the utility of data.[33] Data that are not information are considered noise in that they detract from rather than aid the decision-making process. Thousands of pieces of data about individual welfare recipients, for example, may be of little help in deliberations about changing the funding formula for federal welfare aid to state and local governments.

A term related to MIS is decision support systems (DSS), which usually is used in reference to a computer information system that facilitates nonroutine, semistructured decision making.[34,35] In other words, routine activities are excluded, such as simple record keeping for patient appointments at a mental health clinic, but so are unstructured decision-making processes, such as setting overall funding priorities of mental health vis-à-vis narcotics law enforcement and national security interests in Central America.

Categorization of Information. From Chapter 1 forward, we have emphasized that there are basically two types of information used in budgetary and financial decision making: program information and resource information.[36] That typology can be seen in Figure 11-1, which is a schematic representation of the types of information used in the federal government, as suggested by a report prepared by GAO. The figure shows how public concerns and those of the legislative and executive branches determine the information requirements of government. Four columns of boxes are depicted, with the first column representing program information; that column includes social indicators, impacts, outputs, and other program-related information (see Chapter 5). The other three columns involve resource information— personnel, finances, and property (land, buildings, and equipment).

The illustration also has several rows depicting the nature of the decisions or the types of transactions involved. The highest level includes strategic planning information along with programming information. The second level shows operational planning, and the third, execution and control. The fourth level depicts relatively routine transactions, such as employee payroll, debt service, and construction management.

Structure. The design or structure of an MIS is dependent on the intended users and their information needs. Figure 11-1 is oriented toward the executive branch and its roles in budget preparation and execution. Other major users are the legislative branch in its budget approval and oversight roles and a comptroller office in its audit capacities.[37] In addition to needing information pertaining to appropriations and expenditures, legislatures want information on fiscal notes, the status of bills in each chamber, the receipt of grants, and the like.[38]

Organizations vary in how much information they need and how it will be used. A line agency needs much more data about itself than the budget office needs about the agency. Similarly, a personnel department needs much information on agency personnel while the budget office needs some but not nearly as much. Some users need data simply to have them, not to study them. Congress, state legislatures, and city councils often demand detailed financial data that will not be analyzed. Legislative bodies sometimes suspect the executive of hiding something important unless they force the executive to produce detailed expenditure data. The fact that legislators could look at any particular detail helps keep the executive honest.

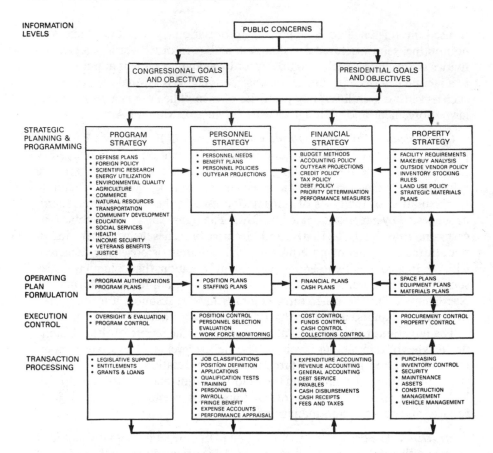

Figure 11-1 Federal Information Requirements Planning Chart. *Source: Managing the Cost of Government*, General Accounting Office, Vol. 2, p. 21, Government Printing Office, 1985.

Timeliness is another criterion. Some data need to be maintained on a daily basis. An accounting department needs daily reports on the status of funds, cash balances, and the like, whereas some agencies may need only weekly or monthly reports about their budgets. A central budget office does not need daily reports from agencies on program performance, such as outputs and impacts. Some information may need to be available only upon request, with a lag time of perhaps a week or more before the requested information is provided.

While numerous approaches exist to designing an MIS, seemingly the most viable approach is to develop modules or subsystems that can be linked with each other. Each subsystem need not be computer based, but as computer technology advances, more and more subsystems will be converted from paper and microfiche files to computer files. A central subsystem to any financially oriented MIS is an accounting system. As has been seen, large governments may have many accounting systems with varying degrees of standardization among them; over time, standardization will be more prevalent, given the need to compare and analyze data from different accounting systems.

Other subsystems may exist largely independent of the accounting system(s). There is no compelling need to have program impact information as part of an accounting system. Having both types of information in the same set of files may unnecessarily complicate data input, storage, and manipulation. On the other hand, computer-supported information systems that contain program data can be linked to accounting systems as needed. One approach is to download selected information from various subsystems into a temporary file. A state budget office that wanted to examine the economic impact of tourism might assemble information from a variety of sources from within the state government but also from external data bases.

The modular approach is attractive in concept but difficult to implement. The problem is linking the modules to each other, and in the real world it is not just a matter of literally plugging one module into another. Although a financial module may be suitable for capturing financial transactions, the problem remains of linking that data with program information. In other words, there might be no easy linkage between what a city department spends and what it produces.

Computers

The rapid advances in computers and related technology are making possible information systems that were only concepts a few years ago and are making these systems affordable for most governments.[39] Powerful mainframe computers, of course, have been a staple for federal agencies, states, and large cities for many years. With the advent of microcomputers, small governments were introduced to computer technology. By the late 1980s, probably almost every government in the United States had at least one computer.[40] What exists may well be a hodgepodge of equipment and software to run it. Large jurisdictions may continue to find great use in mainframe equipment but also find need for mini- and microcomputers that may run independent of the mainframes.[41] In some instances, agencies create microcomputer systems that duplicate mainframe files because either the central data processing office takes too long to respond to user requests or the mainframe files are not as user friendly in allowing for manipulation of data.

Acquisition Planning. During the 1990s, governments can be expected to exert greater planning over their computer installations and information systems. Once having entered the realm of computing through the purchase of one or more computers, a government must decide what steps to take next; planning for the introduction of new computer-based financial information systems is essential.[42] The vastness of the federal government has made this point quite apparent. As a result of the Paperwork Reduction Act of 1980, a rolling-forward five-year plan is developed annually for automatic data processing and telecommunications needs. OMB Circular A-127 emphasizes that agencies should use wherever possible "off-the-shelf" systems rather than paying vendors to develop unique configurations of hardware and software.

Software Packages. Computer use in budget preparation is becoming routine, with the most common type of application being the spreadsheet software program. A spreadsheet is a chart in which the rows can be organizational units within a department or at a more detailed level can be major and minor objects within a bureau or office. Columns in the spreadsheet can be time units, such as past year actual figures, current year projected figures, and proposed budget year and out-year figures. Other columns can be included such as expenditures by quarter; columns can be designated for appropriated amounts and actual expenditures. Spreadsheets can be used for budget proposals and for multiyear budget plans.[43]

The advantage of the spreadsheet program is that it can calculate thousands of adjustments in a few seconds. The spreadsheet can quickly adjust personnel costs to reflect possible pay increases, such as an across-the-board 5 percent pay adjustment. While pay is adjusted, the computer also can be instructed to recalculate employee benefits. Spreadsheet programs can accommodate numerous assumptions, such as a pay increase at one level and price increases for supplies and equipment at another level. Among the more popular spreadsheets in use for microcomputers are Lotus, Quattro, and Ecel.

Agency budget requests can be submitted to a central budget either electronically or by submitting the requests on floppy disks. If the central budget office decides to cut a request, the computer can readjust figures, such as recalculating all subtotals and totals, without having to spend hours of staff time. At the federal level, OMB is moving toward use of the Budget Preparation System (BPS), a network system that allows agencies to submit budget data via computer directly to OMB.[44]

Word processing also is an integral part of budget preparation, since substantial textual materials must be drafted each year. Perhaps the biggest advantage of any word processing software package is that it frees staff of retyping portions of the budget countless times as decisions, such as whether to fund a particular activity and at what level, are made and adjusted. Changes can be made, the computer can be instructed to check for spelling errors, and the new material then is ready to be presented in a variety of formats that include one, two, or more columns per page, justified right margins, and text that wraps around graphs and charts.

Data base managers are another type of software widely used in budget and financial operations. These software packages are intended to handle data pertaining to cases, such as characteristics of welfare clients, paychecks issued to employees, and the status of corporations inspected for compliance with air and water pollution regulations.

Issues and Problems

Access to information and MISs constitutes one of the most critical problems in the field. The federal government has hundreds of data banks that contain more than a billion records on individuals. Who should have access to these files? The Privacy Act is intended to protect individuals about whom federal agencies maintain files; on the other hand, the Freedom of Information Act opens many federal records to public inspection. Balancing these two objectives obviously is difficult. Agencies that collect information about individuals may be reluctant to share that information with other governmental units and indeed may be legally prohibited from such sharing.

Another aspect of access is the security of information systems and the computers that support them. Lack of security can result in unwarranted invasions of personal privacy, fraud, as in situations involving tampering of financial records, or a breach of national security. The Federal Managers' Financial Integrity Act requires federal agencies to test their information systems for "integrity," meaning the ability of unauthorized users to access and alter records. Additionally, the Computer Security Act of 1987 requires federal agencies to develop security plans for computer systems containing sensitive information.[45] When security measures can be circumvented, the information systems can be subjected to so-called viruses, in which programs are introduced that can shut down systems, alter data, or totally destroy data banks.

Computers have greatly expanded the ability of governments to collect, store, and manipulate data; a problem that arises from this is the burden imposed on others in supplying the information. As noted in Chapter 10, the federal government uses an Information Collection Budget to impose limits on federal agencies in their pursuit of data; the intent is to make federal agencies defend their need for data before requiring state and local governments, corporations, or individuals to supply the data.

When new technology is introduced, people need to be taken into account. Computers can be dehumanizing; working all day at a video display terminal can be as tedious and unrewarding as many assembly-line jobs. At the same time, technological changes can greatly increase worker productivity.[46]

Technological changes and particularly computers can affect relationships among the branches of government and levels of government.[47] Computers hold the potential for increasing the powers of legislative branches, which previously may have become dependent upon executives for information. New technology may increase the powers of the federal government over state and local governments and increase the powers of states over their local governments.

SUMMARY

Governmental accounting is characterized by procedures intended to avoid fraud and to guarantee agency conformance with legal requirements. Information from accounting systems is used in decision making and can help improve the efficiency and effectiveness of services. The Governmental Accounting Standards Board was established to help improve the nature of public sector accounting systems. Generally accepted accounting principles include provision for using several different types of funds, with the general fund usually being the most important for any government.

Accounting systems are structured by having a general ledger and subsidiary ledgers and follow a relatively simple formula of assets equaling the total of liabilities and fund balance. Within these ledgers, expenditures are accounted for in a variety of ways, including major and minor objects of expenditures.

Bases of accounting include cash, encumbrance, accrual, and cost. Some jurisdictions use project-based accounting and cost finding as distinguished from more comprehensive cost accounting methods. Regardless of the basis for accounting, reports summarizing transactions are prepared at intervals. Two of the most common types of reports are balance sheets and operating statements.

Auditing focuses upon whether financial statements are accurate reflections of the status of accounts and/or whether an organization is operating efficiently and effectively. Auditing is used for compliance purposes, namely to assure that financial transactions are in accordance with revenue and appropriation legislation. Generally accepted auditing standards constitute the guidelines for auditing in the public sector; in addition, generally accepted government auditing standards are used by the General Accounting Office.

Management information systems, as used in budgeting and finance, include program and resource information. These systems are used by executives, legislatures, and auditors for all four phases of the budget cycle—preparation, approval, execution, and audit. Computers, ranging from mainframes to powerful microcomputers, are greatly increasing the ability to provide the information needed for budgetary decision making. Problems exist with the introduction and expanded use of computer technology, including negative impacts on workers and changes in the relationships among branches and levels of government.

NOTES

1. Leo Herbert, Larry N. Killough, and Alan W. Steiss, *Accounting and Control for Governmental and Other Nonbusiness Organizations* (New York: McGraw-Hill, 1987), p. 7.

2. Robert J. Freeman, Craig D. Shoulders, and Edward S. Lynn, *Governmental and Nonprofit Accounting*, 3rd ed. (Englewood Cliffs, N.J.: Prentice-Hall, 1988), pp. 6–7.

3. Richard E. Brown and Hans-Dieter Sprohge, "Governmental Managerial Accounting," *Public Budgeting and Finance* 7 (Autumn 1987): 35–46.

4. Frederick C. Mosher, *A Tale of Two Agencies* (Baton Rouge: Louisiana State University Press, 1984).

5. General Accounting Office, *Financial Integrity Act* (Washington, D.C.: Government Printing Office, 1987), p. 50.

6. Gerald Riso, "Role of the Federal Chief Financial Officer, *Public Budgeting and Finance* 8 (Autumn 1988): 55–62.

7. *Governmental Accounting, Auditing, and Financial Reporting* (Chicago: Government Finance Officers Association, 1988).

8. Relmond P. Van Daniker and Kay T. Pohlman, *Preferred Accounting Practices for State Governments* (Lexington, Ky.: Council of State Governments, 1983).

9. James F. Antonio, "Role and Future of the Governmental Accounting Standards Board," *Public Budgeting and Finance* 5 (Summer 1985): 30–38.

10. Larry P. Bailey, *Miller Comprehensive Governmental GAAP Guide, 1988* (New York: Harcourt Brace Jovanovich, 1987).

11. *Governmental Accounting, Auditing, and Financial Reporting*, p. 11.

12. Unpublished data from survey conducted by the Department of Public Administration, The Pennsylvania State University, and the Budget Office of the Commonwealth of Pennsylvania and with the cooperation of the National Association of State Budget Officers.

13. Herbert A. O'Keefe and Pete Rose, "Overview of the Issues Involved in Measurement Focus and Basis of Accounting for Governmental Funds," *Government Accountants Journal* 36 (Summer 1987): 41–45.

14. General Accounting Office, *Financial Management: Responses to 17 Questions* (Washington, D.C.: Government Printing Office, 1988), p. 42.

15. General Accounting Office, *Financial Integrity Act*.

16. Karney A. Brasfield, "The Role of Accounting in Cost Budgeting," *The Federal Accountant* 4 (December 1954): 20–31.

17. Joseph T. Kelley, *Costing Government Services* (Washington, D.C.: Government Finance Officers Association, 1984).

18. *Governmental Accounting, Auditing, and Financial Reporting*, pp. 99–130.

19. Freeman, Shoulders, and Lynn, *Governmental and Nonprofit Accounting*, pp. 626–52.

20. Robert W. Ingram, Walter A. Robbins and Mary S. Stone, "Financial Reporting Practices of Local Governments," *Government Finance Review* 4 (April 1988): 17–21.

21. Elizabeth Voisin, "Locals Could Be Hurt by GAAP Changes," *City and State* 5 (June 20, 1988): 42.

22. *Governmental Accounting, Auditing, and Financial Reporting*, p. 131.

23. Marc A. Rubin, "Contracting for Municipal Audits," *Government Accountants Journal* 37 (Spring 1988): 25–29.

24. Alan Reinstein and David R.L. Gabhart, "The Internal Auditor's Role in Public Sector Audit Committees," *Public Budgeting and Finance* 7 (Summer 1987): 72–80.

25. John J. Adair and Rex Simmons, "From Voucher Auditing to Junkyard Dogs: The Evolution of the Federal Inspectors General," *Public Budgeting and Finance* 8 (Summer 1988): 91–100.

26. Mark H. Moore and Margaret J. Gates, *Inspectors-General* (New York: Russell Sage Foundation, 1986).

27. General Accounting Office, *Financial Integrity Act: Continuing Efforts Needed to Improve Internal Control and Accounting Systems* (Washington, D.C.: Government Printing Office, 1987).

28. Richard E. Brown and James B. Pyers, "Putting Teeth into the Efficiency and Effectiveness of Public Services," *Public Administration Review* 48 (1988): 735–42.

29. *Audits of State and Local Governmental Units*, rev. ed. (New York: American Institute of Certified Public Accountants, 1986).

30. General Accounting Office, *Single Audit Act: First-Year Reporting Has Been Extensive* (Washington, D.C.: Government Printing Office, 1988).

31. General Accounting Office, *Single Audit Act: First-Year Reporting Has Been Extensive*.

32. Barry Bozeman and Stuart Bretschneider, eds., "Symposium on Public Management Information Systems," *Public Administration Review* 46, Special Issue (November 1986): 473–602.

33. John M. Stevens and Robert P. McGowan, *Information Systems and Public Management* (New York: Praeger, 1985), p. 7.

34. Peter G.W. Keen and Michael S. Scott Morton, *Decision Support Systems* (Reading, Mass.: Addison-Wesley, 1978).

35. Robert P. McGowan and Gary A. Lombardo, "Decision Support Systems in State Government," *Public Administration Review* 46, Special Issue (November 1986): 579–83.

36. Ronald W. Johnson and Arie L. Lewin, "Management and Accountability Models of Public Sector Performance," in Trudi C. Miller, ed., *Public Sector Performance* (Baltimore: Johns Hopkins University Press, 1984).

37. Charles K. Coe and A. Faye Borthick, "Computer Auditing in the Federal Government," *Public Budgeting and Finance* 4 (Autumn 1984): 67–74.

38. Robert D. Miewald and Keith J. Mueller, "The Use of Information Technology in Oversight by State Legislatures," *State and Local Government Review* 19 (1987): 22–28.

39. James A. Hall, "Computer Applications," in J. Richard Aronson and Eli Schwartz, eds., *Management Policies in Local Government Finance*, 3rd ed. (Washington, D.C.: International City Management Association, 1987), pp. 176–97.

40. John W. Ostrowski, Ella P. Gardner, and Magda H. Motawi, "Microcomputers in Public Finance Organizations," *Government Finance Review* 2 (February 1986): 23–29.

41. Stanley B. Botner, "Utilization and Impact of Microcomputers in State Central Budget Offices," *Public Budgeting and Finance* 7 (Autumn 1987): 99–108.

42. Blue Woolridge and Claire L. Alpert, "Improving the Implementation of Computerized Financial Management Information Systems in Local Government," *Government Accountants Journal* 36 (Spring 1987): 43–50.

43. Edward F. Doezy, "Linking a Strategic Plan to the Budgetary Process," *Government Finance Review* 3 (December 1987): 11–15.

44. Office of Management and Budget, "Preparation and Submission of Budget Estimates," Circular A-11, June 17, 1988.

45. General Accounting Office, *Computer Security: Status of Compliance with the Computer Security Act of 1987* (Washington, D.C.: Government Printing Office, 1988).

46. Arie Halachmi, ed., "Symposium on New Information Technology and Productivity," *Public Productivity Review* 11 (Summer 1988): 33–99.

47. Kenneth L. Kraemer and John L. King, "Computers and the Constitution," *Public Administration Review* 47 (1987): 93–105.

12

Financial Management: Capital Budgeting and Debt

Every year, governments spend resources on the construction of facilities or the purchase of equipment that will continue to be used for many years beyond the year of purchase. The construction of a new water treatment plant will serve a community for decades although the actual construction itself may take less than two years. In addition, during the construction phase, the construction costs may be a large portion of the community's total budget. Because of the large outlay required, many communities elect to finance the construction costs over a long period by borrowing.

Through the water treatment plant construction, the community has acquired a capital facility that will operate for perhaps 30 years. It has purchased an asset. This chapter focuses attention on the decision to purchase that asset and related decisions on whether and how to finance that asset through borrowing. We examine in this chapter both the rationale for public sector capital budgeting and the general form of capital budgeting processes. Second, since state and local governments finance much of their capital spending through various forms of borrowing, we examine the various forms of bonds and other debt instruments. The chapter concludes with a discussion of debt management. We defer discussion of federal borrowing, which is largely unrelated to capital investments, to Chapter 15.

CAPITAL PLANNING, BUDGETING, AND ASSET MANAGEMENT

In this section we define capital and capital investments, discuss the reasons for considering capital spending separately from operating budgets, describe the general form for a capital investment planning and budgeting process, and conclude with a discussion of potential problems arising from separating capital from operating budgets. We focus mainly on state and local governments.

Capital versus Current Expenditures

Physical Nature and Time Duration. Businesses think of capital expenditures as the purchase of physical assets that will be used over a period of several years. Public sector capital expenditures typically share those two characteristics: a physical asset is purchased, and its use extends over a number of years.[1]

Examples of capital expenditures are easy to find. A school building is physically present, and it will last for many years. On the other hand, paper, pens, pencils, staples, and mimeograph ink, while they have a physical presence, are used up and have to be purchased again next year. The former expenditure easily is classified as "capital" and the latter as "current." Similarly, water mains extending from a treatment plant to neighborhood lines have a physical presence and will serve for many years. Their construction is a capital expenditure. On the other hand, chemicals used in the treatment process will be used up and purchased again and again. Purchase of these chemicals is an operating or current expenditure.

Classification Problems. These examples illustrate that capital expenditures normally have a physical aspect and a long life. Current expenditures may have a physical aspect, but they typically do not last beyond the current budget year. Other examples, however, illustrate that the distinction between capital and current is sometimes ambiguous. A big-city police department may purchase more than 50 vehicles a year, and most of these may replace vehicles purchased the previous year. That city may classify those police cars as current expenditures. A small town may purchase two police cars of the same type as the big city's but expect those two cars to last for three to five years. The small town probably would consider the police cars a capital expenditure.

Even within the same city, some classification problems occur. Books and periodicals purchased for a library can be expected to be of use for many years and can be treated as capital investments. On the other hand, a periodical purchased by a department of public works may have a short useful life and would be an operating expense. Every government and every business establishes some kind of arbitrary cutoff point that distinguishes current from capital expenditures. In most cases, the cutoff is a combination of the amount of the expenditure and the useful life. Anything expected to be consumed (or destroyed) during one year normally will be a current expenditure, no matter how large it is. In addition, small expenditures, even for goods that will last several years, also are classified as current. But the size of the government's budget usually determines how small is small. A small town may classify expenditures under $1,000 as current, regardless of the useful life. A larger city may use $25,000 as a cutoff below which anything is a current expenditure regardless of useful life.

Although some purchases may be arbitrarily classified one way or the other, what constitutes a capital purchase and what is a current one usually is not controversial. One major category of exception should be noted, however. Although the federal government does not have any separate process for deciding on capital versus current expenditures, since 1951 it has produced annually *Investment and Operating Outlays* as part of a separate document known as *Special Analyses*. Included along with more conventional capital expenditures are expenditures on research and development and education and training.[2] The rationale for considering these latter classes as capital expenditures is that they will yield benefits in the future.

Capital Investments. The purchase or construction of a long-lasting physical asset is a capital investment. For a business, the investment typically means acquiring new productive capacity. Many public sector physical assets also represent investment in the ability to provide more or higher-quality services in the future. This "investment" quality of some expenditures helps explain why capital expenditures often are distinguished from current.

Focusing some attention on the "investment" component of a government budget is politically useful because it draws attention to the fact that many public spending programs build for the future. However, it becomes difficult to draw the line between investment and noninvestment. Although the federal budget includes education and training in the investment category, it does not include many other elements that it logically could. For example, mental health programs, programs for juveniles, and family counseling programs may be considered investments in preventing future social and economic problems. A major rationale for the Supplemental Feeding Program for Women, Infants and Children is that the investment in health helps prevent some future federal expenditures for Medicaid.[3]

Capital versus Current Decisions

Separate Capital Budgets. The size of the expenditure and its investment quality are used to distinguish a capital expenditure from a current one. A third distinction, the method of financing the expenditure, leads most state governments and a majority of local governments to pay at least some separate attention to capital expenditures in the annual budget decision-making process. All but eight states and more than half of city governments have separate capital budgets.[4-6] Table 12-1 shows state and local capital expenditures for 1987 as a proportion of total expenditures.

Considering only direct capital outlays, about 13 percent of state and local expenditures are for capital purposes. With interest included, the figure is closer to 19 percent. Local governments' capital outlays are a slightly higher proportion of total outlays than state governments' outlays, 20 percent to 18 percent, respectively. However, these gross percentages obscure the real nature of the decisions to undertake the capital projects. Capital expenditures cluster in only a few governmental functions. For local governments, of the $61 billion in direct capital outlays in 1987 (Table 12-1), almost $13 billion was for utility capital outlays. The remainder was clustered in schools, roads, and housing construction.

State governments' capital outlays also cluster in only a few functional categories, and decisions made in one year affect future-year budgets. Of the $37 billion in direct state government capital outlays in 1987, over $21 billion alone went to highway construction. That level of capital construction implies significant future-year expenditures for highway maintenance. In addition to the $21 billion in new capital spending, state governments' 1987 current operating expenditures for highways were just over $10 billion, a direct consequence of prior years' capital spending decisions.

Table 12-1 Direct Capital Outlays as a Proportion of Total Outlays, by Level of Government, 1987 (Billions of Dollars)

Government	Total Direct Outlays[1]	Capital Outlays	Capital as Percent of Total	Interest on Debt[2]	Combined Capital Outlays[3]	Combined Capital as Percent of Total
All	1,810	195	11	N.A.	N.A.	N.A.
Federal	1,037	97	9	N.A.	N.A.	N.A.
State and Local	773	98	13	50	148	19
State	314	37	12	19	56	18
Local	459	61	13	31	92	20

[1]Outlays shown are for the level of government making the final expenditure even if the source of finance is a transfer from another level of government.

[2]Only interest on general debt and interest on utilities' borrowing is included here.

[3]For state and local governments, interest on general debt plus interest on utility borrowing is attributed in this table to borrowing for capital investment. Federal debt is not considered borrowing for capital investments.

N.A. = Not Applicable.

Source: Government Finances in 1986–87, Bureau of the Census, pp. 9–11, Government Printing Office, 1988.

Separate Capital Budgeting Processes. These illustrations demonstrate that decisions about capital spending at the state and local levels can have large consequences for future financing. As we have discussed in previous chapters, particularly Chapter 5, it is difficult to incorporate a long-run perspective into budget decisions, especially when the decisions tend to focus on personnel budgets and only on the current-year implications of starting a new program (Chapter 6). The fact that current-year capital budget decisions have significant implications for future operations and maintenance suggests that the effects of capital decisions on future operating budgets must be an important element of any capital budgeting process. For state and local governments, the logic of having some kind of process for examining capital spending decisions in more detail seems compelling. That does not necessarily imply separate capital budgets, however. In the next section, we illustrate a general approach to capital investment planning and budgeting that satisfies both the requirement to examine capital decisions in more detail and the requirement to consider implications for future-year operating budgets.

Capital Investment Planning

Multiyear Capital Investment Plans. Many governments that distinguish between capital and current budget decisions have an established process for developing a multiyear capital investment plan (CIP) and incorporating elements of that plan into a capital budget. Five years is a common period for projecting capital expenditures, although a longer period often is included in a statement of a long-range program. For example, the Orange County (North Carolina) Water and Sewer Authority (OWASA) distinguishes between its fifteen-year Capital Improvements Program and its five-year Capital Improvements Budget.[7] The long-range plan focuses on the expected needs for water supply and sewerage treatment for the next decade and a half, while the Capital Improvement Budget includes detailed cost estimates only for the next 5 years.

Asset Management. Long-term capital investment plans may be a part of a larger program of asset management. Concern for the condition of America's deteriorating infrastructure base emerged in the early 1980s.[8] The president of the Urban Institute summarized the crisis.

> In the last few years, the United States has suddenly "discovered" its infrastructure crisis. The physical plant on which our cities rely has been aging steadily, and in many cases its condition has deteriorated. A few spectacular events—such as the collapse of the

Mianus bridge in Connecticut—have heightened our understanding
of the vulnerability of the urban infrastructure.[9]

Whether or not a crisis existed, the publicity given to the need to replace or
rehabilitate state and local infrastructure and a dramatic decline in federal
aid to state and local governments brought new attention to the condition
of the nation's infrastructure. For budgeting purposes, decisions about capital
planning and spending cannot take place without adequate information about
the current condition of the existing capital facilities or asset base. Until 1982,
Washington, D.C., did not have an inventory of the city's capital facilities,
much less an analysis of the condition, rate of deterioration, and cost to
rehabilitate or replace. In conducting its inventory, the city discovered that
some of its water lines were still the original wooden conduits put in place
in the last century.

Some state and local governments have adopted elaborate systems for assessing the condition of capital assets and linking these "inventories" with the
capital planning and budgeting process. Dallas, Texas; King County,
Washington; and Milwaukee, Wisconsin, for example, have systems of varying sophistication for measuring street conditions and maintaining an updated inventory.[10] Cities throughout developing countries that have
underinvested in both maintenance and reconstruction of such critical urban
infrastructure as pavement, water systems, and drainage also have begun to
develop more complete systems for taking inventory of existing assets and
developing capital investment plans based on a schedule of needed
improvements.[11,12] These innovations in public sector "asset" management
have begun to alter the way some cities plan, budget, and manage their
finances, with capital planning and budgeting playing a more leading role.
Practices vary considerably from city to city, but it is possible to describe
a general form. A model for a capital investment planning and budgeting
process, linked to an inventory of existing facilities, consists of eight steps
illustrated in Exhibit 12-1.[13,14]

Identifying Present Service Characteristics. The first step involves an inventory of existing physical or infrastructure facilities and an assessment of
the service provided. For a state or local government that has not previously
conducted an inventory, this first step is neither simple nor inexpensive,
although maintaining the inventory once established need not be burdensome.
Such an inventory includes listing both all physical facilities and elements
of physical infrastructure and such related information as date of construction, date of last major rehabilitation, type of construction material (such
as type of road surface), and, where relevant, such characteristics as size and
capacity.

Quantity of service includes such characteristics as the absolute number
of people served, the proportion of total population served, the geographic

Exhibit 12-1 Capital Facilities Planning and Budgeting

1. Identify present service characteristics (inventory facilities and service levels)
   a. Coverage (quantity)
   b. Quality
   c. Cost per unit of service (efficiency)
2. Identify environmental trends
   a. Population growth projections
   b. Changing regulatory environment
   c. Employment and economic development trends
3. Develop service objectives
   a. Extension of service to new population or area (coverage)
   b. Improvement in quality of service
   c. Opportunities to stimulate economic growth
4. Develop preliminary list of capital projects and cost estimates
   a. Rehabilitation of existing facilities
   b. Replacement of existing facilities
   c. Addition of new facilities
5. Identify financial resources
   a. External assistance
   b. Projected growth in present revenue base
   c. Potential for direct cost recovery for individual projects
   d. Use of credit
6. Select subset of projects for inclusion in five-year capital investment plan (CIP)
7. Identify future recurrent cost impact of CIP on operating budget
8. Include first year of CIP in annual budget estimate

area covered (area, density, spatial distribution), and various socioeconomic groupings related to coverage, such as number of business and residential clients. Different quantity characteristics are appropriate for different services. Quality of service may be determined through an assessment of the type of service provided, with different types considered qualitative differences. For example, water treatment systems that remove only bacteriological contaminants are qualitatively less effective than those that remove toxins and heavy metals as well as bacteria. Quality also may be indicated by such things as the age of the facility and its condition. The latter may be measured by the frequency-of-repair record. Qualitative assessments of quality of service, including records of citizens' complaints and structured citizen satisfaction surveys, are as appropriate as quantitative measures.[15]

Identifying Environmental Trends. Most city and state governments develop long-range planning forecasts for such barometers of future requirements for service as population growth, commercial and industrial growth, changing demographic and economic composition of the jurisdiction, and so forth.

These forecasts are linked to the capital facilities planning process to develop plans for required service expansion or contraction. In addition, more detailed analyses of recent trends in business location may indicate that the lack of assurance of future supply of critical services, such as adequate water, may be a factor in slowdowns in new business investments. In that case, the capital facilities planning process can provide a means for the jurisdiction to plan expansion of service in an orderly way and serve as a promise to potential investors that the jurisdiction is anticipating future business and residential requirements.

Developing Service Objectives. The process of developing service objectives that define the need for capital investments can be as varied as the community served. Extensive citizen input in the form of representation on long-range planning groups, open forums to discuss the need for community facilities, referendums to approve a specific bond issue to finance a capital investment (see next section), and a variety of other channels are common to city governments in the United States. Even in jurisdictions with regularly established channels for citizen input, a special group often is convened every two to three years just to review the current CIP and establish new priorities.[16]

Preliminary Listing of Capital Projects and Cost Estimates. Based on the service objectives established in the previous step, a preliminary list of capital projects can be developed representing what meeting those objectives entails and the time frame for accomplishment. Typically, the preliminary list includes rehabilitation of existing facilities to improve the quality and/or efficiency of service; replacement of existing facilities, also for quality and efficiency; and addition of new facilities or expansion of existing facilities to meet expansion objectives. The preliminary list typically will not be screened for financial feasibility at this stage.

Identifying Financial Resources. Identifying the financial resources potentially available to carry out the preliminary list of capital projects involves analyzing the jurisdiction's overall financial condition and some of the individual capital projects for possible sources of financing specific to them. In the 1980s evaluation of the financial condition of local governments became an important aspect of overall financial management.[17,18] In the wake of public pressure to hold steady or to cut back state and local taxes, major new revenue initiatives in the form of tax increases were not possible even in the face of the need to build new infrastructure and rehabilitate existing facilities. However, because of the expansion of tax bases, making long-range projections of tax yield increases and assessing the performance of other ordinary revenue sources sometimes reveal potential revenues that will be available at some point in the future for capital investment financing.

More commonly, however, state and local governments, particularly the latter, rely increasingly on revenue sources specific to individual capital projects for additional funding needed for capital investments. User fees and property assessments traditionally have been used to finance the major portion of water and other utility capital investments, as well as operating expenses. More recently, cities have levied special impact fees and other charges to residential and commercial developers to pay for required investments in roads, water, and sewer lines and drainage to serve new developments (see discussion in Chapter 4).[19,20]

Still other sources of revenues tied to particular projects are external assistance in the form of grants from other levels of government and borrowing, typically in the form of issuing bonds. Although federal funding cutbacks were significant starting in 1980, state aid to local governments has in some cases made up for some of the deficit, and federal funds are still available on a more limited programmatic basis (see Chapter 14 for discussion of intergovernmental grants and other transfers).

Selection of Projects for Inclusion in Five-Year Capital Investment Plan. Step 6 involves matching available financial resources with the set of projects included in the preliminary investment plan. Steps 3 through 6 may be an iterative process of narrowing down the list of projects, re-examining financial alternatives, and finally selecting a feasible set. Re-evaluation of desired service objectives sometimes is necessary during this iterative process as financial realities make it clear that some objectives are impossible without major new financial initiatives. For most state and municipal governments, the application of complex analytical tools such as cost-benefit analysis or rate of return analysis plays only a small role in the selection of projects.[21,22] Instead, the most influential priorities are based on such ranked criteria as first, replacing deteriorated facilities; second, meeting population growth requirements; and third, improving quality of services.[23]

Identifying Implications for Future Recurrent Costs. This step in the analysis and planning process often is neglected.[24] It sometimes is difficult to anticipate the future maintenance costs to keep a facility operating, and the usually valuable public relations aspects of a new project tend to overshadow the longer-run impact on the general fund's budget for operating costs. The problem is exaggerated especially by the fact that the operating and maintenance costs of any new infrastructure or facility are lower in the early years of operation, with heavier costs falling outside the range of normal five-year capital planning cycles. Without such analysis, a state or local jurisdiction may find itself in 10 to 20 years facing the dilemma of forgoing new capital investments because of the need to budget greater funds for maintenance or neglecting maintenance in favor of politically more popular capital projects.

The analysis of future operation and maintenance costs is not all negative. If the analysis of the current capital facilities base in step 1 has been carried out well, the jurisdiction will have an idea of the present operation and maintenance costs of existing facilities. Replacing some facilities that require expensive maintenance expenditures may produce significant reductions in operation and maintenance costs in the operating budget.

Including Year One of CIP in Annual Budget. After arriving at a feasible set of investments, including the ability to finance both the investment and future operating costs, the last step is to incorporate the first year of the capital investment plan in the annual budget. To this point, the process has been one of planning and programming that may have involved representation of the legislative body, but no legal appropriation of funds will have taken place. Some jurisdictions submit the CIP to the legislative body (state legislature, city council, etc.) for formal approval, but the CIP may not include actual appropriation of funds. A survey of state capital budget practices found great variation in how state legislatures appropriate funds for capital projects.[25] Some states appropriate the full costs of capital projects, at least for smaller ones, whereas other states appropriate only the annual costs of a project. For the latter, only a single year's cost actually shows up in the appropriations acts.

Evaluation of Capital Budgeting

Much of the argument over the value of capital budgeting at the state and local government level hinges on whether there should be a separate capital budgeting process. There is little argument over the need to examine the full, long-term implications of capital spending, not just focus on a single budget year. It is possible to have a comprehensive capital planning process that concludes with a capital budget plan or statement without a separate capital budgeting process. The amount the city council or state legislature is then asked to appropriate may be for only one year, but the budget request is made in the context of future-year requirements.

Pros and Cons of Separate Capital Budgeting. Capital budgets and statements indicate the extent to which investments are being made with current expenditures. From a political perspective, this indication has value as governmental officials can show citizens that much of government spending is going for acquisition of useful assets, not solely to such unpopular items as bureaucrats' salaries.

On the negative side, capital budgeting can encourage political logrolling, in which various political interests agree to help each other. A capital budget can be a political grab bag, a fund in which every interest can find a project. A state capital budget may provide highway projects in every county, even though real need is concentrated in a small number of counties. In providing everyone with something, some important needs will not be met while less pressing needs are. Furthermore, if capital costs are presented in a completely separate budget, particularly when financed by borrowing, it may appear as if capital decisions are "costless" in the current year.

On balance, however, the arguments in favor of special attention to capital spending, at least at the state and local level, seem overwhelming. While capital budget decisions are no less political than other budget decisions, the logic of focusing attention on long-run financial and economic consequences of spending or failing to spend for capital facilities is compelling. More than current operating budget decisions, decisions to invest in infrastructure help shape the future direction, location, and extent of private economic investments in the community. Local governments' capital investments may in some cases play a leading role in encouraging future local economic development (see Chapter 15). State and local governments compete for location of major federal facilities, and they sometimes offer large incentive packages of infrastructure and other financial assistance to induce private companies or federal agencies to locate major facilities in their jurisdictions. One of the facilities "plums" of the 1980s was the Supercollider, a several-mile underground circular facility for particle physics research won by the state of Texas in large part because of the widespread financial and citizen support.[26] Sometimes states or localities will fight against the location of a large facility in the "neighborhood," as, for example, in the case of a disposal facility for low-level nuclear waste.

Once built, major facilities largely will be limited to the uses for which they were designed; inadequately conceived facilities can result in inadequate services, major financial burdens, or the need for expensive alterations. Excess capacity built into a community sewer system cannot be converted into other uses. Too little acquisition of land for parks in a rapidly growing suburban area may later result in a shortage of recreational opportunities or may force the local government to pay far more for space than it might have earlier.

These arguments do not imply the need to separate capital budgets from operating budgets. In fact, the opposite is implied. While capital spending requires attention to some issues that are not germane to operating budgets, capital and operating expenditures are inevitably interrelated. In fact, some even argue for capital budgets that include all operation and maintenance costs, leaving general fund budgets a fraction of their present size covering administration and the costs of those services which have few capital requirements.[27]

Federal Capital Budgeting. For the federal government, the logic of capital budgeting is less compelling. First, much of the "capital" side of the federal budget goes toward defense acquisitions, which are not investments in the same sense as state and local expenditures for water systems or highways. This difference does not mean that such investments as nuclear-powered aircraft carriers do not have significant implications for future operation and maintenance. But the need to replace a weapons system often is generated not by its being worn out but by its inability to cope with new offensive or defensive systems of a potential enemy. Furthermore, the federal government may undertake many nondefense capital expenditures for macroeconomic policy reasons more than for investment purposes. The federal government's role in stimulating the economy may lead to capital spending with the primary objective of assisting a state or local economy rather than providing a needed facility. Unfortunately, this kind of logic often leads to the pork barrel decisions that place these types of investments in every congressman's district.

In the 1980s concern for improved federal financial management led to a reconsideration of the question of federal capital budgeting. The General Accounting Office (GAO) initiated a series of studies of the federal budgetary process that supported capital budgeting.[28] The general argument advanced in support of separate federal capital budgeting has focused on improved accounting practices and more businesslike management of federal funds. The director of the GAO's Accounting and Financial Management Division stated the case:

> Under the current unified budget, a dollar spent is a dollar spent. The current budget treats outlays for capital and operating activities the same, even though they are different in a key respect—capital outlays do not reduce the resource base of the government the way current outlays do because they represent asset exchanges. When an outlay is made to acquire an asset, whether it is a building or a loan note, it produces a future stream of benefits to the government.[29]

The main support for a federal capital budget process currently comes from these concerns about introducing a financial management perspective into the process. Paralleling GAO's interests in improved financial management, in 1985 the executive branch appointed a White House task force to examine capital budgeting issues. The same concerns that motivated the 1967 President's Commission on Budget Concepts to recommend against a federal capital budget prevailed in the 1985 task force. Principally, the 1967 commission concluded that a separate capital budget for the federal government would understate the extent to which any federal expenditure, capital or current, draws resources away from alternative private sector uses of the resources and that it might lead to too heavy a priority for "brick and mortar projects relative to other Federal programs for which future benefits could not be capitalized . . . ."[30,31] The argument that the federal budget should not be fragmented into two parts that might obscure the economic consequences of federal spending seems likely to continue to prevail in support of a unified budget statement.[32,33]

STATE AND LOCAL BOND FINANCING

State and local governments finance a major portion of their capital investment spending through long-term debt instruments. In 1987 state and local governments combined issued $132 billion in new long-term debt.[34] Most state constitutions or statutes limit the issuance of long-term debt for both state and local governments to capital investment-type expenditures. The two major categories of long-term debt are "full faith and credit" or general obligation bonds and "nonguaranteed" bonds. Full faith and credit debt is guaranteed by the general revenues of the issuing jurisdiction without regard to the purpose of the expenditures or the potential for direct cost recovery through user charges. Full faith and credit debt thus is considered guaranteed in that the full resources of the jurisdiction are pledged as security to potential investors. Nonguaranteed bonds do not have the full backing of the issuing jurisdiction's resources.

Types of Bonds

General Obligation Bonds. Since general obligation bonds typically are considered safer investments than nonguaranteed bonds because of the full backing of the jurisdiction's resources, these bonds carry lower interest rates than nonguaranteed bonds. The interest rate is critical in large bond issues, for which a difference of 0.1 percent can affect total interest payments by millions of dollars. However, constitutional and statutory provisions (such as Proposition 13 in California) may set limits on income, sales, and property tax rates, limiting the amount jurisdictions may borrow regardless of the purpose. For this reason, other types of bonds not backed by the general revenue resources of a state or local government have become much more common. In 1987, 68 percent of state governments' outstanding long-term debt was in the nonguaranteed category.[35]

Nonguaranteed Bonds. Nonguaranteed debt generally is restricted to the revenue earnings of the specific facility created by the investment. A wide variety of sources are used to repay these so-called nonguaranteed bonds.[36] The most common are revenue bonds, in which charges to users generate the funds necessary to repay the loans. Other sources include special assessments, in which the properties affected by an investment are assessed charges, such as property owners assessed for sewer installations.

Revenue Bonds. Revenue bonds pledging the revenue from a specific tax, such as those using the revenue from taxes on gasoline to finance highway construction, have the advantage of placing the burden for financing a facility on those who will use it. Similarly, using the parking fees from a parking garage to finance its construction places the burden on those who park in the garage. From an intergovernmental perspective, the revenue bond device forces nonresidents who use the parking garage or the highways to pay their fair share.

Private Purpose Bonds. In the early 1980s considerable use was made of state and local bonds to finance private construction and ownership of facilities such as buildings, which in turn were leased for governmental use. Similar use has been made of government bonds for lease and subsequent purchase of privately constructed facilities. In some cases, government bonds have been issued to finance a facility that then is leased or purchased by the private sector. This last device often has been used to finance industrial development facilities such as industrial parks and incubator facilities to help small businesses get started.

Other so-called "private purpose" bonds have been used to subsidize home mortgages. Tax-exempt home mortgage revenue bonds are used to generate funds for low-interest mortgages. They are controversial because they compete with traditional mortgages issued by commercial banks and savings and loan associations and because their use has not been restricted to low-income housing. State- or local government-issued bonds for these largely private purposes were quite popular because the interest on state or local bonds is tax exempt. By 1985, more than one-third of state and local tax-exempt bonds issued were for private facilities.[37] The 1980 Mortgage Subsidy Bond Tax Act limited such bonds to low-income facilities and placed a limit on the amount that could be issued in any one state.[38]

The 1986 Tax Reform Act contained several provisions to limit the deductibility of such private purpose facilities.[39] Interest earned on general purpose bonds for construction of facilities or infrastructure to provide essential services remain tax exempt. Private activity bonds for construction of exempt facilities such as airports, docks and wharves, hazardous waste treatment plants, and water supply facilities also retain their tax-exempt status, although the interest is included in the alternative minimum tax base. No longer tax exempt is the interest on bonds for construction of industrial parks, parking garages, sports facilities, and convention or trade show facilities. In addition, each state and its local governments are limited in the amount of private purpose bonds that can be issued in a year, and interest on any otherwise qualified bond issue is subject to tax if the bond issue exceeds the state cap.[40] How to determine which facilities to include in the exempt category—for example, ports—and which would lose tax exemption—for example, air and water pollution control facilities—was one of the controversial issues in the closing stages of the fight for approval of the 1986 reform.[41] It is unlikely that such bonds will continue to be as popular as they once were now that limits on their tax advantages make them less attractive than other investments.

Overall, the use of bonds to finance state and local investments continues to grow as state and local financial conditions improve and federal transfers to assist state and local governments decrease.[42] The distinction between general obligation bonds and limited revenue bonds is less important in practice than the financial condition of the borrowing entity. In fact, many water utilities and other users of more limited revenue bonds are in better financial shape than are general purpose state and local governments.

Bond Issuance Process

Voter Approval. The process of securing financing via a bond issue involves several steps. In many states, a general obligation bond or full faith and credit obligation generally requires a referendum to secure voter approval. Revenue bonds and other forms of limited obligation financing generally do not require voter approval. In some cases, to avoid state limitations on general municipal borrowing, cities have established nonprofit building authorities to issue bonds and construct facilities. Such facilities are then rented to the municipality, and the rental payments secure the bond principal and interest.[43] These special authorities, because they are not legally obligating in a direct way the general revenues of the municipality, can issue bonds without voter approval and without the debt's counting as part of the municipality's overall debt limit.[44] Of course, the municipality's source of funds to pay for renting the facility is in fact the general revenue fund.

Underwriter. Typically, the authority issuing a bond will secure the services of an underwriter whose role is to arrange the actual sale of bonds to financial institutions. Individuals, banks, insurance companies, and bond funds invest in state and local bonds. Legal counsel retained by the issuing authority also will provide a legal opinion on the status of the issue, the legal authority to issue the bond, and the tax-exempt status of the bond.

Bond Features. A variety of differences characterize bonds. Some bonds, called term bonds, may be due and payable to the investors on a single date. Serial bonds are due on a specific schedule of payments over a number of years. In recent years, serial bonds have largely replaced term bonds in part because of statutory prohibitions against term bonds. Investors holding term bonds obviously must be concerned with whether a jurisdiction is annually setting aside sufficient funds to be able to repay its debt.[45,46]

Another difference is between coupon and registered bonds. Coupon bonds have coupons attached indicating the bond's maturity date and the amount of payment. Whoever presents the mature coupons receives payment. Registered bonds require that the owner register with the government issuing the bonds. The advantage of the coupon bond is that it is easily transferred from one owner to another, while the registered bond offers protection against loss or destruction of the bond itself. States and municipalities prefer coupon bonds because the issuing jurisdiction is not responsible for keeping records of the purchasers. However, a provision of the Tax Equity and Fiscal Responsibility Act of 1982 requires that state and municipal bonds be registered to retain their tax-exempt status. The state of South Carolina and the National Governors' Association challenged the constitutionality of the requirement (*South Carolina vs. Baker*), but the Supreme Court upheld the provision in 1988.[47] As a consequence, unless Congress revises the statutory requirement, future issues of coupon bonds will be limited.

Interest Rates. Interest rates, of course, are usually the most critical element of the bond. As a hedge against changing interest rates or financial condition, the state or municipal authority may sometimes use what is called a "call" feature. This feature means the authority may call or repay the bond in part or in full before the maturity date. The issuer can thus take advantage of falling interest rates by paying off all or part of the bond issue. Exercising this feature usually involves the payment of some premium, such as payment of 103 percent of par value. Callable bonds typically carry a higher rate of interest since investors would otherwise be less attracted to an investment that may be repaid sooner, and therefore at a lower profit.

The actual interest the jurisdiction will have to pay on a bond issue depends on many factors related to the financial condition of the state or local authority and the general market for other investments at the time of the issue.[48] The tax-exempt status of the interest earned by state and local bonds means that the interest rate paid will be lower than comparably safe investments that do not enjoy tax-exempt status. If the jurisdiction has a good record of previous debt management, it will be perceived as a lower risk than one that has had trouble meeting its financial obligations. Likewise, if the jurisdiction is located in a good regional economy with low unemployment rates and a high tax base, it will be able to sell its bonds at lower interest rates.

The issuing jurisdiction also will provide potential investors with information about other long-term obligations, including not only other debt but also the extent of any unfunded pension liabilities (see Chapter 13). General reputation for good financial management is cited as evidence of good credit risk.[49-51] Investors rely heavily on standard ratings provided by two independent services, Standard and Poor's Corporation and Moody's Investors Service. Standard and Poor's uses nine ratings from AAA for the highest rating (best risk) to C for the worst risk. C ratings apply to bonds that pay no interest. In addition to these nine ratings, Standard and Poor's has a D classification for bonds in default status. Moody's scale ranges from Aaa to C in a similar fashion.

Bond Ratings. The importance of the bond rating is illustrated by a change from an AA rating to AA+, a change of less than a full category. For the town of Chapel Hill, North Carolina, such a change in 1988 meant a decrease of half a percentage point in interest on bond issues totaling $11.8 million.[52] If the entire $11.8 million in bonds had been issued for only a 10-year period, the savings from the rating change would have been approximately $400,000; for a 20-year period, the savings would have been almost $850,000.

Public Sale versus Negotiated Sale. Actual interest at the time of sale is determined by the offering purchasers. Two purchase methods are used: public sale or private negotiations. Public sales are initiated by a widely published notice of sale. The notice of sale typically includes information such as the denomination of bonds, bid conditions and requirements, and provisions for payment. Sealed bids are submitted by interested institutional investors, brokerage firms and even individuals, although individuals typically purchase through intermediaries. The issuing jurisdiction then is free to accept the lowest bid interest rate or reject according to the terms and conditions of sale. Jurisdictions with good ratings prefer this method as they are likely to attract numerous bidders and thus be able to choose lower interest rates.[53-55]

Negotiated sales are conducted between investment banks and the issuing government. The underwriter acts as a broker between the issuing jurisdiction and the investment community. If the issuer thinks the rates quoted by potential buyers through the underwriter are too high, the issuer is free to reject the bids as in a public sale. A key advantage to the negotiated sale is that the bond issue can be spread over a period of time. If the interest rates bid are high but the issuer cannot postpone the project, the issuer may sell only a portion of the total issue to start the project while the underwriter continues to seek additional bids. One disadvantage to negotiated sales, however, is that some investors, such as some pension funds, cannot purchase state or municipal securities except through public sale.

DEBT CAPACITY AND MANAGEMENT

Since the federal government's borrowing is for purposes other than capital investments, we continue in this section to focus on state and local governments, reserving a discussion of federal debt for Chapter 15. Media discussions of the federal debt and the size of the federal deficit raise citizens' consciousness of governmental debt, but locally people are often asked to approve bond issues for financing everything from schools to new fire stations. More importantly, citizens are not given the opportunity to vote on an even larger component of state and local debt that is issued by special authorities or that does not involve the pledge of full faith and credit of the jurisdiction. The issues to be addressed in this section involve how much debt can be managed safely and what efficient debt management practices will ensure sound future financial condition.

Size of Debt

The size of debt can be assessed in several ways. The total amount of debt is probably the least meaningful measure. The statistic that state and local governments' total outstanding debt at the end of 1987 was $719 billion sounds staggering but is not really instructive. Interest payments on general debt in 1987 amounted to $42 million, or only 5 percent of total state and local expenditures. Individuals with home mortgages, car loans, and occasional credit card interest may easily exceed 5 percent of their total expenditures on interest payments. Interest for state governments alone was 6 percent and for local governments 5 percent in 1987. In 1980, the comparable percentages were 3 and 4 respectively.[56]

Per Capita Debt. Per capita debt figures help put the total in perspective. How much per capita did state and local governments owe in 1987? State governments owed $1,092 and local governments $1,861. Is that too much, too little, or just about right? Is it growing, declining, or remaining more or less stable? The latter questions are easier to answer than the former. Figure 12-1 charts state and local per capita debt in five-year intervals from 1970 through 1985. Per capita debt has risen both at the state and local government levels, with local debt rising somewhat more rapidly than state debt. In addition, the rate of increase in the five-year period 1980–85 was equal to the rate of increase for the preceding *ten*-year period (1970–80). Thus, state and local debt is rising faster than population, but is that cause for alarm?

Debt/Personal Income. Relating debt to income instead of population makes the picture begin to clear. Total debt outstanding per $1,000 of personal income is one way of measuring whether debt is in danger of becoming an unreasonable burden. In 1987, state debt per $1,000 in personal income was $75; local debt per $1,000 was $128. These numbers are considerably less alarming. Over a 30-year period, combined state and local debt per $1,000 in personal income has remained very stable. Figure 12-2 charts this historical trend. State and local debt per $1,000 of personal income, although higher than in 1982, was no higher than the previous high of $204 per $1,000 15 years ago.

Distribution of Debt

Ultimately, whether the size of state and local debt is reasonable is a subjective judgment of how much financial burden is imposed on the individual

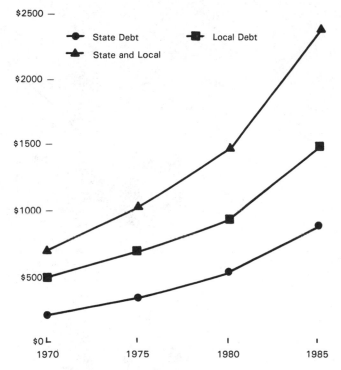

Figure 12-1 State and Local Debt per Capita, 1970–85. *Sources: Statistical Abstract of the United States: 1985*, Bureau of the Census, p. 274, Government Printing Office, 1984; and *Statistical Abstract of the United States: 1988*, Bureau of the Census, p. 263, Government Printing Office, 1987.

taxpayer and the economy and what the perceived value is of the facilities and services purchased by the debt transactions. Generally, debt is distributed somewhat as income and state and local services are. The state with the highest per capita debt in 1987, Alaska ($21,285), also was ranked 4th in personal income per capita ($17,796).[57] By this measure, presumably Alaska has the income level to support a higher debt. Alaska's cost of living tends to inflate all of its statistics, of course. New York ranked 6th in per capita income and 8th in per capita debt. There is wide variation, however. Connecticut ranked 1st in per capita income and only 18th in per capita debt; California was similar, with a per capita income ranking of 8th and a debt ranking all the way down to 33rd. Massachusetts ranked 5th in per capita income and 21st in per capita debt. California and Massachusetts were two of the leading states in enacting tax and spending limitations in the late 1970s (see Chapter 4).

Indebtedness is not distributed evenly among the various types of local governments. Municipalities account for the largest share of local debt—

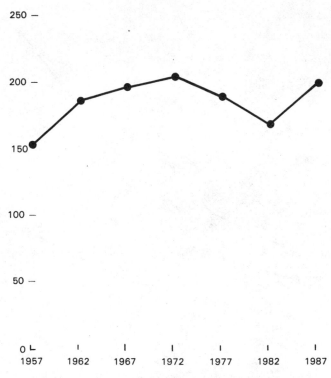

Figure 12-2 State and Local Debt per $1,000 Personal Income, 1957–87. *Sources: Historical Statistics on Governmental Finances and Employment,* Bureau of the Census, p. 113, Government Printing Office, 1984; and *Government Finances in 1985–86,* Bureau of the Census, p. 3, Government Printing Office, 1988.

more than 40 percent. Special districts, such as water and sewer authorities, accounted for an additional 29 percent, followed in declining order by county governments, school districts, and townships.[58] The low ranking for school districts is a misleading indicator of debt related to education, as both municipalities and counties borrow for construction of school facilities.

Debt Default

It should be noted that the figures on debt do not reflect the full scope of future financial obligations of governments. As will be seen in the following chapter, pension programs for public workers constitute a form of debt and often are not adequately funded. It also should be noted that there have been few defaults on state or local indebtedness since the Depression of the 1930s. In that decade, about 4,800 state and local units defaulted on their debt obligations. While that number may seem large, the total number of governments was 150,000. Most of the defaults involved small jurisdictions; less than 50 had populations more than 25,000.[59] Since that time, the number of defaults has been low.

In recent years, few public bond issuers have faced financial insolvency, although the exceptions have been large. In the mid-1970s, New York City came close to bankruptcy as a result of extensive borrowing to meet current or operating budget requirements. Only intervention by the state government and the banking community prevented outright default on several bond issues. The largest failure has been the Washington Public Power Supply System (WPPSS). In 1983, after a more than decade long program of construction of five nuclear power generating plants, WPPSS defaulted on over $2 billion in revenue bonds.[60] The revenue bonds were issued in anticipation of the sale of electricity. WPPSS got caught in the situation faced by the power industry in many parts of the country in the 1970s—a drop in the rate of growth in electricity demand, rapid escalation in the costs of nuclear power plant construction, and rising interest rates.[61] In reality, the cases of default by state and local governmental institutions recently have been far exceeded by failures of banking and savings and loan institutions.

Debt Capacity

Measuring Debt Capacity. Measuring debt capacity is an art rather than a science. In recent years, the public finance and budgeting profession has given considerably more attention to raising the level of the art. Three main factors influence debt capacity: "resource availability, expenditure needs, and willingness of lenders to purchase the debt."[62,63] Resource availability involves the analysis of all potential sources of revenues to the jurisdiction, including own-source revenues, transfers from other levels of government, and potential for project self-financing, including user charges, special assessments, impact fees, and a variety of other measures to collect fees or revenues sufficient to support the specific project or facility (see Chapter 4 for a discussion of revenue sources).

Expenditure analysis involves the present and potential future commitments of the jurisdiction in question. Population growth, changing economic conditions, state of the current capital facilities and infrastructure base, and socioeconomic characteristics of the population are important influences on potential future expenditures. The willingness of lenders to purchase debt is reflected ultimately in the interest rate they will require to lend.

Debt Burden. The most common overall measure of debt burden is the ratio of debt service to annual revenues, reflecting the extent to which revenues are sufficient to cover debt service in addition to operating expenses.[64] The World Bank often looks at the ratio of debt service to current revenues, the ratio of capital expenditures to total expenditures, and the excess of current revenues over ordinary operating expenditures as indicators of the ability of a city to incur additional debt.[65] More refined measures focus not on actual revenues but on the revenue base itself. Frequently cited indicators of potential debt capacity problems include net debt in excess of 10 percent of assessed valuation (property), net debt in excess of $1,200 per capita, and marked debt increases from the previous year.[66] These quick indicators are all useful, but ultimately they are interpretable only in the context of a jurisdiction's overall debt management strategy.

Debt Management. In general, good debt management at the state and local levels involve restricting debt primarily to financing long-term investments. A general rule is that such borrowing should not be used to meet current operating expenses. The much-publicized financial crisis for New York City involved short-term borrowing to finance current expenses.[67,68] Occasionally, short-term borrowing is used to finance emergencies, but often is refinanced as part of a long-term debt issue. Moreover, the payout period of the debt should correspond to the useful life of the facility or infrastructure financed.[69]

Restricting debt to long-term capital financing does not apply to such financial emergencies as disaster relief for major floods or unusually heavy snow in one winter that requires more sand, salt, and overtime labor than was budgeted. But this concept, along with matching the payout period for the debt with the useful life of the facility, is a useful rule of thumb. Following these two principles ensures that the jurisdiction is more or less matching the benefit flows from capital facilities with the opportunity costs (see Chapter 7 for more detailed discussion of cost and benefit streams and the concept of opportunity costs).

One of the major positive results of the financial difficulties of cities, such as New York in the late 1970s, followed by major cutbacks in federal aid in the 1980s has been growth in both the need for and the tools for analyzing governments' financial condition. Effective debt management involves using debt financing in a manner that balances competing claims against both the current annual budget and future annual budgets. As a consequence, state and local governments increasingly rely on methods to assess overall financial health and place potential bond issues in that context.[70]

SUMMARY

Our most common contact with government is the daily use of physical facilities and infrastructure provided most often by state and local governments. Few of us stop to analyze how those facilities are paid for or what impact their construction has on state and local taxes unless the extension of new water and sewer lines or a major street repaving project brings a hefty assessment on our property. However, it is increasingly common for state and local governments to highlight capital facilities' planning and budgeting and to involve citizens more directly in the planning process. Most of the services the ordinary citizen enjoys from government, such as roads, water, recreation facilities, libraries, and solid waste collection, involve major investments in facilities or equipment that will last for many years. As a result, almost all state and larger municipalities have identifiable capital planning and budgeting processes. Many of these are closely integrated with the annual current budget planning and decision-making process as well, and the trend is toward greater integration.

Because of the long life of capital facilities and infrastructure, extensive use is made of long-term financing in the form of various types of bond issues. While some local governments still consider it financially prudent to borrow little or not at all, state governments and virtually all large cities are unable to provide the services demanded by citizens without resorting to some debt financing for capital investments. While a common ethic is still that future generations should not be saddled with unreasonable debt burdens about which they have no say, most citizens recognize that capital facilities will be enjoyed by future generations. Debt financing provides a means for those future generations to share the costs as well as the benefits.

Effective debt management requires that the amounts of debt incurred not impose infeasible burdens on future taxpayers and that it not force future cutbacks in operation and maintenance expenditures necessary to maintain capital facilities. State governments, through constitutional provisions and statutory requirements, regulate their own as well as local governments' borrowing. These regulations mainly focus on the commitment of the "full faith and credit" of the jurisdiction. In response partly to the restrictions imposed on general obligation bonds and partly to the efficiency of tying repayment of debt to specific revenues generated by the investment, there has been tremendous growth in the use of a wide variety of debt instruments. Overall, however, state and local debt has grown little over the past 30 years in relation to income. State and local governments also have become more sophisticated in their financial analysis of capital investments and debt financing. As a consequence, state and local governments weathered severe crises brought on by declining federal aid in the early 1980s and emerged near the end of the decade in apparently sounder financial health than the federal government.

NOTES

1. Leo Herbert, Larry N. Killough, and Alan Walter Steiss, *Governmental Accounting and Control*, (Monterey, Calif.: Brooks/Cole, 1984), pp. 133–35.

2. Stephanie Goldman, ed., "AABPA Symposium: Capital Budgets," *Public Budgeting and Finance* 7 (Autumn 1987): 8.

3. See, for example, "Study of Savings in Medicaid or Indigent Care for Newborns from Participation in the WIC Program," Request for Proposals FNS 88-63WP, Food and Nutrition Service, U.S. Department of Agriculture, June 13, 1988.

4. Lawrence W. Hush and Kathleen Peroff, "State Capital Budgets," *Public budgeting and Finance* 8 (Summer 1988): 67.

5. C. Bradley Doss, Jr., "Capital Budgeting in U.S. Cities," *Public Budgeting and Finance* 7 (Summer 1987): 61.

6. A General Accounting Office survey, also in 1986, reported similar results, with 37 of 45 states responding reporting separate capital budgets. General Accounting Office, *Budget Issues: Capital Budgeting Practices in the States* (Washington, D.C.: Government Printing Office, 1986).

7. *Capital Improvements Program for the Period 1987–2001 Including Five Year Capital Improvements Budget for the Period 1987–1991* (Carrboro, N.C.: Orange Water and Sewer Authority, 1986).

8. Pat Choate and Susan Walter, *America In Ruins: Beyond the Public Works Pork Barrel* (Washington, D.C.: Council of State Planning Agencies, 1981).

9. William Gorham, in Preface to Harry P. Hatry and George E. Peterson, *Guides to Managing Urban Capital: Summary* (Washington, D.C.: Urban Institute, 1984), p. xi.

10. Stephen R. Godwin and George E. Peterson, *Guide to Assessing Capital Stock Condition* (Washington, D.C.: Urban Institute, 1984), pp. 7–9.

11. Ronald W. Johnson, "Asuncion Municipal Development Project: Financial and Institutional Analyses" (Washington, D.C.: The World Bank, 1984).

12. Ronald W. Johnson, "Montevideo Municipal Development Project: Financial and Institutional Issues" (Washington, D.C.: The World Bank, 1986 and 1987).

13. See, for example, Donald Levitan and Michael J. Byrne, "Capital Improvement Programming," in Jack Rabin and Thomas D. Lynch, eds., *Handbook on Public Budgeting and Financial Management* (New York: Marcel Dekker, 1983), pp. 585–600.

14. J. Richard Aronson and Eli Schwartz, "Capital Budgeting," in Aronson and Schwartz, eds., *Management Policies in Local Government Finance*, 3rd ed. (Washington, D.C.: International City Management Association, 1987), pp. 400–21.

15. Harry P. Hatry et al., *How Effective Are Your Community Services? Procedures for Monitoring the Effectiveness of Municipal Services* (Washington, D.C.: Urban Institute and the International City Management Association, 1977).

16. See A. John Vogt, *Capital Improvement Programming: A Handbook for Local Government Officials* (Chapel Hill, N.C.: Institute of Government, 1977), pp. 56–60.

17. Robert Berne and Richard Schramm, *The Financial Analysis of Governments* (Englewood Cliffs, N.J.: Prentice-Hall, 1986).

18. Sanford M. Groves and Maureen Godsey Valente, *Evaluating Financial Condition: A Handbook for Local Government* (Washington, D.C.: International City Management Association, 1986).

19. "Paying the Piper: New Ways to Pay for Public Infrastructure," in Jeffrey I. Chapman, ed., *Long-Term Financial Planning: Creative Strategies for Local Government* (Washington, D.C.: International City Management Association, 1987), p. 173.

20. Maureen B. Valente and Clayton Carlisle, "Developer Financing: Impact Fees and Negotiated Exactions," *Management Information Service Report* 20 (1988): 1–15.

21. Robert Kee, Walter Robbins, and Nicholas Apostolou, "Capital Budgeting Practices of U.S. Cities: A Survey," *The Government Accountant's Journal* 36 (Summer 1987): 16–22.

22. Ronald Chapman, "Capital Financing: A New Look at Old Techniques," in John Matzer, Jr., ed., *Practical Financial Management: New Techniques for Local Government* (Washington, D.C.: International City Management Association, 1984), p. 141.

23. Harry P. Hatry, Annie P. Millar, and James H. Evans, *Guide to Setting Priorities for Capital Investment* (Washington, D.C.: Urban Institute, 1984).

24. Michael A. Pagano, "Notes on Capital Budgeting," *Public Budgeting and Finance* 4 (Autumn 1984): 32–40.

25. Hush and Peroff, "State Capital Budgets," pp. 71–72.

26. See *Dallas Morning News and Dallas Times Herald,* November 11, 1988, for numerous feature articles and news analyses.

27. Pagano, "Notes on Capital Budgeting," p. 39.

28. General Accounting Office, *Managing the Cost of Government: Building an Effective Financial Management Structure* (Washington, D.C.: Government Printing Office, 1985).

29. Frederick D. Wolfe, "Capital Budgeting for the Federal Government," testimony before the Subcommittee on Economic Development, House Committee on Public Works and Transportation, 100th Cong., 1st sess., December 8, 1987.

30. *Report of the President's Commission on Budget Concepts* (Washington, D.C.: Government Printing Office, 1967), p. 34.

31. Goldman, "AABPA Symposium," p. 8.

32. General Accounting Office, *Pros and Cons of a Separate Capital Budget for the Federal Government* (Washington, D.C.: Government Printing Office, 1983).

33. General Accounting Office, *Budget Issues: Capital Budgeting for the Federal Government* (Washington, D.C.: Government Printing Office, 1988).

34. Bureau of the Census, *Government Finances in 1986–87* (Washington, D.C.: Government Printing Office, 1988), p. 16.

35. Bureau of the Census, *Government Finances in 1986–87, p. 16.*

36. *George C. Kaufman, "Debt Administration," in Aronson and Schwartz, eds., Management Policies in Local Government Finance,* pp. 302–27.

37. Joseph A. Pechman, *Federal Tax Policy,* 5th ed. (Washington, D.C.: Brookings, 1987), p. 125.

38. See Mortgage Subsidy Bond Tax Act of 1980; Subtitle A, Title XI of the Omnibus Reconciliation Act of 1980, 94 Stat. 2599; Susannah E. Calkins and Jeanne R. Aronson, "The Home Mortgage Revenue Bonds Controversy," *Publius* 10 (Winter 1980): 111–18.

39. John E. Peterson, "The Municipal Bond Market in a Changing Economy," *Public Budgeting and Finance* 8 (Winter 1988): 22–34.

40. Linda J. Mittermaier and Jeffrey L. Patterson, "Exclusions from Income are Narrower after the Tax Reform Act of 1986," *Taxation for Accountants* 41 (August 1988): 90–98.

41. Jeffrey H. Birnbaum and Alan S. Murray, *Showdown at Gucci Gulch: Lawmakers, Lobbyists and the Unlikely Triumph of Tax Reform* (New York: Vintage, 1988), pp. 199–201.

42. John M. Kamensky, "Budgeting for State and Local Infrastructure: Developing a Strategy," *Public Budgeting and Finance* 4 (Autumn 1984): 15.

43. Alex G. Brown, *The Municipal Bond Primer* (Denver: Kirchner Moore, 1987), p. 10.

44. Robert Lamb and Stephen P. Rappaport, *Municipal Bonds,* 2nd ed. (New York: McGraw-Hill, 1987).

45. Andrea Lubov, *Issuing Municipal Bonds: A Primer for Local Officials* (Washington, D.C.: Government Printing Office, 1979).

46. Jeffrey G. Madrick, *Fundamentals of Municipal Bonds* (New York: Public Securities Association, 1981).

47. *State of South Carolina v. Baker*, 108 S.Ct. 1355 (1988).

48. Steven R. Wilson, "Credit Ratings and General Obligation Bonds: A Statistical Alternative," *Government Finance Review* 2 (June 1986): 19–22.

49. Robert Bland, "The Interest Cost Savings from Experience in the Municipal Bond Market," *Public Administration Review* 45 (1985): 233–37.

50. Cathy Daicoff Macsherry, "Infrastructure and S&P Credit Rating," *Public Budgeting and Finance* 4 (Autumn 1984): 41–45.

51. Unfunded pension liabilities also affect bond ratings (see Chapter 13). Linda J. Martin, et al., "Pension Obligations and Municipal Bond Ratings," *State and Local Government Review* 18 (1986): 26–30.

52. John Myers, "Chapel Hill Retains Strong Bond Rating," *The Chapel Hill Newspaper,* September 8, 1988.

53. Phillip Cagan, "The Interest Saving to States and Municipalities from Bank Eligibility to Underwrite All Nonindustrial Municipal Bonds," *Government Finance* 7 (May 1978): 40–48.

54. Michael D. Joehnk and David S. Kidwell, "A Look at Competitive and Negotiated Under-writing Costs in the Municipal Bond Market," *Public Administration Review* 40 (1980): 22–25.

55. George C. Kaufman, "Improving Competitive Bidding Procedures for Municipal Bonds," *Governmental Finance* 3 (August 1974): 22–27.

56. All 1987 figures in this and the following paragraph are from Bureau of the Census, *Government Finances in 1986–87* (Washington, D.C.: Government Printing Office, 1988), pp. 16 and 10–11. For 1980, figures are from *Governmental Finances in 1979–80* (Washington, D.C.: Government Printing Office, 1981), p. 5.

57. All per capita debt and personal income figures in this paragraph are from Bureau of the Census, *Government Finances in 1986–87*, pp. 110 and 111.

58. Bureau of the Census, *Government Finances in 1986–87*, p. 16.

59. George W. Mitchell, "Statement before the Committee on Banking, Housing and Urban Affairs," *Federal Reserve Bulletin* 61 (1975): 729–30.

60. James Leigland and Robert Lamb, *WPP$$: Who Is to Blame for the WPPSS Disaster* (Cambridge, Mass.: Ballinger, 1986).

61. David Mybra, *Whoops!/WPPSS: Washington Public Power Supply System Nuclear Plants* (Jefferson, N.C.: McFarland, 1984).

62. Berne and Schramm, *The Financial Analysis of Governments*.

63. *Evaluating Local Financial Condition* (Washington, D.C.: International City Management Association, 1988).

64. Berne and Schramm, *The Financial Analysis of Governments*, p. 262.

65. Johnson, "Montevideo Municipal Development Project."

66. George G. Kaufman and Philip J. Fischer, "Debt Management," in Aronson and Schwartz, eds., *Management Policies in Local Government Finance*, pp. 287–317.

67. Joseph Asher, "The Lessons of Cleveland," *ABA Banking Journal* 72 (Fall 1980): 44ff.

68. Lynn E. Browne and Richard F. Syron, "The Municipal Market Since the New York City Crisis," *New England Economic Review* (July/August 1979): 11–26.

69. Terry Nichols Clark, G. Edward DeSeve, and J. Chester Johnson, *Financial Handbook for Mayors and City Managers* (New York: Van Nostrand Reinhold, 1985), pp. 52–102.

70. Advisory Commission on Intergovernmental Relations, *Measuring State Fiscal Capacity: Alternative Methods and Their Uses* (Washington, D.C.: Government Printing Office, 1986).

13

Government Personnel
and Pensions

In his classic work on government budgeting, A.E. Buck wrote, "Personnel is the most important single factor in government both from the operating and the fiscal point of view."[1] Yet, despite the importance of personnel to budgeting, rarely has there been any attempt to integrate the two. Budget literature has been almost silent on government personnel policies and procedures, and personnel literature has been similarly silent on budgeting.[2,3]

Government personnel is reviewed here in two main sections. The first section reviews the impacts of personnel decisions and expenditures on the budget and discusses the structure of personnel retirement systems. The second section suggests some of the reasons why budgeting and personnel administration have been separate activities and discusses budget staffs, including sizes, skill mixes, and training.

PERSONNEL IMPACTS AND PENSION PLANS

Personnel Considerations in Decision Making

Importance of Personnel Expenditures. The largest portion of any government's operating budget is typically for personnel. In 1986–87 direct personal services for salaries and wages cost government on the average 22 percent of direct expenditures. That figure does not include costs for employee insurance and pension benefits. Local governments spent the highest proportion (42 percent) and the federal government the lowest (11 percent), with the states being near the average (18 percent). The federal percentage is low because Social Security costs are part of total expenditures.[4]

Public employment has been important for welfare purposes. The awarding of positions to the economically needy and to the politically faithful has been a common practice. Patronage appointments have been common at all levels of government.

Administrators have used personnel tactics to build empires. A large staff is often regarded as evidence of success for the administrator. Moreover, when staff is increased, the administrator can make claims on other resources, namely increases in budget items for supplies, equipment, and the like. All administrators, of course, are not would-be kings. Empire building results in part from sincere convictions that increases in personnel will increase the effectiveness of an agency.[5,6]

Given the magnitude of personnel expenditures, the use of employment for patronage purposes, and tendencies toward empire building on the part of agencies, it becomes obvious why budgeting decisions often have focused on personnel practices. Budgets of many years ago indicated the names of individuals and their earnings. The purpose was to guarantee that individuals were not receiving exorbitant salaries.

Today the practice of naming employees in the budget is far less common, although information on the wages and salaries of individual employees is available to the public for most government employees. In contemporary budgets, salaries of heads of agencies are often reported in budgets, but itemized earnings of lower-ranked employees are not. Still, budgets usually at least report personnel expenditures by agency and may provide more detail. Table 13-1 displays position and salary information for a correctional youth center in Illinois; the table is taken from a separate document on personnel prepared by the Illinois Bureau of the Budget.

Personnel Complement. One item to note from the Illinois table is that it reports the number of positions. Similar displays may be found in some state budgets and local budgets. The federal government in its *Budget Appendix* once reported the number of positions at each pay level for each agency, but that practice has been replaced by summary information indicating the total number of full-time positions and full-time equivalent workyears.

Sometimes personnel tables are included in budgets only for information purposes, that is, to provide the legislative body and the general public with information about the size of the personnel complement of agencies. In other cases, these displays exist for decision purposes. An agency may not be permitted to hire a new staff member, even though funds are available in its budget, without first receiving authorization for a new position. Budget offices and personnel departments often exercise such control, and sometimes the legislatures are involved. Exercising complement control is considered one method of limiting growth in the bureaucracy and the budget.

Table 13-1 Positions and Salaries, Pere Marquette Youth Center, Illinois, 1986–88

Position Title	Monthly Salary Range (Dollars)	Number of Positions (Fiscal Years)			Annual Salary Rates in Dollars (Fiscal Years)	
		1986	1987	1988	1987	1988
Account Technician I	1331–1677	2	2	2	38,520	40,252
Business Administrator I	2115–3209	1	1	1	28,848	29,653
Chief of Security I	2115–3209	1	1	1	33,456	35,388
Clerk Typist III	1160–1423	1	2	2	31,020	32,763
Correctional Casework Supervisor	2006–3012	1	1	1	26,004	26,608
Correctional Counselor II	1813–2373	3	3	3	77,542	81,845
Corrections Assistant Superintendent	2494–3852	0	1	1	35,880	38,184
Corrections Food Supervisor I	1709–2215	3	3	3	72,216	76,116
Corrections Food Supervisor II	1873–2454	1	1	1	28,176	29,443
Corrections Leisure Activities Specialist II	1813–2373	1	1	1	24,114	25,354
Corrections Maintenance Craftsman	1785–2321	1	1	1	26,652	27,851
Corrections Superintendent I	2647–4123	1	1	1	37,344	38,164
Nurse I	1691–2234	1	1	1	23,537	24,785
Secretary I	1331–1677	1	1	1	15,864	16,684
Storekeeper I	1371–1731	1	1	1	19,872	20,766
Youth Supervisor II	1559–1999	18	18	18	388,777	410,414
Youth Supervisor III	1785–2321	3	3	3	76,731	80,543
Youth Supervisor IV	1904–2495	2	2	2	55,172	58,448
Youth Supervisor Trainee	1331–1677	0	2	2	34,512	36,065
Subtotals		42	46	46	1,074,237	1,129,326
Budgetary Adjustments Overtime and Other Adjustments		+0	+0	+0	+30,245	+67,195
Vacancies		+0	−2	−3	−46,782	−75,321
Totals		42	44	43	1,057,700	1,121,200

Source: Illinois Personnel Detail, Fiscal Year 1988 (State of Illinois, 1988).

Labor-Management Relations. Labor unions have come to play important roles in personnel matters and budgeting. Overall salary and wage levels, as well as other benefits, particularly retirement benefits, are set by governments in a variety of ways, with the two primary ones being through legislative action and collective bargaining. Unions obviously are deeply involved in collective bargaining, but they also are influential in the legislative process of determining compensation—salaries, wages, and benefits. Through lobbying efforts, unions have been able to persuade state legislators to pass laws setting minimum salary levels for teachers in local school districts, to impose standards for retirement systems, and to pass other related personnel legislation, such as mandating regular training for police officers.

Collective bargaining is well established in many governments. At the federal level, about 60 percent of the workers are covered by exclusive bargaining units; membership in unions is lower than that figure, since some workers covered by a bargaining agreement often choose not to join a union. At the state level, nearly 40 percent of full-time workers are unionized, and the comparable figure for the local level is 50 percent.[7,8]

Collective bargaining greatly complicates the process of budgeting.[9] Given the proportion of expenditures committed to personnel, a wage settlement can have a massive impact on the budget. Many labor contracts are valid for only one year, meaning that year-round negotiations are likely to occur and result in great uncertainty over what personnel costs will be for the budget that is being prepared.

The number of bargaining units and unions further complicates the situation. Employees bargain as a unit that is said to have a "community of interests," as in the case of clerical workers for a city. Determination of the bargaining unit is made by an independent agency, such as a state labor relations board for both state and local governments within the state or, in the case of the federal government, the Federal Labor Relations Authority. Those responsible for budgeting, then, have no control over the number of bargaining units and correspondingly the number of unions that will be involved in negotiations.

The greater the number of bargaining units, the more complex budget planning becomes. The federal government has well over 2,000 units, with some having thousands of employees and others only a handful. A major difference between the federal government and other governments is that federal workers generally do not have the power to bargain over salaries, although there are important exceptions such as the Postal Service.[10] About half of the states have ten or more bargaining units.[11]

Although collective bargaining unquestionably has great influences on the budgeting process, there is conflicting evidence on whether collective bargaining leads to higher personnel costs.[12] One factor is that the economic "health" of a jurisdiction will affect its ability to grant wage and salary increases to workers. During the recession of the early 1980s, for instance, wage increases at the state and local levels were kept to a minimum largely because of tight budgets, regardless of worker unionization. Further complicating matters during that period were budget restrictions, such as Proposition 13 in California, that curtailed local governments from raising taxes.

Another factor in wage determination is the spillover of decisions within a community and from one community to others. If unionized police in a city win wage increases, clerical workers in the same city are likely to benefit even if they are not unionized. Similarly, if a union is successful in bargaining for increases in compensation in one city, other cities in response may grant increases to their workers in order to remain competitive in recruiting and retaining employees and in some cases possibly to avert unionization.

Labor Negotiations. To bargain for compensation increases, union leaders have had to learn about budgeting. Without a thorough understanding of a jurisdiction's budget, unions can be persuaded by management that funds simply do not exist to grant increases. The job of the union is to "find" budget surpluses that can be used to increase employee compensation. Some national unions help their state and local affiliates to analyze their respective governments' budgets.[13]

Since the mid-1970s, there have been some important changes in the nature of bargaining between unions and management. In the early years of public sector collective bargaining, one of labor's main arguments was that salaries and wages in the public sector needed to be increased to match the private sector. While that thrust continues, especially in regard to teachers' salaries, negotiations have come to focus more on productivity of workers. In some jurisdictions, wage increases have been dependent on measurable improvements in worker productivity. According to the concept of "productivity bargaining," workers are entitled to benefit from the financial savings accruing from greater productivity.

Another change in bargaining has been management demands for concessions.[14] As budgets have become tighter, some jurisdictions have demanded that workers take pay reductions. In other cases, agreements have been developed for hiring new workers at pay rates lower than current ones; this occurred in the Postal Service. Some negotiations have concentrated on job security, in which unions have tried to protect workers from layoffs. While these practices are not nearly as common in government as in the private sector, the point is that collective negotiations in the public sector no longer are characterized by unions simply demanding greater pay and benefits.

Comparable Worth. One other matter that casts considerable confusion on the personnel-budgeting arena is that of "comparable worth" or "pay equity." Simply stated, the concept of comparable worth maintains that workers should receive compensation according to their intrinsic contribution to an organization. Where a problem arises is that many occupations in government that are held by women tend to be low paying. Included are clerical secretaries, librarians, nurses, and teachers. Demands are being made that compensation levels be greatly increased in these areas to avoid such situations as paying someone who tends lawns or drives a trash truck more than a secretary, who is expected to master sophisticated office equipment and a variety of computer software programs. Labor unions often are torn on this issue. On the one hand the unions want to be strong advocates for comparable worth, but on the other hand they do not want to lose the support of workers in other occupations.[15,16]

Pension Plans

The most expensive part of an employee benefit package in a government is pension plans. There are approximately 200 state-administered plans, some of which include local government employees as well as state employees, and over 2,300 locally administered plans.[17] The federal government has a variety of plans, with the main one being the Federal Employees Retirement System (FERS) for persons hired on or after January 1, 1984. Employees hired before that date may opt for FERS or remain in the Civil Service Retirement System (CSRS); most have chosen to continue with CSRS coverage.

Structure of Plans. Retirement systems generally are based on an assumption that a person will use a variety of measures to cover living expenses during retirement. First, living expenses may decline as the individual becomes less active and has fewer demands on income, such as supporting dependents. Second, savings are used to cover expenses. Third, many government workers are covered by Old-Age and Survivors Insurance, Disability Insurance, and Health Insurance (Medicare) of the Social Security Administration. Members of FERS are required to participate in Social Security, while federal employees who belong to CSRS do not participate. In addition to these supports, then, retirement systems are intended to aid former employees. In FERS, workers may pay up to 10 percent of their earnings into a tax-deferred plan and the government matches part of the amount.[18]

One area that is not controllable is contributions of employees and state and local governments into Social Security. These governments once had the option of joining and withdrawing from Social Security; governments withdrew when their calculations indicated greater returns could be made on their own investments than what Social Security paid in benefits. In the 1980s, however, Congress passed legislation barring withdrawal from Social Security, and the Supreme Court upheld the law.[19] The result is that state and local governments must budget each year for increased Social Security costs regardless of their budget situations.

Benefits under pension plans normally are determined according to some combination of wages or salaries and years of service. The longer one has worked for a government and the higher one's salary, the higher pension benefits will be. In addition, cost-of-living increases are usually assigned pensioners, sometimes on an automatic basis according to an economic barometer, such as the consumer price index, and other times on an ad hoc basis.[20] In the latter instance, a government might decide one year to increase retirement benefits by the same percentage as salary increases being awarded current employees. Other benefits are provided for disability retirement, namely for people who retire early because of poor health, and for survivors' benefits, covering family members who continue to live after the death of retirees. About three-quarters of benefits paid each year go to elderly retirees, with the remaining quarter divided evenly between disability retirees and survivors.[21]

Funding. Pension plans are funded by a combination of contributions from government and employees and investment earnings on those contributions. In some cases, the retirement program is financed exclusively by government, but that practice is an exception to the rule. In 1985–86, earnings constituted 56 percent of receipts for state and local retirement systems. Government contributions accounted for another 32 percent, and employee contributions for the remaining 12 percent.[22]

There are basically two means of financing retirement programs—pay-as-you-go and advance funding. In the former case, all that is required in any one budget year is to raise sufficient revenue to cover retirement benefit checks. This method is generally discouraged in that it allows for the accumulation of debt, namely that persons in the future will be owed benefits and taxpayers at that time will be forced to meet those costs.

The preferred method is advance funding, in which monies are accumulated for workers while they are working and those monies generate income through investments while workers are on the payroll and during retirement as well. In such a case, a retirement system would not have an "unfunded liability" and therefore would be "actuarially sound." Advance funding uses the concept of "present value," in which future receipts, particularly contributions and investment earnings, are compared with anticipated costs (benefits) in terms of current dollars.[23] The concept is analogous to the discount rate used in analysis (see Chapter 7). According to a survey of state and local governments, nearly three-fourths of the systems have unfunded liabilities.[24]

Pension fund liabilities can cause serious problems. Meeting current operating needs and covering the costs of retiree benefits can easily put a budget out of balance and force a tax increase. Where jurisdictions are at their legal or political limits on tax rates, severe program cuts may be the only alternative. Pension fund liabilities can increase the cost of doing business, namely, interest rates may be higher for jurisdictions that have large outstanding pension debts.[25]

Several options are available for improving the funding situation of retirement systems.

1. An obvious option is to increase government and employee contributions.[26]
2. Another is to take advantage of economies of scale by combining systems; this may reduce administrative costs and make possible more lucrative investments.[27]

3. Retirement systems can pool their funds for investment purposes.[28]
4. A jurisdiction can accept more risk in investments with the expectation of achieving a greater return; the stock market crash of 1987, however, is a sobering reminder of the loss that can result from nonguaranteed investments.
5. In some cases jurisdictions have sold bonds in order to obtain funds needed to cover retirement liabilities.[29]

For private sector retirement systems, Congress has insisted on advance funding; the Employee Retirement Income Security Act of 1974 mandated such action. The problem of unfunded liability was more acute in the private sector, where some companies incurred debt to their employees, went bankrupt, and left the workers without any retirement benefits. Whether Congress has the legal authority to extend a requirement for advance funding of state and local systems is uncertain.

PERSONNEL OPERATIONS

Personnel Administration and Budgeting

Because decisions related to personnel have major effects upon budgeting, some linkage between the two is needed. However, just as constant tensions exist between budget offices and line agencies, so do tensions persist between the budget and personnel systems.

Historical Differences. A fundamental problem is that budgeting and personnel administration stem from differing historical backgrounds. As has been seen in earlier chapters, budgeting has arisen to provide information to executive and legislative decision makers. Central budget offices are intended to aid the chief executive, an elected politician. Budgeting is frankly political. Personnel administration, on the other hand, is a product of a reform movement designed to minimize political concerns, to base personnel actions—appointments, promotions, and the like—on what one knows and does on the job rather than on whom one knows. Personnel administration is expected to be apolitical.

Not only are budgeting and personnel distinct in their historical roots, but these differences have resulted in differences in organizational structures. Since passage of the Pendleton Act of 1883, which established a merit system of employment in the federal government, the personnel function at all levels of government has tended to be organizationally separate from control by political executives. The justification for this independence has been that it insulates personnel matters from the caprices of politics.[30]

Some staunch advocates of merit systems have concluded that these independent commissions have outlived their usefulness and should be abandoned.[31] Commissions often are seen as having negative influences and rarely being innovative and supportive of improvements in managerial practices.

Reforms. At the federal level, action was taken in 1978 with passage of the Civil Service Reform Act. The Civil Service Commission was dissolved, and taking its place were the Office of Personnel Management (OPM) and the Merit Systems Protection Board (MSPB). The OPM, which reports directly to the president, is expected to take personnel actions that are conducive to implementing the policies of the political leadership, while the MSPB in effect is a watchdog guarding against political influences on hiring, firing, and other personnel actions.

Even when the central personnel agency reports to the chief executive, tensions persist between that unit and the budget office. The two offices must deal with each other on such matters as reclassification of jobs, complement control, collective bargaining, and reductions-in-force (RIFs), in which employees are laid off, usually for financial reasons.[32]

Personnel in Budgeting

It takes people to operate budgeting systems, people at the central location of a budget office, in line agencies, and in the legislative body. While only some personnel are assigned full time to budget matters, all personnel are inevitably involved with budgeting and budget decisions. In this section, we discuss the size and skill mix of budget staffs.

Federal Staff. At the federal level, both the executive and legislative branches have sizable staffs. The Office of Management and Budget has a staff of about 550, and each department has personnel whose main function is budgeting. Congress has the Congressional Budget Office, staffs for standing committees, staffs for each congressman and senator, the General Accounting Office, the Library of Congress (including the Congressional Research Service), and the Office of Technology Assessment. Staffs exist for the House and Senate Budget Committees, the House Ways and Means Committee, the Senate Finance Committee, and the House and Senate Appropriations Committees.

Altogether Congress has about 38,000 employees. Most of the people who work for Congress do not work on budgeting, such as employees of the Government Printing Office (5,100 employees) and the Architect of the Capitol (2,200 employees), but many are assigned to work on budgeting and substantive matters with budgetary implications.[33]

State Staff. The sizes of state budget staffs vary greatly. New York State has about 200 professional staff members, while California and New Jersey each have approximately 100 staff members. Other states with more than 40 professional budget office personnel include Florida, Illinois, North Carolina, Ohio, Virginia, and Wisconsin. On the other hand, many states have fewer than 20 professionals.[34]

Professional fiscal staffs are to be found in virtually all state legislatures. However, detailed information is not available on this matter, nor are there data on professional staffs working in municipal budget offices and for city councils and other local legislative and executive bodies. Local staffs generally are small, with local legislative bodies—city councils, school boards, and the like—often having to rely mainly on executive branch staff for budget information and analysis.

The question of how many budget staff members are needed on either the executive or legislative side of government can be answered only in terms of the expectations for the budget units. Small staffs handling multimillion- or multibillion-dollar budgets obviously can be expected to do little more than superficially review materials prepared by agencies and perhaps devote in-depth effort to selected "hot" issues.

Skill Mixes. Budget offices vary in the purposes that are pursued and the activities undertaken, both of which are linked with the skill mix of budget personnel. A budget office emphasizing the control function of holding agencies accountable for spending in accordance with appropriations may prefer persons with business skills and particularly accounting training. At the federal level and to a lesser extent at the state level, skills in public finance may be important for developing policies for economic growth. Still other skills may be sought by budget units engaged in policy and program analysis.

Budget office staffs at the state level have been increasing in their professionalism, especially in the last 10 to 20 years. Today, few offices hire people with less than a baccalaureate degree, except for clerical workers and technicians. Many state budget offices routinely hire persons with master's and doctoral degrees.

There has been a trend away from staffing state offices with persons having accounting and other business degrees. Whereas in 1970 the typical state budget office had two-thirds of its staff trained in these fields, only 14 states reported in 1985 having half or more of their personnel trained in accounting and business. The states tended to be southern and/or less populated (examples include Alabama, Georgia, Iowa, Maine, Oklahoma, and Wyoming).[35]

Conversely, the social sciences have increased their representation in state budget offices. In 1985, 15 states reported that half or more of their staff were trained in public administration, economics, or other social sciences.

Included in this grouping were Colorado, Illinois, Kansas, Michigan, Pennsylvania, Texas, Virginia, and Washington.

The typical state budget office staff now has a blend of educational backgrounds. Both business and the social sciences are represented along with other professional disciplines that include engineering, law, education, and labor relations. Indeed, categorization of staff has become difficult in that a staff member often has a baccalaureate degree in one field and one or two master's degrees in other fields.

Whether the composition of the staff has any bearing upon the way a state budget system operates is not clear. Certainly, a staff cannot do something for which it is not trained. Only those trained in program analysis would be expected to be able to conduct analysis. On the other hand, it is possible that budget offices might recruit program analysts and not use their talents. The available evidence suggests that the use of effectiveness analysis in decision making is not significantly greater in social science–oriented budget units than in business-oriented units.[36]

Training. Aside from recruiting personnel with new talents, existing personnel can be upgraded through training programs. Budget offices routinely invest in training their staff either as a whole or selectively, such as sending a few employees to special courses each year. The effectiveness of this training depends in part upon whether employees are given the opportunity to use newly developed knowledge and skills. Training an employee in a budget technique that is not used by the jurisdiction may have limited benefit. On the other hand, training can be an effective means of a budget office acquiring the type of talent needed in serving its mission.

SUMMARY

The impacts of personnel costs on the budget are immense. Because labor costs are a large segment of every operating budget, personnel may be the first to be cut during financially tight periods. Collective bargaining, while helping employees, has greatly complicated budgetary planning at the state and local levels; unresolved negotiations at budget time mean that personnel costs are unknown.

Many retirement programs at the state and local levels are not actuarially sound and may present severe problems in coming years. In granting workers improvements in retirement benefits, government officials need to assess the current and projected impacts on budgets. Advance funding is preferred over pay-as-you-go methods of financing retirement plans.

Despite the apparent linkages between the budget and personnel functions, the administration of these systems has often not been integrated. Tensions persist between the two, in part the result of differing histories. Budgeting is openly a political process, while personnel administration has a penchant for the apolitical.

Executive and legislative staffs in recent years have expanded in size and changed in terms of their capabilities. Congress has substantially increased its budget staffs with the creation of the Congressional Budget Office and the House and Senate Budget Committees. State budget offices have shown a shift toward persons with social science backgrounds, whereas business administration types previously tended to dominate. Many local governments face the problem of needing more budget staff but not having the resources to acquire it. Training can be a useful method of acquiring needed talent.

NOTES

1. A.E. Buck, *Public Budgeting* (New York: Harper and Brothers, 1919), p. 539.

2. Robert D. Lee, Jr., *Public Personnel Systems*, 2nd ed. (Rockville, Md.: Aspen, 1987).

3. Felix A. Nigro and Lloyd G. Nigro, *The New Public Personnel Administration*, 3rd ed. (Itasca, Ill.: Peacock, 1986).

4. Bureau of the Census, *Government Finances in 1986–87* (Washington, D.C.: Government Printing Office, 1988), p. 8.

5. Dennis D. Riley, *Controlling the Federal Bureaucracy* (Philadelphia: Temple University Press, 1987).

6. Francis E. Rourke, ed., *Bureaucratic Power in National Policy Making*, 4th ed. (Boston: Little, Brown, 1986).

7. Lee, *Public Personnel Systems*, pp. 333–34.

8. John F. Burton, Jr. and Terry Thomason, "The Extent of Collective Bargaining in the Public Sector," in Benjamin Aaron, Joyce M. Najita, and James L. Stern, eds., *Public-Sector Bargaining*, 2nd ed. (Washington, D.C.: Bureau of National Affairs, 1988), pp. 1–51.

9. David Lewin et al., eds., *Public Sector Labor Relations* (Lexington, Mass.: Lexington Books, 1988).

10. Charles J. Coleman, "Federal Sector Labor Relations: A Reevaluation of the Policies," *Journal of Collective Negotiations in the Public Sector* 16 (1987): 37–52.

11. See Bureau of the Census, *Labor-Management Relations in State and Local Governments* (Washington, D.C.: Government Printing Office, 1985).

12. Daniel G. Gallagher and Peter A. Veglahn, "The Effect of Collective Bargaining on Wage Dispersion Between Municipal Police Departments," *Journal of Collective Negotiations in the Public Sector* 16 (1987): 327–41.

13. Llewellyn M. Toulmin, "The Treasure Hunt: Budget Search Behavior by Public Employee Unions," *Public Administration Review* 48 (1988): 620–30.

14. Daniel J.B. Mitchell, "Concession Bargaining in the Public Sector," *Public Personnel Management* 15 (1986): 23–40.

15. Stephen L. Mangum, "Comparable Worth and Pay Setting in the Public and Private Sectors," *Journal of Collective Negotiations in the Public Sector* 17 (1988): 1–12.

16. Elizabeth C. Wesman, "Unions and Comparable Worth," *Journal of Collective Negotiations* 17 (1988): 13–25.

17. Bureau of the Census, *Finances of Employee-Retirement Systems of State and Local Governments in 1985-86* (Washington, D.C.: Government Printing Office, 1987), p. 10.

18. For details on federal retirement systems, see Lee E. Sharff, Sol Gordon, and Al Ungerleider, *Federal Personnel Guide* (Washington, D.C.: Federal Personnel Guide, annual).

19. *Bowen v. Public Agencies Opposed to Social Security Entrapment*, 477 U.S. 41 (1986).

20. John E. Petersen, "Public Pension Fund Administration," in J. Richard Aronson and Eli Schwartz, eds., *Management Policies in Local Government Finance*, 3rd ed. (Washington, D.C.: International City Management Association, 1987), pp. 318-41.

21. Ann K. Bixby, "Benefits and Beneficiaries Under Public Employee Retirement Systems, Calendar Year 1985," *Social Security Bulletin* 51 (May 1988): 29-32.

22. Bureau of the Census, *Finances of Employee-Retirement Systems*, p. 1.

23. Robert Berne and Richard Schramm, *The Financial Analysis of Governments* (Englewood Cliffs, N.J.: Prentice-Hall, 1986): 274-313.

24. Paul Zorn, "Public Pension Funding: Preliminary Results from a Survey of Current Practices," *Government Finance Review* 3 (August 1987): 7-11.

25. Linda J. Martin et al., "Pension Obligations and Municipal Bond Ratings," *State and Local Government Review* 18 (1986): 26-30.

26. James M. Ferris, "Local Government Pensions and Their Funding: Policy Issues and Options," *Review of Public Personnel Administration* 7 (Summer 1987): 29-44.

27. Ralph A. Pope, "Economies of Scale in Large State and Municipal Retirement Systems," *Public Budgeting and Finance* 6 (Autumn 1986): 70-80.

28. Sandra C. Whiston, Joseph Martin, and Paul Todisco, "A Pooled Investment Fund for Local Public Retirement Systems: The Start-up Experience in Massachusetts," *Government Finance Review* 1 (June 1985): 19-22.

29. Renee Wentela, "Tax-Exempt Bonds: A New Method of Financing Unfunded Pension Liabilities," *Government Finance Review* 1 (April 1985): 19-21.

30. Lee, *Public Personnel Systems*, pp. 24-35.

31. National Civil Service League, *A Model Public Personnel Administration Law* (Washington, D.C.: National Civil Service League, 1970), p. 7.

32. Gary C. Cornia, William M. Timmins, and David A. Varley, "Cooperation Between Personnel and Budget Offices During Position Requests and Reclassifications," *State and Local Government Review* 17 (1985): 180-87.

33. Office of Personnel Management, *Federal Civilian Work Force Statistics: Employment and Trends as of September 1988* (Washington, D.C.: Government Printing Office, 1988), p. 11.

34. Data from 1985 survey of state budget offices conducted by the Department of Public Administration, The Pennsylvania State University, in conjunction with the Budget Office of the Commonwealth of Pennsylvania and with the endorsement of the National Association of State Budget Officers.

35. 1985 data from survey cited in footnote 50. 1970 data are from comparable survey conducted in 1975 in which budget offices were asked about their staffs five years earlier.

36. Unpublished data; and Robert D. Lee, Jr., and Raymond J. Staffeldt, "Educational Characteristics of State Budget Office Personnel," *Public Administration Review* 36 (1976): 424-28.

14

Intergovernmental Relations

Each level of government has discrete financial decision-making processes that determine matters of revenue and expenditure. In another sense, however, decisions about revenues and expenditures at different levels of government are interdependent. Budgetary decisions made at one level are partially dependent upon budgetary and nonbudgetary decisions made at other levels.

This chapter examines the financial interdependencies among the federal, state, and local governments.[1-4] The first section examines some of the basic economic and political problems that stem from having three major levels of government providing various services and having differing financial capabilities. The second section considers the patterns of interaction among the different levels, and the third section considers the main types of grant-in-aid programs. The chapter concludes with a discussion of alternatives for restructuring these patterns of financial interaction.

BASIC PROBLEMS

For convenience purposes, we have commonly referred throughout this book to the three levels of governments, but at this point this simplification must be set aside. In this section, we consider the problems associated with the functioning of these governments.

Areal and Functional Relations

Multiple Governments. In addition to the federal government and the 50 state governments, there are somewhat more than 80,000 local governments and the District of Columbia. The local "level" is not a level in that most states have county governments, and within their boundaries are municipalities and sometimes townships as general-purpose governments. Superimposed over these are numerous independent school districts and special districts such as irrigation and sewer districts.

These various local governments are not merely subunits of their respective state governments, nor are the states subunits of the national government. Each government has substantial decision-making authority. The nation does not have a centralized system in which policies are set by the national government and their administration is delegated to the states, which in turn delegate responsibilities to local governments.

The use of this myriad of governments can be defended in several ways. By having multiple governments, an omnipotent, despotic type of government may be avoided. Another presumed advantage is that the diversity of governments allows for differing responses according to the divergent needs of citizens in different locales.

The existence of numerous units of government increases the probability that greater choice will be afforded individuals in their own preferences. People may locate in specific communities that offer desirable mixes of taxes and services; of course, it is not suggested that such economic calculations are the sole criteria upon which location decisions are based.[5,6]

Another advantage of multiple governments is that economies of scale may be achieved; functions may be performed by the unit of the size that is most capable of performing them. Just as it may be advantageous from the standpoint of efficient resource utilization for private, profit-oriented organizations to grow to a large scale, it may also be more efficient for one unit of government to conduct some governmental activities on a large scale.

On the other hand, to perform all governmental functions at the central level might result in inefficient conduct of some activities. Lessened flexibility of operations and other diseconomies suggest the need for some functions to be performed by units of government smaller than the federal government. Probably many services can be provided most efficiently at the local level.

Of course, all of these governments are not free to do whatever they please. The Constitution provides for the federal government's powers (especially Article I, Section 8) and reserves all other powers to the states (Tenth Amendment). Local governments have fewer constitutional protections, because these governments have been created by their states. Within these legal parameters, a higher-level government may impose standards upon lower levels.

Coordination Problems. The existence of thousands of governments results in coordination problems both geographically and functionally. Municipalities in a metropolitan area need some coordinative mechanisms. Road networks, for example, need to be planned in accordance with commuting patterns within a metropolitan area, and such plans should not be restricted to the geographical boundaries of each municipality. Recreation and parks programs, for example, may be provided on a metropolitan or area basis and thereby achieve economies of scale.[7]

Functional coordination also is a problem in that the three main levels of government share responsibilities within program fields or functions. Criminal justice, for instance, is a function of all three levels; some type of police, court, and prison system exists at the local, state, and federal levels. The independent pursuit of similar objectives by these governments can result in ineffective services and wasted resources. Therefore, increasing emphasis has been given to developing mechanisms for functional integration. While program specialists stress functional integration, however, policy generalists may stress areal integration.[8] This conflict has been popularized by Deil S. Wright as picket fence federalism, with each picket being a function such as mental health or education and all three levels of government being part of each picket.[9]

Fiscal Considerations

Vertical Imbalance. The conflict between area and function is played out within the context of the need for services and the corresponding need for revenues, with differences in capabilities existing within levels of government and among levels.[10] Vertical imbalance, or noncorrespondence, refers to the relative abilities of different levels of government to generate needed revenue. Although one level of government may have a comparative advantage in its efficiency in providing a particular service, it may not have the revenue capability to provide the service. Another level of government, on the other hand, may possess sufficient revenue capability but not be the most efficient unit to provide certain services. In the United States, it is typically the federal government that possesses the revenue capacity but not the comparative advantage in providing many governmental services, while states and local governments are in the position of having functional expenditure obligations that are greater than their ability to raise revenue.[11]

This disparity is attributed largely to the different revenue sources used by governments. The federal government, relying upon personal and corporate income taxes, has a more elastic tax structure in which revenues increase with any increase in economic activity. While state and local revenue sources are relatively inelastic, the demand for services provided by these governments is quite elastic.

Superior fiscal capacity can be used by one level of government to entice or persuade another to provide a given service. This is the case in the federal government's persuading the states to build an interstate network of freeways.

Had the federal government not been willing to pay 90 percent of the cost of the system, certainly there would be far fewer freeways today.[12]

State and Local Fiscal Capacities. Problems exist among governments at the same level with regard to fiscal capacities. From state to state there are clearly differences in income and wealth, which are the basic sources of governmental revenue. Differences in income and wealth lead to differences in revenue-generating abilities, tax burdens, and levels of public services, although there is not a simple direct correlation between income on the one hand, and taxing and spending on the other.[13] For example, U.S. per capita personal income in 1986 was $14,641, but Connecticut's was $19,600, or 134 percent of the national average, and Mississippi's was $9,716, or only 66 percent of the national average.[14]

If the distribution of the demand for governmental services was similar to the distribution of income and wealth, then there would be no problem with differences in revenue capacity among the states. Citizens theoretically could choose states with the level of services most corresponding to their own preferences. Unfortunately, the need for many governmental services is greatest in those states where the fiscal capacity to meet those needs is lowest. The problem is even more acute with respect to different local jurisdictions within the same state. Central city governments within large metropolitan areas are faced with demands for services that increase at a faster rate than does the value of revenue sources.

Fiscal Responsibilities. At issue is the extent to which one government with greater revenue-generating capacity should be responsible for aiding other lower-level governments. The issue is whether and to what extent governments should redistribute resources among different segments of the population and geographic areas; during the 1980s, there was seemingly less support for redistributive activities, especially at the federal level, than in previous decades.[15,16]

One governing principle is that a government should engage in such funding only when the problem addressed corresponds to its level of responsibility, namely that the federal government should deal with national problems and the states with state problems. President Ronald Reagan issued Executive Order 12612 in 1987, which read in part: "It is important to recognize the distinction between problems of national scope (which may justify Federal action) and problems that are merely common to the States (which will not justify Federal action because individual States, acting individually or together, can effectively deal with them)."[17] This executive order can be used to derive an extremely narrow definition of when the federal government should assist states and localities.

Disparities in fiscal capacity among governments at the same level lead directly to another problem, that of external costs and benefits of governmental functions. People of low income moving from states with low services to states with high services create new burdens on the high-service states. This fact is especially evident in the migration of the 1930s from impoverished areas to the West Coast and in the more recent migration from the rural South to cities in the North and West. Proportionately, more people who move from the lower-income to the higher-income states receive welfare payments and generate greater demands on other public services than do those moving from states with similarly high levels of income and services.

In the above example, some of the costs of the failure to provide comparable levels of service across state lines are borne by those outside the low-service states. The problem has an opposite side too. Providing services at the level at which it is most economical to do so may also result in the benefits' spilling over into larger areas. The most obvious example is education. Higher levels of education generally yield higher levels of income. Given the mobility of the population, the benefits produced by one local educational system may spread far beyond the local boundaries.

Economic Competition. Governments compete with each other in attracting businesses and industries. Firms locate for a variety of reasons, such as access to markets, labor supply, and other resources. Because businesses seek to minimize production costs, advantages lie with jurisdictions that have high services and low taxes for industry. Whether businesses actually move for these reasons or not is irrelevant to the argument. As long as governments compete with taxes and services, the effects are the same.

Competition for businesses among political jurisdictions has important consequences, one being distortions in revenue and expenditure patterns. When special concessions are granted to firms, needed revenues must be obtained elsewhere or the level of services must be reduced. Devoting resources to special facilities, such as industrial parks, that are frequently financed by long-term debt instruments, may affect a community's ability to finance other capital projects, such as a civic center or a new sewage treatment plant.

Overlapping Taxes. The taxes of jurisdictions overlap with each other in that ultimately the same people and firms must pay the various governments. Tax overlapping also occurs when all levels of government tax the same specific source, such as federal, state, and local taxes on income.[18]

Overlapping, or multiple taxation, in some sense is unavoidable and not necessarily undesirable. It causes serious problems only when one jurisdiction in effect pre-empts another lower level's ability to raise sufficient revenue. This can occur if the state sales tax rate is so high that it discourages local jurisdictions from levying such a tax; indeed, states may preclude their local governments from having sales taxes but may provide them alternative sources of revenues. The same kind of problem is evidenced in the federal use of personal and corporate income taxes vis-à-vis states and local governments. These jurisdictions, while often criticized for failing to raise sufficient revenue to meet needs, may be largely pre-empted by the federal government from major reliance upon income taxes.

PATTERNS OF INTERACTION AMONG LEVELS OF GOVERNMENTS

Direct Expenditures and Taxes

Discussions of intergovernmental finance too often concentrate exclusively on financial assistance and neglect the more important factor of direct expenditures. Federal expenditures are not made in a vacuum but rather have varying geographical impact. The same is true for state expenditures.

Nongrant Spending. The location of facilities becomes particularly important. Political considerations are crucial at the state level over the location of highways, state hospitals, and parks. At the federal level, military installations, the awarding of defense contracts to corporations, which of course are geographically based, and other civilian installations arouse much lobbying. Local and state governments work actively to obtain federal projects in their jurisdictions as one means of guaranteeing future economic prosperity.

Beyond the physical items are various loan and grant programs to individuals and corporations that greatly affect jurisdictions. At the federal level these include Social Security, Medicare, support to farmers, small-business loans, and Aid to Families with Dependent Children. States also make large welfare and other human services payments.

Tax Collections. In addition to spending, tax collections have varying effects on locales, and the resulting balance between federal expenditures and revenues has significant effects upon jurisdictions. Generally, federal revenues raised in the Northeast and Midwest have tended to be greater than the federal expenditures in these regions, while the opposite pattern has existed in the South and West.[19-21] Table 14-1 indicates the states with the highest and lowest ratios of federal expenditures to taxes in 1987. New Mexico was at the top of the list; for every $1.00 paid by individuals and corporations to the federal government, $1.93 was received. New Jersey was at the other end, receiving $0.66 on every $1.00 paid to the federal government. Where the balance is less than even, federal finance has a negative influence on a state's economy. This has been the case of the Great Lakes states, which are part of the so-called "rust belt." Federal taxes exceeded expenditures in 1987 in each of these states—Illinois, Indiana, Michigan, Ohio, and Wisconsin.

In recent years efforts have been made to gauge somewhat systematically the ability of the states to raise revenue and particularly tax revenue. The Advisory Commission on Intergovernmental Relations has been a leader in this

Table 14-1 States with Highest and Lowest Ratios of Federal Expenditures to Taxes, 1987

Highest Ranked			Lowest Ranked		
1	New Mexico	1.93	41	Indiana	0.88
2	Missisippi	1.62	42	Connecticut	0.87
3	Virginia	1.56	43	New York	0.85
4	North Dakota	1.52	44	Texas	0.83
5	South Dakota	1.51	45	Wisconsin	0.82
6	Vermont	1.42	46	New Hampshire	0.80
7	Hawaii	1.40	47	Michigan	0.75
8	Alabama	1.36	48	Delaware	0.74
9	Arkansas	1.32	49	Illinois	0.71
10	Maine	1.31	50	New Jersey	0.66

Sources: *Federal Expenditures by State for Fiscal Year 1987*, Bureau of the Census, p. 1, Government Printing Office, 1988; and "Estimated Total and Per Capita Federal Tax Burdens by State," *Tax Features*, Vol. 31, p. 4, Tax Foundation, Inc., © April 1987.

area, developing a measure called the representative tax system (RTS). "Tax capacity" is defined as "the dollar amount of revenue that each state would raise if it applied a nationally uniform set of tax rates to a common set of tax bases."[22] States are ranked from highest (or 1st) to lowest (or 50th) in their ability to raise taxes. Table 14-2 compares state rankings on the RTS with the ratios of federal expenditures to taxes. If the federal government's spending and taxing patterns were aimed at redistributing resources toward states with lower taxing ability, then one would expect that states ranking low on the RTS would rank high on the ratio of expenditures to taxes. Table 14-2 indicates some tendency in this direction but not a strong one. States in the upper-left quadrant of the table have the distinct disadvantages of comparatively weak tax bases and weak support from the federal government as gauged by the expenditures/taxes ratio.

Intergovernmental Assistance

State Aid. The literature on intergovernmental relations sometimes tends to overemphasize federal aid to state and local governments and underemphasize state aid to local government. In 1986–87, federal aid to states was $95.5 billion and to local government was $19.5 billion. State aid to local government was $136.8 billion, more than one-third more than what the federal government provided to these governments. Of course, state aid probably would be much smaller were states not receiving substantial federal support. As was seen in Chapter 2, states receive about a fifth of their revenue from the federal government. Local governments receive about a third of their revenue from state government and only 4 percent from the federal govern-

Table 14-2 Ranks of States on Representative Tax System Scale and Ratio of Federal Expenditures to Taxes

	Low Rank on Representative Tax System	High Rank on Representative Tax System
Low Rank on Expenditure/ Tax Ratio	Illinois Indiana Iowa Michigan North Carolina Ohio Oregon Pennyslvania Rhode Island Wisconsin	California Colorado Connecticut Delaware Florida Louisiana Minnesota Nevada New Hampshire New Jersey New York Oklahoma Texas Vermont Wyoming
High Rank on Expenditure/ Tax Ratio	Alabama Arkansas Georgia Idaho Kentucky Maine Mississippi Missouri Montana Nebraska South Carolina South Dakota Tennessee Vermont West Virginia	Alaska Arizona Hawaii Kansas Maryland Massachusetts New Mexico North Dakota Virginia Washington

Sources: Measuring State Fiscal Capacity, Advisory Commission on Intergovernmental Relations, p. 7, Government Printing Office; *Federal Expenditures by State for Fiscal Year 1987*, Bureau of the Census, p. 1, Government Printing Office, 1988; and "Estimated Total and Per Capita Federal Tax Burdens by State," *Tax Features*, Vol. 31, p. 4, Tax Foundation, Inc. © April 1987.

ment; except for school districts, each type of local government obtains half or more of its revenue from its own sources.[23]

Differences in federal and state support exist among the types of local governments (Figure 14-1). As of 1986–87, nearly half of all federal aid to local governments went to cities, but these monies constituted only 7 percent of city revenues. Special districts such as sewer and water districts are the type of local government most dependent upon federal aid—16 percent of

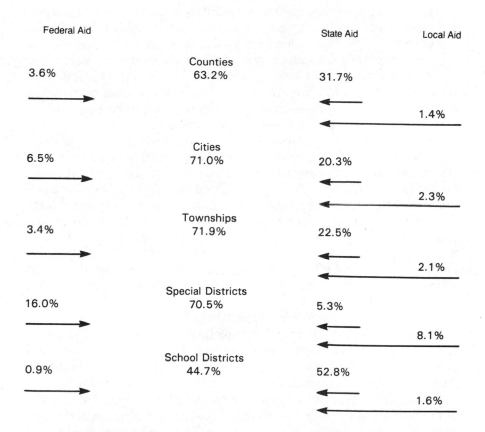

Figure 14-1 Intergovernmental Sources of General Revenue for Types of Local Governments, 1986–87. *Source: Government Finances in 1986–87*, Bureau of the Census, p. 46, Government Printing Office, 1988.

their budgets. Slightly more than half of state aid went to school districts, with these monies accounting for more than half of school district revenues, making school districts the only type of local government that does not raise a majority of its revenues by itself. Most of the other state aid was divided evenly between counties and cities.

These summary figures, of course, do not convey the great variety in state aid patterns.[24] Some states provide much greater assistance to local governments than other states; some states may provide a given service and thereby make direct expenditures, whereas other states may fund local governments to provide a service. New Hampshire, for example, provides only 12 percent of local government general revenues, compared with New Mexico at 49 percent.[25]

Aid to elementary and secondary education, as noted, constitutes the largest portion of state aid to local governments. States use a formula for distributing these funds.[26,27] The foundation plan, as it is called, is geared to guaranteeing a minimal amount of educational expenditures either per pupil or per classroom. Formulas typically are geared to real estate property assessments, with districts having low assessments receiving more aid than districts having high assessments. Additional formulas may be used for programs serving preschool, disadvantaged, and handicapped children.

These formulas were attacked in the courts starting in the 1970s as discriminatory, that is, the foundation plans were accused of failing to equalize educational opportunity among jurisdictions.[28] While recognizing the great importance of education, the Supreme Court decided in a Texas case that the allocation of funds for education was a state responsibility and was not controlled by the Constitution.[29] Nevertheless, cases have been won in state courts, so that many states have been required to alter their educational financing schemes to minimize disparities in per-pupil expenditures among districts. One line of argument is that the states should assume responsibility for all school finance, with the possible exceptions of enrichment programs and capital equipment.[30]

Other state aid programs are comparatively small. Education is followed in size by welfare and highways.[31] Aid for these functions is usually geared to some type of formula, the former often being a per-client reimbursement program. Virtually all states have some form of motor fuels tax-sharing formula in which local governments as well as the states benefit.[32]

Overall, state assistance has been more predictable than federal aid because of the extensive use of formulas. They facilitate budget planning at the local level because jurisdictions from year to year have some knowledge of what state funds will be. The only major controversies have centered on the factors used in the formulas.

Federal Aid. Functional or categorical grants have characterized federal aid. The categorical grant is the provision of resources by one party, the federal government in this case, to others, states and localities, with the condition that the recipients spend the money in a particular fashion and for a particular function.

Federal grants have been aimed at inducing state and local governments to increase the level of services in specified areas. During the 1960s, about 80 percent of all federal aid went for transportation and income security. As can been seen in Table 14-3 there have been substantial shifts since that time. General purpose aid, including general revenue sharing, which was enacted in late 1972, climbed from almost nothing to 16 percent in 1975 but has since dwindled back to almost nothing. Transportation, which accounted for more than 40 percent of the aid in the 1960s, is projected to decline to less than

15 percent, while health programs will rise to 37 percent and income security will account for about a quarter of the aid.

Categorical grant programs have gone to areas where significant externalities exist. As was seen in the previous section, the incentives in some functional areas are for governmental units to provide less of a service than is warranted by national interests because the benefits fall outside the jurisdiction providing the service. Grant programs are used to offset these parochial interests. Matching provisions are usually required as a means of ensuring that grants will not merely result in a lessened tax effort by the recipients of the grants; without matching provisions, a $1 million federal grant could be offset by an equal reduction in local revenues supporting a program, thereby producing no increase in the level of services. A study conducted in the mid-1980s by the Treasury Department, however, concluded that federal grants have only a minor effect on state and local expenditures, since matching requirements in federal grants have the effect of limiting spending by recipient governments as well as the federal government.[33]

Federal aid to state and local governments is not of equal importance to all federal agencies. As can be seen in Table 14-4, the Department of Health and Human Services (HHS) is by far the most important department, accounting for nearly half of all federal grants. A different perspective, however, is gained when considering the portion of an agency's budget committed to grants. While HHS spends about a quarter of its funds on grants, the Depart-

Table 14-3 Percentage Function Distribution of Federal Grants-in-Aid, 1960–93

	1960	1970	1980	1987	1988	1989	1991	1993
Natural Resources and Environment	2	2	6	4	3	3	3	2
Agriculture	3	3	1	2	2	1	1	1
Transportation	43	19	14	16	15	15	14	12
Community and Regional Development	2	7	7	4	4	4	3	2
Education, Training, Employment, and Social Services	7	27	24	17	18	18	18	17
Health	3	16	17	24	28	29	33	37
Income Security	38	24	20	28	27	27	26	27
General Government	2	2	9	2	2	2	1	1
Other	*	1	1	1	1	1	1	1
Total†	100	100	100	100	100	100	100	100

*0.5 percent or less
†Totals may not equal 100 percent due to rounding.

Source: Special Analyses, Budget of the United States Government, 1989, Office of Management and Budget, p. H-18, Government Printing Office, 1988.

ment of Education spends half (52 percent) and the Department of Transportation, the Environmental Protection Agency, and the Department of Housing and Urban Development spend two-thirds or more on grants. HHS spends comparatively little because much of its budget is committed to Social Security payments to individuals.

Regional Differences. Just as total federal outlays are not uniform from state to state, so, too, are grants not uniform. In 1987, the national average was $439 per capita in federal grants to state and local governments. The region receiving the highest per capita grants ($623) was New York and New Jersey along with Puerto Rico and the Virgin Islands. The lowest group ($353) consisted of Arkansas, Louisiana, Oklahoma, New Mexico, and Texas.[34]

These per capita grant figures must not be interpreted simply as revealing what regions are winners and losers in the federal aid game. A state and its local governments might receive comparatively small amounts of grants but extensive economic support by direct federal expenditures, resulting in the state becoming a winner. Another consideration is what the corporations and individuals in a state pay in taxes. The winner might turn loser when taxes paid are compared with federal dollars returned either as direct expenditures or as grants.

Assuming that the federal graduated income tax has the effect of drawing proportionately greater resources from wealthy states than from less wealthy

Table 14-4 Federal Agency Outlays and Grants to State and Local Governments, 1987 (Billions of Dollars)

Department or Unit	Total Outlays	Grants	
		Outlays	Percent of Total
Agriculture	50.4	10.9	21.6
Commerce	2.1	0.4	19.0
Education	16.8	8.7	51.8
Energy	10.7	0.2	1.9
Health and Human Services	202.4	47.9	23.7
Housing and Urban Development	15.5	10.9	70.3
Interior	5.0	1.3	26.0
Justice	4.3	0.2	4.7
Labor	23.5	5.6	23.8
Transportation	25.4	16.9	66.5
Treasury	180.3	0.4	0.2
Environmental Protection Agency	4.9	3.3	67.3
Other	463.3	1.9	0.4
Total	1,004.6	108.4	10.8

Sources: Budget of the United States Government, 1989, Office of Management and Budget, pp. 6, 40–137, Government Printing Office, 1988; and *Special Analyses, Budget of the United States Government, 1989,* Office of Management and Budget, p. H-18, Government Printing Office, 1988.

states, federal aid could amplify or dampen this effect. Were the effect amplified, per capita federal aid to state and local governments would increase as per capita personal income declined. This pattern, however, is not evident. As income increases, per capita federal grants neither consistently increase nor decrease, suggesting that grant programs do not redistribute income in favor of either wealthy or poor states. The lack of a consistent pattern is explained by the numerous federal grant programs that tend to offset each other in benefiting particular types of states.[35]

Responsiveness to Need. Studies that have compared federal and state aid to urban areas have concluded that, while both are responsive to need, state aid is more responsive. Cities with greater fiscal problems receive greater per capita state assistance.[36-38]

Federal programs for aiding localities can be provided directly to these communities or indirectly through the states. In the latter case, state officials are allowed some discretion in distributing federal funds, although federal regulations may require that a given amount "pass through" to localities and that some of this money be distributed according to set criteria such as population. State enabling legislation often is required before a local government may receive funds directly from the federal government.

Future Trends. The dollar volume of federal grants-in-aid continues to climb each year, but a peak was reached in the 1970s and is not expected to be reached again in the foreseeable future. As is indicated in Figure 14-2, federal aid in 1978 was approximately 27 percent of state and local outlays; since then, that percentage has been slipping and could drop to 11 percent by the end of the 1990s. On various comparative measures, federal aid is expected to decline. It will drop from about 16 percent of the federal budget in 1980 to 10 percent by 1990. Federal aid will drop from 3.4 percent of gross national product in 1980 to 2 percent in the 1990s. These trends began in the Carter administration and were accelerated in the Reagan years.[39,40]

Coping with these trends has been difficult at best for many governments and nearly devastating for others, especially when juxtaposed with other problems such as reductions in revenues due to economic recessions and taxing limitations (for example, Proposition 2½ in Massachusetts). Governments have had to scramble to keep services operating and in many situations have had little or no choice but to cut programs and sometimes eliminate them.[41] On the other hand, the Treasury Department's study of the mid-1980s concluded that the long-term fiscal outlook for state and local governments was better ". . . than it has been at virtually any other time in recent history."[42] Flowing from such a conclusion could be the view that there is little need for federal aid in the future, a view that probably would be attacked by most state and local officials.

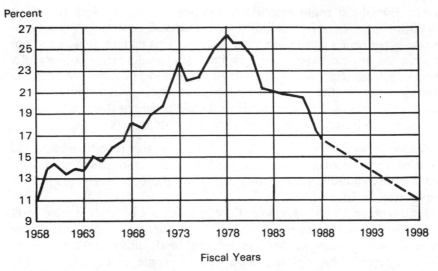

Percent

Figure 14-2 The Rise and Decline of Federal Aid, 1958–88--1998, as a Percentage of State-Local Outlays. *Source:* "Federalism 1986–87: Signals of a New Era" by R. Gleason, *Intergovernmental Perspective*, Vol. 14, p. 13, U.S. Advisory Commission on Intergovernmental Relations, Winter 1988.

TYPES OF FISCAL ASSISTANCE

Grant Characteristics

Of the numerous aspects of grants-in-aid, at least four are particularly important: the purpose of the award, the recipient, the amount, and the method of distribution. The purpose of awards will be discussed in some detail in this section, but for the moment it should be noted that purpose ranges from narrowly defined aid to that of general support.

Second, recipients can be individuals or families who receive financial aid, as in the case of welfare payments or Medicaid payments to the poor and medically needy. When programs provide guarantees of aid to individuals and families, they are referred to as "entitlements." Sometimes the term "entitlement" is used for programs providing funds to state and local governments, as in the instance of community development block grants (see below), in which funds are promised in advance to local governments.

The third aspect is the amount of aid that is made available. Some programs are open ended in the sense that aid is provided to the extent to which recipients qualify. All persons meeting a needs test based on income, for instance, might qualify for aid; if the number of qualified applicants increases, then the amount of aid available must be increased. This type of grant, of course, complicates budgeting in that administrators do not know in advance what funds will be needed. An alternative is for the legislature to predetermine an amount that will be available, regardless of the number of potential recipients.

Fourth, there are different distribution methods. One is for would-be recipients to compete for awards by submitting proposals to indicate how funds will be used. Another method is to use a formula that allocates funds among eligible recipients.[43] Formulas can be used to help target money to where it is needed the most.[44,45] Gaining agreement on specific provisions in a formula among legislators can be difficult; for example, members of Congress evaluate proposed provisions of a formula in terms of how home districts or states will be affected. Sometimes the distribution is set by the legislative body, particularly in instances of providing funds for specified public works projects.

Categorical Aid

At the federal level, there are hundreds of grant programs, with categoricals being one of the most common types; states also have an extensive array of narrow grant programs. Categorical programs have a narrow focus to target aid to deal with perceived problems. If rat infestations are seen as a major problem in poor neighborhoods, an aid program can be established to support efforts to eliminate or control rat populations. Categorical programs presumably allow the federal government to target aid to problems that are perceived to be national in scope and to allow the state governments to do the same in regard to state problems.

Categorical grants typically require would-be recipients to apply for aid by preparing proposals. These proposals indicate how problems will be addressed and what the expected benefits will be. Through the application process, applicants are required to engage in considerable preplanning, which is expected to help increase the chances for the money to be spent effectively. Funding agencies, through the application review process, can weed out many unsound projects.

Criticisms of categorical aid programs abound. Grants may skew local priorities. A jurisdiction might apply for funds for one type of project, even though some other project, for which no funding was available, would provide greater benefits to the jurisdiction. Another criticism is that much time and energy are consumed in drafting grant proposals. Sometimes the complaint is made that jurisdictions do not obtain their "fair share" of federal dollars simply because of inadequate staff for proposal writing; small jurisdictions, in particular, may have little "grantsmanship" capability. Categorical grants make budget planning difficult, because proposals may be held pending for months. Complaints also are made about grants not being coordinated.

One frequently made proposal is that the application process should be simplified.[46] Simplification includes reducing the amount of paperwork involved and standardizing some forms and procedures to make the process comprehensible to applicants who may wish to seek funds from two or more agencies. Office of Management and Budget (OMB) Circular A-102 standardizes some forms and procedures.[47]

To deal with the problem of coordination among grants, Congress passed the Joint Funding Simplification Act in 1974. The law provided for federal agencies to work with local governments that sought funding from more than one agency, including state as well as federal agencies. OMB, by executive order, was put in charge of the process. The law met with considerable difficulty in implementation and was allowed to expire in 1985.

Revenue Sharing

General Revenue Sharing. A dramatic alternative to categorical grants is general revenue sharing (GRS), which at the federal level was created by the State and Local Fiscal Assistance Act of 1972.[48,49] Under the original legislation, the federal government shared some of its revenue with states, counties, cities, and townships; in subsequent years, the states were dropped from the list of beneficiaries, in part because many had surpluses in their budgets and could hardly claim to be in need of general federal support.

Although general revenue sharing was allowed to expire in the fall of 1986, the topic is worthy of consideration in that it represents the opposite end of the spectrum from categorical grants. Three key characteristics of the now defunct grant program were

1. pre-established amounts of aid
2. use of formulas for distributing the aid
3. considerable latitude to spend funds in terms of local priorities

When renewing the program, often for three years at a time, Congress set specific dollar amounts to be disbursed in given time periods. Such provisions allowed local governments to plan well in advance as to how GRS monies would be used; of course, the drawback to the federal government was that this portion of the budget was relatively uncontrollable.

GRS allocations were made by a series of complex formulas. A ceiling was set to limit how much any jurisdiction would receive, as well as a floor to guarantee that most jurisdictions would receive some funds. A distinguishing feature of GRS was that jurisdictions received funds without having to make application for these monies.

GRS attempted to solve some of the problems associated with categorical grant programs. Jurisdictions had great freedom in deciding which functional areas would receive funds. Another benefit was that time and energy were not wasted in proposal writing. Jurisdictions that needed funds but did not have the staff capability to make application for categorical grants received GRS funds.

In contrast, there were many criticisms of GRS. The formula was said to provide monies to some jurisdictions that were not in need. The floor provision may have propped up basically inefficient jurisdictions that might otherwise have been forced by economics into consolidating their services with other governments. The ceiling, on the other hand, possibly denied needed funds to many deserving jurisdictions, particularly central cities. Communities allegedly were allowed to squander their GRS funds, whereas categorical grants required more planning.

GRS expired in 1986 because a compelling case could not be made for its continuation. As the federal government faced budget deficits in excess of $200 billion, federal officials could convincingly argue that there simply was no revenue to share with local governments.[50] Additionally, proponents faced the difficult task of identifying a national purpose being served by GRS.

While revenue sharing is no longer in operation at the national level, it is at the state level. States provide funds to local governments through a variety of means that include formulas based on population and income.[51]

Block Grants. A form of compromise between GRS and categorical grants is special revenue sharing, or block grants. Under this system a higher-level government shares part of its revenue with lower-level governments, but the use of funds is restricted to specified functions, such as law enforcement or social services. Sometimes a distinction is made between block grants and special revenue sharing, with the former requiring submission of an application and the latter not, but more often the terms are used interchangeably or the term block grants is used to cover both situations. State aid to education, using various formulas, is an example of a block grant, with the funds coming largely from state general revenue. In contrast, state aid for local roads is another form of block grant, with monies coming from earmarked taxes on motor fuels.

Block grants at the federal level have been used as a method for consolidating categorical grant programs. These categoricals are grouped together so that jurisdictions have greater flexibility within specified program areas. The application process is greatly reduced, because a jurisdiction applies for only one grant instead of several. Early block grants include the Partnership for Health Act of 1966, the Law Enforcement Assistance Act of 1968, and the Comprehensive Employment and Training Act of 1973.[52,53]

A landmark in block grants is the Housing and Community Development Act of 1974.[54,55] The program provides entitlement funding to medium and large cities through the use of a formula and gives funds to states to award on a discretionary basis to small cities.[56,57] The law phased out programs for open space, public facility loans, water and sewer grants, urban renewal, model cities, and rehabilitation loans. Block grant funds may be used for these types of projects as well as such activities as clearing property and constructing public works. Under the original legislation, entitlement cities were required to submit an application for funding; the process was considerably less detailed than had been required for the previous categorical programs. During the Reagan administration, the application process was dropped for these entitlement cities.

In 1981, the Reagan administration recommended numerous consolidations of categorical grants into block grants.[58] Congress obliged by passing the Omnibus Budget Reconciliation Act of 1981, which among other things created nine block grants to be administered by the states. Seven of the grants are controlled by the Department of Health and Human Services (HHS) and the other two are controlled by the Department of Housing and Urban Development and the Department of Education.[59,60] In subsequent years, other consolidations of categorical grants into block grants occurred.

A distinctive feature of the block grants created during the Reagan administration was that monies were granted in lump sums to states, which could determine how the money was to be divided among governments within each state. This approach was championed as restoring power to the states. Available evidence indicates that states used this opportunity to improve the management of programs.[61,62] States standardized forms and the procedures used for local governments making application for funds; the standardization sometimes cut across block grants. Mechanisms were established for auditing these grants to ensure that local governments were operating according to provisions established in law and regulation.

The other distinctive characteristic of the Reagan block grants was a substantial reduction in funds.[63] These cuts were in part defended in the name of efficiency. Since the block grants would provide more flexibility to state and local governments, fewer federal officials were needed to administer the programs, and similarly fewer state officials were needed to oversee local government operations. Another rationale was that since the federal budget had massive deficits, grant programs should not be immune from budget cuts.

State and local governments selectively replaced some lost federal dollars, but overall the pattern was for programs to be reduced in scope to reflect the cuts made in Washington.[64,65] Some cuts were postponed while categorical grants were being phased out and block grants phased in, but once the affected categoricals had been terminated, cuts took place in programs.[66] States were more likely to increase their support of health and social services programs, in which they had been involved for many years, than other programs such as community services and low-income energy grants.[67] Central city governments tended to be harder hit by cuts than suburban and rural governments, since the former have a history of greater reliance on federal funding.[68]

RESTRUCTURING PATTERNS OF INTERGOVERNMENTAL RELATIONS

In addition to changing the mix of categorical grants, block grants, and revenue sharing, there are other techniques and organizational arrangements that have been used to improve intergovernmental relations. One is the Advisory Commission on Intergovernmental Relations (ACIR) created in 1969 and consisting of federal, state, and local officials.[69] The commission is strictly an advisory body and has no authority to initiate changes. Nearly half of the states have created similar state-level bodies, and many metropolitan areas have comparable organizations, some of which include representatives of state and federal agencies.[70]

Tax Laws

Tax Deductions. A substantive change that could be made is to adjust taxes in ways that would reduce the need for financial assistance. By increasing the taxing powers of lower-level governments, the need for grants-in-aid may be reduced. For example, taxpayers currently may deduct many state and local taxes from gross income before computing federal tax liabilities.[71] Included are state and local income taxes, property taxes, and some other, lesser taxes. Federal tax law could be altered either to increase or decrease deductibility.

Economists have been particularly critical of deductions for property taxes in that this benefit is felt largely by middle-income families. Lower-income families are less likely to own homes and therefore are unable to benefit from deductibility, and higher-income families do not benefit appreciably from such deductions.

On the other side of the argument, tax deductions do provide some measure of latitude for state and local taxation. They reduce somewhat the differentials among states and among localities, and they mitigate some of the problems of tax overlapping. At least overlapping taxes may be held to a level that is not confiscatory. The strongest argument in favor of tax deductibility is one of practicality. The principle is firmly entrenched; any effort to eliminate deductibility for property taxes, for example, would be politically unacceptable without compensating tax relief.

Tax Credits. A potentially more substantial shift in revenue sources than tax deductions would be provided by tax credits. These allow individual taxpayers to apply taxes paid to one jurisdiction as credits against the tax liability to another jurisdiction. One proposal sometimes made is to allow such credits for the federal income tax; the effect would be to redistribute revenue from the federal government to state and local governments. A tax credit on income taxes could encourage those states without income taxes to adopt them because the taxpayer would be less affected. However, if the tax credit is uniform regardless of income, it would benefit the wealthier states even more than the poorer ones.

Unemployment Insurance. The federal government has enticed or forced states to impose unemployment insurance taxes on employers by providing that most monies from such taxes may stay within each state; in the event that a state did not have an approved system, a tax presumably would be imposed by the federal government. Until the 1986 Tax Reform Act, unemployment benefits were not treated as income under federal tax law, thereby providing an important benefit to individuals and a costly tax expenditure to the federal government. These benefits are now taxable.

Taxes and Bonds. Another important benefit that has been afforded state and local governments through federal tax law has been the tax exemption on interest earned on bonds issued by these governments.[72] Tax exemption has had the effect of allowing governments to pay lower interest rates to bondholders than if the bonds were taxable. As was explained in Chapter 12, that benefit has been greatly reduced in that only special types of bonds now qualify for exemption.

Grant Requirements

Mandates. Other proposals to improve intergovernmental fiscal relations pertain to mandates.[73] For instance, when a state legislature passes a law requiring school districts to adopt certain procedures in dealing with gifted children, a mandate has been established that has budgetary implications.[74] The complaint is that often funds are not provided to assist jurisdictions in complying with mandates. The federal government has tended to tie mandates to grants, making the stipulation that a government must meet specified conditions to qualify for funds. Notable cross-cutting mandates—requirements that apply to most federal agencies and grant programs—require jurisdictions to pay locally prevailing wages, meet federal standards for architectural barriers for handicapped persons, and prevent discrimination based on race, sex, and the like.[75,76]

Civil Rights. One particular controversy has concerned the extent to which a jurisdiction's operations must comply with such stipulations. In *Grove City College v. Bell* (1984), the Supreme Court ruled that only that portion of an organization affected by federal dollars had to comply with standards protecting against discrimination based on race, sex, age, and handicapping condition; in that instance, since the college's only federal support was identified as being for student-aid activities, only those had to comply. Congress in 1988 reversed that decision by passing the Civil Rights Restoration Act, which provides that all operations of a recipient government must meet federal standards; the law was passed over a veto by President Reagan.

A disturbing trend for state and local governments is that during the 1980s the federal government selectively increased some mandates without linking them to the availability of grants-in-aid.[77] Federally imposed environmental standards regarding waste water treatment, for example, are independent of the availability of federal funds to local governments.

Paperwork. Related to mandates are various reporting requirements that create paperwork and thereby create costs. States require local governments to submit numerous reports each year, and the federal government requires the same of state and local governments. The federal Paperwork Reduction Act of 1980 granted authority to OMB over federal agency requests for information from state and local governments; the purpose is to limit agencies in asking for information.[78] The Regulatory Flexibility Act of 1980 and Executive Order 12291 of 1981 require agencies to conduct regulatory impact analyses to determine the effects of proposed rules or regulations, including effects on state and local governments. Executive Order 12498 of 1985 further requires agencies to develop annual regulatory plans that must be submitted to OMB; while it may not legally "veto" agency plans to issue regulations, by using this review process OMB can stall, if not block, plans that would increase the paperwork burden on state and local governments.

Another provision that attempts to deal with the mandate/paperwork problem is contained in the State and Local Government Cost Estimate Act of 1981. The law requires the preparation of fiscal notes for proposed legislation that would cost state and local governments $200 million or more annually. Such fiscal notes, which explain the effects of proposed legislation, are intended to aid legislators in their deliberations and especially to avoid unintentionally imposing severe financial burdens on these governments.

Other Possible Improvements

Information Availability. Besides the reduction of mandates and paperwork, several other intergovernmental devices have been proposed and used.

One concern has been that jurisdictions have inadequate information about grant programs. In response, the General Services Administration, working with OMB, annually publishes the *Catalog of Federal Domestic Assistance;* the catalog, which gives capsule descriptions of grant programs, is useful for a local government that is attempting to determine whether it might be able to secure federal funding for a contemplated project.

Grant Coordination. Another concern is that federal grants should be coordinated at regional and statewide levels. If a community is applying for a federal grant to assist elderly citizens, how would that grant complement other programs for the elderly in the region and how would the grant relate to state-level programs? In response to this type of question and as an outgrowth of the Intergovernmental Cooperation Act, the Bureau of the Budget (now OMB) issued in 1969 Circular A-95, which provided for the establishment of areawide and state clearinghouses responsible for reviewing and commenting on proposed projects. The review and comment process offered the potential for eliminating waste in the use of federal funds. The jurisdiction applying for these funds was expected to respond to any objections made by the clearinghouses and, where appropriate, modify the proposed project.

On the negative side, A-95 produced delays in the grant process and frustrated mayors, their budget offices, and line agencies. For all of the time devoted to A-95, projects in many cases were implemented much as originally intended, perhaps over the objection of various clearinghouses.

In 1982, President Reagan rescinded A-95 by issuing Executive Order 12372, which was in turn amended the following year by Executive Order 12416.[79-81] As part of an effort to provide "regulatory relief," the Reagan executive orders gave states responsibility for establishing such review processes and allowed considerable flexibility to state and local elected officials in determining what grant programs were to be submitted to the state single point of contact (SPOC) for comment and review. As a result, far fewer reviews are conducted than was the case under A-95.

Federal counterparts to various state-level coordinating bodies have included Federal Regional Councils (FRCs) organized around the ten federally standardized regions of the United States.[82] The FRCs, consisting of representatives from federal domestic agencies, were intended to bring greater coordination among federal programs; these bodies, however, were eliminated by executive order in 1983 on the grounds that they were no longer needed.

Federal-state, interstate, and interlocal arrangements have been developed for the provision of services, as distinguished from forums for discussion, where, for example, some metropolitan councils of governments involve officials from various communities in the region. One of the most successful interstate organizations is the New York Port Authority, established in 1921 by New York and New Jersey.[83,84] The authority operates terminals, bridges, tunnels, and the World Trade Center.

At the local level, there are numerous types of cooperative arrangements. Some counties provide services such as water and sewage treatment on a contract basis for municipalities within their jurisdiction. This arrangement may be at the choice of municipalities, as in the case of the Lakewood Plan, whereby communities can contract with Los Angeles County for virtually all city services, or at the insistence of state governments, which may require city-county cooperation for services such as police and fire protection.[85] As some cities and their suburbs have grown into complex mazes of jurisdictions, there have been attempts at consolidation into metropolitan governments. Miami-Dade County, Florida; Nashville-Davidson County, Tennessee; and Indianapolis, Indiana, are three examples.

Management Capacity. With the increasing emphasis upon block grants and GRS, greater attention has been focused upon the abilities of state and local governments to manage themselves. The granting of decision-making power over the use of federal funds—sometimes called "devolution"—has led to concerns for improving management capabilities at these levels.[86] There have been suggestions that the federal government assume a responsibility for "management capacity building," but during the 1980s the federal government showed only limited inclination in this direction.[87,88] One should not jump to the conclusion that Washington has superior management capabilities that, if only transferred to the state and local levels, will produce quick results.

Realigning Responsibilities. A far more comprehensive suggestion for relieving both states and localities of some of their financial burdens involves reconfiguring responsibilities for major functions among the three levels of government.[89] President Reagan in 1982 advocated major revisions involving what he called "swaps and turnbacks."[90,91] The "swap" proposal entailed the states accepting financial responsibility for Aid to Families with Dependent Children (welfare) and food stamps, and in return the federal government would relieve states of the financial burden for Medicaid.

The "turnback" proposal involved having the states assume financial responsibility for 40 or more federal aid programs in social services, education, transportation, and community development. According to the proposal, over a period of several years these programs would be transferred to the states and federal funding eventually would be eliminated. A basic rationale of the proposal was that if these programs were important to the states, they would be willing to commit their own dollars for continuance; on the other hand, there was the presumption that lower-priority programs would be phased out by the states.

Neither the swap nor the turnback concept was well received by state and local governments. The administration's position called for a drastic cut in federal grants at a time when state and local governments were suffering through a major economic recession that had depleted their treasuries. Additionally, the "turnback" term was a misnomer in that programs were not being turned back or returned to state and local governments; many, if not most, of the programs proposed for elimination by the federal government had never been handled exclusively by state and local governments. The Reagan administration proposals were not enacted into law, but the idea of a major reorganization of governmental responsibilities remains an important proposal for improving how the overall governmental system meets the needs of citizens.[92,93]

SUMMARY

Fundamental problems exist over how to structure intergovernmental relations. Functional integration results in picket-fence arrangements that may deter geographic integration. Fiscal capacities differ among and within levels of government, so that the government that perhaps should provide services often lacks the necessary funding capability. Failure to provide services results in externality problems.

Both direct spending and grants-in-aid are important for intergovernmental relations. Decisions by federal and state agencies on the location and expansion of capital facilities affect the economic viability of local jurisdictions. Despite more extensive attention often being devoted to federal aid programs, state aid to local government is larger. Some states provide much of their local governments' revenue while others provide little, a point that should be stressed to avoid unwarranted generalizations. Aid to education constitutes the largest portion of state aid, with monies typically allocated on a formula basis. Federal aid is concentrated in the areas of education, income security, health, and transportation.

Intergovernmental grants can have at least four characteristics: their purpose (narrow, broad, and general), the type of recipient, the amount, and the method of distribution. Categorical grants are criticized as deterring coordination, skewing local priorities, and needlessly wasting time in proposal preparation. On the positive side, the categoricals are said to force planning in the preparation of proposals and to allow for screening out inadequately conceived projects. General revenue sharing supported local priorities and provided funds to jurisdictions that did not have staff available to apply for categorical grants. GRS was criticized as not meeting any national purpose and giving funds to many undeserving jurisdictions. The program was terminated at the federal level, but states engage in revenue sharing with their respective local governments. Block grants, a cross between categoricals and GRS, have the advantages and disadvantages of both.

In addition to grant programs, numerous other devices are employed. These include provisions in federal tax law that are to the advantage of state and local governments and processes involving the review and comment on grant proposals. Also, mechanisms have emerged for providing services on an intergovernmental basis, such as with the New York Port Authority or the Lakewood Plan in California. Proposals have been made for major reconfiguring of program responsibilities among the federal, state, and local governments.

NOTES

1. James M. Buchanan and Marilyn R. Flowers, *The Public Finances*, 6th ed. (Homewood, Ill.: Irwin, 1987).

2. Parris N. Glendening and Mavis M. Reeves, *Pragmatic Federalism*, 2nd ed. (Pacific Palisades, Calif.: Palisades Publishing, 1984).

3. David N. Hyman, *Public Finance*, 2nd ed. (Chicago: Dryden, 1987).

4. Deil S. Wright, *Understanding Intergovernmental Relations*, 3rd ed. (Pacific Grove, Calif.: Brooks/Cole, 1988).

5. Charles M. Tiebout, "A Pure Theory of Public Expenditures," *Journal of Political Economy* 44 (1956): 416–24.

6. Larry H. Long, *Migration to Nonmetropolitan Areas: Appraising the Trend and Reasons for Moving* (Washington, D.C.: Government Printing Office, 1980).

7. Tony Travers, *The Politics of Local Government Finance* (Boston: Allen and Unwin, 1987).

8. James W. Fesler, "The Basic Theoretical Question: How to Relate Area and Function," in Leigh E. Grosenick, ed., *The Administration of New Federalism* (Washington, D.C.: American Society for Public Administration, 1973), pp. 4–10.

9. Wright, *Understanding Intergovernmental Relations,* pp. 83–86.

10. The discussion is based in part on Bernard P. Herber, *Modern Public Finance*, 5th ed. (Homewood, Ill.: Richard D. Irwin, 1983).

11. Harold Wolman and Edward Page, "The Impact of Intergovernmental Grants on Subnational Resource Disparities," *Public Budgeting and Finance* 7 (Autumn 1987): 82–97.

12. John E. Chubb, "The Political Economy of Federalism," *American Political Science Review* 79 (1985): 994–1015.

13. Office of State and Local Finance, Department of the Treasury, *Federal-State-Local Fiscal Relations* (Washington, D.C.: Government Printing Office, 1985), pp. 207–49.

14. Bureau of the Census, *Statistical Abstract* (Washington, D.C.: Government Printing Office, 1987), p. 417.

15. Demetrios Caraley, "Changing Conceptions of Federalism," *Political Science Quarterly* 101 (1986): 289–306.

16. Martha Derthick, "American Federalism: Madison's Middle Ground in the 1980s," *Public Administration Review* 47 (1987): 66–74.

17. Executive Order 12612 in 52 F.R. 41686 (October 30, 1987).

18. Robert Gleason, "Federalism 1986–87," *Intergovernmental Perspective* 14 (Winter 1988): 9–14.

19. Advisory Commission on Intergovernmental Relations, *Regional Growth: Flows of Federal Funds, 1952–76* (Washington, D.C.: Government Printing Office, 1980).

20. Eleanor H. Erdevig, "Federal Funds Flow No Bargain for Midwest," *Economic Perspectives* 10 (January/February, 1986): 3–10.

21. Office of State and Local Finance, *Federal-State-Local Fiscal Relations,* pp. 142–52.

22. Advisory Commission on Intergovernmental Relations, *Measuring State Fiscal Capacity*, 1987 ed. (Washington, D.C.: Government Printing Office, 1987), p. 4.

23. Bureau of the Census, *Government Finances in 1986–87* (Washington, D.C.: Government Printing Office, 1988), p. 2.

24. Steven D. Gold, *State and Local Fiscal Relations in the Early 1980s* (Washington, D.C.: Urban Institute, 1983).

25. Bureau of the Census, *Government Finances in 1986–87*, pp. 76 and 78.

26. Charles S. Benson and Kevin O'Halloran, "The Economic History of School Finance in the U.S.," *Journal of Education Finance* 12 (1987): 495–515.

27. Steven D. Gold, "State Aid for Local Schools: Trends and Prospects," *Public Budgeting and Finance* 4 (Winter 1984): 30–40.

28. Richard G. Salmon, "State/Local Fiscal Support of Public Elementary and Secondary Education," *Journal of Education Finance* 12 (1987): 549–60.

29. *San Antonio School District v. Rodriquez*, 411 U.S. 1 (1973).

30. Martin W. Schoppmeyer, "Full State Assumption in Arkansas," *Journal of Education Finance* 13 (1987): 174–81.

31. Bureau of the Census, *Government Finances in 1986–87*, p. 12.

32. See current issue of *Highway Statistics*, prepared annually by the Federal Highway Administration.

33. Office of State and Local Finance, *Federal-State-Local Fiscal Relations*, pp. 154–57.

34. Office of Management and Budget, *Special Analyses, Budget of the United States Government, 1989* (Washington, D.C.: Government Printing Office, 1988), p. H-19.

35. Office of State and Local Finance, *Federal-State-Local Fiscal Relations*, pp. 193–202.

36. Thomas R. Dye and Thomas L. Hurley, "The Responsiveness of Federal and State Governments to Urban Problems," *Journal of Politics* 40 (1978): 196–207.

37. John P. Pelissero, "State Aid and City Needs: An Examination of Residual State Aid to Large Cities," *Journal of Politics* 46 (1984): 916–35.

38. Robert M. Stein and Keith E. Hamm, "A Comparative Analysis of the Targeting Capacity of State and Federal Intergovernmental Aid Allocations: 1977, 1982," *Social Science Quarterly* 68 (1987): 447–65.

39. Office of Management and Budget, *Special Analyses, Budget of the United States Government, 1989*, p. H-20.

40. Advisory Commission on Intergovernmental Relations, *Significant Features of Fiscal Federalism*, 1988 ed., vol. 1 (Washington, D.C.: Government Printing Office, 1987), p. 15.

41. Richard P. Nathan and Fred C. Doolittle, *The Consequences of Cuts: The Effects of the Reagan Domestic Program on State and Local Governments* (Princeton, N.J.: Princeton University Press, 1983).

42. Office of State and Local Finance, *Federal-State-Local Fiscal Relations*, pp. 420–21.

43. General Accounting Office, *Grant Formulas: A Catalog of Federal Aid to States and Localities* (Washington, D.C.: Government Printing Office, 1987).

44. General Accounting Office, *Local Governments: Targeting General Fiscal Assistance Reduces Fiscal Disparities* (Washington, D.C.: Government Printing Office, 1986).

45. Senate Committee on Governmental Affairs, *Targeting Federal Aid: Hearing*, 99th Cong., 1st sess. (Washington, D.C.: Government Printing Office, 1986).

46. John W. Kalas, *The Grant System* (Albany: State University of New York Press, 1987).

47. Office of Management and Budget, "Grants and Cooperative Agreements with State and Local Governments," OMB Circular A-102, 53 *Federal Register* 8028 (March 11, 1988).

48. General Accounting Office, *Changes in Revenue Sharing Formula Would Eliminate Payment Inequities; Improve Targeting Among Local Governments* (Washington, D.C.: Government Printing Office, 1980).

49. Richard P. Nathan and Charles F. Adams, *Revenue Sharing: The Second Round* (Washington, D.C.: Brookings, 1977).

50. House Committee on Government Operations, *The Impact of the Proposed Elimination of the General Revenue Sharing Program on Local Governments*, 99th Cong., 1st sess. (Washington, D.C.: Government Printing Office, 1985).

51. John P. Pelissero, "State-City Revenue Sharing Policy," in Benton and Morgan, eds., *Intergovernmental Relations and Public Policy*, pp. 175–88.

52. General Accounting Office, *Lessons Learned from Past Block Grants* (Washington, D.C.: Government Printing Office, 1982).

53. Richard P. Nathan and Paul R. Dommel, "Federal-Local Relations Under Block Grants," *Political Science Quarterly* 93 (1978): 421–42.

54. General Accounting Office, *The Community Development Block Grant Program Can Be More Effective in Revitalizing the Nation's Cities* (Washington, D.C.: Government Printing Office, 1981).

55. Donald F. Kettl, *Managing Community Development in the New Federalism* (New York: Praeger, 1980).

56. General Accounting Office, *States Are Making Good Progress in Implementing the Small Cities Community Development Block Grant Program* (Washington, D.C.: Government Printing Office, 1983).

57. David R. Morgan and Robert E. England, "The Small Cities Block Grant Program," *Public Administration Review* 44 (1984): 477–82.

58. George E. Peterson, *The Reagan Block Grants* (Washington, D.C.: Urban Institute, 1986).

59. General Accounting Office, *Education Block Grant Alters State Role and Provides Greater Local Discretion* (Washington, D.C.: Government Printing Office, 1984).

60. Deborah A. Verstegen, "Two Hundred Years of Federalism: A Perspective on National Fiscal Policy in Education," *Journal of Education Finance* 12 (1987): 516–48.

61. General Accounting Office, *Block Grants: Overview of Experiences to Date and Emerging Issues* (Washington, D.C.: Government Printing Office, 1985).

62. General Accounting Office, *State Rather than Federal Policies Provided the Framework for Managing Block Grants* (Washington, D.C.: Government Printing Office, 1985).

63. John W. Ellwood, ed., *Reductions in U.S. Domestic Spending* (New Brunswick, N.J.: Transaction Books, 1982).

64. Richard P. Nathan and Fred C. Doolittle, *Reagan and the States* (Princeton, N.J.: Princeton University Press, 1987).

65. George E. Peterson and Carol W. Lewis, eds., *Reagan and the Cities* (Washington, D.C.: Urban Institute, 1986).

66. General Accounting Office, *Block Grants Brought Funding Changes and Adjustments to Program Priorities* (Washington, D.C.: Government Printing Office, 1985).

67. Paul Posner, "State Managerial Responses to the New Federalism," in Lewis G. Bender and James A. Stever, eds., *Administering the New Federalism* (Boulder, Colo.: Westview, 1986), pp. 96–123.

68. Nathan and Doolittle, *The Consequences of Cuts*.

69. House Committee on Government Operations and Senate Committee on Governmental Affairs, *Twenty-Five Year Record of the Advisory Commission on Intergovernmental Relations*, 98th Cong., 1st sess. (Washington, D.C.: Government Printing Office, 1984).

70. Robert Agranoff and Valerie L. Rinkle, "The New Federalism and Intergovernmental Problem Solving," in Bender and Stever, *Administering the New Federalism*, pp. 295–328.

71. Daniel R. Feenberg and Harvey S. Rosen, "The Interaction of State and Federal Tax Systems: The Impact of State and Local Tax Deductibility," *American Economic Review* 76 (1986): 126–31.

72. Office of State and Local Finance, *Federal-State-Local Fiscal Relations*, pp. 284–323.

73. Catherine Lovell and Charles Tobin, "The Mandate Issue," *Public Administration Review* 41 (1981): 318–31.

74. Joint Legislative Audit and Review Commission, Virginia General Assembly, *State Mandates on Local Government and Local Financial Resources* (Richmond: Commonwealth of Virginia, 1984).

75. Marshall R. Goodman and Margaret T. Wrightson, *Managing Regulatory Reform* (New York: Praeger, 1987).

76. Jane Massey and Jeffrey D. Straussman, "Another Look at the Mandate Issue: Are Conditions-of-Aid So Burdensome?" *Public Administration Review* 45 (1985): 292–300.

77. W. John Moore, "Mandates Without Money," *National Journal* 18 (1986): 2366–70.

78. General Accounting Office, *Implementing the Paperwork Reduction Act* (Washington, D.C.: Government Printing Office, 1983).

79. Cole B. Graham, Jr., "State Consultation Processes after Federal A-95 Overhaul," *State and Local Government Review* 17 (1985): 207–12.

80. Irene F. Rothenberg, "Regional Coordination of Federal Programs," *Journal of Policy Analysis and Management* 4 (1984): 1–16.

81. Irene F. Rothenberg and George J. Gordon, " 'Out with the Old, in with the New': The New Federalism, Intergovernmental Coordination and Executive Order 12372," in Bender and Stever, *Administering the New Federalism*, pp. 74–95.

82. Robert W. Gage, "Federal Regional Councils: Networking Organizations for Policy Management in the Intergovernmental System," *Public Administration Review* 44 (1984): 134–45.

83. General Accounting Office, *Federal Interstate Compact Commissions: Useful Mechanisms for Planning and Managing River Basin Operations* (Washington, D.C.: Government Printing Office, 1981).

84. Richard C. Kearney and John J. Stucker, "Interstate Compacts and the Management of Low Level Radioactive Wastes," *Public Administration Review* 45 (1985): 210–20.

85. Howard L. Chambers, "Intergovernmental Cooperation: Lakewood, California," *Public Management* 70 (July 1988): 8–9.

86. Beth W. Honadle and Arnold M. Howitt, eds., *Perspectives on Management Capacity Building* (Albany: State University of New York Press, 1986).

87. Study Committee on Policy Management Assistance, *Strengthening Public Management in the Intergovernmental System* (Washington, D.C.: Government Printing Office, 1975).

88. Patricia M. Crotty, "Assessing the Role of Federal Administrative Regions," *Public Administration Review* 48 (1988): 642–48.

89. Advisory Commission on Intergovernmental Relations, *Pragmatic Federalism: The Reassignment of Functional Responsibility* (Washington, D.C.: Government Printing Office, 1976).

90. J. Edwin Benton, "Economic Considerations and Reagan's New Federalism Swap Proposals," *Publius* 16 (Spring 1986): 17–32.

91. Timothy J. Conlan and David B. Walker, "Reagan's New Federalism," *Intergovernmental Perspective* 8 (Winter 1983): 6–22.

92. Advisory Commission on Intergovernmental Relations, *Devolving Federal Program Responsibilities and Revenue Sources to State and Local Governments* (Washington, D.C.: Government Printing Office, 1986).

93. Advisory Commission on Intergovernmental Relations Staff Report, "Public Assistance in the Federal System," *Intergovernmental Perspective* 14 (Spring 1988): 5–10.

15

Government, the Economy, and Economic Development

The sheer size of the government sector in the U.S. economy guarantees that government action will have a major impact on overall economic performance. As stated in Chapter 2, total government's share of gross national product now exceeds 40 percent. This chapter focuses on the impact of the government's budget on the overall economy.

The first section considers the U.S. economy and its interdependence with other nations. Not only do such nongovernmental economic events as the stock market crash of 1987 ripple throughout the world, but also other governments and private individuals in other countries react to actions taken by the federal government, such as attempts to hold interest rates down. These external reactions sometimes can cause economic changes within the United States that are completely contrary to the original decision to hold interest rates down. To understand government and the economy, one first has to understand the conditioning factors of the world economy.

Section two summarizes the major objectives sought by government economic policy. Included in economic policy objectives is a discussion of deficit control and management of the federal debt. In contrast to Chapter 12's discussion of state and local borrowing as a means to finance capital investment, this chapter describes federal deficit spending and subsequent borrowing as a macroeconomic policy tool, not a question of investment financing.

The third section is a brief discussion of how governments and businesses attempt to forecast the future. Section four follows with an examination of the principal tools used to affect the economy. For the federal government, these tools conventionally include fiscal and monetary policy, and for state and local governments, infrastructure investments and taxing or spending decisions that are intended to affect the local and state business climate. The chapter concludes with a discussion of the distributional effects of overall economic policy. This section focuses on the role of government in influencing the distribution of income in society.

THE UNITED STATES AND THE WORLD ECONOMY

OPEC Control of Oil Production

Most citizens have long thought of the United States as a significant contributor to the world economy. It took the shock of the Organization of Petroleum Exporting Countries (OPEC) cartel's holding production off the world market in 1973–74 to bring many to the realization that the world economy is a significant contributor to the U.S. economy. Long gas lines and gasoline prices that more than doubled at the pump forced many people to recognize that many major economic conditions are not completely in the United States' own hands. Since that first OPEC production cut, citizens are more attuned to how much of the United States' economic well-being depends on the economic behavior of hundreds of millions of individuals around the world, and on the economic policy decisions of dozens of other governments.

The United States as a Debtor Nation

A second dramatic event, although less immediately apparent to many citizens, occurred in 1985. For the first time, the United States became a net debtor nation. Technically, foreign investments in the United States exceeded U.S. investments abroad by a little over $100 billion, or nearly 3 percent of gross national product (GNP).[1] Claims of foreign investors, both private and governmental, on assets in the United States exceeded the claims of U.S. investors, private and governmental, on assets in other countries.[2] That phenomenon is not all bad. The inflow of foreign capital helped keep U.S. interest rates low because it filled part of the demand for borrowing created by the federal budget deficit.

On the other hand, when the net inflow of foreign capital replaces domestic investment, it represents a short-run fix with a potentially serious long-run disadvantage. The potential long-run problem is that the United States is increasingly dependent in a major way on the confidence of foreign investors in the U.S. economy. Any major threats to their confidence, such as an unmanageable budget deficit, could cause that source of external investment to dry up. A related problem is that those investments crowd out domestic investment capital and produce benefits that flow outside the United States.

Value of the U.S. Dollar in the World Economy

The third phenomenon, noticed by many citizens, occurred in two phases in the 1980s. First, many U.S. residents enjoyed low prices on imported goods or low-priced vacations in Europe as the value of the dollar relative to other currencies climbed to record highs. Then late in 1987 residents watched the flood of tourists reverse as European and Asian visitors came to the United States while prices for comparable trips for U.S. residents abroad climbed to new highs. Imported cars, stereos, and televisions that had been bargains a year before became unaffordable for many.

Competitiveness of the U.S. Economy

A fourth key economic issue of the 1980s was the competitiveness of the U.S. economy relative to other emerging industrial powers. While "cheap foreign labor" had been a cry for many traditional U.S. industries, such as textiles, for more than two decades, the 1980s saw problems in industries in which innovation and technology had been the hallmark of the U.S. competitive edge. For the first time, the United States saw competitors in computer design, electronics, and other high-technology products begin to produce not only cheaper but, in the minds of many consumers, better products.

These events certainly do not show that the U.S. economy has failed. Nor do they necessarily mean there are insurmountable problems. What they do signal is that the U.S. economy is so interdependent with those of other nations that no significant actions the United States takes are without significant repercussions around the world. Likewise, no significant economic events in other major industrial nations or groups of developing nations are without repercussions in the United States. Understanding the role of the government in the U.S. economy thus means casting a wider net and considering also the actions and reactions of major trading partners and of major creditors.

OBJECTIVES OF ECONOMIC POLICY

The government's role in the economy consists of several interrelated functions. First, the government provides the legal framework in which economic transactions take place. Second, governments directly produce goods and services and regulate private production. Third, governments purchase significant quantities of goods and services, and fourth, government redistributes income among individuals and groups.[3] Government's regulation of economic transactions through setting the legal framework is the subject of texts on regulation, business, and constitutional law. The government's role in producing and purchasing goods and services is the subject of most of the chapters of this book. This and the following section focus on the government's effects on the economy's performance.[4]

While Franklin D. Roosevelt's 1932 election platform promised to involve the government in the solution to economic problems brought on by the Depression, it was not until after World War II that the overall role of government in stimulating the economy was formalized. The Employment Act of 1946 set several macroeconomic policy objectives for the federal government. Primary among these were full employment, price stability, and steady economic growth. To these have been added in practice, if not formal legislation, equilibrium in the balance of payments and debt management.[5,6] Most industrial nations share these objectives, whether they rely primarily on the private market, central planning, or a mix of central control and market activity to achieve them.[7] Less industrial, developing countries also share these objectives, but the most prominent economic policy objective for these nations is the promotion of economic development.[8,9]

The first three objectives are a related set of primarily domestic policy objectives. In many respects, they can be reformulated into a single prescription: achieve a level of economic growth that produces full employment without unacceptable inflation. Economic growth is the engine that drives demand for employees. However, running that engine at too high a rate of speed or with too rich a fuel mixture may cause prices to rise unacceptably fast. The reformulation of the first three objectives into a single, conditional statement shows a causal connection between economic growth and employment. It also reveals two key, value-loaded terms: *full employment* and *unacceptable inflation*.

Full Employment

Definition of Full Employment. As a measure of economic performance, employment refers to the number of civilians over age 16 outside of institutions (the work force) who are working in formal, income-producing jobs. The most commonly used measure of employment is the complement of employment, unemployment. Employment then refers to the proportion of the work force employed at a given time, and the measure used is the unemployment rate. There is no legislated definition of full employment, although an unemployment rate of 3 to 4 percent has often been cited as full employment since the 1946 Employment Act. It generally has been accepted that about 3 to 4 percent of the work force at any given time will be between jobs or otherwise temporarily unemployed, so this level of unemployment is considered full employment. In recent years, however, that numerical definition has eroded. Some members of the work force are considered at least temporarily unemployable because of changes in the nature of jobs and skill requirements. These "structurally" unemployed, while members of the work force, are not counted by some economists as part of the base for calculating full employment.

Political Acceptability of Higher Unemployment Rates. The political system has a varying capacity to accept unemployment. A nationwide unemployment rate of 9 or 10 percent, a rate reached in the early 1980s, is clearly unacceptable by current standards but a marked improvement over the peak of 24 percent unemployment during the Depression. As the rate declines toward 5 percent, acceptance increases. The extent to which society tolerates unemployment is partially dependent upon who is unemployed. Though there may be a tendency to accept high unemployment among low-skilled, minority-group, or younger workers, tolerance for unemployment may quickly dissipate when it reaches middle-income, white-collar workers.

Politically, the rate itself also may not be the criterion of acceptability. After two years of unemployment rates exceeding 9 percent, the need to lower the rate was a key issue in the 1984 presidential election. However, later in the decade, when the rate was close to 5 percent, citizens were concerned not with the rate but the types of new jobs that were being created in the economy. The argument was that most of the new jobs created were service occupations that paid only the minimum wage.

Controlling Inflation

Relationship between Unemployment and Inflation. As the unemployment rate declines, the more difficult it becomes to find workers, and as a result wage rates may be bid up, creating inflationary pressures. Certainly, through the mid-1960s the traditional assumption that rising employment leads to price increases and declining employment to price decreases seemed to hold up. Figure 15-1 illustrates that assumption. However, the mid-1970s recession saw both rising unemployment and rising prices. At the peak, 1974 prices rose 11 percent over the year before, and 1975 prices 9 percent over 1974. During 1975, unemployment peaked at over 8 percent. As the economy came out of the recession, as measured by a gradually declining unemployment rate, the inflation rate held high. The 1980s seemed to show a return to previous patterns with the unemployment rate moving opposite to the direction of inflation.

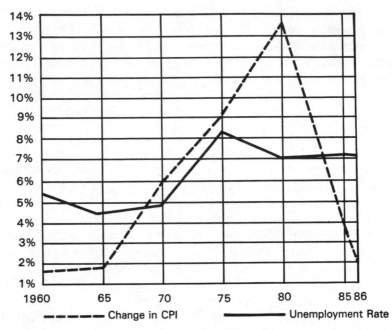

Figure 15-1 Inflation and Unemployment, 1960–86. *Sources: Economic Report of the President, 1988*, Council of Economic Advisors, p. 292, Government Printing Office, 1988; and *Statistical Abstract of the United States: 1988*, 108th ed., Bureau of the Census, p. 445, Government Printing Office, 1987.

Trade-off between Stable Prices and Full Employment. If inflation and unemployment are to some extent trade-offs, then a major issue is how much inflation will accompany a full employment economy or, alternatively put, how much unemployment will accompany stable prices? During the 1950s and 1960s, a 3 percent inflation rate was thought necessary to reduce unemployment to 4 percent. Later analyses in the 1970s suggested that the unemployment rate would have to be much higher to achieve a 3 percent inflation rate.[10] That analysis seemed to be borne out later when inflation fell to only 3 percent for the first time in over a decade (1983 and 1985). During those two years, the unemployment rate was more than 9 percent and more than 7 percent respectively. Following the peak of 1983, however, the unemployment rate began to decline slowly, reaching nearly 5 percent in 1988 while inflation fell to just below 5 per cent. The record of the 1980s suggested to the President's Council of Economic Advisers that there was insufficient evidence to support an absolute trade-off between inflation and unemployment.[11] However, the same council acknowledged that once unemployment and inflation both approach 5 percent, any further movement in one often will be accompanied by an opposite movement in the other. What worried many economists in the late 1980s was the nation's apparent inability to pass the point of 5 percent inflation and 5 percent unemployment.[12] Compared with rates in 1982–83, both rates were much improved. However, a steady 5 percent rate of inflation masks an almost static condition of no growth in economic productivity.

Economic Growth

Economic Productivity. It must be noted that unemployment is not the only, and perhaps not the best, measure of the economy's health. Even if the rate of unemployment and the rate of inflation are both at acceptable levels, it still is possible for the overall productivity of the economy to be seriously declining. Although growth for growth's sake is not a goal, economic growth under stable price conditions signals a higher standard of living.

For the United States, the average annual growth rate in productivity as measured by GNP from 1965 through the 1980s was 3 percent. For Japan, the comparable figures varied between 4 percent and 6 percent.[13] Just as important, during the period the average annual rate of inflation in the United States varied between 4 percent and 6 percent. Thus, the productivity of the U.S. economy, measured not in inflated dollars but in terms of real output, was virtually stagnant. Productivity in terms of output per worker was only 1.6 percent for 1965 through 1986, compared with 2.6 for Canada, 4.3 for Japan, 2.5 for Germany, and 2.4 for the average of 20 industrial countries.[14]

Impact of Government on Productivity. Most economists think that the primary impact of the government on economic productivity and long-term growth is due to influences on knowledge development and investment in productive capacity. The importance of the government's role in contributing to knowledge development is underscored by the fact that a major chapter on knowledge and progress was introduced into the *Economic Report of the President*. In the United States, as well as most developed and developing nations, the government is the primary provider of education. In addition to this human capital investment, the government also invests directly in research and development (R & D) to produce technological breakthroughs and indirectly affects private investment in R & D. One mechanism for influencing private R & D has been to allow a 20 percent tax credit for increases in R & D expenditures over prior-year levels.[15] The impact of both the direct and indirect actions of government on improving the productivity of the economy can be measured only in the long run. For example, even if businesses substantially increase their expenditures for R & D as a result of government incentives, the payoff in terms of reversing any decline in productivity will show up years into the future.

Equilibrium in the Balance of Payments

Understanding the reason why productivity declines lies partly in understanding how the U.S. economy has shifted in its relation to the world economy, and partly in understanding how domestic budget deficit management has contributed to the overall economic situation. The U.S. balance of payments position is discussed in this section. A discussion of the overall deficit situation and debt management follows.

U.S. Transition from Creditor to Debtor. As noted earlier, in 1985 the United States became a net debtor nation. In the context of this chapter, net debtor means that there are more foreign demands on U.S. assets than there are U.S. claims on assets in other countries. Traditionally, that situation has been brought about by a country or its citizens purchasing more abroad than is sold to other countries. That is a contributing factor for the United States. As the value of the dollar climbed in the middle 1980s, the dollar earnings of U.S. residents could buy more imported goods, whose prices, while stable or rising in their countries of origin, were falling measured in dollars. While that situation seemed favorable from the U.S. consumers' point of view, it was a disaster from the producers' point of view. Producers of goods in the United States found their products rising in cost to foreign consumers, with no compensating improvements in the product nor rising incomes abroad. Furthermore, the temporarily happy consumer situation was masking more serious underlying problems with the balance of payments.

Balance of Payments. The balance of payments consists of several components or measures. The net balance of goods purchased abroad versus goods sold abroad is the simple trade balance. In the early 1980s, the net excess of imports over exports stood at just under $30 billion. By 1987, it had risen to over $150 billion.[16] As with GNP, one also needs to distinguish between "nominal" net exports and "real" net exports, adjusting for inflation. Real net exports, eliminating price inflation, fell even faster than nominal net exports from 1982 through 1986. The difference between nominal and real in this case meant that the quantity of imports was rising faster than the dollars being spent because the prices of the imports were falling simultaneously. After 1986, the situation reversed as the value of the dollar relative to other currencies fell and the actual quantity of imports began to fall.

To remedy the imbalance in real net exports, either real GNP must rise faster than domestic demand, domestic demand must fall, or some combination of the two must occur. The equation is deceptively simple. Domestic investment plus foreign investment equals total production. In late 1987, the net export deficit, in real terms, was 3 percent. GNP would have to grow faster than domestic demand by 3 percent to redress the balance. A 3 percent excess of real GNP over domestic demand, however, has never been achieved in the post-World War II era. If, on the other hand, the import/export imbalance is solved by a slower growth in demand, then U.S. production capacity is underutilized and unemployment increases. Considerable pressure, therefore, was placed on other major industrial countries to adjust their currencies upward against the dollar. By 1988, the dollar had declined to the point where more U.S. goods were being sold abroad than foreign goods were being imported.

Financing the U.S. Economy. The importance of these movements in the two measures of trade balance lies in their implications for how the economy is being financed. Historically, the U.S. economy has been financed domestically. National saving has been sufficient to provide funds for national investment, with the surplus national saving being invested abroad. The result was U.S. claims on foreign assets that exceeded foreign claims on U.S. assets. Since the early 1980s, however, the reverse has been true. Part of the economy has been financed not by domestic savings but by foreign investments in the United States. These foreign investments represent a claim on U.S. assets that now exceed U.S. claims on foreign assets. The concern about this situation is not a matter of nationalistic pride. Foreign investments in the U.S. economy represent foreign confidence in the economy. However, the 1980s evidenced a flow of external funds to finance the federal government budget deficit rather than foreign confidence. In macroeconomic terms, this external financing of the deficit creates a situation in which a greater quantity of U.S. goods and services has to be sold abroad in the long term to meet payments to foreign holders of U.S. debt. That quantity then is not available for U.S. consumption. Thus, the trade balance, and the overall balance of payments disequilibrium, is intertwined with the domestic federal government budget deficit.

Deficits and Debt Management

Chapter 12 described state and local debt primarily as long-term investment in physical infrastructure and other capital assets. Prudent financial management for state and local governments suggests that short-term borrowing be restricted to meeting short-term contingencies and that long-term borrowing should be related to the expected life of the investments financed. Federal debt policy, on the other hand, relates more to macroeconomic policy considerations than to capital investment requirements. Deficits in the federal budget accumulate as spending exceeds revenues whether or not the spending finances investments in long-term growth or provision of current goods and services. While it is possible to make a numeric comparison between the investment levels in the federal budget and the size of the deficit, a meaningful argument that the deficit results from conscious investment planning cannot be made.

Developing Country Debt Management. For developing countries, prudent debt management is more comparable to that of U.S. state and local governments. Developing countries as a rule have excess or idle labor capacity. The long-run economic strategy is to invest in education to improve the productivity of labor and in physical infrastructure. Typically, a shortage of physical infrastructure retards the economic investment that would employ the excess labor capacity. Governments in developing countries borrow, from donor agencies such as the World Bank and from developed country banks, to increase physical infrastructure and other capital investments. If they are economically sound, the investments will produce the long-run economic growth necessary to repay the foreign debt. Similarly, U.S. state and local governments borrow to finance capital investments in order to produce economic growth sufficient to repay the indebtedness. More often than not, developing countries encounter debt troubles when borrowing finances current consumption rather than investment and when physical infrastructure investments that have been built are not maintained. The economy then does not maintain a sufficient level of growth, revenues do not increase as expected, and debt exceeds capacity to repay.

U.S. Federal Use of Debt. In the post-Depression era, the federal budget deficit has been used as an overt tool to influence total demand in the economy and thus overall economic performance. According to the prevailing economic theory of that era, deficits should be managed to provide the appropriate stimulus to the economy without creating inflationary pressure. However, in the 1980s the size of the deficit reached proportions that were out of step with economic policy objectives.

Size of the U.S. Federal Debt. To understand the most recent decade, it is first important to understand the relative size of the federal debt and then to consider its origins and implications. Figure 15-2 illustrates the debt as a percent of GNP, a useful measure of whether the debt is growing more slowly or faster than the overall economy. Total federal indebtedness in 1950 was equal to 93 percent of GNP, reflecting the financing of World War II. Until the 1970s, that figure steadily declined and leveled off for a decade at around 35 percent. The postwar low of 34 percent was reached in 1980 (fiscal year 1981). Rapid increases after that brought federal debt to over 54 percent of GNP in 1987, the highest since 1960.

Effects of Economic Performance on Size of Federal Debt. Two circumstances explain the rapid rise in the federal government's debt after a long period of decline. First, the federal budget is affected by the overall performance of the economy in terms of both revenues and expenditures (see discussion

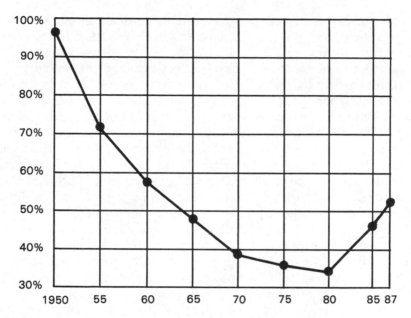

Figure 15-2 Federal Debt as Percent of GNP, 1950–87. *Source: Statistical Abstract of the United States: 1988*, Bureau of Census, p. 291, Government Printing Office, 1987.

below in Tools Available to Affect the Economy).[17] The recessionary period of the early 1980s held overall growth in the economy to virtually zero in real terms. This lack of growth created pressure on the budget for automatic increases in expenditures for some social welfare programs that expand as unemployment goes up. It also caused a decrease in federal revenues.

Effects of Tax Cuts on Size of Federal Debt. The second circumstance was a set of overt decisions. On taking office, the Reagan administration initiated a sweeping set of economic reforms that involved a major series of tax cuts beginning in 1981 and significant budget reductions in nondefense spending. However, as the program evolved, it proved impossible to reduce nondefense spending sufficiently to match increases in defense, and overall spending levels remained at prior levels or higher. The theory behind the tax cut was that the funds not collected by the government would be better invested by the private sector, yielding in fact a future revenue dividend in the form of increased tax yields from the heightened economic activity. The fiscal dividend never occurred. Estimates of the revenue loss from the Economic Recovery Tax Act of 1981 for the first five years placed it at $635 billion, unaccompanied by matching expenditure cuts.[18] Federal revenue levels fell to the lowest levels since the 1960s, while expenditures soared to new heights.[19]

Economic Effects of 1980s Deficit Levels. Deficits create pressure on prices and may lead to inflation. Financing the deficit through borrowing places demands on available capital for private investment financing and state and local borrowing, driving up interest rates. To some extent, both pressures are reduced if the borrowing is from foreign sources, as domestic markets are then left with more resources for private investment and consumption. Indeed, as discussed in the preceding section, that is what happened during the 1980s.[20] Foreign borrowing by both the private and public sectors increased until the United States became a major debtor to other countries. Mainly, foreign capital served to replace the lack of domestic savings as a source of private investment. In 1970 foreign direct investment in the United States was less than 3 percent. By 1986 it had climbed to nearly 9 percent.[21] In the long run, the foreign borrowing will reduce the aggregate level of consumption in the United States because the ultimate claims on resources will be from outside the country rather than from domestic consumption.

The consequence of the rapid deficit increase and the resultant borrowing has been renewed demand for legislative and constitutional mechanisms to limit or prohibit deficits (see Chapter 9). Although proposed and enacted limitations on deficit spending have been a part of American budgetary history since the 18th century, the current period reflects the fact that major adjustments now seem unavoidable.[22] A balanced budget requirement prohibiting federal borrowing altogether probably is impossible to administer. The federal budget's link to the economy and the variety of programs that change automatically as the economy moves up and down make it extremely difficult for revenue or expenditure adjustments to achieve balance. On the other hand, more explicit attention to how the deficit is financed could be a positive outcome of balanced budget discussions. With or without legislative or constitutional changes, no one in the late 1980s was willing to argue that the size of the deficit was no cause for concern.[23]

ANTICIPATING ECONOMIC CONDITIONS

Both the private and public sectors need tools to anticipate economic trends and to measure economic change. If businesses are to make sound investment decisions, including hiring new workers or building new plant capacity, they have to be successful in anticipating future economic developments. If interest rates are expected to fall, it is not the time to borrow to buy new production equipment. If a tax incentive that reduces overall tax liability when funds are invested in new productive capacity is about to expire, it is a good time to make new investments. Some of these events can be predicted with relative certainty. An investment tax credit may have a specific expiration date, and it may be easy to see that Congress is not likely to renew it. On the other hand, it may not be as easy to predict how much change will occur in interest rates. Forecasting tools are a vital ingredient in business economic planning.

If government is to achieve its economic policy objectives, it too needs sensitive and valid measures with which to predict the direction of the economy. With those measures, it also needs models of change that predict what will happen if specific policy changes, such as a change in the maximum corporate income tax rate, are enacted. Although forecasting techniques are beyond the scope of this text, some understanding of the change measures that are watched closely by business and government and of the analytical models used by forecasters is important to our discussion of government's economic policy.[24,25]

The several indices or barometers of economic change that have been developed can be classified roughly as lagging, coincident, and leading. Leading indicators presumably show in advance what the economy will do, whereas lagging indicators report what already has occurred.

Coincident Indicators

Gross National Product. Coincident indicators, those that report what the economy is doing now, are the ones that most commonly reach the public's attention. GNP is one of the most important; it is a measure of the total goods and services produced by the nation. GNP is the aggregate of personal consumption expenditures, gross private domestic investment, net exports of goods and services, and government purchases of goods and services. Most commonly reported is the rise or fall in GNP. For example, U.S. GNP grew 5.9 percent in 1987 over GNP in 1986. Care must be taken in interpreting that growth, however. Some was not an increase in production but rather was an increase in the prices of goods and services. Adjusted for inflation, GNP growth in 1987 was only 2.9 percent. Just over half of the nominal growth was due to inflation. For analysis purposes, therefore, both nominal and real (adjusted to remove effects of inflation) figures are used.

Net National Product and National Income. Two other coincident indicators, both derivatives of GNP, are net national product (NNP) and national income (NI). GNP includes all capital investment, some of which does not produce new productive capacity but only replaces capacity that is being used up. NNP is the measure of investment after depreciation is removed. A GNP of $4.5 trillion in 1987 equals an NNP of $4.0 trillion, or approximately $.5 trillion of GNP represented no new capacity. NNP thus tells what consumption and investment is net of capital stock replacement. NI is derived from NNP by eliminating indirect business taxes included in the price of goods sold and business transfer payments.[26] Table 15-1 summarizes the relationships among GNP, NNP, and NI from 1950 through 1987.

The three measures of national product and income indicate what is happening to the levels of production and income. Prices are another measure

Table 15-1 Relationships among Gross National Product, Net National Product, and National Income, 1950–87 (Billions of Dollars)

Item	1950	1955	1960	1965	1970	1975	1980	1985	1987*
Personal Consumption Expenditures	192.1	257.9	330.7	440.7	640.0	1012.8	1732.6	2629.4	2966.0
Gross Private Domestic Investment	55.1	69.7	78.2	116.2	148.8	219.6	437.0	641.6	716.4
Net Exports of Goods and Services	2.2	3.0	5.9	9.7	8.5	31.1	32.1	–79.2	–119.9
Government Purchases of Goods and Services	38.8	75.3	100.6	138.6	218.2	335.0	530.3	818.6	923.8
Equals:									
Gross National Product	288.3	405.9	515.3	705.1	1015.5	1598.4	2732.0	4010.3	4486.2
Less:									
Capital Consumption Allowances	23.6	34.4	46.4	57.4	88.8	161.8	303.8	437.6	479.4
Equals:									
Net National Product	264.6	371.5	468.9	647.7	926.6	1436.6	2428.1	3572.7	4006.8
Current Surplus	.1	.0	.4	1.6	2.9	2.4	5.7	6.3	13.1
Indirect Business Tax and Nontax Liability	23.4	32.2	45.3	62.5	94.0	140.0	213.3	333.2	367.6
Business Transfer Payments	.8	1.2	2.0	2.8	4.1	7.4	12.1	21.6	23.2
Statistical Discrepancy	.8	1.8	–2.8	–1.2	–1.1	2.5	4.9	–5.6	–6.8
Equals:									
National Income	239.8	336.3	424.9	585.2	832.6	1289.1	2203.5	3229.9	3635.9

*Preliminary.

Note: Subtotals may not add up to totals due to rounding.

Source: *Economic Report of the President, 1988*, Council of Economic Advisors, pp. 248–249, 272, Government Printing Office, 1988.

of what is happening. Wholesale prices may provide an earlier warning of potential problems than measures of national product because they indicate probable changes in prices about to be paid by consumers. The wholesale or producer price index covers about 2800 commodities. The consumer price index (CPI) is for goods and services bought by urban wage and clerical workers. It is estimated from a sample of urban areas around the country. Although often cited as a measure of inflation, it tends to overstate actual price increases because of the heavy influence of housing prices. Consumers not buying new homes will not experience as much an increase in prices in a year as the CPI would indicate. The CPI also is influenced heavily by oil prices so that a large drop in fuel costs may bring the CPI down even while food and other necessities are increasing, as happened in the fourth quarter of 1988. For that reason, analysts often use other indices to adjust for inflation.

Unemployment. Two other measures provide good indications of the current state of the economy, unemployment and industrial production. Unemployment, a percentage measure of the people within the labor force who are not employed, is a common public policy target indicator. The measure is politically charged. A change in the unemployment rate of half a percent up or down is enough to send the president before the news media to announce significant economic progress or to have opposition leaders charge that the economy is failing. However, unemployment is subject to wide seasonal fluctuation, and the measurement of unemployment is subject to manipulation. Some job seekers may become discouraged and fall out of the count altogether. Women and members of ethnic minority groups may not be well represented in the count of job seekers because they may perceive that there are no jobs to seek or no jobs worth seeking. Therefore, unemployment always has to be interpreted with some care.

Industrial Production. The industrial production index is a measure of the manufacture of durable and nondurable goods and is prepared by the Federal Reserve System. The durable portion of manufacturing is watched closely, particularly key industries such as steel. Steel sales reflect future intentions of manufacturing concerns. Falling sales may indicate lack of confidence in the economy and attempts by firms to keep inventories low. The value of this index has declined somewhat as the size of the manufacturing segment of the economy relative to the services segment has declined.

Leading Indicators

Though the above measures are useful measures of the current state of the economy, or what it has been, they often do not provide the lead time necessary to devise intervention strategies. The forecaster as a result turns to the leading indicators. A nonprofit research group, the National Bureau of Economic Research, identifies more than 30 leading indicators, only a few of which are discussed here.

Employment-Related Indicators. A key leading indicator is the average workweek of production workers in manufacturing. Its usefulness is based on the practice of most manufacturers to cut back on the length of the workweek rather than lay workers off if the demand for production starts to fall off. A somewhat later indicator is the average weekly initial claims for unemployment insurance. This indicator senses the extent to which layoffs are increasing or decreasing. Both measures indicate employers' estimates of the direction of change in the economy.

Housing Starts. Private, nonfarm housing starts provide a measure of the faith of builders and financial investors in the health of the economy. A decline in the number of starts can signal future economic decline. Housing is thought to be sensitive in that it reflects willingness to tie up investment dollars for several months to a year in an expensive commodity for which there may be no buyer at the time construction begins. However, housing starts are extremely sensitive to mortgage rates. During periods of extremely high rates, such as the early 1980s, many potential buyers were forced out of the market. In recent years, housing starts have become a somewhat less reliable leading indicator. Growth in the use of adjustable rate mortgages allows home buyers to hedge against cyclical swings in interest rates, which in turn keeps demand for housing higher in the initial stages of rising interest rates. Continuing interest rate increases can lead to the onset of a recessionary period, but housing starts would not be affected as early.[27]

Stock Markets. Stock markets are watched closely by the business community and government analysts, but their volatility makes them hard to use as a leading indicator. The New York Stock Exchange (NYSE) is the market most carefully watched, but the Tokyo and London markets also are watched closely. Several composite indices of stock exchange transactions are used, the most notable being the Dow-Jones and Standard and Poor's Indices.

Stock transactions are useful as leading indicators in that they reflect the faith of investors in the stocks traded on the open market and thus in the companies whose stock is traded. As a barometer of investor confidence, stock transactions may be helpful. In principle, the value of a stock is a reflection of the health of the firm. However, stocks may surge or decline wildly as a result of corporate takeover attempts and fights to prevent takeover. Furthermore, the crash of 1987 indicates that factors such as the mechanisms by which some firms automatically buy or sell stocks by computer (program trading) may sometimes have more to do with surges than with any underlying economic factors. To the extent that stock prices reflect these other circumstances rather than the economic health of the corporation, they may be misleading as an economic indicator.

Composite Indices. A variety of combined indices exist for increasing the sensitivity of measures of economic changes and trends. The Bureau of Economic Analysis of the Commerce Department publishes a monthly series of indices.[28,29] These composites combine several individual indices, such as the composite of 12 leading indicators. A related composite is a diffusion index. Diffusion indices measure the percentage of components of an index that are moving in the same direction. For example, in the Dow-Jones averages, if industrials, transportation, and utilities increase in price but general stocks decrease, the diffusion index is 75 percent.

Forecasting

Despite the availability of a wide range of indicators and extensive historical series, forecasting remains a risky business. It is common to find two or more major federal organizations in substantial disagreement over expected economic trends. Rarely do the Office of Management and Budget (OMB) and the Congressional Budget Office (CBO) agree, for example, on the forecast of the federal deficit. One analyst noted that OMB and CBO averaged errors of $58 billion and $35 billion respectively in estimates of the size of the deficit for fiscal years 1979–83.[30]

Major economic directions are forecasted by judgment or a combination of judgment and sophisticated econometric models (see discussion on forecasting revenues in Chapter 4). Several major university-based research groups and several private organizations employ econometric models that include variables numbering from as few as 100 to as many as 1,200. Among the more famous private models are those of Wharton Econometric Forecasting Associates, Data Resources, Inc. (DRI), and Chase Econometrics. Several organizations, including the Institute for Survey Research, University of Michigan, conduct surveys of ordinary consumers and expert analysts to obtain "judgment" estimates of economic trends. Judgment regularly is used to adjust the sophisticated mathematical models.

The models themselves consist of two types of variables, endogenous and exogenous, and systems of simultaneous equations specifying the linkages among these variables. Endogenous variables are those whose values are determined within the model. Values of exogenous variables are determined outside the system of equations; in other words, exogenous values are "given" to the model. The models are based on theories of economic behavior that link aggregate economic variables to produce predicted values of those variables of interest, such as GNP. If a model does not predict accurately, it may be due to a failure of the fundamental theory, the conditions in which the theory accurately models behavior may not be met by the economy at the time, or the data may be inadequately or inaccurately measured.

Not surprisingly, during major economic changes controversy frequently erupts over why both business and government could not have anticipated the degree of change or sometimes even the direction of change. The recession year of 1982 had been predicted in 1981 to be a year of modest economic growth. The recovery in 1983 was predicted to be a period of slow growth, whereas actual growth in GNP turned out to be more than twice that predicted.[31] Models seem to fail when major structural changes are happening to the economy, such as OPEC's successful control over oil production in the early 1970s. When the economy is behaving with stability, various models are fairly successful.

Given the conflicting interpretations possible even with sound information, economic forecasters as well as political leaders interpret the data from their own perspectives. The technical problems involved are great, but inevitably forecasting succumbs not to technical problems but to political resolutions. The president and his staff may attempt to focus attention upon one indicator that shows signs of progress, while members of Congress from the opposing party may focus on another. The issues involved in conflicting theories of economic behavior and the implications for government economic policy are returned to in the next section.

TOOLS AVAILABLE TO AFFECT THE ECONOMY

Automatic Stabilizers

Governmental actions used to effect economic policy objectives can be either discretionary or automatic. When discretionary action is taken, some policy making has occurred that results in decisions to intervene or not to intervene in specific circumstances. The automatic or built-in features, on the other hand, require no immediate action on the part of decision makers.[32,33]

The progressivity of the tax structure is an example of a built-in or automatic stabilizer. As the economy declines, corporate profits decline, and workers' salaries decrease. Both corporate and personal taxes thus go down, with the result that more funds are left available to the private sector for investment, stimulating demand. Similarly, tax revenues rise as the economy expands, providing some brake on too-rapid growth that might lead to inflationary pressures.

Discretionary Policies

There are also nongovernmental stabilizers that are an inherent part of the economy and individual economic behavior. Recessions are resisted by individuals and corporations that use savings to maintain established levels of activities. Conversely, expansionary trends are resisted. As income rises, greater proportions of income are placed in savings rather than being used for consumption.

Discretionary interventions range widely. They are based on economic theories of behavior, both micro- and macroeconomic, that anticipate the economy's responses to governmental actions involving taxing and spending and alterations in the flow of funds through the monetary system. The former actions are called fiscal policy; the latter, monetary policy. Fiscal and monetary policy are discussed separately first, followed by a discussion of their integration into an overall strategy. A separate section then considers the public investment role of government, a role particularly important for developing countries and for U.S. state and local governments.

Fiscal Policy Instruments

The essential tools of fiscal policy are revenues, expenditures, and the implied surplus or deficit. Their use has evolved over the 20th century, changing as different views of the role of government in the economy have held sway. The prevailing view early in the century was that little government intervention was necessary. If the economy seemed to be faltering, the government's role should be limited to an incremental increase in expenditures over revenues to "prime the pump." During the Depression, demand fell off so rapidly and to such a depth, however, that small actions by the government had virtually no effect. It was only the extraordinary production demands of World War II that stimulated sufficient growth to pull the economy out of the depths. The immediate postwar period rode on the demands for consumer goods that had been in short supply during the war, and there seemed to be little for the government to do for the economy one way or the other.

Keynesian Economics. Ideas for what the government *should* do in the event of a downturn, however, had not stood still. John Maynard Keynes had argued in 1936 that the problem was lack of demand.[34] Government's role should be to stimulate demand by spending, thus ensuring that idle productive capacity is used. By 1946, the federal government had been assigned a formal role in the economy, and that role was guided by the prescriptions of Keynesian economics. Keynes focused on the problem of cuts in production in response to declining demand, which result in less purchasing power for consumers, which further reduces demand for goods and services. This still further reduced demand results in further reductions in production levels. The emphasis, according to Keynesians, should be upon maintaining demand levels. The fiscal mechanism for maintaining demand levels, according to this view, is to spend at a level higher than revenues, in other words, to incur a deficit at those times where the economic fluctuation threatens to reduce demand to levels that will generate unemployment and general economic decline.

Supply-Side Economics. It was almost 40 years before a major contrasting view of the basic problem in a fluctuating demand cycle was given wide circulation. Focusing not on the demand side, some economists began to argue in the 1970s that the basic problem lay on the supply side.[35] So-called "supply-side economics" became the dominant viewpoint of the Reagan administration. Briefly, the supply-side view has held that high tax burdens are the major contributor to reduced economic performance. The more government taxes, the less money is available for private investment and the less incentive there is to produce. If taxes are cut, production will be stimulated and in turn additional workers will be hired. Although the tax rates are lower, the actual revenue yield will be higher because of increased corporate profits and increased take-home pay for workers. Furthermore, the increased supply of goods and services available should have a dampening effect on inflation.

The supply-side view held sway in the 1981 tax cuts (Economic Recovery Tax Act of 1981). However, the expected revenue windfall did not materialize. The reconstruction of events suggests that the principal deficiency in the supply-side view has not been that tax reductions do not stimulate the economy, but rather in the faith that the response will be great enough to generate offsetting revenues.[36] Only under extremely burdensome conditions would taxes seem high enough to meet the conditions suggested by the theory and hence produce the expected revenue increase. To date, there has been no evidence of any tax system meeting those conditions.

Contemporary Fiscal Policy. The contemporary view of fiscal policy seems to have become more pragmatic than theoretical. Budgetary deficits that overwhelm incremental fiscal adjustments have overshadowed theoretical debate among fiscal policy theorists. The current approach to fiscal policy calls for moderate fiscal efforts on the tax or expenditure side to counter trends rather than massive tax cuts or expenditure increases. Modest increases in government expenditures during periods of economic decline are expected to stimulate demand, which in turn will stimulate a higher level of production. Similarly, modest tax reductions should have a similar stimulative effect on the supply of funds available to individuals. Of the two, expenditure increases and decreases are more easily implemented than changes in tax rates or bases.

Multiplier Effects. The effect of fiscal policy is based not only upon the taxes extracted from the economy and the expenditures put into it, but also upon a multiplier. This means that any transaction will generate several other transactions. For each government expenditure paid to industry or an individual, part is taxed while the remainder is divided between consumption and investment. The private citizen or firm spends, and in doing so places dollars in the hands of others, some of which will be taxed and the rest spent or invested. Therefore, an increase of $100 in government expenditures will be multiplied in its effect on the economy.[37]

The stimulative effect of expenditures comes from expenditures exceeding revenues, or the deficit. The initial government expenditure financed by the deficit puts money in the hands of producers and consumers who in turn pay a portion in taxes, save a portion, and spend a portion. The dampening effect occurs from an excess of revenues over expenditures. Economists now divide the surplus or deficit into two components: a structural deficit and a fiscal component. To arrive at those two components, the concept of a "full employment surplus" is used. This concept is based on a hypothetical calculation of the budget surplus or deficit, if the economy were operating at full employment. Any deficit or surplus beyond this calculation is a "structural" imbalance between expenditures and revenues.

Structural Deficit. The notion of a structural deficit, which generally is to be avoided, and a stimulative deficit, one that would tend to move the economy back to full employment, is related to the concept of a "prudent" fiscal deficit. The World Bank defines a prudent fiscal deficit as one that can be financed consistently with objectives to maintain external credit-worthiness, growth in private sector investment, and stable prices.[38] The principle translates into practical guides that suggest that a prudent fiscal deficit is low when economic growth is stagnating or low and can be higher as the rate of economic growth increases.

Response Lags in Fiscal Policy. The problem with the implementation of a modest fiscal policy is the gap between the time a revenue or expenditure response is necessary and the time it actually can occur. The lack of complete information about the economy produces a perception lag, the period of time that elapses between an event—such as the beginning of an inflationary period—and its recognition. The perception lag contributes to a reaction lag, the time that is consumed between recognition and the decision(s) to act. Pluralistic or decentralized political systems may have rather substantial reaction lags associated with them. For example, in January 1967 President Lyndon Johnson proposed a surtax on income to dampen the inflationary effects of Vietnam War spending. The proposed legislation was not introduced in Congress until August, and though finally approved was not signed into law until July 1968. To close this gap, several presidents have attempted to gain congressional approval for moderate discretionary authority to raise or lower taxes. However, Congress has jealously guarded its prerogative to initiate and approve tax actions.

Beyond the reaction lag is the implementation lag, the time required before action actually affects the economy. Tax measures clearly are felt within a short period of time. The introduction of a new tax does require time to establish the specific regulations and mechanisms for collection. Once the tax is established, however, comparatively little time is required to make adjustments for a larger or smaller tax rate.

In contrast, extended implementation lags are likely when expenditures are adjusted for fiscal policy purposes. In the short term, the apportionment process that allocates funds to agencies may have some marginal influence on spending patterns during the various quarters of the fiscal year (see Chapter 10). Potentially more influential tools are budget impoundments, which, within certain limits, allow the president to defer or rescind expenditures (see Chapter 9). Many expenditures, however, are basically uncontrollable in the immediate future because of previous commitments, such as entitlement programs for assistance to the elderly and the poor. Furthermore, a large component of the federal budget now is directed strictly to meet interest payments on the debt or to refinance previous debt.

Capital construction has been suggested on occasion as one discretionary area where government expenditures could be used for fiscal policy purposes. Construction would be initiated during slack periods and curtailed during periods of high employment. To some extent, public construction has been used for this purpose, particularly by the federal government during the Depression. Developing-country governments, where the central government has a much larger role in public infrastructure construction, are often in a better position to use this type of discretionary expenditure control.[39]

Monetary Policy

Control Over the Money Supply. Both demand-side and supply-side economists focus on the role of taxing and spending in the economy. Although fiscal policy economists did not launch a major critique of demand-side theories until the late 1970s, other economists since the 1950s have argued that the government's main effect on the economy should not come through fiscal policy at all. Led by the work of Milton Friedman, these economists argue that the main effects of government policy on the private sector come through control over the money supply.[40] In a simple economy, governments control the money supply through their monopoly power over the printing of money. As an economy expands, demand increases for the supply of money, and ultimately government meets this demand by printing more money. In simplistic terms, a government literally can print currency and use that currency to meet its spending requirements. The increase in the money supply, over and above printing replacements for worn currency, is called seignorage.[41] Clearly, if the government resorts simply to printing money without regard to demand, the value of the currency printed declines in value. U.S. news media in the early 1980s showed film footage of individuals in Bolivia actually pushing carts full of currency to pay for a few dollars worth of goods as the annual inflation rate reached several thousand percent.

In a more complex economy, paper money and coinage in circulation is not the major component of the money supply controlled by government. In the United States, only 25 percent of the principal money supply is paper money and coinage. The remaining 75 percent is demand deposits in banking institutions. Most financial transactions, from those by individuals through those by the largest financial institutions, are conducted with checks and other paper documents that transfer bank account balances from one individual or institution to another. This major component of the money supply expands through credit or borrowing. When an individual borrows to purchase a new car, the bank increases the individual's bank balance, which allows a check to be written to the car dealer. In this way, the money supply increases by the amount of the loan. Similarly, banks can borrow from the Federal Reserve System and the money supply is thereby increased.

Role of the Federal Reserve System. In the United States, control over the money supply, and hence monetary policy, is exercised by the Federal Reserve System, a quasi-public institution. The system is headed by a board of governors consisting of seven members appointed by the president with the advice and consent of the Senate. The chairman is designated by the president. The Federal Reserve Banks and branches are augmented by all national banks, and by state banks and trust companies that wish to join.

The Federal Reserve System serves as banks to the banking community. Financial transactions among banks and other financial institutions are cleared through the Federal Reserve System. The system lends money to the member banks, which member banks then can relend to their customers. The system also buys and sells government bonds ranging from short-term Treasury notes (90 days) to long-term bonds (open market operations). The Federal Reserve also controls the reserve requirements for member banks, the amount of money the bank has to have available as a proportion of the total demand deposits of customers (the reserve requirement). Using these three tools— lending, open market operations, and control of reserve requirements—the Federal Reserve controls the money supply.

Importance of Open Market Operations. Open market operations are the most prominent operations because they occur daily. As the Federal Reserve purchases bonds, it increases the reserve holdings of the member institutions selling the bonds and hence increases the supply of money available to be lent. This increase in turn stimulates economic activity as more investment funds are made available. As member banks buy bonds from the Federal Reserve, their cash reserves decrease, reducing the total supply of funds available to the economy.

Discount Rate. Frequently adjusted during the 1980s, the Federal Reserve's lending rate to member institutions, called the discount rate, has increased in prominence as a monetary tool. Banks borrow from the Federal Reserve to meet customers' demands for money. As the Federal Reserve increases the interest rate, the rate charged to final borrowers increases, which in turn decreases the demand for funds.

Reserve Requirement. Changing the reserve requirements of member institutions is the least frequently used tool. For every dollar in customer deposits, member banks are required to retain a specific percentage. By increasing this percentage, the Federal Reserve can curtail immediately the amount of money available. Historically changed only every few years, the reserve requirement in the 1980s became a more prominent feature of monetary policy, with adjustments occurring more often on an annual basis.

Putting these monetary tools together, the government's monetary policy is described as loose or tight, or expansionary or contractionary. A loose monetary policy implies a lower prime rate, perhaps a lowering of reserve requirements, and the Federal Reserve's purchasing securities from member banks. These actions increase the money supply, which permits banks to lend more to customers. As a result, private investment goes up and unemployment falls. The side effects are lower interest rates and higher prices.

A tight monetary policy implies the reverse—the prime rate increases, reserve requirements may increase, and the Federal Reserve sells securities. These actions reduce the ability of banks to lend. Tight monetary policy is pursued generally to dampen inflationary pressures and to slow down a speeding economy. Loose monetary policy is pursued to stimulate growth and reduce unemployment.

Combining Fiscal and Monetary Policy

An Example from the Early 1980s. Although economists differ on the emphasis given to fiscal versus monetary policy, the two sets of tools operate in concert, whether deliberately or not. Sometimes the effects of fiscal policy actions are offset by monetary policy actions. One example from the 1980s was the rapidly increasing budgetary deficit, brought on mainly by the 1981 tax cut, and an expansive monetary policy. In 1982 possible major losses to the U.S. banking system stimulated a loosening of the reserve requirements of member banks. The losses stemmed from the inability of Mexico to meet its interest payments to U.S. banks because of the drop in world oil prices. One would expect the result of the rapidly increasing budget deficit to be increased interest rates and higher prices. As it borrows more money to finance the deficit, the federal government competes with other potential borrowers, which pushes interests up. Similarly, as the federal government purchases additional goods and services financed by the deficit, price pressures increase. However, one also would expect interest rates to fall as a result of looser monetary policy. In the early 1980s, the effects of deficit spending far outweighed the effects of monetary policy, at least as measured by long-term, real interest rates, which increased more than 8 percentage points from 1979 through 1984. Inflation effects were confused also, as price increases were selective rather than general. Consumer goods increased in price, but fuel prices fell as a result of the drop in world oil prices. Higher interest rates slowed demand for housing, so the prices of building materials dropped. Thus, the mid-1980s showed results that were mixed and difficult to interpret.

The response of the rest of the world economy also complicated matters during that period. Higher interest rates in the United States relative to other industrial countries caused the U.S. dollar to appreciate in value against other major currencies. As already discussed, this appreciation in the value of the dollar resulted in sharply increased imports.

The other economic impact of the combined expansive fiscal policy and loose monetary policy was to reverse a previously rising unemployment rate. By the mid-1980s, the looser monetary policy began to have the expected effects on interest rates, which fell from 1984 through 1986. By then, the loosened controls over money supply produced dramatic changes. Currency and non-interest-bearing checking accounts increased over 15 percent in 1986 alone.[42] This rapid increase by any measure exceeded the rate of economic growth. One of the results was the expected but delayed trade-off in inflation. By late 1986, the Federal Reserve began to tighten controls on the banking system to respond to the inflationary pressures.

The experience of the 1980s, plus the significant increase in the complexity of world economic linkages, has made many analysts wary of overadvocating overt fiscal or monetary policy responses to changing economic conditions. The inability to predict economic change sufficiently far in advance and the slow response period suggests to many economists that fiscal policies may best be restricted to gradual, long-term economic objectives, with faster monetary policy responsiveness oriented to short-term adjustments. In either case, the size of the aggregate federal debt and the annual deficit at the end of the 1980s overshadowed debate about fiscal versus monetary theory, with no one willing to argue that the current size of the deficit was appropriate by any theoretical measure.

Public Investment Role of Government

Government Investment in Infrastructure. Fiscal and monetary policy are basically tools of central governments. State and local governments typically have balanced budget requirements, making it impossible to incur debt strictly for fiscal policy reasons, and neither have major influence on the overall money supply. However, state and local governments have significant impacts on regional economies, and increasingly state and local governments adopt explicit economic development strategies. In this regard, state and local governments are not unlike central governments in many developing countries. Developing-country central governments and many U.S. state and local governments pursue strategies to create an effective economic climate to foster economic growth. One of the major strategic elements available is public sector investment in the physical infrastructure necessary to business expansion.[43]

As discussed in Chapter 12, serious concern emerged in the United States during the early 1980s on the loss in economic productivity due to the deterioration in the infrastructure base of roads, bridges, streets, water and sewer systems, and other public facilities. According to some, fewer technological innovations, decrease in labor productivity, and inadequate capital investment in infrastructure have been the major contributors to an overall worsening of the U.S. economy.[44] In developing countries, inadequate operation and maintenance of existing facilities has in many cases led to deterioration of physical facilities long before their expected depreciation. This deterioration has in turn led to a decline in economic production.[45] Those developing countries that have been able to maintain a reasonable growth rate and meet debt repayment schedules restricted the use of foreign borrowing and the profits from exports of natural resources to infrastructure investments, as opposed to consumption expenditures. Indonesia, for example, was able to weather the loss of revenue from oil sales in the 1980s because its primary use of that revenue had been for investment rather than consumption. In the late 1980s, foreign borrowing substituted for oil profits, but the continued use of these funds for economic infrastructure investments allowed Indonesia to sustain a level of economic growth capable of meeting repayment obligations.

State and Local Incentives to Private Investment. Governments are a major source of total capital formation in many developing countries. For all developing countries, public sector investment in infrastructure represents an average of 25 percent of all capital formation and as much as 60 to 70 percent in some countries.[46] While state and local governments in the United States do not invest nearly as high a proportion of their capital formation in infrastructure, their role in creating favorable economic climates also is important. State employee pension funds, for example, have been used as sources of venture capital and to capitalize industrial development funds to attract new business in some states.[47]

Similarly, even in the face of reduced federal revenue transfers and difficult fiscal circumstances, state and local governments have increased both their relative share of infrastructure financing and the absolute amounts spent on public infrastructure.[48] State and local governments also actively compete with each other over the location of major federal facilities.

To the extent that state and local governments offer special incentives, such as tax breaks and below-market-cost facilities for industrial expansion, little national economic growth is stimulated. Certainly it may be possible to induce a business to relocate or to locate a planned expansion by offering special incentives, but such a move represents for the national economy as a whole only a relocation of economic activity rather than net new economic growth. When the public investment creates possibilities for new investment, however, not only the local economy but the total economy expands. A joint public-private venture, for example, participated in the redevelopment of the Baltimore harbor area, which created conditions in which net new economic investment was attracted. Similar ventures have occurred in Portland and Seattle. The Kingston, Jamaica, inner-city redevelopment project has followed a similar model.[49]

Linkage between Public Infrastructure and Economic Growth. The causal linkage between public infrastructure investment and real economic growth depends on two conditions. The lack of facilities or infrastructure has to be a barrier to investment, and the costs of the investment have to be in principal recoverable through economic gains.[50] For example, if poor road conditions slow the movement of goods and services, then the costs of those goods and services reach levels higher than their economic value. In addition, firms may hold back on new investments because of the expected difficulty in transportation. Investment in road improvements under these conditions then reduces transportation costs, which in turn either provides additional funds for investment or is passed on in savings to consumers, who in turn can increase either savings or investment. If the economic returns on the road improvements exceed their costs, it is a net economic gain to the economy. On the other hand, if there are insufficient centers of production and consumption linked by those roads, then the volume of transportation will not be sufficient to yield sufficient economic gain and the investment will not have been warranted.

Unfortunately, determining when the investment will yield sufficient economic return is often not easy. Many local governments in the United States have invested in downtown revitalization without sufficient analysis of the business conditions in the local economy and have been disappointed with the returns. Similarly, inadequate consideration of whether there are genuine economic opportunities to be stimulated by an infrastructure investment at times has led to indiscriminate construction of roads and markets in developing countries where there were no real markets and production centers to link.[51]

REDISTRIBUTIONAL EFFECTS OF ECONOMIC POLICY

Unintentional Redistributive Effects

To this point in the chapter, we have been concerned with the overall performance of the economy. Governmental involvement in the economy also has specific objectives focused on subsectors or individuals. Fiscal and monetary policy actions taken to affect overall economic growth and price stability are not necessarily neutral in their effects on individuals and industries. If the government lowers corporate tax rates to stimulate business investment, but increases other taxes in order to neutralize the effects on the budget balance, then those for whom taxes are raised are paying for the economic benefits whether they share in the benefits or not. Many developing country governments have attempted to address problems of the urban poor by imposing price controls on agricultural products. While the short-run effect may be to lower food prices in urban areas, the longer-run effect is to decrease agricultural production. In the short run, economic costs are imposed on one group, rural producers, for the benefit of other groups, urban consumers. In the long run, overall economic performance is reduced.

Economic policy for stabilization purposes, whether passive or active, also can result in unintentional redistributive effects. Under inflationary conditions, persons on fixed or relatively fixed incomes are penalized. This is especially true for retired persons living on pensions, but it is also true for workers who cannot command increases in wages. If the government takes no action to slow the rate of inflation, its inaction "redistributes" income from those on fixed incomes to those whose wages or other income rises with inflation. Concern over the differential effects of changing prices has led to growing interest in so-called "incomes policy," in which the federal government would be responsible for stabilizing the distribution of income. Closely related is the idea of a guaranteed annual income, or a "negative income tax."[52]

Negative Income Tax

There are three components of the negative income tax: the income guarantee, the benefit reduction rate, and the breakeven income. The income guarantee is the amount of the transfer when the family income is zero. The benefit reduction rate is the rate at which the amount transferred is reduced as family income increases, and the breakeven income is the point where family income reaches a level that no longer qualifies for a transfer. The United States has no negative income tax, but its principles are incorporated to varying degrees in several income-related transfer programs.

Transfer Programs

Several transfer programs (Aid to Families with Dependent Children [AFDC]; Food Stamps; Supplemental Feeding Program for Women, Infants, and Children [WIC]; Medicaid) provide a minimum or floor level of benefits comparable to the income guarantee. Benefits decrease according to an established schedule as the income of the eligibility unit goes up and cease when income reaches a specified point. Although criticism of these programs increases as budget deficits increase, both major parties agree that it is in the public interest and in the interest of economic growth to provide some minimum or safety net of income-related assistance. Criticism of the loss of incentive to work that might be a consequence of these programs has been met by imposing work requirements. In 1988, the Welfare Reform Act provided a mandatory work requirement for all physically able recipients of several forms of welfare assistance, even if the only work available was in public service jobs. Provision was made for child care assistance and job training.

Tax Policies

Expenditure programs are not the only form of income redistribution. As noted in Chapter 4, different taxes have different impacts on various groups. In addition, the overall structure of the entire tax system may operate to redistribute income among different groups.[53] The Tax Reform Act of 1986 was in one basic aspect almost exclusively a redistributive act.[54] Throughout consideration of various possible changes, the basic principle followed was that the act had to be revenue neutral. In the face of huge budget deficits, neither political party was prepared to support a tax reform that reduced revenues as the Economic Recovery Tax Act of 1981 had. As a consequence, lower income groups benefited from sharply reduced taxes, middle-income groups benefited from modest reductions, and upper-income individuals and corporations faced tax increases.[55]

The increase in corporate taxes continued to be controversial. One issue is the extent to which corporate taxes are a form of double taxes. After corporate taxes have been paid, the dividends paid out to stockholders also are subject to taxation. To some extent, then, double taxation occurs. The 1986 tax reform made the issue even more prominent as taxes went up on corporate income and on individual earnings from stock dividends and sales. The argument also can be made that corporate taxation discourages capital investment, first by taxing the corporations that make profits and second by taxing the dividends paid to investors. Almost before the ink was dry on the 1986 act, various proposals to reduce corporate taxes were introduced. The major tax component of the Republican Party platform in the 1988 election was to reduce corporate tax obligations by reinstating the investment tax credit repealed in 1986. The justification for the platform plank was based on the proposition that overall economic productivity is lower because of lower investment. However, the elimination of the investment tax credit was the largest single revenue-producing component of the 1986 act, estimated to yield $150 billion by 1991.[56] In order not to contribute to the huge federal deficit, a reinstatement of that provision would have to produce sufficient increases in corporate profits to replace the $150 billion.

While economic policy affects the distribution of income, it cannot be expected to address structural features of the labor market. For example, workers with minimal or obsolete skills will have difficulty finding employment even during periods of rapid growth. Economic policy also is of limited assistance in coping with readjustments in the economy, such as might occur if defense spending is reduced significantly through the 1990s. Other policies, of course, are designed to affect more basic structural problems. Expenditures on education, both academic and vocational, are expected to increase the overall human resource base for the economy. Regulatory policies are expected to reduce the private incentives to pollute the environment, which imposes a long-run economic cost when conditions have to be resolved remedially.

SUMMARY

Representing over 40 percent of total economic activity in the United States, the combined effects of federal, state, and local governments' budgets on the economy are enormous. The federal government acts deliberately to intervene in the economy to achieve aggregate economic objectives. The major economic policy objectives followed by most central governments are economic growth, full employment, stable prices, and balance in the flow of funds into and out of the economy. Because of the huge size of the present U.S. federal budget deficit, management of the deficit and the overall government debt has been added as a major economic policy objective.

Fiscal policy and monetary policy constitute the tools used to influence macroeconomic performance. Fiscal policy consists of the use of the government's taxing and spending powers to stimulate or dampen economic activity. An excess of expenditures over revenues—a deficit—stimulates demand and thus employment. A possible consequence, however, may be inflation. An excess of revenues over expenditures—a surplus—has a dampening effect on the economy. Monetary policy affects economic activity through control over the money supply. Through influence over interest rates, reserve requirements, and the purchase and sale of bonds, government monetary policy can speed up or slow down the pace of economic activity. In the latter half of the 1980s, debates over the theory and detail of fiscal and monetary policy were overshadowed by the huge federal budget deficit.

While state and local governments do not exercise fiscal and monetary policy, their role in providing the basic infrastructure required for private sector business activity is important to regional economic performance. In this respect, state and local governments and developing country governments pursue similar ends. For developing country governments, their effective use of borrowed funds from donor agencies and commercial banks depends on putting the funds to use in increasing economic productive capacity.

Government policy interventions also have objectives and consequences for income redistribution. Changes in tax policy and increases or decreases in expenditures are almost never neutral with respect to who is affected. In addition, there is general agreement that some level of redistribution of income is appropriate to address the problems of the very lowest income individuals. How extensive these programs should be, however, has been controversial. A major welfare reform in 1988 made it official policy that all able recipients of various forms of welfare are required to perform some kind of work.

NOTES

1. Stuart Auerbach, "U.S. Becomes World's No. 1 Debtor Nation," *Washington Post*, June 25, 1986, p. G-21.

2. Henry J. Aaron et al., *Economic Choices 1987* (Washington, D.C.: Brookings, 1986), p. 23.

3. Joseph E. Stiglitz, *Economics of the Public Sector*, 2nd ed. (New York: Norton, 1988), p. 24.

4. Naomi Caiden, "The Boundaries of Public Budgeting: Issues for Education in Tumultuous Times," *Public Administration Review* 45 (1985): 495–502.

5. Richard A. Musgrave and Peggy B. Musgrave, *Public Finance in Theory and Practice*, 4th ed. (New York: McGraw-Hill, 1984).

6. James D. Savage, *Balanced Budgets and American Politics* (Ithaca, N.Y.: Cornell University Press, 1988).

7. A. Premchand, *Government Budgeting and Expenditure Controls: Theory and Practice* (Washington, D.C.: International Monetary Fund, 1983).

8. Bruce Henrick and Charles P. Kindleberger, *Economic Development* (New York: McGraw-Hill, 1983).

9. World Bank, *World Development Report 1987* (New York: Oxford University Press, 1987).

10. Arthur M. Okun and George L. Perry, eds., *Curing Chronic Inflation* (Washington, D.C.: Brookings, 1978).

11. Council of Economic Advisers, *Economic Report of the President, 1988* (Washington, D.C.: Government Printing Office, 1988), p. 83.

12. Louis Uchitelle, "Inflation Seems Only a Shadow: Increase Sticks at Around 5%; Consumers Are Complacent," *The New York Times News Service*, October 16, 1988.

13. World Bank, *World Development Report 1988* (New York: Oxford University Press, 1988), p. 225.

14. World Bank, *World Development Report 1988*, p. 223.

15. Stiglitz, *Economics of the Public Sector*, p. 687.

16. Unless otherwise noted, figures in this section are from Council of Economic Advisers, *Economic Report of the President, 1988*, pp. 91–93.

17. Lance T. LeLoup, Barbara Luck Graham, and Stacey Barwick, "Deficit Politics and Constitutional Government: The Impact of Gramm-Rudman-Hollings," *Public Budgeting and Finance* 7 (Spring 1987): 83–103.

18. Ibid., p. 84.

19. Paul N. Van de Water and Kathy A. Ruffing, "Federal Deficits, Debt and Interest Costs," *Public Budgeting and Finance* 5 (Spring 1985): 54–66.

20. Stephen Marris, *Deficits and the Dollar: The World Economy At Risk* (Washington, D.C.: Institute for International Economics, 1987).

21. Tax Foundation, *Facts and Figures on Government Finance: 1988/89* (Baltimore: Johns Hopkins University Press, 1988), p. 84.

22. Savage, *Balanced Budgets and American Politics*.

23. For a good discussion of the need to pace a deficit reduction program with overall economic conditions, see Aaron et al., *Economic Choices 1987*.

24. Jan Kmenta and James B. Ramsey, eds., *Evaluation of Econometric Models* (New York: Academic Press, 1980).

25. William Ascher, *Forecasting: An Appraisal for Policy-Makers and Planners* (Baltimore: Johns Hopkins University Press, 1978).

26. General Accounting Office, *A Primer on Gross National Product Concepts and Issues* (Washington, D.C.: Government Printing Office, 1981).

27. Henry F. Myers, "Housing Cycles Balance Economy: Buying Decline Cools It, Rise Leads Recovery," *The Wall Street Journal News Service*, October 16, 1988.

28. Department of Commerce, Bureau of Economic Analysis, *Business Conditions Digest* (Washington, D.C.: Government Printing Office, monthly).

29. Department of Commerce, *Economic Indicators: Historical and Descriptive Background* (Washington, D.C.: Government Printing Office, 1980).

30. Robert McNown, "On the Uses of Econometric Models: A Guide for Policy Makers," *Policy Sciences* 19 (1986): 359–80.

31. McNown, "On the Uses of Econometric Models," p. 363.

32. C. Stephen Wolfe and Jesse Burkhead, "Fiscal Trends in Selected Industrialized Countries," *Public Budgeting and Finance* 3 (Winter 1983): 97–102.

33. Stiglitz, *Economics of the Public Sector*, p. 395.

34. John Maynard Keynes, *The General Theory of Employment, Interest and Money* (New York: Harcourt Brace, 1936).

35. Arthur B. Laffer and Jan P. Seymour, eds., *The Economics of the Tax Revolt: A Reader* (New York: Harcourt Brace Jovanovich, 1979).

36. David N. Hyman, *Public Finance: A Contemporary Application of Theory to Policy*, 2nd ed. (Chicago: Dryden, 1987), pp. 425–28.

37. David J. Ott and Attiat F. Ott, *Federal Budget Policy*, 3rd ed. (Washington, D.C.: Brookings, 1977), pp. 80–85.

38. World Bank, *World Development Report 1988*, p. 58.

39. Premchand, *Government Budgeting and Expenditure Controls*.

40. Stiglitz, *Economics of the Public Sector*, p. 681.

41. World Bank, *World Development Report 1988*, pp. 56–59.

42. Council of Economic Advisers, *Economic Report of the President: 1988*, p. 33.

43. A. Premchand, "Government Budget Reforms: Agenda for the 1980s," *Public Budgeting and Finance* 1 (Autumn 1981): p. 16, contrasts developing and industrial country central government economic objectives.

44. Pat Choate and Susan Walter, *America in Ruins: Beyond the Public Works Pork Barrel* (Washington, D.C.: Council of State Planning Agencies, 1981).

45. Dennis A. Rondinelli, Ronald Johnson, and James McCullough, "Analyzing Decentralization Policies in Developing Countries: A Political-Economy Framework," forthcoming in *Development and Change* 20 (1989).

46. World Bank, *World Development Report 1987*, p. 48.

47. Lawrence Litvak, *Pension Funds and Economic Renewal* (Washington, D.C.: Council of State Planning Agencies, 1981).

48. Hugh O'Neill, *Creating Opportunity: Reducing Poverty Through Economic Development* (Washington, D.C.: Council of State Planning Agencies, 1985).

49. George E. Peterson, G. Thomas Kingsley, and Jeffrey P. Telgarsky, "Urban Economic Development: Orientation to Policy," (Washington, D.C.: Urban Institute, 1988).

50. Warren C. Baum and Stokes M. Tolbert, *Investing in Development: Lessons of World Bank Experience* (New York: Oxford University Press, 1985).

51. Dennis Rondinelli, *Applied Regional Analysis: The Spatial Dimensions of Development Policy* (Boulder, Colo.: Westview, 1985).

52. Edgar K. Browning and Jacqueline M. Browning, *Public Finance and the Price System*, 3rd ed. (New York: Macmillan, 1987), pp. 256–93.

53. Hyman, *Public Finance*, pp. 336–73.

54. Jeffrey H. Birnbaum and Alan S. Murray, *Showdown at Gucci Gulch: Lawmakers, Lobbyists, and the Unlikely Triumph of Tax Reform* (New York: Vintage, 1988).

55. Joseph A. Pechman, *Federal Tax Policy*, 5th ed. (Washington, D.C.: Brookings, 1987).

56. Browning and Browning, *Public Finance and the Price System*, p. 525.

Concluding Remarks

Five major themes are likely to characterize the field of public budgeting and finance in the coming years and warrant the attention of both scholars and practitioners. These themes are

1. added emphasis on integrating planning, budgeting, accounting, and performance measurement systems
2. increased emphasis on financial management
3. continued legislative-executive conflict over budgetary roles
4. continued concern for achieving an acceptable balance for providing public services and paying for them within an intergovernmental framework
5. increased concern for promoting economic growth within an international context

A risk-free prediction is that budgetary decision systems will have increased capabilities to utilize program information. The steady development of systems oriented toward program information since the late 1950s shows no signs of abating. Whether the use of program information is desirable has been a moot question for years. The issue involves how to use program information, not whether to use it.

Advancements in computer technology—both hardware and software—help strengthen the trend toward use of program data. Microcomputers make possible relatively sophisticated information systems for small governments and may even give them an advantage over larger jurisdictions that still operate largely within a mainframe environment.

As planning, budgeting, accounting, and evaluation systems become increasingly developed in their own independent ways, the need for better integration increases. One of the essential emphases in program budgeting was, and is, to link budgetary, program, and accounting information into an integrated decision system. This trend, however, does not include the notion that political realities will be removed from budgetary decision making, as some critics have contended. All that is suggested here is that a greater array of information will be more readily available than in the past and that decision makers will need to choose among that information in determining what positions to take on difficult problems.

Financial management gained increased attention in the 1980s and can be expected to continue to be a central concern in the 1990s. Earlier, unrepressed inflation and serious taxpayer recalcitrance forced government leaders to realize resources were limited and budget trimming was essential. Economic problems at the local, state, and federal levels have continued to make for "tight" budget situations that place emphasis upon frugal decision making. Budget execution, therefore, will receive greater attention. Can savings be achieved through closer monitoring of program spending? Can improvements in accounting systems lead to savings? What alternative financial arrangements hold promise for reducing costs? To what extent should governments pursue contracting out of services, privatization, and lease rather than purchase arrangements?

As the 1990s unfold, executives and legislative bodies will continue their struggles with one another over their relative roles in budgetary decision making. The increased ability to collect, store, and manipulate data through computer technology makes possible legislative involvement in far greater depth and detail than was possible only ten years ago. Will that increased ability be translated into greater legislative authority and control, and in what ways? On the other hand, both executives and legislatures may be less than assertive in dealing with the most intractable problems. When the White House is controlled by one political party and Congress by another, neither is eager to deal with major problems on its own if the remedies are likely to be viewed unfavorably by the electorate. In the case of the federal budget deficit problem, neither side has been willing to take responsibility for increasing revenues by endorsing greater taxation.

If Congress is to play an increased role in decision making, then an imperative must be some realignment of powers and procedures within the two chambers. As was seen in earlier chapters, legislative bodies have changed their operations, added staff, and more generally increased their ability to handle policy making. At the same time, Congress is a complex maze of committees, processes, and political considerations that make difficult any coherent approach to policy making. Gramm-Rudman-Hollings (GRH) may force action to bring budgets more into balance than they would be, but the GRH process does not alter the fundamental means by which Congress operates.

During the 1990s governments will continue to be confronted with competing programmatic needs that must be met within a context of limited resources and intergovernmental relationships. National security and defense along with programs for the elderly (Social Security and Medicare) will continue to demand the attention of the federal government, while all levels of government will be called upon to deal with such problems as AIDS, drug trafficking and drug abuse, and poverty and related conditions, such as homelessness. Difficult choices must be made over how programs are to operate and how they are to be financed. Presidents, governors, and mayors may all lament the afflictions of AIDS or drug dependencies, but where are funds to be obtained for dealing with these problems? Local governments may be willing to provide programs for the poor, but only if state and federal funds are available to support these efforts.

Promoting economic growth will continue as a priority objective. So-called rust belt states will continue their struggle to survive under conditions of fiscal distress. Other areas, such as those dependent upon the price of petroleum, will continue through periods of boom and bust as petroleum supplies and prices fluctuate. The extent to which state and local governments can affect their economic futures will remain uncertain.

One of the most important causes of the uncertainty in promoting economic growth by all levels of government is the rapidly emerging international economy. International considerations have had major impact on the United States throughout the 20th century, but in the 1980s a new level or magnitude of impact emerged. What the U.S. economy makes and sells is intimately influenced by the economies of other nations. The industrial mix of the U.S. economy and its labor force will be forced to change in the 1990s. These changes will occur at a time when the U.S. labor force is aging due to the aging of the World War II baby boomers. How budget systems will be able to respond to these challenges is unknown.

These themes do not capture all that is likely to transpire over the coming years. At the same time, the themes reflect many of the concerns of the future. One certainty is that budget systems will continue to undergo change as they are called upon to serve the needs of decision makers.

Bibliographic Note

This bibliographic note is intended to assist in finding materials for further reading on public budgeting systems. Because the preceding chapters are footnoted extensively, we make no attempt here to recapitulate everything cited earlier. Readers will find the index a handy guide to footnote references. This bibliographic note is meant as an aid in identifying both general references and sources that have produced and can be expected to continue to produce literature on public budgeting.

Several periodic publications provide much of the basic analytic literature on budgeting as well as current information, including both interpretive description and basic data. *Public Administration Review* (American Society for Public Administration) often produces scholarly articles on budgeting. *Policy Studies Journal* and *Policy Studies Review* (Policy Studies Organization) include occasional articles related to budgeting in their regular issues and in related special symposia issues. *State and Local Government Review* (University of Georgia) frequently includes budget-related articles that are particularly helpful to practitioners as well as scholars. *Public Budgeting and Finance* (American Society for Public Administration and American Association for Budget and Program Analysis) focuses especially on financial management and budgeting as does *Public Budgeting and Financial Management* (Dekker). *Government Finance Review* (Government Finance Officers Association) provides brief analytic pieces and news items on budgeting and finance.

There are numerous journals that deal with public finance and with policy analysis and evaluation. Although occasional articles related specifically to budgeting systems appear in these journals, their usual focus is on specific budgetary subtopics. *Public Finance Quarterly* (Sage) and *Public Finance/Finances Publiques* both publish empirical and theoretical analyses of economic policy concerns, including government growth and size, tax policy, fiscal and monetary policy, and economic analysis. *Public Finance* is more international in orientation. There are a large number of journals devoted to policy analysis and policy evaluation. In addition to *Policy Studies Review* and *Policy Studies Journal*, the journals *Evaluation Review* (Sage), *Evaluation and Program Planning* (Pergamon), and *Journal of Policy Analysis and Management* (Association of Public Policy Analysis and Management) all share that focus.

In addition to the periodicals focusing centrally on budgeting or related topics, other professional journals include occasional articles of relevance. These include *Administration and Society, Administrative Science Quarterly, American Economic Review, American Political Science Review*, and *Management Science*. The Washington-based *National Journal* provides weekly news and analysis of the federal government including budgetary events, and the *C. Q. Weekly Report* (Congressional Quarterly, Inc.) covers congressional actions in particular. Most of the journals listed have annual or occasional indices to facilitate general search. However, indices such as the *Social Science Index to Periodicals* (SSI) and the *Public Affairs Information Service Bulletin* (PAIS) are more useful.

A second major source of up-to-date analysis and data is government publications. An excellent reference work that explains various types of documents and their sources is Joe Morehead's *Introduction to United States Public Documents*, 3rd ed. (Littleton, Colo.: Libraries Unlimited, 1983). An annual index to many state, local, and federal documents is *Bibliographic Guide to Governmental Publications—U.S.* (Boston: Hall). Federal documents can be located through the *Monthly Catalog of United States Government Publications* (Government Printing Office) and the *Congressional Information Service Index* (CIS). For statistical information, refer to the *American Statistics Index* (Congressional Information Service); this index, although covering only federal documents, includes many materials containing state and local data.

Students of budgeting and finance will generally find themselves returning regularly to several key government sources. The Office of Management and Budget, Council of Economic Advisers, Treasury Department, Congressional Budget Office, and General Accounting Office produce publications of major import to the field.

Several annual volumes from various agencies contain basic data on revenues and expenditures for local, state, and federal levels and intergovernmental transfers among levels. Considerable care must be exercised when working from more than one source since the figures do not always agree. The Census Bureau in the Department of Commerce publishes *Government Finances, Statistical Abstract*, and *Survey of Current Business*. In addition, the Census of Governments is conducted every five years and contains not only financial data but also a wealth of organizational information. The Advisory

Commission on Intergovernmental Relations has a varied publishing program, including its annual *Significant Features of Fiscal Federalism*.

Analyses of federal budgeting and finance are published by private organizations such as the American Enterprise Institute (Washington), the Committee on Economic Development (New York), the Heritage Foundation (Washington), the National Bureau of Economic Research (New York), the National Industrial Conference Board (New York), and the Tax Foundation (New York). The Brookings Institution (Washington) publishes numerous books on budgeting and taxation.

Books, of course, are an important source of information. Four of the classics in public budgeting, no longer subject to revision and updating, are William F. Willoughby's *The Problems of a National Budget* (New York: Appleton, 1918); A.E. Buck's *Public Budgeting* (New York: Harper and Brothers, 1919); Arthur Smithies's *The Budgetary Process in the United States* (New York: McGraw-Hill, 1955); and Jesse Burkhead's *Government Budgeting* (New York: Wiley, 1956). Histories of budgeting include Vincent J. Browne's *The Control of the Public Budget* (Washington: Public Affairs Press, 1949); Bertram M. Gross's "The New Systems Budgeting", *Public Administration Review*, 29 (1969): 113–37; and Carolyn Webber and Aaron Wildavsky, *A History of Taxation and Expenditure in the Western World* (New York: Simon & Schuster, 1986).

General works on budgeting with emphasis on the political process include Richard F. Fenno, Jr.'s *The Power of the Purse: Appropriations Politics in Congress* (Boston: Little, Brown, 1966); Joel Haveman's *Congress and the Budget* (Bloomington: Indiana University Press, 1978); Lance T. LeLoup's *Budgetary Politics*, 3rd ed. (Brunswick, Ohio: King's Court Communications, 1986); Howard E. Shuman's *Politics and the Budget: The Struggle between the President and the Congress*, 2nd ed. (Englewood Cliffs, N.J.: Prentice-Hall, 1988); and Aaron Wildavsky, *The New Politics of the Budgetary Process* (Glenview, Ill.: Scott, Foresman, 1988). Other general works include Donald Axelrod's *Budgeting for Modern Government* (New York: St. Martin's, 1988); Fremont J. Lyden and Marc Lindenberg's *Public Budgeting in Theory and Practice* (New York: Longman, 1983); Thomas D. Lynch's *Public Budgeting in America*, 2nd ed. (Englewood Cliffs, N.J.: Prentice-Hall, 1985); John L. Mikesell's *Fiscal Administration*, 2nd ed. (Chicago: Dorsey, 1986); and Alan W. Steiss' *Financial Management in Public Organizations* (Pacific Grove, Calif.: Brooks/Cole, 1989). A book that focuses upon the various types of analysis that are used in budgeting is Robert Berne and Richard Schramm's *The Financial Analysis of Governments* (Englewood Cliffs, N.J.: Prentice-Hall, 1986).

Edited volumes provide reports of journal articles and originally prepared pieces. Among these are *Management Policies in Local Government Finance*, 3rd ed., by J. Richard Aronson and Eli Schwartz, eds. (Washington: International City Management Association, 1987); *Casebook in Public Budgeting and Financial Management*, by Carol W. Lewis and A. Grayson Walker III, eds. (Englewood Cliffs, N.J.: Prentice-Hall, 1984); *Public Budgeting*, 4th ed., by Fremont J. Lyden and Ernest G. Miller, eds. (Englewood Cliffs, N.J.: Prentice-Hall, 1982); and *Contemporary Public Budgeting*, by Thomas D. Lynch, ed. (New Brunswick, N.J.: Transaction Books, 1981).

For literature on decision making, program budgeting, zero-base budgeting, accounting, economic policy, personnel management, program evaluation, and the like, the reader is encouraged to turn to the footnotes for each chapter.

Happy reading.

Index